Plains Families

Exploring
Sociology
Through
Social History

Scott G. McNall

University of Kansas

Sally Allen McNall

University of Kansas

Plains Families

Exploring Sociology Through Social History

St. Martin's Press · New York

To our parents

Library of Congress Catalog Card Number: 82-60479
Copyright © 1983 by St. Martin's Press, Inc.

All Rights Reserved.

Manufactured in the United States of America.

76543

fedcba

For information, write St. Martin's Press, Inc.,
175 Fifth Avenue, New York, N.Y. 10010

book and cover design: Jeremiah Lighter

cloth ISBN: 0-312-61391-1
paper ISBN: 0-312-61393-8

Contents

2

The Martins   42

3

Culture and Social Structure   67

4

The Wades and the Patchens   101

5

Communities and Associations   128

6

The Higbees and the Davises   151

7

Socialization and Sex Roles 182

8

The People of Baker 213

9

Social Class and Stratification   246

10

Vi Mercer   277

11

Social Change and Stability 287

Preface

S TUDENTS in introductory sociology courses may all too easily form the impression that the substance of the discipline is simply a set of abstractions. Caught up in an effort to master essential concepts, theories, and definitions, students often lose sight of the fact that underneath these formulations is a society in motion; that it is located in time and space; that its various segments are interconnected; and, above all, that it has been created by people much like themselves. We have found over the years that an exciting way to bring sociological concepts to life is to link them concretely to history.

Plains Families is the story of real people and of their society and culture. The book uses the Great Plains region of the United States, from the 1860s to the present, as a sociological laboratory— as a base to investigate how and why the settlers came to the Plains, to examine the values and beliefs they and their descendants held, how the economy and polity affected them, and how all of these factors worked in concert. Through the use of diaries, letters, and interviews, members of Plains families themselves present first-hand accounts of their day-to-day lives, and of the impact of local, national, and world events.

Beginning with Chapter 2, the book is divided into alternating "historical" and "sociological" chapters. Each even-numbered, historical chapter presents the original documents of one or more Plains families. It is then followed by a chapter that explains the basic sociological concepts and principles illustrated by the lives of the individuals in the preceding chapter.

The book opens with a section on methodology that explains the means by which data and concepts are derived, how sociologists discover and analyze patterns of human behavior, and how they link these concepts with social history. By allowing students to explore a given set of data, we also show how sociological terms and concepts can be used to describe everyday occurrences.

Following the introduction, Chapter 1 shows how the people in the Great Plains were shaped by historical circumstances, and how the social institutions they developed were affected by events such as the Civil War, by laws such as the Homestead Act, and by climate and geography. Thus, we develop a model of society as a complex whole, a model to which we refer throughout the book.

Chapter 2 presents the diaries and letters of Henry and Lucy Martin, who left Illinois in the 1870s for a homestead in western Kansas. These personal records describe the couple's arrival on the Plains, their feelings about their new home, and their values. Their letters and diaries also reveal how the Martins were influenced by the larger political and economic institutions. The analysis that follows in Chapter 3 focuses on culture and social structure. In Chapter 4, the personal documents of Nebraska ranchers Arthur and Henrietta Wade are excerpted, along with those of their offspring; the following chapter looks at their lives as it explores communities and associations. Chapter 6 shows what it was like growing up in the small town of Cooley, Kansas, as seen through the eyes of members of two farm families; Chapter 7 uses their experiences to discuss socialization and sex roles. Chapter 8 presents original documents of residents of a midwestern college town, which are used in Chapter 9 to illustrate the issues of social class and stratification. The final historical chapter (10) consists of an interview with an eighty-eight-year-old Minnesota farmwoman who lived through most of the years spanned by the book. Chapter 11 then examines her life to recap the social processes explored throughout the book and to develop a general theory of social change.

We are grateful to many people for their assistance in the preparation of *Plains Families.* We would especially like to thank Sharon Cox, who cheerfully typed several versions of this manuscript, and Karyn Zarley, who filled the breach when Sharon wasn't there. Paula Nixon and Marcia Gaston managed to turn up almost all of the obscure references we sent them searching after and often found additional material as well. The staffs of several libraries were most patient and helpful, and we owe a special debt to Sherry Williams of the Kansas Collection at the University of Kansas; Pat Michaelis and Janet Sherbert at the Kansas State Historical Society in Topeka; Philip Brown of the Hilton M. Briggs Library at South Dakota State University in Brookings, whose enthusiasm and thoroughness were truly remarkable; and Anne Trump of the Brookings Public Library. Gary Mason's generous help with the illustrations was invaluable, and we are also grateful for the assistance of Steven Jansen at the Watkins Community Museum in

Lawrence and Earl Van Meter of the Douglas County (Kansas) Extension Office. Another debt is owed to the people who were interviewed for this book and to the participants in the Lawrence Arts Center's "Images of Aging" project.

The critical comments of several reviewers added significantly to the quality of the book. For these contributions, we thank Jerry G. Bode, Ball State University; Clifford V. Colman, Miami Dade Community College, South Campus; Richard Levinson, Emory University; Paul Lockman, Jr., University of Colorado; Charlotte O'Kelly, Providence College; Bartolomeo J. Palisi, California State University—Fullerton; Hallowell Pope, The University of Iowa; and Elizabeth Useem, University of Massachusetts at Boston. Any errors in fact or interpretation, of course, are solely our responsibility.

Scott G. McNall

Sally Allen McNall

Plains Families

Exploring
Sociology
Through
Social History

Introduction

THE purpose of this book is to wed sociology and social history. It uses history to illuminate sociological theory, and sociological concepts and theory to explain history.

History is the "fragmentary by-products of social routines" (Tilly, 1981:18). History reveals what people made, said, wrote, and did, and to understand these things, we need to have some means of organizing them. That is what theory is for. Yet we should heed Stinchcombe (1978:1), who stated, "one does not apply theory to history; rather one uses history to develop theory." If we attempt to apply theory mechanically, without constantly checking it against the living, changing data of human societies, it will not be able to tell us much. For example, such terms as *rationalization, bureaucratization*, and *urbanization* merely describe processes; they do not tell us why they occur. If we want to study urbanization, we must move beyond these labels to ask why people moved from the farm to urban centers, why they settled there in the first place, and why jobs and other opportunities were concentrated in the urban areas.

What we must do is look for what Stinchcombe called *deep analogies*—relationships among sets of facts. For sociological concepts to have meaning, they must be grounded in actual history. We therefore must use history to modify and extend theory, whereas we use theory to discover deep analogies.

Our text draws on the words and experiences of the American families, and their descendants, who settled the Great Plains. Many of them recorded a wide variety of information. For instance, the Great Plains settlers wrote down what they planted, how much they paid for seed, when they planted it, what the yield was, and how much they paid for the feed for their livestock, as well as what they did during the day. By examining these records, we have been able to determine what the average settler or farmer did.

Many of the settlers also kept diaries. For the most part, those kept by the men were running accounts of what happened each day and what the weather—which determined the farmers' welfare—was like. Occasionally, a man might record joy over the birth of a child, love for his wife, or grief over a family or friend's tragedy, but usually it was only a major life event that called forth such emotion. The women, on the other hand, were more likely to comment in their diaries on the vicissitudes of farm life and also on what they and others thought and felt. Thus these personal accounts can tell us about such things as sex roles, socialization, and family life in the early rural communities.

The letters that the Great Plains settlers wrote and received are also a rich source of information. Those traveling to an unsettled region often wrote long letters home describing their daily experiences and reactions to new circumstances and expressing their concerns about their relatives and acquaintances. Many of these letters are now part of the archives of state historical societies, and we drew heavily on them. They helped us to determine what people in a particular locale did and how they responded to changing circumstances and crises.

Each even-numbered chapter presents the original documents of one or more families and is followed by a chapter which describes the forces at work. Because the settlers themselves often did not comment on events outside their own world, we have tried to identify those events and to show how they affected the settlers' actions. If a chapter deals with a family living on a farm in Nebraska during the early 1900s, we read the available literature on that state for that period. In addition, we examined accounts of what was happening in the country as a whole, as well as relevant sociological and psychological studies. If newspapers were available for the towns we discussed, we read those too. In short, we did everything possible to place the written records in their historical context.

In examining numerous diaries and letters, we tried to identify the references to particular people, places, and events. For example, when we came across a pejorative comment about a Populist leader, we researched the history of Populism. Neither did we take anyone's recollections at face value. Instead, we double-checked the accuracy of anything the diarists and letter writers presented as fact. For instance, one immigrant reported that on entering the vast inland prairies for the first time, he noticed that no birds could be heard singing; so we checked to see if others had noted this and if it was generally accepted by scholars of the period. The bibliography lists the materials we used to establish the historical context.

The families in this book are composites. We have changed names, merged one family's set of records with those of another, moved passages from diaries into letters and vice versa, rearranged and combined interviews, and generally revised the materials to tell coherent and vivid stories. For example, in Chapter 6, Ed Higbee reminisces about his childhood. His words are taken from letters, retrospective materials, and diaries, combined so as to allow Higbee to "tell" his own story. Although we often quote directly from diaries and letters, we have eliminated redundant or irrelevant material. Often we have edited the material, standardizing grammatical forms, spellings, and punctuation.

For the more recent historical periods, the material we have on any given family is more complete, because the family members themselves have been accessible. Accounts of life after 1910 are also based on personal interviews with rural families and on their responses to specific written questions.

What does this book tell us about the American family? About social changes? About our general value system? Can we extend our observations about the settlers of the Great Plains and their descendants to other populations, to families on the eastern seaboard, to nonwhites, or to urban dwellers? Can we talk about processes common to the entire United States? Our answers to these questions will emerge as we work through the materials, examining facts in the light of theory and theory in the presence of facts.

This book focuses on typical individuals who settled in Iowa, Kansas, Minnesota, Nebraska, Oklahoma, and the Dakotas and on their descendants who continue to live in rural areas and small towns. Their experiences have provided a stereotype of the American family: their survival of hardship and catastrophe by means of optimism, endurance, ties with their community, and plenty of hard work. Politicians, television, and novels for both adults and children still promote this stereotype of the "real American family." What should it mean to us?

This book relates the actual conditions that the American settlers survived. It describes how some of them endured through hard times and how some of their children and grandchildren did the same. Yet throughout this book, the documents that we used refer to those who were unable to survive or succeed in farming. In particular, the material from the years after World War I often cites family members and acquaintances who went to live in the cities and whose life-styles there were very different from those of the farms and the small towns. Finally, this book documents how life on an American farm has changed over time. In every case, we can see a complex interplay between what people believe they can and should do and the actual circumstances that determine what happens to them.

Beginnings 1

THE settlers who entered the Great Plains after 1860 met an alien world. Ways of life well adapted to the eastern seaboard, to the forest lands, to the small farms of New England, and to European countries were left behind, together with friends, relatives, and security. When the pioneers crossed the Mississippi River in Minnesota or the Missouri River on the eastern edge of Kansas, they left civilization behind. For the few families who ventured forth on their own, the only sounds heard for days, even weeks, were the turning of their wagon wheels, the heavy breathing of their oxen, and the talk they kept up to fill the hours. The "great inland sea," as the prairie was called by early explorers, seemed to have an endless horizon, unbroken by the friendly sight of another wagon train, a homestead, or even animal life. According to their own accounts, the singing of birds was not a sound that awoke the early travelers.

Although the pioneers had received general directions about where to head and at which stream to turn, they often lost their way. Some of those with sailing backgrounds adapted methods developed at sea, in order to prevent traveling in circles. They trailed a long rope behind their wagons, and their families made sure that it stayed straight. The pioneers fixed their bearings from the evening stars and the morning and evening sun in order to keep headed ever westward. Their wagons' tongues were pointed in the proper direction for the morning run, which usually began before the sun came up.

Destinations were often vague. Some pioneers simply traveled until they found either free land on which to settle or villages that had been established by those who had come ahead of them.

The travelers' diets were limited. They were seldom able to supplement their stores with game and fish, for the great herds of

5

buffalo roamed farther west, and their methods of hunting and trapping or fishing often did not work here.

Life was particularly hard for the frontier women. Taken away from friends, family, and community, they were dropped on the prairie, as one woman put it, "without even a tree to hide behind." They were left alone in crude dwellings built as shelter from the fierce winds that blew across the plains. The loneliness was often unbearable. Food was often scarce, and feeding a family was difficult. It also was impossible to keep clean in the blowing dust. Childbearing was especially hazardous. As a result, some pioneer women had nervous breakdowns, and because of the strain of the work and the uncertain weather, so did some of the men. Many simply gave up and returned to more familiar settings or moved on to what they considered more favorable locations.

Yet the development and growth of the area were astonishingly rapid. By the late 1800s, cities, towns, and communities on the Great Plains were well established, and the patterns of living that would affect the great-grandchildren of the early settlers had also been laid down.

In this chapter, we will outline the social institutions of the frontier and show the relationship between values and norms and the economy, geography, climate, and technology to which they were adapted. For example, certain technological innovations, such as barbed wire, permitted the farmers to enclose their land, thus protecting it from the range stock of the early ranchers. The moldboard plow permitted tough prairie sod to be cut and turned under, which contributed to rapid settlement. In short, technology helped to define prairie farming; it also shaped the value system. For instance, farmers were concerned with transforming and civilizing the wilderness. The ranchers, on the other hand, accepted the environment as they found it and prided themselves on adjusting to it. The ranchers looked with scorn on the "sodbusters" who contributed to dust storms and erosion, whereas the farmers considered the ranchers to be totally uncivilized. This rivalry between the two groups later influenced the politics of the region.

OPENING THE FRONTIER

By 1850, the Great Plains had become one of America's last frontiers. Settlers had already pushed westward from the eastern seaboard into Ohio, Missouri, Illinois, and Arkansas toward the Missouri River, which served as a boundary of the untouched lands lying toward the west. The land comprising the Upper Midwest and the central prairies—Minnesota, northwest Iowa, the Dakotas, the Nebraska and Kansas territories, and northern Oklahoma—was coveted by the inhabitants of more settled areas. But its development was somewhat sporadic and was affected by local conditions, such as the Sioux Indian uprising in the Dakotas and Minnesota in 1862 and the severe frosts of 1866 which drove many farmers in Minnesota to more hospitable climates. But by 1900 the area was settled: between 1850 and 1900 the population of the seven-state region (Kansas, Minnesota, North Dakota, South Dakota, Iowa, Nebraska, and Missouri) rose from 880,000 to 10.3 million (U.S. Department of Commerce, 1961:12–13). As Billington (1949:703) noted, this was the greatest movement of people in the history of the United States:

> Millions of farmers, held back for a generation by the forbidding features of the Great Plains, surged westward between 1870 and 1890. They filled Kansas and Nebraska, engulfed the level grasslands of Dakota, occupied the rolling foothills of Wyoming and Montana, and in a desperate bid for vanishing lands, elbowed Indians from the last native sanctuary in Oklahoma. A larger domain was settled in the last three decades of the century than in all America's past; 407,000,000 acres were occupied and 189,000,000 improved between 1607 and 1870; 430,000,000 acres peopled and 225,000,000 placed under cultivation between 1870 and 1900.

The Homestead Act of 1862, the railroads, and the higher price of agricultural goods added to the rapid growth of this area.

The Homestead Act

The Homestead Act of 1862 was directly responsible for the rapid development of the Great Plains. The intentions of the act were to relieve urban crowding; to promote settlement of the land by people with few resources; and to provide an opportunity for all Americans to own their own property. The act was also designed to encourage and pay for the construction of a transcontinental railroad. Under the terms of the act, any male or female citizen over the age of twenty-one, the head of a family, or anyone declaring his or her intention to become a

citizen could file on a quarter section (160 ac___ ____) ___ _____-
owned land, for a fee of $10.00. The homestead__ ___ _____-
live on the land for five years, make certain impro__ ___ ____ ____
file for a final title. However, he or she could w___ ___ ____ ____
requirement by living on the land for six months ____ ____ paying
the government $1.25 an acre.

The settlers could acquire land by other mea___ ___ ___ ____
instance, under the preemption law of 1841, s____ _____ ____
acquire 160 acres of government land for $1.25 an ____ __ ____
agreed to live on the land and improve it. A perso_ _____ ___ file_
both a homestead claim and a preemption clai__, __ereby
acquiring up to 320 acres. Many people did, but not all of them
intended to farm the land.

During the 1870s, after extensive lobbying efforts, Congress
enacted several laws that facilitated the transfer of government
land into private hands, although not necessarily those of the
farmer. The Timber Culture Act of 1873 allowed homesteaders
to apply for 160 acres, in addition to those they could obtain
through homesteading and preemption, by agreeing to plant
one-fourth of the land to trees. The Desert Land Act of 1877,
which had been lobbied through Congress by the ranchers,
allowed individuals to claim up to 640 acres at $1.25 an acre if
they would irrigate it. And in 1878 the Timber and Stone Act
allowed land defined as unfit for cultivation and valuable
chiefly for timber and stone to be bought at the rate of 160
acres for $2.50 an acre or, as one person noted, "the price of a
log."

A considerable amount of creativity was shown by those eager
to claim the land. In some areas, in order to fulfill the requirement
that a dwelling place be built on each homestead, entrepreneurs
rented houses on wheels that could be moved from claim to claim.
Until they were prevented from doing so, couples sometimes built
their house across the line separating two claims. Companies hired
people to file claims, with the understanding that the companies
would then buy the land from them. Under the Homestead and
Preemption acts, an individual who acquired a claim could sell it:
the land did not revert to the government. The Timber Culture Act
encouraged "innovation," as did the Desert Land Act. People were
paid to testify that they had observed water on a certain tract of
land; of course, the water might have been poured from a bucket.
And the Timber and Stone Act, lobbied through Congress by the
logging companies, was used by these companies to acquire massive
stands of timber in the West. In port cities, the logging companies

vied for agreements with sailors who would take out claims on timberlands and then "sell" them to the companies.

Despite these abuses, the Homestead Act still helped to open up the Great Plains. Much of the land owned by private speculators was settled because they had a vested interest in seeing that it was.

The Railroads

By 1869, the Central Pacific and Union Pacific railway lines reached San Francisco, and other companies had lines running through all of the midwestern states. Between 1850 and 1871, to encourage the development of the western territories, Congress awarded to the railroads vast tracts of public land. The usual procedure was to give the railroads alternating, 640-acre sections of land in a checkerboard pattern along the entire length of a line. Sometimes, however, all of the property along a line was reserved for the railroads until they completed it and chose the sections they wanted.

In an effort to encourage agricultural education, the federal government gave each state 30,000 acres of land for each of its senators and representatives in Congress in order to help the states finance the construction of colleges. And though it contradicted the intent of the Homestead Act, the government also sold land to investors in huge blocks of 10,000 or more acres, before the practice was ended in 1889. In these and other ways, the land was concentrated, not in the hands of independent small farmers, but in the hands of a few people with similar interests.

By the turn of the century, public lands had been disposed of in the following fashion (Gates, 1936:657–662):

Grants to railroads	183 million acres
Grants to states	140 million acres
Direct sales by Land Office	100 million acres
Indian lands sold	100 million acres

Although many people believe the United States was open to free homesteading during this period, probably less than one acre in nine went to the small pioneers. Cochrane (1979) concluded that out of the billion acres distributed, only 147 million became homesteads. Whether these were homesteads that people settled to farm or property purchased for speculation is irrelevant. What is important is that a relatively small number of acres was set aside for the pioneer farmer. What did the large land owners, such as the railroads, do with their land? In most cases, they sold it to people who, lured by tales of free or cheap land, wanted to move to the new frontier.

The railroads were a key factor in the development and sale of this land. The value of a tract of land was directly related to whether a rail line went through it or through a nearby property. Thus both the federal and state governments were encouraged to pass legislation that gave the railroads the most favorable conditions for selecting land and, at least initially, for setting rates for freight and passengers. Often, the liberal legislation for the railroads was pushed by the land speculators. The states could not enlarge their tax coffers unless they could sell the lands they owned, and this sale depended on the railroads.

The railroad companies spared no effort to attract immigrants to the lands they held. They dispatched agents to foreign countries to paper the walls with bills advertising the virtues of such far-removed lands as Kansas, Nebraska, and Minnesota. Railroad brochures circulating in the eastern United States told of land in the West selling for between $2.50 and $6.00 an acre. Some railroad companies even offered credit, which was extremely important to some of the cash-poor residents of eastern cities.

Prospective immigrants were told of cattle grazing on well-developed farms in lush river valleys. Yet, in reality, nothing like this awaited them. Instead, the early settlers often discovered that they had to drill deep wells, find firewood, build houses out of sod, and brave the elements—seldom with any other settlers nearby to turn to for comfort.

The states and towns also competed for immigrants and distributed booklets to attract newcomers, for new people meant that land values would go up. Some speculators even offered free land in order to increase the local population. Once the wagon trains were on their way or people reached the end of their railway journey, they were often confronted by agents for a particular town.

The railroads had a dual impact on the development of the frontier: they encouraged immigration and offered transportation to and from the eastern markets for the new settlers' crops and goods. The railroads were thus directly linked to the economic welfare of those settling the Midwest. So important were the railroads that existing towns offered inducements to them to run a spur in their direction. If that failed, the towns would sometimes move to the rail line. In one Kansas town, all of the buildings were put on rollers and moved several miles so that they could be next to a line.

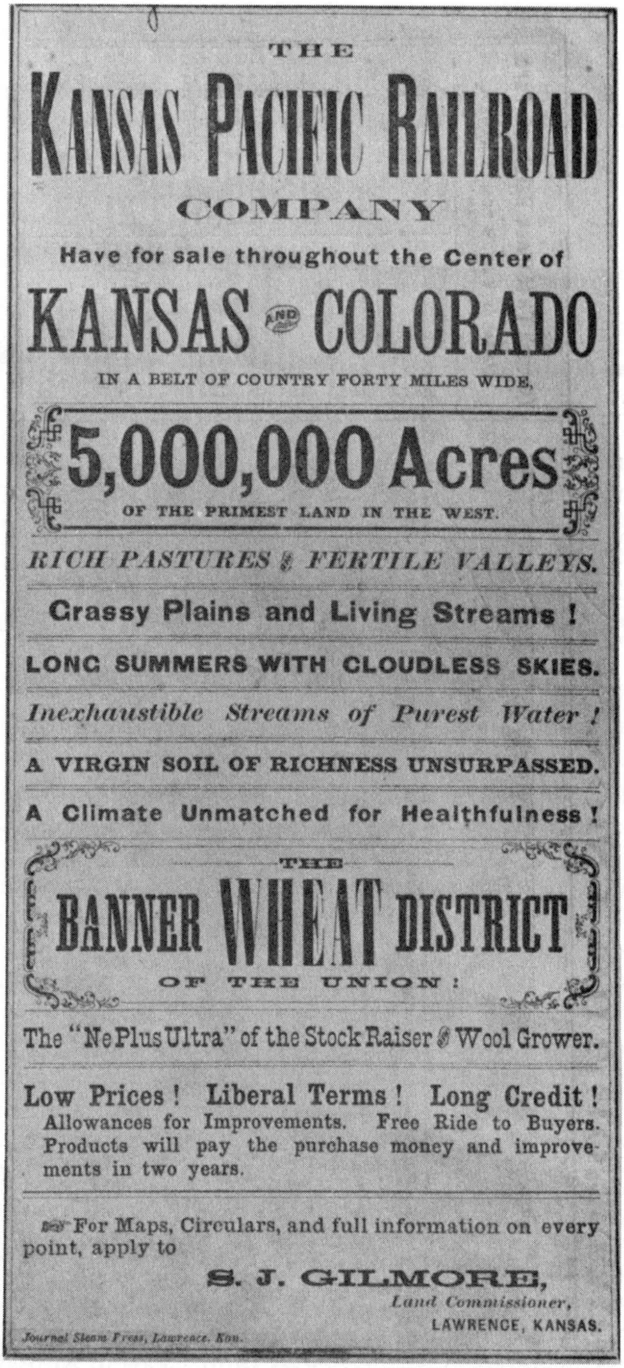

Courtesy of the Kansas State Historical Society

As we will see later, attitudes toward the railroads varied considerably. Farmers found themselves hard pressed to meet the costs of moving their crops to market and demanded federal and state regulation of the railroads. The townspeople, however, did not usually side with the farmers, because their economic interests were linked to the railroads.

The Boom Mentality

After the Civil War the population of the Midwest grew because of opportunities to get rich. Farm prices rose fairly consistently from 1860 onward, in great part because of the influx of European immigrants to the East Coast and new opportunities to sell agricultural products to Europe. Ranchers in Texas could now sell their cattle to eastern markets for twenty times what they were paid locally.

The railroads, anxious to sell their land, were quick to point to the ease with which newcomers could make their fortunes. In *Settler's Guide* (circa 1870), the Kansas Pacific Railway touted the virtues of its lands:

> The plain facts as they exist today...the sober story of our actual climate and soil, rolling prairies, fertile fields, meadows and uplands, running streams and winding brooks, the content and prosperity of our people, our cheap lands, the splendid prizes of home, wealth, and friends which this country offers the industrious in whatever business engaged, our churches, schools, etc., the warm welcome accorded all newcomers, the assurance that there is room for all here—it is these plain facts which we wish to get before the young, the ambitious, the stout-hearted sons and daughters of the East; before parents wishing to make a new home for themselves and family where the evil influences and associations of the saloon are and will be forever unknown; before the business man seeking new fields for investment and enterprise, before the stock-raiser who wants more land, and corn, and cattle, and hogs. It is these classes, the heart, strength, and mind of the land, whom we wish to interest and assure that an intelligent, progressive community...bids them welcome, thrice welcome....
>
> We are eager to speak of our soil—deep as an old ocean's bed and rich as her coral caves, dark as the orbs of an orient princess, watered by special dews from Heaven, to make the

grasses long and juicy and the cattle strong and fat. To harvest, one has but to plant corn, oats, wheat, sorghum, barley, rye, buckwheat, potatoes, broom-corn, millet, clover, and timothy, and each year seems to add some new cereal, fruit, or shrub; apples, peaches, pears, cherries, plums, and small fruits of almost every description are grown in this valley, and although comparatively new, we have as promising orchards and vineyards here as can be found in any country, East or West.

The guide compared prairie lands with the gold fields of California, and as expected, people and money flowed in. The guide hastened to assure its readers that it was not a product of the writer's imagination and recommended that those who wanted to read about impossible dreams consult other railroads' guides to Florida and California.

Many of the new farms, especially the larger ones, were financed with eastern money. Louis Watson, a Kansas doctor whose practice had fallen on hard times because "the people were either too healthy, or they went to the naturopath," began a large experimental farm with the help of the Kansas Pacific Railway. In a letter to his mother, dated August 1, 1879, he explained:

The "Kansas matter" is a contract I effected with the Kansas Pacific Railway to make an experimental farm 300 miles west of the Missouri river. The contract is a good one, but it requires money to carry it out. I have raised enough to make the first payment on 3200 acres of land which I have selected immediately surrounding an important station on the railroad. The land is good with plenty of good water but no timber. That has to be planted. I organized a corporation with capital stock of $25,000 assigned my contract upon the company's agreement to pay me a certain amount therefore and pay me a salary as General Manager for two years. It would be all right were the stock all taken. I hope it will be soon. If not, it's possible I may go East or send somebody on that business. The fare to Boston being only $20.00. (Diary of Dr. Louis Watson, Kansas State Historical Society, 1879)

Many large farms had been started before the Civil War, and there had been plantation holdings of several thousand acres since colonial times. Many people were familiar with the large holdings of the western cattle kings, but most were unaware of the large size of the farms west of the Missouri River. As early as 1860, for example, there were 501 farms of 1,000 acres or more in the nine North Central states or territories (Shannon, 1945:155). The major development of large or "bonanza" farms, as they were called, occurred between 1870 and 1890 in the Red River Valley of the North. The valley ran in a 300-mile strip, up to 40 miles wide in some places, from the Dakotas through northern Minnesota.

The development of large farms, which were originally financed by railroad capital, began when wheat prices were high. One organization hired Oliver Dalrymple, a Minnesota wheat farmer, to oversee its first venture. The organization furnished all of the capital, and when the farms had returned the original capital, plus interest, Dalrymple was to receive half the land and all the improvements. In the first year, 1,280 acres were cultivated, and the yield was 23 bushels to the acre. As Shannon (1945:157) wrote, "These results were widely advertised, and the Dakota boom was on." By the second season, Dalrymple was farming 4,500 acres, which eventually grew to 100,000 acres.

Other farms were equally large—40,000- to 60,000-acre operations were not uncommon. Shannon (1945:158) estimated that the average cost per acre of land, machines, and labor was about $9.50. Most of the pioneers did not have this much money, but they often furnished the labor for these large enterprises.

The interconnectedness of events during this period should be clear. So far we have seen that the opening of the frontier was accomplished in a remarkably short time, though not by the yeoman farmer of legend. Resources—capital in substantial amounts—were necessary for taking up a claim or developing it. Land speculators, the railroads, and the federal government all helped open the frontier, but little of this would have occurred were there not rapidly expanding markets for agricultural products.

THE PEOPLE

The Question of Slavery

The settlement of the Great Plains was bound up with the issue of whether a state, on being admitted to the Union, would be a free or a slave state. This conflict shaped the Great Plains' politics and the norms and values of those who settled the area. Congress had been debating the route of the future transcontinental railway and was set to authorize a southern one. Stephen Douglas, a senator from Illinois and a heavy speculator in western lands and Chicago real estate, wanted a northern route running from Minneapolis–St. Paul, through what is now North Dakota, and across the northern part of the United States to Portland, Oregon. In order to persuade Congress to decide on this route, Douglas had to show that it passed through an area of settlement. Hence, in January 1854, he introduced a bill to create the Nebraska Territory, which more or less encompassed the present states of North Dakota, South Dakota, Wyoming, Montana, and Nebraska.

To entice the southern senators into voting for this bill, Douglas introduced the concept of "popular sovereignty." This meant that once the people in an area had formed a territorial legislature, they could vote on whether they wanted the territory to be free or slave. The bill flew in the face of the Missouri Compromise of 1820, which prohibited slavery north of the 36th parallel. Some of the southern senators wanted to repeal the Missouri Compromise so that any western state could choose slavery. The "solution" was the Kansas-Nebraska Act, which divided the area into the Kansas and Nebraska territories, with Nebraska free and the fate of Kansas left to popular sovereignty.

"Bleeding Kansas," as it came to be called, was up for grabs. In 1854, even before the Indians' claims had been settled, the federal government opened a land office. Both proslavery and antislavery forces competed to settle the area. The New England Emigrant Aid Company and other societies financed the settling of entire antislavery towns. The first such town, Lawrence, Kansas, was involved in battles with proslavery forces from Missouri. The Kansas-Missouri border was, in fact, the scene of many pre–Civil War skirmishes. Senator David R. Atchison of Missouri boasted of these times: "We had at least 7000 men in the Territory on the day of the election, and one-third of them will remain there. The proslavery ticket prevailed everywhere. Now let the Southern men come on with their slaves. . . .We are playing for a mighty stake; if we win, we carry slavery to the Pacific Ocean" (cited in Morison, 1965:591).

But slavery did not prevail. In what was called the "Great Exodus," many southern blacks, most of whom had been born slaves, migrated to Kansas in the late 1870s and the 1880s. Like many immigrants before them, they came as much to escape persecution as to seek opportunity. Like other immigrants, when possible, they traveled as families (Gutman, 1976: 433-438).

Ethnicity

Many of the antislavery settlers were not new immigrants to the United States, but people who were already established in eastern areas. After the Civil War, however, foreign settlers flooded into the Great Plains and helped to shape its political, religious, and economic institutions. Sometimes, because of the diverse number of foreign settlers, people found it difficult to talk to one another. As one woman immigrant said in 1854:

> We came to America that year with a Mr. LeFeaver from Belgium. He brought along provisions, also a milk cow to supply our food, but finding conditions different from what he had anticipated, started back to Belgium the latter part of the same year, leaving us on the prairie. . . . We had some bedding and a few ears of corn brought from Belgium, but no shelter whatever. My father was sick and we were found by a trapper. As my folks could speak only French they could not converse with the trapper, but he took a piece of charred coal and on his hands made characters and signs which told my father that down on the Shunganunga Creek we would find a Frenchman living with a black woman. (Letters of Clara Frost, Kansas Collection, University of Kansas, 1854)

By 1890, the percentage of foreign born in some states was as high as one-third to almost one-half of the total population (see Figure 1-1). But this percentage declined around 1900, because by then the American-born children of these immigrants helped to reduce the proportion of foreigners.

The midwestern frontier states attracted many German immigrants because of political and economic unrest in Germany during the early nineteenth century. These states also absorbed an influx of immigrants from Ireland, many of whom fled during the potato famine of the late 1840s; many Irish communities were established in Illinois, Wisconsin, Iowa, Nebraska, and Minnesota. Minnesota and the Dakota territories also had heavy concentrations of Scandinavian settlers. In many of these communities, there is still a generation of people who speak the language of their forebears. Festivals are held in many of these towns in tribute to their ethnic heritage. For instance, in the old Swedish community of Lindsborg, Kansas, an annual festival features folk dancing and the sale of Swedish items and foods. Similar events are observed in Czech, Irish, Russian, Norwegian, and German communities throughout the Midwest. Ethnicity shaped the lives of those who grew up in

Figure 1-1
PERCENTAGE OF FOREIGN BORN FOR SELECTED STATES: 1890

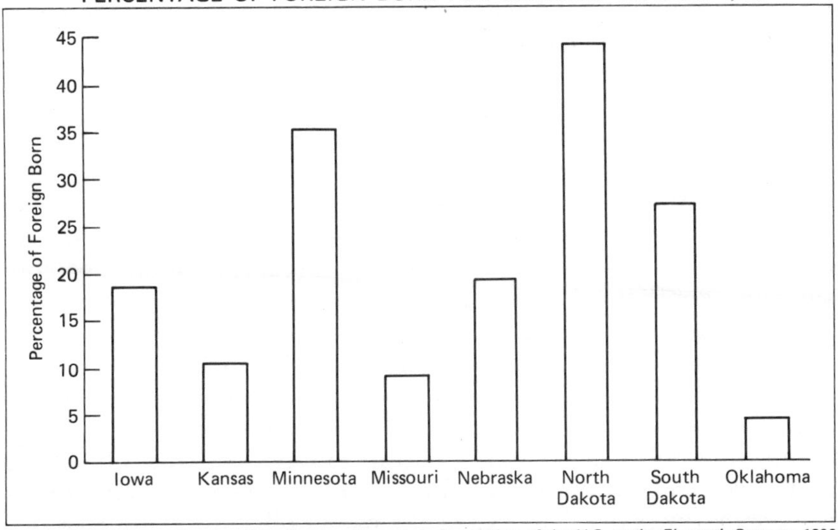

Source: United States Bureau of the Census. *Report on Population of the U.S. at the Eleventh Census: 1890*
(Washington, D.C.: U.S. Government Printing Office, 1893).

these communities; it was, and still is, a vital part of our historical experience.

Many communities were settled by members of a single religious faith, such as the Mennonites. Descendants of Swiss Anabaptists and followers of Menno Simons, most Mennonites came to the United States from Russia and Germany. In Russia, Empress Catherine II had guaranteed the sect religious and economic independence. But with the onset of the Franco-Prussian War in 1870, they were told to leave the country or become citizens within ten years. Because they were pacifists, Russian citizenship was not acceptable to the Mennonites. Cornelius Jansen, a leader of the Russian Mennonite community, came to the United States in 1872 to find a new home for his people. He met the foreign immigration agent of the Atchison, Topeka and Santa Fe railroad, which had recently acquired 3 million acres of Kansas land. Indeed, in 1874, the new government of Kansas, eager to attract immigrants, even passed a law exempting Mennonites and Quakers from military service. And like many foreign immigrants to the Middle West, the Mennonites arrived with their own assets: "The first arrival of Mennonites in Kansas...consisted of 400 families, 1900 people, who brought with them two and a quarter million dollars in gold, and purchased 60,000 acres of land in the counties of Marion, McPherson, Harvey and Reno" (cited in Sheridan, 1956:108–109).

The Mennonites also made important contributions to the culture and economy of the Midwest. Their communalism—their way of helping one another—saw them through difficult economic periods and stabilized many agricultural areas. Above all, they changed the prevailing agricultural customs. The Mennonites brought with them the wheat that still dominates world markets, Russian red winter wheat, which was better adapted to the climatic conditions of the Great Plains than either spring wheat or corn was.

The ethnicity and religious beliefs of the early settlers also influenced the politics of their region. For instance, the use of liquor, which varied by ethnic group, became a source of considerable conflict. Certain religious groups were reform minded, which led to the foundation of local and national movements aimed at improving the moral and physical lot of humanity. Of course, each group thought differently about how this might best be accomplished. The Temperance movement, religious reform movements, and political-economic reform movements were all shaped by the settlers' ethnic backgrounds, and as a result, communities were sometimes divided against themselves. Finally, ethnicity also influenced family size and structure.

The Family

The 1880 diary of Harry E. Kelly, an early settler in Kansas, described his neighbors:

> The Dubin family came here from the German section of Pennsylvania some time during 1878. This family consisted of two rather large sons, and a daughter. In fact the eldest son was already married and his young wife was at that time one of the members of the immediate family.
>
> Mr. Dubin was of the typical Prussian type and exceedingly fixed in his manners and opinions as most such men are, and although this might be acceptable in the East, it did not serve to make men very popular in the West at the time.
>
> He built his house about three miles southwest of our own immediate settlement. This was a small stone house at first, but very soon afterward a larger building was constructed, also several up to date farm buildings. His fields and gardens were always the best to be found on the prairies and his stock, both horses and cattle, were always above the average of his neighbors. He was one of the very first men to demonstrate the fact that tame fruit trees could grow on these prairies in spite of hot winds and little rain.

His married son, Amos, took up a claim about one mile north of his father's home where he lived the balance of his life. Eventually, the other children married and settled close by.

After the death of his wife, the elder Mr. Dubin returned to his home in the East where he later died. . . . (Papers of Harry E. Kelly, Kansas Collection, University of Kansas, 1887)

This account reveals much about frontier families. Many families with grown children came to the region from settled towns and farms on the eastern seaboard and often maintained close ties to the East. Sometimes one member of the family, usually the father, would travel to the area to be settled, locate a homesite, make certain improvements to it, and then return for his family.

Although popular myth tells another story, the size of the Dubin family is typical of that of the early American farm families. For instance, between 1850 and 1880, whether living on a farm or in a town, the average family consisted of about five people (Seward, 1978:85). This family was, for the most part, a *nuclear family*, that is, one made up of a husband and wife and their children. In this country's history, there has never been a significant number of extended families or several generations living under the same roof. Households have included nonfamily members, such as servants or laborers, but again, their numbers have not been significant. When two generations lived together, it was usually only for a limited period of time, and then for economic reasons. For example, the Dubins' son and his new wife lived with his parents, but only until they could establish their own home.

Although children certainly did help on the farm, they were not a principal economic asset. A couple did not have more children in order to expand their farming operations. Family size seems to have been determined less by economic factors than by individual decisions—or the failure to make such a decision (Seward, 1978).*

Frontier marriages, like those of today, were subject to strain and, consequently, to separation and divorce. In 1880, Kansan P. J. Jennings noted:

Rush was a bootmaker by profession, which made him a useful individual for the community to have. He had a wife and two children, one boy and one girl—named Willie and Maud. Domestic difficulties persuaded him, too, and another home on the prairie was thus abandoned.

These separations at that early date were very frequent on

*See also Smith (1974) for a discussion of how such decisions were made.

the prairies as many men and women could not seem to fight the battles of poverty and loneliness that was the portion of all of those who were trying to conquer the untamed West. (Diaries of P. J. Jennings, Kansas State Historical Society, 1880)

There are few reliable statistics on the number of marriages that were dissolved, however, because, like Rush, a husband or wife often left without obtaining a divorce.

Technology

A family's resources and size in part determined the amount of land they could farm and how they farmed it, as did the available technology. The families who settled the Great Plains in the mid-1800s often arrived with only an ox pulling their wagon and the family cow, and perhaps a horse, trailing behind.

After locating a suitable homesite on their 160-acre claim, the newcomers began cutting into the heavy prairie sod. In this one operation, they acquired arable land and, if they wanted a sod house, building material. Blocks of sod, about 12 by 18 inches in size, were piled on one another like bricks and "cemented" together with water to form walls about 4 to 5 feet high. Then the family organized an expedition to a creek or

Kansas sod house
Courtesy of the Kansas Collection, Kenneth Spencer Research Library, University of Kansas. Photograph by William Long, Hoxie, Kansas. From the collection of John R. Neuenschwander.

riverbed where they cut small saplings, often cottonwood, for rafters. The rafters were then overlaid with sod to form the roof. Over the years, the roof often became indistinguishable from the rolling hills around it, save for its chimney rising above the plain.

Before the introduction of the moldboard plow, turning the sod in order to plant corn or wheat was extremely difficult. Finding water for crops and livestock was also a problem. During especially dry times, water had to be carried by bucket from the well to the family garden; irrigating the larger crops was not yet feasible.

Seldom could any family keep more than twenty acres in production at one time. The farms, which were literally one-horse—or one-ox—operations, were basically self-sufficient: families consumed what they produced, and they produced only for themselves. Some were fortunate enough to live near streams where they could catch fish to preserve for the long winters. Others had money to buy chickens, hogs, or a milk cow. But most farmers had spent their cash buying their farms, and there was not much for them to buy, anyway, as community stores were few and far between.

The nature of farming and the farm family's well-being changed dramatically between 1860 and 1900 because of advances in technology. In 1866 Joseph Glidden patented a modern form of barbed wire, which was made commercially available during the 1880s. Before that time, farmers had used other types of fencing to protect their crops from cattle, but the materials were so costly that only small areas could be enclosed. Cheap wire meant the end of both the long cattle drives and the open range, as well as the beginning of a new pattern of settlement organized around small towns and the farmers who frequented them for supplies and entertainment. Cattle were no longer driven to market but were pastured out and fed over the winter. All these factors changed the characters of such towns as Dodge City, Wichita, and Abilene, which had been organized around the cattle drives, and altered the needs of those involved in the cattle industry (Dykstra, 1976).

Mechanized agriculture forever changed the way in which people related to the land. The midwestern states particularly welcomed the new machines, for the farms there were large, level, and contiguous. According to an 1899 report compiled by the United States commissioner of labor, it took a person about

61 hours to sow and harvest wheat by hand, whereas it took only 3 hours and 20 minutes with a machine. Moreover, machine labor was five times cheaper than hand labor. With inventions such as the McCormick reaper, patented in 1834, a farmer could harvest fifty times more land than with a sickle and flail.

Labor costs dropped, more land was cultivated, and the farmers' welfare was enhanced by still other inventions, such as gangplows that could be drawn by teams of up to forty horses. With these plows, farmers could turn several furrows at once. Spring-toothed harrows allowed them to break up the furrows and clods but at the same time retain the moisture in the ground. Grain drills could seed several furrows at once, and binders freed farmers from having to tie the shocks of wheat together by hand. The overall impact of these and other technological developments on the values, educational system, and economy of the Great Plains states should not be underestimated. Shannon (1945:145) noted:

> The most obvious result was the reduction in spirit-deadening toil. This helped the man who was fortunate in his selection of soil and wise in management...to acquire prosperity and leisure, and give his family added cultural advantages. Certainly, the academies, high schools, colleges, and universities which sprung up in all the predominantly agricultural states, after 1860, were created out of the wealth produced, directly or otherwise, primarily by the farmers. So were the churches, the small-town industries, and many of the cultural activities.

The Economy

The machine age introduced the age of credit. Early farmers were short of cash; yet, if they were to increase their levels of production, and thereby their incomes, they needed to bring more ground under cultivation. This could be accomplished only by using machines. In 1890, a simple walking plow cost $13, a gangplow cost $55, a three-disc plow $70, a drill about $55, and a twine binder an average of $150 (U.S. Department of Agriculture, 1901:15–23). Hicks et al. (1965:169) estimated that the average northern farmer of the pre-1900 period had to invest about $785 in machinery, which was far more than a year's income.

Optimism, expanding markets in the East, and simple need meant the farmer had to borrow. Although data were never kept systematically, Shannon (1945:185) determined that in 1880 the average farm mortgage was $1,224. These figures do not include those farms in the United States—at least half of them—that were not solely owner operated but were run by tenants or sharecroppers.

From the beginning, then, farmers participated in a cash economy. Limited at first, as we have noted, this economy grew along with the growth of the region. The farmers had to sell their produce on the open market in order to pay the interest and principal on their debts. Although they participated in a cash economy, the farmers did not participate directly in a capitalist economy. Farm labor was significantly different from factory labor. Farmers engaged in simple commodity production, that is, they produced a product, sold it, and realized the full benefit of their own labor. Most farmers owned or controlled their own farms and seldom used hired labor. If they made a surplus or a profit, it belonged to them alone.

Initially, women contributed substantially to their families' income, often by selling butter and eggs. In some diaries, we find accounts of sums as high as $300 a year earned in this way. In the account books of P. J. Jennings, for example, we find that his cash income for the year of 1881 amounted to $400; of this amount about $200 came from sales that his wife made to the town's general store (Jennings Collection, Kansas State Historical Society).

As well, the farmers were affected by the larger society, but the ways in which they labored and produced supported values different from those of people who had only their labor power to sell. The value system of the American farmer, which developed during this period, from 1860 to 1900, is still relatively intact and must be taken into account in explaining the social movements that have flourished in this region.

The farmers' needs for credit introduced several long-lasting conflicts between those in the cities and those on the farms. From the farmers' perspective, the system favored the ranchers. Drovers (cattlemen) were able to borrow at rates of close to 5 percent with no collateral, whereas the farmers were often charged rates of from 36 to 50 percent, depending on whether or not the money was from a bank, and they were required to put up their entire farms as collateral. The terms of the loans were harsh, because the interest was taken out of the principal before it was lent. A loan of $1,000 meant that the farmer would have, at a 40 percent rate, $600 in hand. One farmer complained to the Wichita, Kansas, *Beacon* in 1874: "The farmer can't borrow a dollar from the banks on his land or anything that is his except his note with undoubted security from thirty to ninety days, but the Texas cattleman can borrow ten thousand dollars on his individual note without endorsement" (Dykstra, 1976:185). The farmers were viewed as poor credit risks by the banks because they were subject to many economic uncertainties, such as droughts, insects, and illness.

The grasshopper plagues, which struck Kansas, Nebraska, and the Dakotas during the 1870s, were the undoing of many families. One farmer described what happened to him and his family:

I don't know how we are going to make it through the winter. We were almost ready to bring in the wheat, but it now looks as though we'd run a reaper over it. We had been out working and all of a sudden the sky began to get dark and we saw this cloud moving toward us. First, we thought it was a storm, but then it turned out to be hoppers. They ate everything. There's nothing left. But the oddest sight is the peach tree, which has been stripped of all the fruit and its leaves. The only thing left on the tree is the peach pits, swaying in the breeze. (From the private collection of the Engler family, Topeka, Kansas)

The devastation wrought by grasshoppers led to the first organized attempts at public relief. After passing a law citing the grasshopper as a public enemy, the state of Nebraska voted a bond issue to buy seed for the next year; Kansas spent $70,000 on a similar measure; and the Dakota territories spent $25,000. The federal government, through the United States Army, distributed food and clothing worth approximately $150,000 (Shannon, 1945:153). In some of the more prosperous towns, women formed relief societies and raised money to help the poor farmers.

There were many arguments as to whether the farmers should be helped. Those against helping them often lived in towns that depended on the farmers' trade, but they did not understand that their own long-term interests would be served by a stable and prosperous agricultural sector. These people wanted to use public funds to improve facilities in the town and to enhance property values. And so taxes and bonds were usually used to build courthouses, jails, parks, streets, bridges, and waterworks. Although the farmers did sometimes succeed, they did not yet see themselves as a distinct political and economic class; that was to come with the rise of Populism. Furthermore, in some areas, communication among the farmers was hindered by distances, poor roads, or language and ethnic barriers, which made political organization difficult. The farmers' economic welfare, then, initially depended on factors other than the political system.

Credit was necessary for the farmers—to tide them over difficult times, to purchase the machines necessary to increase their productivity, and to bring more land under production. For most farmers, accumulating capital was a long and slow process. When they did have money, it usually went to pay off outstanding debts and then to expand the farming operation. Many a farmer's wife commented in her diary, with some chagrin, that "the barn is the finest building we have."

The money that the farmers did have came from a variety of sources. Sometimes immigrants arrived with money and were able to purchase land and machines. Others borrowed eastern dollars, which constituted the major source of capital for development in the Midwest. Eastern money came with the small entrepreneurs who moved West to establish mercantile stores, livery stables, or hotels. Eastern dollars provided the capital for many midwestern banks, and some was available to the farmers. The penetration of the Midwest by eastern capital meant that credit was not a local matter and that the fortunes of the Midwest were tied to a national and, ultimately, international economic system. Finally, the farmers, through their own labor, increased the value of their holdings, which often were their principal capital. Between 1860 and 1900, the number of farms in the United States doubled, growing from about 2 million to 5.7 million (U.S. Department of Commerce, 1949:95). The value of food exports rose from $12.2 million in 1860 to $305 million in 1897 and declined after that. (These figures are relative and not in current dollars.) Farm productivity grew steadily between 1860 and 1920, meaning that the advances in technology increased the output per acre and per worker. Fewer farmers, therefore, were needed to feed the growing urban populations.

The farmers were also tied to the national economy through mechanisms other than the credit system. With the construction of the railroads and through their systems of credit, farm products were sold to the growing market of urban workers in Chicago, St. Louis, and New York, as well as in Europe. The farmers had begun to diversify and fed some of their grain to their cattle and hogs.

In addition, the invention of the refrigerated railroad car meant that live hogs and cattle could be sent to Chicago for slaughtering, where they then were chilled and sent to the East. The meat-packing industry represented a tremendous concentration of wealth and monopolization. "Inevitably the trend toward monopoly, so evident in the steel and oil industries, also affected the meat packers, whose activities tended to revolve about the names of Philip Armour, Nelson Morris, and Gustavus F. Swift" (Hicks et al., 1965:132). This meant that the buyers, not the growers, dominated the early agricultural markets.

During this same time, other fertile lands throughout the world, in Canada, Australia, New Zealand, and Argentina, were being brought under production, and their products began to compete with American goods. All might have gone well had the population of the United States continued its rate of growth, but, although high until 1900, it began to fall after about 1870: "In the decades of the seventies and eighties the increase was just over 25 percent, and in the nineties it was more than 20 percent, a substantial growth in the number of mouths to feed" (Robertson, 1973:307). An offsetting factor was that a smaller percent of total per-capita income was spent on food, dropping from about one-third in 1870 to one-fifth by 1890. Many factors operated in concert to make things increasingly uncertain for the farmers: they were heavily mortgaged, they did not control the markets, and many new producers were entering the world market and driving down prices. And then came the panic of 1873.

Jay Cooke, a prestigious banker, had spent a major portion of his bank's resources on the Northern Pacific Railroad, whose expansion depended on foreign capital, which in turn had disappeared with the Franco-Prussian War of 1870. In May 1873, there was a panic on the Vienna stock exchange in which European investors sold most of their American holdings, chiefly railroad stocks. On the American side, many had been speculating in railroad securities, allowing the railroads to build in unpopulated areas and operate at a loss. American banks had lent them millions of dollars for expansion. And so with the worth of their railroad securities in doubt, Cooke's partners shocked the public by closing the doors of Jay Cooke and Co. on September 18, 1873. The resulting panic on the New York Stock Exchange drove down prices so low that the exchange had to close for two weeks. The result was a six-year depression that affected both the United States and Europe.

The rapid growth of the Great Plains slowed dramatically. Farmers lost their markets, and the railroads responded to their plight by attempting to extract higher transportation rates for the products they did move. And because of their power, the railroads had come to dominate all areas of transporting farm products: they owned the grain elevators, warehouses, and collecting pens.

At the mercy of national markets and unable to control railroad rates, many farmers were driven from their land to the cities. Others stayed but went to work as farm laborers or became tenants. Between 1880 and 1890 the percentage of tenant farmers increased from 16.3 to 35.2 percent in Kansas and also increased dramatically in such states as Oklahoma, Nebraska, and the Dakotas. But despite the falling farm prices, production did not slacken. The result of the boom and bust cycles was a number of social and political movements aimed at controlling some of the farmers' uncertainties.

Politics and Farmers' Movements

National Politics　　The Patrons of Husbandry, or the Grangers, as they became known, were founded in 1867 and reached the height of their popularity shortly after the panic of 1873, when their membership stood at about 1.5 million (Cochrane, 1979:95). The Grangers had two main activities, and in a sense, both were unsuccessful. First, the Grangers were concerned with railroad legislation and in several states managed to pass laws controlling tariffs. They saw these laws being directed primarily at the "Eastern Money Conspiracy" (Thompson, 1969:300). Although many of these laws were judged to be unconstitutional, they did set the precedent for state control of the railroads, but in a different form than the Grangers had envisioned.

The Grangers' second activity was summed up in a portion of their credo, "To foster mutual understanding and cooperation...to buy less and produce more...to diversify our crops...to discountenance the credit system" (cited in Thompson, 1969:300). This took the concrete form of trying to establish buying cooperatives, cooperative elevators, creameries, stores, cooperative selling agencies, and even plants to manufacture their own implements. As one might expect, the Grangers were subject to intense competition from established merchants and implement dealers. The dealers lowered their prices below production costs (which they were able to do because of their monopolistic positions) until they drove the new cooperatives out of business. The Grangers were inexperienced and thus did not have the range of skills and talents needed to sustain their vision. By 1876, when the Greenback issue became prominent, the Grange had become primarily a social club.

Credit problems constantly dogged the farmers. During the Civil War, "greenbacks" (paper dollars) were put into circulation and had an inflationary effect, which was what the farmers wanted because it meant they could pay off their mortgages with cheaper money and receive higher prices for their goods. Basically, the so-called Greenbackers wanted to end all specie payments, which meant that neither gold nor silver would be used in their transactions. Rather, the federal government would issue paper money, which would become legal tender for all debts, and would be convertible on demand into interest-bearing government bonds. (In essence, this is the situation today. Our greenbacks are not redeemable either in gold or silver as they once were but are backed by the power of the federal government to tax.) In any event, the farmers wanted an expanded currency and saw this as a way to get it and also to check the power of the local banks. Related to this was the issue of free silver, although, theoretically, the Greenbackers did not want specie payments of any kind. But for the farmers, the plan of free coinage of silver meant simply more money in circulation. William Jennings Bryan's ringing statement, "Thou shalt not crucify mankind upon a cross of gold," was a challenge by the western farmers to the "monied East" and their recognition that inflation would benefit them.

The Farmers' Alliances were, like the Grange, a means by which farmers attempted to make themselves heard. There were two alliances, Northern and Southern. Although the interests of both were essentially the same, only the Northern will concern us here. The strength of the Northern Alliance, founded in 1880, lay in the wheat-raising section of Kansas, Nebraska, the Dakotas, and Minnesota and was directed against the railroads (Hicks et al., 1965:182). Made up of a loose confederation of representatives from the different northern states, the Alliance ventured into some of the same areas as did the Grange—for example, cooperative buying and selling. The Alliance had originally tried to stay out of politics but was drawn in as it recognized that more and more of the farmers' problems stemmed from corrupt bankers, railroad magnates, and merchants. It called for increased intervention by the federal government and for state and local laws that would help them. The Alliance entered the elections of 1890 (a year of hard times for most farmers) under a variety of names. The name given the movement in Kansas stuck; it was called the People's party, or simply the Populists.

Although the Populists were a political party, Populism was

often less a well-thought-out political response than it was a cry of anguish. Joseph Gusfield (1955), in writing about the Temperance movement, spoke of symbolic crusades, movements begun less for the sake of specific reform than because they offered a way to express frustration with attacks on values or ways of life. In 1890, Mary Elizabeth Lease of Kansas, a strong supporter of labor and a militant Populist, purportedly told an assembled audience of Populist sympathizers: "What you farmers need to do is to raise less corn and more Hell." Barr (1918:1148) also caught the spirit of the gatherings: "It was a religious revival, a crusade, a pentecost of politics in which a tongue of flame sat upon every man, and each spake as the spirit gave him utterance.... The farmers, the country merchants, the cattleherders, they of the long chin-whiskers, they of the broad-brimmed hats and heavy boots had...heard the word and could preach the gospel of Populism." The Alliances' initial foray into politics was quite successful. Although they did not capture complete control of the legislatures, they were able for a limited period to control the balance of power as the third party of Kansas, Nebraska, South Dakota, and Minnesota.

The first convention of the People's party was held in 1891. The delegates called for monetary inflation, specifically the free coinage of silver; they wanted the federal government to own and operate all railroads and telegraph and telephone systems; and they wanted the railroads to return to the government unneeded lands that they had received as bonuses for building in uninhabited territory. The delegates also advocated other reforms, but the issue of free silver became the most visible plank in the platform—for some, the only plank.

The election of 1892 brought to the foreground many of the farmers' problems, but it also effectively spelled the end of the People's party and the Alliances, even though they did enter candidates in the election of 1896. In brief, in 1892 the Republicans renominated President Benjamin Harrison, whose popularity had been declining. The Democrats chose Grover Cleveland, and the Populists ran James B. Weaver. Cleveland won an overwhelming majority in the electoral college, and the control of both the House and Senate passed into Democratic hands.

The Republicans were defeated in part because in many areas of the country the Populists joined with the Democrats, hoping for an alliance that would bring them to power on both local and state levels (Parsons, 1973). They deserted their own candidate, Weaver, believing that if they worked for the Democratic candidates, they would be rewarded with positions of power. Traditional Democratic politicians, however, had little desire to share their power with the Populists and fought with them over the control of resources.

One important discovery in this and the following campaign was the class basis of Populism, which can be considered to be the first class-based political movement in the United States. Its defeat meant, temporarily at least, the defeat of progressivism as a whole (Parsons, 1973). In 1896, the Populists worked to have their candidate, William Jennings Bryan, nominated as the standard-bearer for the Democrats, and they were successful. Bryan was, however, defeated by the Republican candidate, William McKinley.

The elections of 1892 and 1896 provoked a number of local conflicts and problems. First, in many of the midwestern states, the difference between being a Democrat or a Republican originally pertained to whether or not one supported slavery. For many settlers, the Republican party was, indeed, the Grand Old Party of the Republic. After the Civil War, however, the farmers believed that they had been forgotten by the party in power, because the Republicans opposed the free coinage of silver. Many settlers left the Republican fold, moving first to the Populists and then to the Democrats. In the towns, especially those settled by free staters, the population was often solidly Republican, whereas the farmers in the surrounding area were not. This, as we will see, did not contribute to harmony in community politics. But this was not the only important political development of the time.

Between 1860 and the early 1900s, the federal government continued to grow into a major force in the lives of all its citizens. This came about partly because people called for more government intervention. Farmers, because of their economic problems, had been calling for increased governmental control of the railroads as well as other agencies that affected their lives. The national government also began to assume an independence of its own, balancing the interests of the farmers, the urban laborers, and the upper classes. Today's federal bureaucracy is the result of response and adjustment to a variety of historical forces and necessities.

Community Politics   The small town has often been portrayed as the seedbed of American democracy. Following historian Frederick Jackson Turner, who saw the frontier experience as vital to shaping the political spirit of American life, Elkins and McKitrick (1954) argued that American democracy grew out of the experience of small-town life. They felt that people took a hands-on approach to government, directly involving themselves in the decision-making process when the issues concerned them. As the issues changed, so did their involvement and leadership; for example, the person who led the fight for paving the streets might be totally disinterested in building a new schoolhouse. Decisions were made by a relatively homogeneous group of people by means of participation, bargaining, and negotiation. Dykstra (1976) questioned this assumption on a number of counts. First he noted that Elkins and McKitrick viewed the small town as closed, insulated from national pressures and issues. Furthermore, they saw politics as essentially consensual, with decisions that were a summation of different opinions. Democracy became a peaceful mode of settling disputes. But this is not the situation that Dykstra (1976) described in the cattle towns that sprang up on the prairies, nor is it typical of the events mentioned in the letters and diaries presented in later chapters.

Decisions are more than the result of different opinions being distilled until the will of the community is expressed. Very often, one group dominates at the expense of another. As the towns began to grow, their inhabitants developed economic needs different from those of the people who lived on the farms. A bond issue might call for improving the town's streets rather than the rural roads. The farmers would oppose the issue; yet it might pass because the farmers were disorganized or because there were simply fewer of them to vote. Sometimes one town's elite would be pitted against another, and it would solicit the farmers' votes, promising them concessions in return. In short, in most towns, the normal democratic process was conflictual.

The towns' politics reflected the class differences and needs of their people, who were anything but homogeneous. The banker's interests were probably different from the farmer's, whose interests were different from the rancher's, whose interests were different from the hotel owner's. The farmers were looked down upon in many towns, and often there were attempts to manipulate their votes.

Farmers responded to a general sense of rejection by town dwellers with one of the few concrete weapons they had for wielding important power: county politics. Even when a minority in terms of numbers, they sometimes controlled the balance between urban factions contending for political dominance. The initiative, however, was frequently with the townsmen. In 1878, for example, Dodge City's uppermost clique retained its grasp on county offices by shrewdly gaining the endorsement of the rural Greenbacker element, outbidding its rivals for the easily manipulated rural German vote, and in general displaying a cynical affection, as an opposition (newspaper) editor put it, for "the 'dear farmer,' whom they have cursed and abused ever since those honest tillers of the soil have dared to settle on our lands." (Dykstra, 1976:188)

There were, then, many sources of factionalism in these frontier communities: the newcomers versus the old; the farmers versus the townspeople; the Democrats versus the Republicans; the "damned Grangers" against the nonfarmers; the ranchers against the farmers; and the ethnic, non-English-speaking settlers against those of Northern European descent. Some of this mixture was represented by reform movements, which covered a wide spectrum of people.

Early American Puritan religions were unique in their overriding belief that everyone's morals were in constant need of improvement. This drive for improvement might take the form of a crusade to stop drinking, gambling, and/or financial irresponsibility. Many reform movements were an "alliance of evangelical, feminist, anti-liquor idealism" (Dykstra, 1976:245), although the leaders generally were men. At its most moderate, reform could organize relief committees of townspeople to help the "poor farmers." At its most radical extreme, it became the Prohibition movement, which was linked to nativism, Protestantism, and the Republican party. The immigrants often resisted Prohibition, not because they wished to drink—although to some groups, such as the Germans and Irish, drinking was a significant part of their culture—but because the movement was anti-immigrant. It was, as Gusfield (1955) suggested, a last-ditch attempt by rural Protestants to impose their way of life on others. The link between the Republican party and reform meant that many Republicans in small towns came to see themselves as the upholders of American values; thus they were sometimes antifarmer, anti-Grange, anti-Greenback, and certainly anti-Democrat. They tended to represent the elite of their local communities, that is , those who had the most money and were the best educated. On the other hand, the farmers began as Grangers, moved toward the Alliance, then Populism, and finally, in many cases, to the Democratic party. They tended to be poorer and less well educated.

It is not, then, entirely inappropriate to speak of the early Republicans as conservative and supportive of the values of a commercial class and, conversely, of the Democrats as radical and supportive of a laboring population. In many frontier communities, these parties represented important divisions within the population. Time has, of course, blurred these boundaries, but history can help us understand why, for several generations, some families voted a solid Democratic or Republican ticket.

Community

What the immigrants had been led to expect and what they found were often at variance. The land agents for various towns, real and imagined, distributed plans and sketches throughout the eastern states and Europe. An early map of one of the "new Edens" in Kansas, Nebraska, and the Dakotas shows a well-planned town with 250 lots and two rail lines crossing in the middle. It gives the location of Methodist, Baptist, Episcopalian, and Presbyterian churches, as well as the site of a "cathedral" for any Catholics who might want to settle. There was a large park conveniently situated in the center of town, as well as a railroad depot, hotel, merchant's exchange, courthouse, and opera house. In addition, there were a grammar and high school (combined), a "New Eden University," a military academy, and a female seminary. One settler arriving in such a town was thus shocked to discover: "only one rude wooden frame dwelling, which was the town saloon, livery stable, and grocery store, greeted me, and there were scattered among the trees, tents and wagons where people had taken up claim of their lots" (cited in Dick, 1937/1979:49).

Yet the towns did grow rapidly, sometimes almost overnight. An early traveler, John Beadle, described in 1873 the conditions at Benton, 700 miles west of Omaha, Nebraska. After noting that Benton was located in the middle of absolutely nowhere, where no town should ever have been built because of the hostile climate and terrain, he stated:

Yet here had sprung up in two weeks, as if by the touch of Aladdin's Lamp, a city of three thousand people; there were regular squares arranged into five wards, a city government of mayor and aldermen, a daily paper, and a volume of ordinances for the public health. It was the end of the freight and passenger, and the beginning of construction, division; twice every day immense trains arrived and departed, and stages left for Utah, Montana, and Idaho; all the goods formerly hauled across the plains came here by rail and were reshipped, and for ten hours daily the streets were thronged with motley crowds of railroad men, Mexicans and Indians, gamblers, "cappers," and saloon-keepers, merchants, miners, and mulewhackers. The streets were eight inches deep in white dust as I entered the city of canvas tents and polehouses; the suburbs appeared as banks of white dirty lime, and a new arrival with black clothes looked like nothing so much as a cockroach struggling through a flour barrel. (Beadle, 1873:87)

Not all the towns sprang up at the ends of rail lines. The location of most of the early pioneer settlements depended on their geography. Towns might form along the banks of a major river that served as a divide on the way west. Kansas City, Kansas, on one side of the Missouri River, and Kansas City, Missouri, on the other, developed partly because barges carried wagons, supplies, and families across the river on their way west. St. Louis and the twin cities of Minneapolis and St. Paul are on the Mississippi River, and Chicago lies on the shores of Lake Michigan. Denver stands at the foot of the Rocky Mountains and on the divergent trails that led to the Oregon Territory, California, and the Southwest. Towns such as Abilene, Wichita, and Dodge City, Kansas, developed primarily as shipping points for cattle being driven up from open ranges in Texas to be loaded onto boxcars and shipped east.

Those cities situated at the juncture of major railroad lines and waterways grew quickly. The sizes of their populations were also influenced by their states' reception to settlement and the railroads' expansion. As Table 1-1 shows, in 1810 St. Louis was little more

Table 1-1
POPULATION OF PRINCIPAL MIDWESTERN CITIES, 1810-1900

Year	Chicago	Denver	Kansas City, Kansas	Kansas City, Missouri	Omaha	St. Louis
1810	–	–	–	–	–	1,600
1820	–	–	–	–	–	4,598
1830	–	–	–	–	–	5,852
1840	4,853	–	–	–	–	16,469
1850	29,963	–	–	–	–	77,860
1860	109,260	4,749	–	4,418	1,883	160,773
1870	298,977	4,759	–	32,260	16,083	310,864
1880	503,185	35,629	3,200	55,785	30,518	350,518
1890	1,099,850	106,713	38,316	132,716	66,536[a]	451,770
1900	1,698,575	133,859	51,418	163,752	102,555	575,238

[a]Census of 1890 defective; population of 1890 is an estimate of the mean between 1880 and 1900.
Source: United States Department of Commerce and Labor. *Statistical Abstract of the United States, 1909* (Washington, D.C.: U.S. Government Printing Office, 1910).

than a village (1,600 people). Thereafter its population grew slowly until about 1840, to 78,000 people, but rose to 160,000 by 1860 and only ten years later was over 310,000. The major growth for Chicago, Kansas City, Omaha, and St. Louis occurred after the Civil War, when new lands were open and capital was available for expansion westward.

Sara Robinson, wife of the governor of Kansas, said that in sixty days in 1855, fifty-five houses were built in Lawrence, Kansas. The *Kansas Herald*, championing the cause of Leavenworth, Kansas, with a population of eight hundred, noted that the late 1850s had seen "erected one steam saw mill, two brick yards, one three-story hotel, four boarding houses, five dry goods stores, five groceries, five saloons, two boot and shoe stores, two saddlery shops, one tin shop, two blacksmith shops, and one hundred tenanted houses" with twenty or thirty in the process of construction (cited in Dick, 1937/1979:45). In 1857 the *Omaha City Times* sketched the growth of its town:

June 1853. Town claim made by the company by payment to the Indians, whose claim was still in effect.

June 1854. Still no settlements, but a single log house, 16 feet square, built by the company as an improvement to hold the claim.

June 1855. Number of inhabitants from 250 to 300, and the best lots sold at $100.

Main street, Almena, Kansas, in the early 1890s
Courtesy of the Kansas State Historical Society

October 1856. Number of inhabitants 1600, and the best lots sold at $2,500.

April 1857. Number of inhabitants 2000, and best lots sold at $3,500.

June 1857. Number of inhabitants 3000, and best lots sold at $4,000. (Adapted from material presented in Dick, 1937/1979:46)

Most towns were much smaller than those cited above and were built to accommodate the horse-centered economy of the times. In other words, a typical small town had at least a blacksmith, a livery stable, and a harness maker. If it was a cattle town, it would have outfitters to sell the cowboy a new suit of clothes, which he usually purchased once each year after the long cattle drive, and it also would have saddle and lariat makers. There would be hotels that catered to the cattle traders and banks that competed for their business by offering low-interest loans. The cattle towns also had the saloons of television fame. But such towns faded quickly from the scene with the coming of barbed wire and the practice of grazing and feeding cattle within smaller confines.

It is difficult to describe a typical community of this period, because each was unique. It might have been a free-state settlement; it might have been settled by members of only one ethnic group, or it might have been geared to transportation rather than farming. Nevertheless, because the economy and geography of the area were so homogeneous and because the area was settled over approximately the same period of time, there are remarkable similarities among the towns scattered throughout Kansas, Oklahoma, Nebraska, Minnesota, and the Dakotas. The typical town would have had about 1,500 inhabitants. In 1870, approximately 90 percent of the prairie states' population was classified by the United States Census Bureau as rural, meaning that the people lived in towns of under 2,500 in population or on farms (U.S. Department of Commerce, 1949:29).

A person walking down a typical main street in about 1870 would find a livery stable, often connected to a hotel. A settler might stay at an establishment that advertised supper, breakfast, bed, and stable and hay for a horse for 80 cents. But usually one would pay 25 cents for a bed and up to 50 cents for supper, though most establishments offered a $1.00 "package." The finest hotel in town would normally be a two-story building and have private rooms containing washstands and commodes. During the boom periods, a room might simply be divided up by means of blankets and labeled a hotel. Thus the quality of the accommodations would generally depend on the stability of the trade. Some of the hotels built to house the drovers are still in existence today, for they were often luxury accommodations. The same street would also have at least one saloon, which, if one were lucky, would serve food. A small saloon was not a particularly attractive place: "The shelves were ornamented by soiled decanters, dirty glasses, and a few boxes of cigars. In the corner sat a few barrels with spigots in them.... Perhaps a card table had been improvised by laying planks across a whiskey barrel. A fiddler and other loafers hung about drinking, swearing, and whiling away their time" (Dick, 1937/1979:407). Before the town became well developed, the grocery store would be a small structure, probably 10 by 12 feet, with crude planks lined with salt, flour, coffee, dried goods, and other sundries. Often it had been established by a local farmer who wanted to capitalize on a heavily traveled route that ran by or through his property, and so some of the early grocery stores were in sod huts. If the town were large or an important politician came from the area, there might be a post office that a merchant ran as a second business. It might have been located in the town's drugstore, which stocked a wide variety of medicines. There was a serious shortage of doctors in many areas, and people usually had to treat themselves.

If the town had enough people, perhaps two thousand, there would be a doctor who practiced medicine under trying circumstances. The operation by candlelight with a patient "anesthetized" by alcohol and sterilization provided by boiling water was not, unfortunately, uncommon. The diaries of frontier doctors are full of stories and lamentations about how they could have done better, or saved a patient, if only they had had the equipment they had learned how to use in eastern medical schools. Operations were performed only when there was no other alternative.

The other town professionals would be a lawyer or two. Lawyers were plentiful on the frontier and could often be found doing other things, such as teaching school, running a store, or publishing a town's small newspaper. In fact, during this period lawyers constituted the bulk of the town's professionals, partly because qualifications were low, usually consisting of a short apprenticeship to an established attorney. After several months of sweeping out the office, filing the few documents, and acquainting themselves with the small law library kept by the practicing attorney, the future lawyers would present themselves to the court for admittance. With the opening of the frontier and the boom caused by settlement, lawyers were kept busy filing and contesting claims and handling the land speculators' numerous transactions.

If the town was also a place from which goods could be shipped, it would have grain and stock dealers, who were regarded by the farmers as the bane of their existence. The divisions between the town and country were deepened by the farmers' distrust of the grain merchants, who could spell ruin for them. The farmers generally lacked the knowledge necessary to refute the merchants' claims about prices in places as distant as Minneapolis, Chicago, St. Louis, or Kansas City. But the farmers had no other means of getting their goods to market. If the merchants did not own the storage facilities, they might own the wagons on which goods were moved short distances or be the only persons to whom the railroad would lease cars for shipment to distant areas. Sometimes the local merchant was an agent of the railroads, controlling what would be shipped, when, and by whom. With monopolies involved in buying, shipping, and packing the farmers' products, as in the case of the slaughterhouses, it is little wonder that the relationship between farmer and agent was strained.

Every town worthy of its name had a newspaper. Sometimes the paper was established before the drugstore and hotel were opened and before the town's doctor and lawyers arrived. Some early newspapers were subsidized by the company founding the town, in order to attract settlers to the area and thus raise the land values. The first thing that a newspaper did was to adopt a lofty motto for its banner, choose a suitable name (e.g., *Herald, Bugle, News, Enquirer, Platform, Advertiser*) preceded by the name of the town, and begin to detail the town's virtues. More of the newspaper's first copies were distributed in the East than in the town itself. One newspaper boasted of two hundred new subscribers in Tennessee, which meant that the company or the town fathers had sent a bundle of newspapers to a hamlet (with a post office) to be distributed to the population. Some papers made their aim explicit. The Oakdale, Nebraska, *Pen and Plow* declared, "The leading object of the *Pen and Plow* is to call the attention of the emigrant East to the upper Elkhorn Valley as a desirable field of settlement and investment" (cited in Dick, 1937/1979:419). One newspaper office was described as follows:

A visit to the printing office afforded a rich treat. On entering the first room on the right hand side three "law shingles" were on the door; on one side was a rich bed, French blankets, sheets, table cloths, shirts, cloaks, and rugs all together; on the wall hung hams, maps, venison, and rich engravings, onions, portraits, and books; on the floor were a side of bacon carved to the bone, corn and potatoes, stationery and books....In a room on the left, the sanctum, the housewife, cook and editor lived in glorious unity, one person.... The cookstove was at his left, and tin kettles all around; the corn cake was "a-doing" and instead of scratching his head for an idea as editors often do, he turned the cake and went ahead. (Flint, 1916, Vol. I:28)

Many of the small newspapers that depended for their survival solely on the support of subscriptions and advertisements from people in the local community failed. Those that succeeded had to strive mightily to find things to report. Many an editor was reduced to commenting on the quality of vegetables at the town market.

We have looked at the people who settled the Great Plains region, the communities they established, and some of the problems they had. Now we can speak more specifically of value systems that they brought with them and developed.

Values and Beliefs

Education and Religion   A high priority of every small community was its schoolhouse. It usually began as one room with primitive facilities. In the winter it was heated by a cast-iron stove: the students close to it were hot, and those next to the drafty wall were cold. The teacher often had only a sixth-grade education, although there soon were rapid improvements in teacher training and certification programs. The teacher was required to teach, usually by rote, to a wide range of ages and talents. Lessons were written out on a black-painted wooden plank and erased with a damp rag. Students usually attended school for a few months of the year; in most areas the school year was not extended to six months until the end of the century. After six years of school, most students quit rather than continue on to high school or college, which often meant leaving their homes and boarding out in a larger town or city.

Education was held in remarkable esteem. Almost all believed it to be worthwhile, and educated people were highly regarded. There were literary circles in almost every town; library guilds if the town had a library; evening reading groups; and visiting lecturers, both religious and secular. Of course, some of the activities were engaged in for social reasons, but they were educational as well, and people defined their involvement in them as self-improvement.

This desire for self-improvement—moral, intellectual, and spiritual—applies to many activities in this period and reflects the settlers' value systems. Many had moved to the region hoping for better lives, which were to be achieved through hard work, study, and individual effort. The educational movement cannot be separated from the social movements that we have mentioned, such as reform, the Temperance movement, or even Populism. In some respects all of these efforts were aimed at improving the human condition.

The settlers' religious values mirrored their pragmatism and their positive attitude toward progress. Their efforts to establish schools were matched only by their efforts to establish churches. Most of the small communities in the Great Plains were settled by Baptists, Methodists, Presbyterians, and Lutherans. There also were some Catholics, but generally they stayed in the larger urban centers. Small-town America thus was basically Protestant.

Most communities at first could not support separate churches for all of the faiths represented among the settlers. If a Methodist minister, for example, settled in the community, all churchgoers would attend services at the Methodist church until they could have their own church. Often ministers from different faiths circulated from town to town giving sermons.

Dogma, matters of doctrine, did not play a large role in the church services or in deciding who was or was not a member of any given church. This posed a special problem for the frontier preacher. He might want to lead in the area of moral reform but could go only as far as his parishioners would follow. He had, in short, to deliver a religious message that was compatible with the needs of his followers. If he did not, the faithful, on whom he depended for his salary, would stop coming. Preaching well-known messages from familiar biblical texts, therefore, became the rule.

Democracy: The Ideal and the Real   Democratic ideals can be found in the Homestead Act of 1862. As we noted, many congressmen who supported the act did so because they saw a direct link between owning private property and supporting democratic ideals. They believed in the ideal of the yeoman farmer, who was independent and thus would support the principles on which the country was founded. Though their ambitions were sometimes frustrated, thousands of settlers came to the Great Plains from the East and abroad in search of cheap land and their own property. The ideal flourished, then, even though many failed to find land or found that others had taken more than their share.

Although there were hardening economic divisions in many communities, there still were flexible class boundaries. People were judged (as far as we can tell from diaries and other historical accounts) by what they accomplished, not by who their ancestors were. Being a good provider for one's family, staying sober, being a good helpmate, and being a good farmer all ensured acceptance by the community. People thus could be successful: they were what they proved themselves to be.

Nonetheless, democratic ideals also had their costs. Not everyone could succeed, though most believed that everyone had an equal chance to do so. Furthermore, democracy in practice meant conflict and struggle. A community's problems were not settled without a considerable amount of personal involvement. Some issues split communities on lines that would be dissolved and re-formed as other issues became more significant. Some people suffered, and some people gained. Conflict was, then, a normal method of settling disputes.

Fatalism   Although the settlers' value system stressed individual initiative, self-reliance, and improvement, there were limits to individual effort. One might labor to plant one's wheat only to see it eaten by grasshoppers before it could be harvested. Or one's cattle might be lost in a blizzard. A flood could wash away one's home, and a drought could spell disaster for one's crops. Tragedy could also be a serious accident, a woman dying in childbirth, or a provider being sick for a long time. The settler lived with continuous uncertainty.

As a result, a fatalistic attitude became part of the larger value system. "I've done my best, now only God can decide what my fate will be," declared many a diarist. Effort, optimism, and will all were there but were tempered by the realization that failure or disaster was always lurking close by.

We have described the institutions that developed on the frontier between 1850 and 1900, sketched the character of the small towns, and discussed the settlers' value systems, economy, and politics. Although we will return later to some of these themes, we will now turn to the actual lives of individual families.

2 The Martins

Henry Martin was born and raised in Illinois. In 1873, lured by the railroads' description of cheap land and golden opportunities, he left his family and his intended bride, Lucy Kimball, to establish a homestead in the town of Bradley in western Kansas. He built a sod house and started a garden, and after two years he returned for Lucy.

By the standards of the day, Henry was a very successful farmer. Extremely active, he became involved in the Republican party, church activities, and agricultural reform and education.

The diaries and letters from which the material in this chapter was taken were edited to allow the Martins to tell their story chronologically.

Henry Martin

I was nineteen when Lucy Kimball, whom I had known since we were children at school together, promised to be my wife, sealing that solemn promise the next day with her gift of the New Testament which I have kept beside me ever since. Yet it was three long years before we wed, for I determined (in that momentous year of 1873) that we would emigrate to Kansas and homestead there, beginning a new life in earnest hopes of better things for ourselves and our posterity. I had been much taken by the opportunities for purchase of cheap land which were then presented by the railroads, in particular the Atchison, Topeka and Santa Fe line. Lucy, when she read about it with me, learned to share my enthusiasm. The first six months of our betrothal, October through March, I continued at my par-

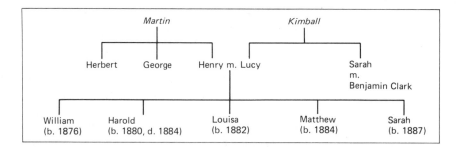

ents' farm outside of Willey, Illinois, at my usual chores, helping to husk corn, hauling ear corn and fat hogs to market, chopping and hauling wood, grubbing stumps, and so forth and so on. The evenings, that mild winter, were another matter, for Lucy and I were part of a lively circle of young people who seldom passed up an opportunity to attend a lecture or musical evening, a social at our Presbyterian Church, or meeting of our small but serious literary society, our singing school, or—since Lucy and I had both signed our pledge—any temperance meeting or rally round about. Plenty of visiting and long buggy rides, as well!

In March I took my leave of my mother, father and brothers, and of the sweetest girl in Illinois and began my journey to Bradley, Tripp County, on the plains of western Kansas. I was on and off the train for five days, getting as far as Watts and continuing thence by cart to Bradley, where I picked out my homestead the first day and took out papers four days later, March 16, 1873. I had made an arrangement with my new neighbors, Mr. and Mrs. Solomon Perkins, who had come out in wagons eighteen years before and run a "road ranch" on the overland trail west of Atchison. Their growing family had decided them to take up a homestead at Bradley, and I was to board with them and work out my board with the spring plowing and whatever other work was handy, at twenty dollars a month, taking what time I needed to break prairie and build a house on my own land.

So I spent a long and, after those first days, uneventful year, enlivened only by my election for the first time as secretary for the local convention of the Republican Party and my attendant responsibilities. Like my father before me, I was always an active worker for that political party. He and my mother had shared from youth a deep sympathy for the noble cause of abolition and passed their loyalties on to their children. I may add that my interest in Kansas was influenced by its early status as a free state. I also witnessed a real "frontier" incident one otherwise peaceful spring day in Bradley—the shooting, in the main street, of two fleeing "hoss thieves." The summer of '74 was memorable for us all as that of the "grasshopper year." I will never forget the sight of them going overhead, for seven hours and more, layer upon layer like a veritable storm of insect life. They stayed with us upwards of a week, and there was nothing they scorned to devour, but the trunks themselves of our few poor trees. All the green corn crop was lost, with every soft crop, on every farm. I lost no crops, as I hadn't yet planted any, but I shared in the discouragement of my neighbors and learned, that first season, a deep admiration for those Kansans who hung on through such disasters and helped to make our state what it has now become.

The second autumn, nevertheless, saw me ill and lonesome, so that I removed to a room in town, where I earned some money at a variety of jobs, in particular at the stables. Small results! but enough to permit me to roof our little house with frame and shingles rather than sod, put in a door and window, put by for a cookstove, and pay my way back to Illinois when I completed the spring plowing and planting and put in our garden, all of which Mr. and Mrs. Perkins had agreed to tend for me, for future considerations, till my return.

I stayed two months in Illinois with my dear bride's family after our wedding day. Despite my girl's courage and eagerness to make her own home "in the wilderness" with me, the parting from the cherished spots of youth together (one woodland aisle in particular!) was hard, and parting from her mother and sister was harder yet for my Lucy. Many tears were shed by the womenfolk of both our families at the final moment of parting.

Our journey took four days, and since we arrived fresh in the early morning at Bradley, we took at once the two mile walk up to our future home in the far west. The house was nearly finished, needing only some final plastering, and our trunks and other household gear, including the seeds from our parents' gardens which we had packed carefully in damp sawdust, awaited us at Watts.

In a week's time, we spent our first night at *Home*, and the next day, Sunday, September 30th, we established our family altar to stand as long as the household should stand and shared our hearts' hopes together there.

That year I began planting fruit trees for fruit and shade

and windbreak and to hold the soil. I also made a dugout for our animals, built our milkhouse, dug our well, helped to build the sod-hill schoolhouse for our little community, killed a wild-cat, fought two prairie fires, and tried our luck with wheat and corn crops. I was also appointed by the probate judge to act as a commissioner to appraise improvements and lots for the township and was elected Sunday School Superintendent for the district. On June 10th that summer another era in our lives began when Lucy, with Mrs. Perkins in attendance, presented me with a nine pound son and heir, whom we named William, after his mother's father. That month was a busy one indeed, for in addition to the shared work of harvesting the wheat and rye crops round about, I tasted the pleasures of housework and baby nursing while the little mother was resting or engaged at the washtub!

An ordinary day for me during those years would consist of a morning spent in the fields or tending to the animals if I were not making some improvements around the place—weather always permitting. Real Kansas rain, cold, or heat can put a pretty effective stop to all but the most essential tasks. On such days it is a farmer's privileged lot to stay indoors with his family and read or write letters. About one day a week was devoted to the transaction of miscellaneous business in and around town, especially as our family and my various other

---

*

Amount and Value of Garden Produce
Marketed in Fall of 1878

			Bushels	Value
Aug.	21	Onions	1 3/5	$1.20
	21	Potatoes	1 3/4	1.00
	23	Beets	1 3/4	.65
	30	Onions	1 5/6	1.80
	30	Potatoes	1 3/4	1.30
Sept.	6	Potatoes	3/4	.60
	6	Onions	1	1.00
	20	Onions	6	5.15
Oct.	25	Onions	1/2	.50
Nov.	14	Potatoes	4	3.70
	14	Onions	2 1/2	1.90

*

responsibilities increased. Church or politics or community work, such as repairs to the school, often came first. Also in those years it was my habit to exchange work as a harvest hand, builder, mason—whatever was needed by my neighbors.

Our evenings were frequently enlivened by one visitor or several—travelers passing through, whom we put up, our friends, callers on matters of business who stayed to sample Lucy's cooking and to enjoy the pleasures of sociable conversation. Social events of a more elaborate nature were scarce during our first years on the prairie. Sunday of course was a day of gathering together, with Sunday School and sometimes prayer meeting in the morning and church service in the evening.

The following year my wife's younger sister, Sarah, not finding—as I thought—any of the young men at home up to snuff, came out to join us and be the schoolteacher for our township. She was to live with us for three years, a cheerful, patient, Christian soul, who worked as hard in the milkhouse or garden as ever Lucy or I did, helped with the babies—indeed, I well remember her, moving little Willy in his basket from row to row with her among the potatoes— and made a fine addition to our new literary society and all our social doings.

The next winter was a hard one, with several bouts of illness for us all, and troubled spirits because of some disgraceful local squabbles over squatter's rights, disgusting to all those who care for the *law*. I found no class of people more reprehensible than the wretches calling themselves "settlers" who merely made shift to live, hand to mouth, on their dubious claims—while waiting to be bought out at a profit and move on again. Moreover, since Bradley became a city of the third class, our town council saw fit to license two of the Devil's mantraps, and we had to witness the results of that. It was two more years before the temperance amendment to the state constitution was carried.

Meanwhile those of us who cared for the better things of life worked to provide for ourselves and new members of our community those social and educational occasions which refresh and elevate the mind. I speak here of the many beautiful church picnics and socials which our womenfolk arranged, our new debating society, church choir, Sunday School, the occasional ice cream supper or sleighing party with like-minded friends, and the regular little "Lyceum" which was begun by those of us who were able and willing to "work up" a subject well enough to teach it to others. I may say that for several years Edward Parkinson and myself did a fair job of teaching the Natural Sciences to those who were

---

Bradley Debating Society, 1878–1880

RESOLVED THAT:

Negro emigration to Kansas is detrimental to the best interests of the state. Negative.

Reading fiction is injurious. Positive, with some dissenting opinion.

All laws should be obeyed. Negative.

That the government should own and operate the railroads. Positive.

Man will do more for love of money than for love of woman. Negative.

The author has done more for mankind than the warrior. Negative.

That the higher criticism is injurious to the church. Positive.

That free trade is in the best interests of the farmer. Negative, with some dissenting opinion.

That travel is more educational than the classroom. Negative.

That the Australian ballot should be adopted in our elections. Positive.

An entry in Henry Martin's diary listing some topics that he and his neighbors formally debated in the schoolhouse as members of the Bradley Debating Society. They met during the first week of each month.

interested, young and old, and of inviting lecturers from other parts of the state, as well.

In the spring, however, we had cause for rejoicing, for our second son, Harold, was born. While 1880 was a year of general drouth and crop failure, we did well enough from our produce, and did not need to join the chorus of grumblers and fretters. Our good neighbor and friend Mr. Perkins succumbed to a feverish flux in the late spring, and his wife, sturdy pioneer that she was, turned to and finished the planting that he had begun, with my help and that of the Mitchell boys. She farmed her own land for ten more years, with no more help than a hired man for planting and harvest, and found time enough beside for her usual visiting, churchwork, and care of new mothers.

Expenditures 1882

For labor		$ 67.30
Dry goods		42.70
Flannel	$1.50	
Calico	2.00	
Oil cloth	.05	
Socks, 3 pair	.50	
Straw hat for Will	.20	
Overalls	.60	
Suspenders	.40	
Collars	.15	
Gingham	.70	
Muslin	.20	
Ducking, ticking, buttons, edging	1.35	
Elastic, thread	.80	
Corset	1.20	
Mittens	.60	
Tapes		19.40
Sugar (98 lbs.)		11.70
Coffee (31 lbs.)		7.00
Hardware		13.75
Furniture		11.00
Blacksmithing		5.50
Boots and shoes		10.00
Farming implements		20.50
Coal oil (16 gal.)		3.35
Salt (138 lbs.)		1.90
Drugs and medicine		2.20
Lumber		5.05
Dried fruit (52 lbs.)		4.70
Canned fruit		.20
Postage stamps and cards		1.50
Stationery		1.30
Books		2.10
Periodicals		13.50
"Drinks from Drugs"	.10	
"Temperance Songs"	.10	
"The Liquor Traffic and Crime"	.10	
Chicago Tribune	1.00	
St. Louis Evangel	.50	
Record and News	3.00	
Louisville Republic	1.50	
Bradley Bugle	1.50	
Cigars		1.00
Matches		.60
Crackers		.90
Garden and field seeds		4.30
Nuts and candy		1.30
Tea (1.5 lbs.)		1.10
Church		8.65
Sabbath School		2.25
Spices (2.5 lbs.)		1.10
Window glass		1.25
Brooms, 2		.50
Toys		2.40
Beans and Rice (18 lbs. each)		3.00
Molasses (5 gallons)		2.00
Post office box rent		.45
Ice cream, lemonade and soda-water		.75
Pens and pencils		.10
Doctor bills		2.25

Copy of a page from Henry Martin's diary

In 'eighty-two, my mother, father, and two younger brothers joined us, homesteading six miles to the south of our farm. They arrived in Kansas in time to greet our daughter Louisa, born that Spring. By then we could welcome them to a flourishing community, in which our church building had been completed, our public roads laid and maintained by our own labors, and a school bond passed. This permitted us to hire a regular teacher upon the occasion of Sister Sarah's marriage and therefore to enrich and enliven the year by a variety of activities at the new schoolhouse, such as evening spelling schools, oratorical contests, and closing and opening day exercises, much enjoyed by all. We had even begun, that year, to hold a regular county fair.

'Eighty-four was a far sadder year, for shortly after the birth of our third son, Matthew, our boy Harold took ill, and after two weeks of ceaseless anxiety and care, we had to lay our little one to rest until the Resurrection Morn. Only the menfolk were at the grave that sad afternoon of his death, for the snowstorm was too heavy for our weary and sorrowing women.

In 'eighty-five the railroad bond passed, and we proudly welcomed it to Bradley.* 'Eighty-seven saw another drouth and short crops, but a memorable Fourth of July celebration in the town, with over six thousand people arriving from five counties round, gathered to hear the bands and the speechifying and to watch the sham battles. That same summer, our second daughter Sarah was born, and we first hired a girl to do housework.

In 1890, a group of our most wide awake and enterprising farmers established together the Farmers' Institute in Bradley, for the purpose of increasing our knowledge of modern farming methods and determining in other ways just where our best interests as farmers lay. I assumed the duties of its president. Also I began work as a census examiner as well as farmer—a busy year indeed, for my brother George moved back to Illinois, and I began to work his land until it could be sold. Indeed, between our own arrival and 1894, when my mother, widowed, went back to Illinois, many of our friends "gave up" on western Kansas and returned to Iowa or Ohio or moved to the eastern portions of our state. My brother Herbert stayed and thrived, though by means somewhat different than my own. He was an active, industrious man, and as disgusted as any with the skimming propensities, the dishonesty, and corruption of too many of our fellow Kansans. Yet this never prevented him from dealing with others in whatever way he deemed honorable

---

*The citizens of Bradley voted a bond to enable a spur (side) line of the railroad to be run to them.

Prairie school, Woodbine, Kansas, 1897
Courtesy of the Kansas Collection, Kenneth Spencer Research Library, University of Kansas.

to *himself*! He lent money as soon as he had it to lend and early acquired a reputation as a man to consult about a purchase of seed, land, stock, notes, or any profitable commodity. He also could regularly get the best price going for any salable item, from wheat to hogs—sometimes traveling a good extra distance to accomplish this and conducting an extensive and growing correspondence with men as far away as Denver and Chicago. He bought and sold farm machinery at a good profit, being the first man in our part of the state to understand how important to farmers such methods were to become. Our fellow Kansans, by and large, would rather deal with a man than a bank; yet I daresay brother Herbert's interest rates were not uncommonly low, for he was a rich man by 1900, owning as much property as anyone in the county and interests in many businesses. He never had a partner.

In 'ninety-three our two eldest children, then aged sixteen and eleven, joined the church, providing their mother and father the occasion for a real struggle between Christian humility and a parent's pride! That same year Lucy and I traveled to the World's Fair in Chicago, where we found much to edify and amaze us. While my interests lay with the exhibits of farm machinery and experimental farming in general, I delighted, with Lucy, in the Women's Building, where I found what is usually found in women's work—a world of indescribable wealth and beauty. That year, also, I was

---

Accounts with H. R. Falkner, 1887

	Debits	Credits
January		
Lumber	$ .25	
Festival	.25	
April		
Planting corn (1 day)		$ .75
May		
Flour (20 lbs)	.70	
Planting corn		.75
July		
Cash for flour		.70
Harvesting (1 3/4 days)		1.75
August		
Stacking wheat (3 days)		3.00
Stacking millet (1 1/2 days)		1.10
Raking hay (1/2 day)	.75	
Hauling and stacking hay (2 days)	3.00	
Stacking hay		.75
Hauling lumber and fixing granary (2 days)	.75	
September		
Stacking hay		.75
Helping thresh		.75
Helping thresh	.50	
February		
Padlock	.25	
March		
Plowing 2 acres	2.00	
Plowing 2 acres	2.00	
Walnut trees (100)	.30	
Plowing and harrowing (3/4 day)	1.50	

In addition to recording sales and purchases, Henry Martin recorded his transactions with others. Often labor was traded. H. R. Falkner, for instance, "owed" Henry $3.00 for stacking wheat, and Henry "owed" Falkner $2.00 because Falkner plowed 2 acres for him.

elected President of the County Sunday School Association and moderator of the Presbytery. One other event of some note was our attendance at a meeting where we heard Mary Lease, the far-famed Populist, give a few calamity howls concerning the "curse of the money power" and the "incubus of bonds."

In the 'nineties my fruit trees did well. I did a good business for some years selling Herbert's fruit-tree sprayers and instructing my neighbors on the subject of rusts, fungi, molds, and the necessity for spraying.

In May of 'ninety-five, due to a disastrous dust blizzard of three days duration, we lost our entire orchard, garden, and field crops as well, including three thousand sweet potato sets (which however I got in again that same week). My appointment as postmaster, with Lucy as my assistant, was another development of note.

In 'ninety-six, son Will, to our joy, declared his intention of studying for the ministry and began work as a teacher in order to save his tuition.

During that decade, my days were more frequently taken up by my duties as President of the County Sunday School Association, president of the cemetery association, county clerk, census enumerator, and secretary of the Republican party (although I resolutely resisted the persuasions of friend and foe to run for any higher political office). Much of the farm work fell on the broad shoulders of our boys, whenever they were home from school. Corn and millet and rye continued as our regular crops, and more of it, as our new binder and cultivator made possible. We also set out more trees and bushes each year.

'Ninety-seven was marked by the entrance of our daughter Louisa at the normal school in Emporia, founded some thirty years before to instruct teachers in our state in the usual educational subjects and in the arts of agricultural chemistry and husbandry. Louisa was young, only eighteen, to have gained her first-grade certificate, but she had worked hard for it, boarding for two years in Salina with Lucy's old friend Mrs. Margaret Lewis, in order to attend the high school there.

That same year I was able to acquire another one hundred and sixty acres and a threshing machine, and a powersheller for corn. Lucy began to can the cherries from our trees—sometimes with my help. One year I recall we put up over three hundred quarts of cherries, gooseberries and currants.

That year also, I was appointed with others to draft a bill for the legislature to appropriate funds to the Farmers' Institute, I think as a consequence of a lecture I delivered for them, entitled "State Control: A Necessity in Successful Institute Work," in which I made the point that Kansas should not be lagging behind Indiana, Illinois, and Wisconsin in the matter of the welfare of her farmers. I have never found it necessary to seriously question my political allegiance to the Republican party, to become one of the "Pops." Yet many good men of Kansas became Grangers in the '80s and "Pops" in the '90s, as well as many fools, which is of course the usual way of the world. As for that motley crew, the Farmers' Alliance, I am *not* so sure that the world needs its kind.*

In 'ninety-eight I was a delegate to the meeting of the State Board of Agriculture at Topeka and visited the State Agriculture College, at which our son Matthew then had formed the intention of studying. In those days, tuition was free, board and books at cost, and I was interested to find that the special course of study for young women (how to cook and sew and care for the home) was based on sound scientific principles. I found the College atmosphere healthy and pure and full of hope for the bright future of our children.

In 'ninety-eight, also, we began our new house and throughout the summer plastered and papered and built furniture, with little help from the young folk, who spent more time visiting and racketing about Matthew's pet croquet lawn than ever before, though in term time they were hard workers at their studies. They made good use in those days of the piano we installed at the completion of the new house. That house, I figure, cost $2,100 altogether, ten times what I had spent putting up the old one.

When the new century began, I well recall standing on the steps of that house and comparing our prosperous and beautiful surroundings with the raw homestead of a quarter-century before. What changes had been wrought in our State, redeeming that wilderness and making it bloom! A land filled with a rapidly growing population, with peace and plenty—truly we had no cause to regret our new life in the West but could only thank a generous God for his goodness to us and to our children.

✳ ✳ ✳

Lucy Kimball Martin

September 14, 1879 Today my little sister Sarah was married, and I know she has got a good husband—maybe not so good as my dear Henry, but Ben Clark is a kind, sober, Christian man, ambi-

---

*Grangers, Populists ("Pops"), and Farmers' Alliance members all were part of the general agrarian revolt that began after the economic disasters of the late 1870s. The Grange gave way to the Farmers' Alliance, which in turn became part of the Populist movement. There were important regional differences among these groups, and in some cases the movements and organizations overlapped, as indicated by Henry's statement. These groups, depending on the region, often formed alliances with the Democratic party, which is one of the reasons Henry did not like them.

tious and independent minded too, and loves her dearly, as any one may see. But oh how I shall miss her, and even though she and Ben will stay in Bradley for as long as he is studying with Dr. Campbell, I know the day must come when they will leave us altogether, and I will again be the only "born Kimball" in Tripp county. How we did want our darling Mother here for this joyous occasion, and I know she too was longing to be with us and that only Father's precarious health could have kept her away. Sarah and I prayed together last night that somehow one or the other of us will be able to see our parents again in this life, but sometimes I am afraid it is not to be.

I had to be my Sister Sarah's mama for a little while last night and talk to her as Mama did to me about the joys and duties of the wedded state. I felt fortunate indeed that I have as good and gentle and considerate a husband as our Mother did. I do not know how a woman with no experience but that of a selfish and arbitrary husband can bear to assume the task of advising another woman on the brink of this great change, and I pray that Benjamin Clark is every bit as careful of his new wife as he has seemed to be of his sweetheart. I told Sarah right out that no mother—and no father either—can do their best these days by a very large family. It is hard enough for us on the farm, I said, but she must think of living in the city, for Ben thinks of it. Well, no one ever need be ashamed of hard work, but I confess I should like to be able to keep my daughters at home rather than see them clerking or making others' hats or clothes! So I told Sarah that any man, glad as he may be to see his little family grow, should have a caution for the health of his wife in these matters. I do not know that being a physician is any guarantee that a man will fully appreciate the dangers a mother and her babes must undergo. Sarah, I guess, had been doing her own thinking about these things, for she replied that there was no fear she would do as poor silly Mrs. Simpson had done and bear eight children in a dozen years. I reminded her that such a decision has to be mutual between husband and wife, and Sarah said she had no doubts of Ben. So then I hugged her close and said I hoped I'd be as good an auntie as she had been, and we cried a little and parted as content as could be.

The marriage ceremony took place in our new little church, performed by Mr. Joseph Courtley, from Salina, and I never saw a bride lovelier than my little sister, in the fine gray dress we have dreamed and worked over so long and her new hat and gloves. I do believe Ben Clark truly knows the prize he has won and that Sarah's faith in him will be justified. Afterwards, we all adjourned to our

For Sarah's wedding outfit

1 hat for church, street or travel, of gray velvet, $4.10	
jet gimp at 20¢ a yard, $2.40	
gray silk ribbon, at 20¢ the yard, $2.40	
narrow silk lace, at $1.00, $8	
2 white face veils at 25¢, 50¢	
1 comb, of tortoiseshell, $1.50	
1 pair white kid gloves, $2.50	

Copy of a list of items purchased for Sarah Kimball's wedding outfit

home, where the wedding supper was quickly laid out by a number of helping hands. Our little community is sad at losing its teacher, although the young man who is to take "Miss Sarah's" place— "Miss Sarah" no more, but "*Mrs. Clark*"—was spoken very well of by the examining board. Time after time, the parents of one or another of the schoolchildren came up to her to say their boys or girls would miss her sorely and then to wish her all happiness. Many of the children themselves did so, and that was the best of compliments! Truly Sarah has much to be proud of in her work, and I only hope that our children, when they come to school age, will have as excellent a teacher.

The new married couple are to live close by the Campbells, so Ben can accompany the doctor on his visits to patients, when possible. I wonder if it isn't this part of his training that makes my new "brother" think of a city practice! Sarah will be lonesome often, I am sure, for I know Dr. Campbell is often out in his buggy or sleigh for a whole day and night at a time, and when there is a great deal of sickness, the doctor can't just take a little time off, as a farmer can, even when it is threshing or plowing time—and he can't stop for the rain or the heat, either.

Yet I know my sweet Sarah will make Ben's home as dear and peaceful a spot as any weary man could desire. How grateful we must be that our beloved Mother taught both of us how precious are cleanliness and order in any home. And Sarah will naturally have an easier time of it in some ways than I, though she won't have the husband I have for helping with the housework and baby-minding (though not the dreaded washing and ironing!). And she won't be able to turn to and help her husband at his tasks as I can, with the vegetables and cows and chickens. I am proud to say my butter and jam have the reputation of the best sold in Bradley, and Henry has

Wedding portrait
Courtesy of L. T. Churchbaugh

sold two winters' worth of my stockings to the soldiers at the Fort at 35¢ the pair!

Sarah will not have those satisfactions, but I know Ben's fame as a physician will be accompanied by the regard of all his patients for the gentle, conscientious Doctor's Wife! I am so glad Sarah has grown to womanhood knowing how precious is any little service performed for the ones we love and what it is to share hardship and gladness and tears with a beloved companion. With what longing I always await Henry's return to his home—with what happiness and relief I shall ever greet him! If it is so for Sarah, all will be well with her.

July 20, 1881   We got up earlier than we usually do this morning because it was to be another very hot day, and I wanted to get ahead of my baking, for I was expecting our new minister to visit, with the whole of the Franklin family, where he had been staying. Also little Harry had a summer cold and was restless all the night, his poor little nose all swollen and sore, and I was up to help him breathe I don't know how often.

So we got up just as soon as it began to get light, which is pretty early in summer on the prairie, you know, and I made my fire and got my bread setting before I even boiled up the coffee. That bread got baked alright, but it was a bad batch, running over the pans, because it went completely out of my mind when I found that Willy was gone I didn't know where! He was just six years old, surely a big enough boy to know better, but he had always been a one to give us a scare, though he always seemed to come out alright.

And so it was this time. I went and got Henry the minute I saw Willy was gone, and we were both out calling for him for about a half hour, I guess, when there he came, running as fast as he could—and the heat was already considerable, so that his little face was shiny and red and damp when he reached us. At first he was so out of breath he couldn't get his words out, but when he did he was so proud of himself!

"I found the cow," said he. "The poor old cow! She's down in a hole in the grass, and I just went looking and I found her, Father, you come and see if I didn't."

Now that old cow had been missing a full week, and I thought Henry had given up on her, although he and Mr. Perkins had made a good search for two days, when she was first missed, and all the men around had been keeping an eye out.

But if he didn't take off running with Willy, back in the direction the child had come from. I followed at a somewhat slower pace myself, since I had poor Harry in my arms, and he was not enjoying the trip one little bit.

That poor animal. She had fallen in an old well, all hidden by the tall prairie grass, and the hole was so small she'd stuck there. Flies were all over her, where she'd worn her hide clear off, trying to get up. I took the boys right back to the house as soon as I saw how it was going to be, and Henry ran off to get Mr. Perkins to help dig her

---

Receipts 1882

Borrowed capital	$ 77.00
Wheat (90 bushels)	84.45
Labor	53.75
Stock	26.65
Eggs (121 dozen)	9.00
Garden produce	4.50
Butter (70 lbs.)	7.50
Flour	2.00
Bran	1.60

out. It wasn't any use, of course, she was too dried out to live, from the sun and no food or water for at least seven days. I thought about if off and on all day—how she suffered, and how easy it is on these prairies to get lost or hurt or both if you are alone, man or beast, so it is certainly best not to be alone if you can manage that!

So I went back and baked that spongy bread, having no time to let it rise again, and I fed the little boys and scolded Will for running off alone without telling. "Suppose *you'd* fallen in the well," I said to him, and I guess I made an impression. All the same he was right to be proud of caring about that old cow enough to go and find her when everybody else had about quit looking, and I told him so, too.

By the time I had the gingerbread and chickens in the oven, and some plum pies ready to go in next, it was near midday. There I was still, in my morning work dress, Harry crying again, Henry I didn't know where, and the churning yet to do, though Henry had finished the milking as always. This isn't what all the husbands round here would do, you know! Many women take all the care of their milk cows and the poultry, beside their other housework.

So there I was, hair falling down and my old washed-out patched-up dress, soaked through in the heat, and down the road came the Franklins and Mr. Flint, as fine as you please, a whole two hours before they were expected. Now I never saw a day since we came out to Kansas that I didn't try to be ready for company. Some days, especially Sundays, I've ended up with a dozen for dinner, when I didn't know when I went to bed the night before that a soul had us in mind to visit. Henry once figured out that we have an average of as many as eighty visitors a month and that I fix fifty meals for company of some kind each month. Now that is all right. I used to shudder at Mrs. Perkins's stories of her first years out west, when a person had no neighbors for twenty or thirty miles and saw

---

✳

Amount of Flour Used by Martin Family
in 1880–1881

	Pounds	*Bushels*
September	116	4
October	174	6
November	296	10
March	400	12
June	214	8

✳

Amount of Butter Sold in Autumn of 1880

	Pounds	Price per Pound	Total
October	5.5	$ .12	$ .70
November	5.0	.15	.75
December	4.25	.15	.64

no one but family for weeks and weeks. I don't know how I would have endured such loneliness. It seems to me that hard times—and in Kansas we have a sufficiency of hard times—are so much more bearable if you can just know that others are there to help if they can and understand if they can't! Sister Sarah's optimistic spirit has done me near as much good as prayer, many a day, and night too. One of my chief joys is to stay in town at the Lewis house or with Sarah or at the Parkinsons' farm, and Henry has always been glad to take me along on his errands and let me and the babies stay over the night, even while he has to go home and tend to the stock.

Well! I had no opportunity to pray for consolation when I saw Mr. and Mrs. Franklin and their four girls and the new minister come rolling up before our house. I just sent up a quick, "Help me to be cheerful now, Oh Lord!" and pushed back my wet hair and went out to explain as best I could.

Naturally it was alright. Beth Franklin is no fool; she saw exactly how I was fixed and simply asked for two aprons and went out and set her biggest girl to churning while she skimmed and gave the butter its first working. I was able to make myself appear a respectable woman, while the younger girls took charge of Will and Harry, and we had a good dinner at a good time, after all, though Henry did come in worn out and struck solemn by the fate of our poor cow.

It turned out that Mr. Flint was not in the least bit difficult to please but praised my plum pies and coffee more than once, and the way our house is roofed properly and even papered inside. Most sod houses, you see, have a sod roof, too—well, that wasn't good enough for Henry, who made a real roof of cottonwood beams and shingles, and those shingles do warp easy; they don't leak as sod roof does. Why, I have seen a woman in a sod-roofed house stirring mush while her boy held an umbrella over her and the stove! So our abode *is* easy to keep nice, compared to many, and we brought furniture and dishes out with us from Illinois, and cutlery and pans, too.

When dinner was over we went outside to see if we could feel a breeze and saw clouds resting on the northwest horizon. About six o'clock we were all doubly glad of Henry's fine roof, for the rain came pouring down, and Will piped up to Mr. Flint, "That's Kansas for you!" which made us all laugh heartily.

The Franklins stayed until the worst of the storm had passed over, and the young people were allowed to read to each other and pop corn.

Meanwhile, the rest of us sat about the stove and talked of the joys and difficulties of providing a Christian education on the prairies.

"Children are fortunate indeed to grow up here," began Mr. Flint, "away from the city, where there are evil temptations of every kind and forced acquaintance with many undesirable sorts of people."

We all gazed proudly at our Kansas offspring, enjoying each other's company.

"And we keep them pretty busy out here, too. No idle hands on the farm!"

"That is true of course. But I'm sure their education is not neglected. I have heard of your excellent work in establishing Sunday Schools for young and old."

"No one's done more than the Martins," said Beth, rocking comfortably in my old chair. "Lucy knows her Bible as well as any woman I know and is past master at teaching its lessons to children. They love to hear her."

"And Beth does as much or more," I said quickly. "We all pitch in; I think that is the greatest virtue of a new little church like ours—of any work done by a few. We all share in it."

"An excellent example, in itself, to your children. Tell me, though, what you consider the most important lessons to teach the little ones?"

"Why," I stumbled along, blushing now I am sure, "I suppose just to work hard at what you must get done, trusting God to take you through your difficulties, not giving up."

"And you know we are all temperance here," added Beth. "We try to give them a firm founding in its principles which will last them through life."

"I shall pray for your success. I can think of no single habit that weakens the moral fiber more surely than the drinking habit. In one home in Chicago, which I will not name, I have seen church members sit down to dinner not a half hour after divine services and take wine with their meal. That is not my idea of a Christian home.

I was shocked, also, to discover that many of the manufactures in that city do not stop work for the Sabbath. The degraded lives of those workers! It is under such conditions that men turn to drink."

"Do you think, then, that it is easier for a farmer to be a sober man?" asked Henry, leaning forward.

Mr. Flint smiled. "I don't know that."

"Surely," said I, "it is easier to be good if there is beauty in your life, such as the beauty of our prairies."

"That is a very good point."

So we talked on, until finally the rain stopped, and we all went outside. Half the sky was clear already and bright with stars, and the wind smelled of our own growing things, and just then I was as glad to be alive as ever I have been.

January 1884   Oh Sarah Sarah how I miss you now, and how very hard it seems that Mama should have gone from us, though I *was* with her at the last, how I want her during these sad days. Our little Harold is dead. If it weren't for baby it would nearly have killed me, too, and I can't seem to stop thinking of [Harold's] thin little arms reaching up to me while he asked me to make it better, and I could not, could not. How do mothers stand it who have just one child? The only peace I feel is with baby at my breast or when Willy says in his manly little voice, can I help you Mama? or when Louisa leans her soft face on my arm and looks up so serious. Oh, no one knows what a child's love is to a mother, not even Henry knows what my poor boy Harry was to me, my second son and never the strong bold one, a worry always and all the dearer to my heart for that. I know Henry loved him too, no one can say he ever favored one child over another, he is as good and loving and careful a father as any in the world. He has been in this darkness with me, he watched with me all those endless anxious days and nights. Dr. Campbell was so hopeful at first, but I think I always knew, and when my darling Harry refused even a spoonful of his favorite peach jam, frowning at me in a puzzle and than turning away his hot little face, I knew we were to lose him.

For a time, all the heart went out of my prayers; I couldn't tell this to anyone; I had just as well not have prayed at all. In that dark time, my Henry held me up with his strength and faith, but oh, he failed too when the last moments came, and then neither of us knew how God could bring us such sorrow. There was no comfort anywhere. Harry loved me more than anyone, and we never got his picture, and he had to be buried without me there, in the frozen ground.

All our good friends, Mr. Flint's prayers and all he had to say of Harry's home in heaven is just no use to me. I can't understand, though I pray hourly that I may, for I don't see how I can go on so. Henry stays by me and helps me with everything. We are so worn with watching and grieving it seems like it takes the two of us to get a thing done. I can take no satisfaction in any of it, though we contrive to get on as usual and eat and wash and get the animals taken care of. Today I even helped Willy with his reading book for an hour, though every minute I saw Harry's head bent over *his* book, at Willy's side, doing the same work and often better too, though he was two years younger. He loved his book so dearly, I had such hopes of him.

Dear Sarah, may this never come to you. It is only holding baby that does me any good at all.

April 1894   I have never been so mad in all my life as I am at Jess Harper for his nonsense this Sunday afternoon. Wouldn't you think a man would know better than to make such a fool display of envy and malice? Henry "takes too much on himself," if you please! Well, I should like to know who would if he didn't. He's kept this Sunday School Association going by main force since its beginnings and worked harder than anyone else as a teacher, and now just because he is President of the County Sunday School Association, he "expects too much," he is not just the "right man" to be a teacher anymore. I have never been so disgusted. If Lizzie Harper weren't an object of my pity, I declare I would not stop at resigning, I would have my say to that man. But there, no one believes what he says, it is only laxity and laziness that helped the Devil's work today, for everyone around knows Harper for a vain and contentious man with none of Henry's zealous concern for the good of the School, he is only out to make himself look fine by dragging others down. And he is a member of that motley troublemaking Farmers' Alliance and a known drinker who keeps whiskey in his house, though I know for a fact that Lizzie has begged him not to set such an example to their poor young ones.

I thought I must burst when he sat down all satisfied with having spoke his nasty piece, and not a soul in the room knew which way to look or had the spunk to tell him what they thought! That is how the Enemy gets hold. And all the grove meetings in the world won't help; it is just *picnicking* they are mostly after these days, I often think. Thank goodness for Henry's quiet way, I had only to follow him and agree that we would not continue as teachers if we were a trouble to the spirit of the assembled.

All the work Henry does, traveling around the county trying to instill the value of organized Christian effort and encourage consecrated and efficient workers, to be told he should leave his own school. Well, it will soon be put to rights, I am sure. Our fainthearted neighbors, for I cannot today call them friends, will see their error in letting us depart so. I am so glad that Will and Louisa are away to college and the Academy and won't have to listen to all the talk there will be, grownups acting like spiteful and cowardly babies, the *silliness*.

Oh, I daresay no one wanted anymore than I to shame Lizzie by trying to talk Harper down in front of her. I remember the very night she took him, it was that New Year's oyster supper and sleigh party when poor Harry was a baby and Sarah stayed home with the boys to let us go, bless her dear heart. I said to myself when I heard Lizzie's news, my girl, you have been bewitched by a black mustache and a fast ride under the stars and a blanket! Oh it is just too aggravating. Henry is right, it is no good tolerating the Devil. Look at me, I have never felt so *un*-Christian in my life.

March 1898   What a turmoil we have had here with poor little Mrs. Turner. I have been grateful time and again to my dear old friend Mrs. Perkins since that day so long ago when she was my sole aid and comfort bringing my firstborn into the world. Though she is no longer among us, we are grateful to her again today, for Flossie Parkinson and I have done as much for another young woman.

Here is how it was: Flossie was spending the night with me in my new house, which she hadn't been in before, because the Parkinsons moved to Topeka six years ago when Ed gave up farming for a job with the State Board of Agriculture. Henry, of course, is fascinated by Ed's work and neglects no opportunity to go visiting him and meeting other "scientifical" men. So this time Flossie and I proposed that she come here while he went there, and we would all have company and occupation to suit us. That is what we did, and I was doubly glad of her presence when I saw the rain begin. Not a storm, just that steady all-day winter's end rain that fills up all the creeks and ponds and makes the roads nigh impassable and is so melancholy besides. Just the time for another woman in the house, to keep one from going to stare stupidly out the window every thirty minutes.

So there we were, safe and snug in the lovely new house, all taken up with each other, and Sarah home from school, for I wouldn't let her ride out in this weather with her weak chest. Montana came as usual to do the outside chores, but Elvira stayed away, and we did not miss her! We played like three girls instead of one girl and two old women—Sarah demonstrated her talent on our piano while Flossie and I sang, we made doughnuts and taffy (though since I got my false teeth I can't *eat* it), we sat around the new parlour chatting and cutting up material for a new quilt and going through the fashion magazines Flossie brought, planning ourselves some fine new outfits.

Not a serious thought in our heads. And then late, night before last, in all the downpour, a knocking on the front door, and who should fall in out of the wet, soaked to the skin, but Mary Turner, the poor forlorn child. George Turner, the young fool, had gone and left her alone in that little old sod house the Perkinses built so long ago, and her so close to her time, while he went to Bradley to pick up lumber. And if the roof didn't fall in on her! Having no place to keep dry, she saddled up the plow horse and came riding along to me, with what results you may suppose.

Once we had her dry and warm in one of my nightgowns, and Sarah back in bed with an explanation meant to keep her there, we had to decide, were we to fetch the doctor? Flossie and I took counsel and decided it was better for us to stay with her, not knowing if we could get to young Dr. Pine in time in that weather. Mrs. Turner, when appealed to, was quite of our mind about this.

"Oh please, yes, do stay with me, please, Mrs. Martin. That's all I need. I don't want the doctor. I don't like the doctor."

Now I was not disposed to quarrel with that, though Dr. Campbell attended the birth of both my Matthew and my Sarah, and I trust the skill of a physician as much as the next woman (perhaps more, because I know my brother-in-law as I do). Yet it was no time to be telling little Mary Turner about advances in medical science. It was time to assure her that her pain was not greater than a woman's usual lot, that all was going well, that Flossie and I had each attended at least a dozen childbeds and knew exactly what we were about.

No matter if not all of that was entirely true! It was truth enough for the occasion, though by morning it did seem to both Flossie and myself that even for a first baby this one was coming slow. Mrs. Turner's pains would come close for a while and then die away again, and while she was grateful for that, we were not. Still, through the night we did not begin to worry much, for Mary is a strong, healthy girl and stayed in a calm and hopeful mood. So when she would lie down and doze off between her pains, Flossie and I carried on the oddest sort of talk as we got sleepier and sleepier.

"Do you remember the first night you spent at our place, Lucy, when Will was just a month or two old?"

"Don't I? It was the first night I spent away from Henry after I came West with him, and in spite of baby it made me feel like a girl again. Weren't we silly, though?"

"It's never taken a lot to make you laugh."

"I thank God for that. There's always enough to cry about."

"I do believe. I can't call to mind one of the things that set us giggling, but I do know that I was dead desperate afraid all that winter, because *I* was going to have a baby; all that night with you I was trying to get my courage up to speak of it to you."

"No! And you never said a word until your girl was *born*, Flossie! How could you be so foolish?"

"Well, I thought, of course, it wasn't just *nice*."

Here two tired old women stifled their laughter, as they had as young ones together.

"Still I am sorry for your being so afraid."

"Oh, but you introduced me to Mrs. Perkins very soon thereafter, and she saw how it was with me and asked me, and so I had good answers to my questions."

"It does seem as if everything was fearful, in those days, doesn't it? We worked so hard to have things as they'd been back home, from clean clothes to the school house, and nothing ever *was* the same. I was so worn out all the time the first ten years out here that I used to wake up afraid because I thought I couldn't get all my work done."

"And always afraid that *this* year all the crops would fail and no one would lend us money, and we'd have to drag back to Iowa—"

"Like any poor-spirited folk! Oh, I tell you Flossie, months on end I'd fight the temptation to pray for just that to happen! just to have some real comfort and fun I hadn't had to make myself—only I knew it would break Henry's heart."

"And the times Ed would go off and leave me alone, the flood, when he was away buying mules, and the time the barn burned with everything in it except the animals, and every time a child was ill or Ed was hurt or ill—"

"Well, it's real different now, though there's never a shortage of worries exactly. It's different for Mary as well, though between you and me George may be no great shakes as a provider. If their farm fails, there are plenty of other opportunities now. Bradley isn't the end of the world anymore, and it's growing so fast that *this* baby, when it grows up, won't hardly believe that people like the Perkinses ever existed."

"I'm not sure my own children do. They are all confirmed town-dwellers, not a one of them is lonesome for the farm."

So we chatted on through the night, recalling this and that hard time and happy time and congratulating ourselves on our superior state of civilization. Morning came, and Sarah got up and had to have a better explanation of what was going on. To my amazement, she simply told Flossie and me to sit still while *she* fixed *us* breakfast, and went to work. I watched her at the big new stove and thought some about how her early married days would likely be easier than mine. A little thought crept in, that I wouldn't change with her, that all the drudgery and anxiety which we hope to see her spared, I wouldn't have spared myself, really, if I could.

But that was asking for it, because just then Mary Turner finally got down to work, and, oh my, I thought my heart would fall through the floor when what should we see but a baby's tiny foot entering the world!

Now this was not something either of us had ever been through with another woman, but I had heard Mrs. Perkins speak of the breech births she'd saved. It took me about two seconds (after my heart began to beat again) to know I must just pretend that Mary Turner was my old cow Matilda the time she calved twins and the second came backwards so, and I helped with it. Oh, but I felt I was not myself at all. Luckily, Mary was clear out of her head with pain and exhaustion by then, and Flossie and I could talk freely without frightening her.

"I have to turn it, you see I have to turn it," said I, feeling as if I had two bodies and one was miles away watching the other.

"Can you?"

"I have to. I want you to do the rest."

"I've everything ready."

Well, I did it, but not in a minute and not easily, and Mary made considerable more of a fuss, the poor thing, than Matilda, and I was terribly afraid of her bleeding badly, but when that blessed baby slid into my hands at last, I forgot my fear and laughed like a crazy woman, because he set up as loud a squawl as I've ever heard the very second his head was free!

Mrs. Turner was all right, as it turned out, thank the Lord, and now she's lying sound asleep with her little boy beside her, and my daughter knows a good deal more than she knew two days ago, and the sun is shining brightly on the brightest green spring fields I have ever seen.

*　　　*　　　*

Culture and Social Structure 3

T HE story of the Martins in Chapter 2 is more than an account of the settlement of the Great Plains; it is also a story of how a distinct culture developed. When we speak of American values or the American way of life, we must understand that behind these terms lies a distinct set of experiences that shaped them. As we will see, the struggle to settle the land, build a house, and raise a family entailed values, attitudes, and opinions that the pioneers brought to the prairie. Yet their experience in settling the land also affected their original attitudes. People changed because of their struggle with the environment, in ways they could not have anticipated and in response to events and circumstances they could not control. Farming methods, which had to be adapted to both the soil and the climate, affected the type of culture that was possible. In addition to their individual efforts, the national economy also affected the pioneers' financial well-being. In short, the social system of the Great Plains was not something given, but something that developed out of the actions of thousands of individuals who were constrained by larger forces: the environment, the economy, and the national political system. People came to the region with one history and there created another history that affects us to this day.

CULTURE

Culture is composed of the patterns of daily living that a person must learn in order to be like others. It can be accumulated and passed on from one generation to the next. We learn our culture. Culture does not refer just to preferences and modes of thought but also to material objects, such as type of house, style of clothing, books, furniture, tools, and instruments. A culture is a design for living that results from the interplay of social, geographic, historical, and individual conditions. Because our culture is the result of this combination, it affects our entire life, and thus we come to support and value it.

Dominant Values

Values are the feelings we have about the events that are basic to our lives; values govern our views of religion, politics, child rearing, and marriage, for example. Values help determine our response to everyday events. Different cultures have different values, and because they do, social scientists have attempted to discern what are called the *dominant value profiles* of individual cultures. By dominant values we mean values that are shared by the majority of a population, that persist over time, and that provide a framework within which people organize their daily lives.

There have been many attempts to describe the dominant values of American culture. For instance, Jules Henry (1963) characterized American society as a *drive* culture, oriented toward achievement, competition, profit, mobility, and an ever higher standard of living. Robin Williams (1961:409–470) compiled an extensive list of American values which we will use, modifying his labels slightly, in order to understand how our present value patterns came about. We will also draw on the material about the Martin family to illustrate these values in operation and in change.

Achievement and Success   Achievement is a central American value that is reflected in our heroes. Often they have been self-made people: Abraham Lincoln split rails, studied by firelight, saved his money, and eventually became president. People often achieve success through their own efforts, and this success is often measured by the amount of wealth that they have accumulated. By the Great Depression of the 1930s, Americans seemed to value financial success over many other central values. But in the Martins' time, the emphasis was still on achievement, which could be measured in ways other than the amount of money that one had amassed. For example, Henry Martin was extremely active in church and community affairs and as a result was admired by his friends.

It was an achievement simply to be able to overcome the odds that stood in the way of becoming a farmer. To migrate to Kansas, to break the soil, to build a sod house, and to harvest one's first crop meant that one had succeeded. If you were a farmer's wife, your success might be defined by your ability to provide a meal for your family or to give birth to healthy children. But whatever the criteria for success, people were preoccupied with achievement.

It has been suggested that the American love of size is related to the dominant value of achievement and success. In the Martins' time, one way of measuring both achievement and progress was to have a larger return on one's investment each year. The investment could take the form of money or labor. A bigger farm, more acres under cultivation, and a larger harvest are all related to the concept of size. In some cases, more was even equated with good. More wheat not only brought in more money to buy more goods, but it also meant success. To be successful, or to achieve, was a driving force for people like Henry Martin. It enabled him and countless others to do the hardest work, starting over again and again after grasshoppers had destroyed all their crops or after drought had burned them out. With a characteristically matter-of-fact air, Henry stated in his diary, "'Eighty-seven saw another drouth and short crops, but a memorable Fourth of July celebration."

Cora DuBois (1955) suggested that the American desire to succeed is characterized by its dominant value, effort/optimism. This is essentially the same as the value of achievement/success, but it also describes an approach to reality that we need to underscore. Americans not only value achievement/success, but they also believe it to be obtainable through their own hard work. (This also has negative consequences, for Americans have a tendency to believe that anybody who is not successful simply has not worked hard enough.)

Henry Martin's diary opens with an explanation of why he decided to emigrate to Kansas, which exemplifies effort/optimism: "I determined...that we would migrate to Kansas and homestead there, beginning a new life in earnest hopes of better things for ourselves and our posterity." We also find throughout Henry's diary and letters, as well as those of other settlers, a considerable number of lists: purchases (including books), income and its sources, and even topics addressed by the local debating society. These lists served several purposes, among them, of course, the settlers' need to keep track of how their money was being spent. The lists also helped them plan for the future, even if only next month. But they were too, in a sense, an accounting of their successes and achievements, what had been acquired and learned. They were a way of saying, "This is how far I've come this year."

A major part of this value system was the settlers' desire for self-improvement, which took several forms. First, participation in "literary" events was highly regarded. Many communities organized debate societies, and others formed study groups whose members prepared and read to one another papers on a wide variety of topics. The programs of the Sunday schools, farmers' associations, and annual institutes are evidence that many of the scheduled activities and topics revolved around achieving success in farming or in one's moral life.

Time was not to be wasted on activities that did not pertain to, or that detracted from, one's achievement of success. Perhaps this was one reason that Henry's debate society decided that reading fiction was injurious. If we examine Henry's lists of purchases, we find that his literary materials consisted of tracts that preached against the evils of drink and books that would aid in self-improvement: Greek and Latin grammars, dictionaries, and geology, geography, and history books. We should emphasize, though, that the Martins were not an unusual family in this respect. There were, as their diaries indicate, a number of families that read widely in texts that many today would consider difficult. As was noted in Chapter 1, a school was one of the community's priorities. Whether education was an individual effort or took place in the public schoolroom, the settlers considered it to be directly related to the dominant values of achievement and success. And they believed that hard work, a striving for self-improvement, and a morality that preaches thrift and self-control were values that often led to worldly success.

Activity and Work The next important dominant value is closely related to the first. In summing up his year's activities, Henry Martin declared, "I began planting fruit trees for fruit and shade and windbreak and to hold the soil. I also made a dugout for our animals, built our milkhouse, dug our well, helped build the sod-hill school house for our little community, killed a wildcat, fought two prairie fires, and tried our luck with wheat and corn crops."

In a frontier environment and in early colonial America, work had survival value; it was also something more. Idleness was not only impractical in the harsh environment of early America, it also was considered sinful. The link between positive feelings for work and morality was fostered by the early Americans' Puritan heritage. The Puritans were distinguished from other religious groups by their concept of a calling. They believed that people were "called" to a particular task in life; the successful pursuit of this calling determined whether they would become a member of the elect, which meant that at death they would join the community of saints. They had no way of knowing whether they would go to Heaven, except that they would have some evidence of whether they were one of the chosen, depending on how successfully they had pursued their calling. This ensured a sort of psychological insecurity that could be relieved only through the active pursuit of a calling, that is, through work.

This Puritan outlook had a subtle, but important, effect on American culture. Individuals stood alone before their God and had nobody but themselves to blame for their failure or success. Individual achievement, reflected in the world of work, was all that counted. As a result, many Americans take more pleasure in individual accomplishments in work and other activities than in group efforts. Among the Great Plains settlers, a family's sense of accomplishment was seldom felt beyond the husband and wife and their children. There are many indications throughout Henry's diaries and letters that he saw his accomplishments as an individual act, his work as the means by which he defined himself. This is why many men today still define their masculinity in terms of their jobs. To be without a job, without work, means to them not to be a man. (The women of Lucy Martin's generation did not, however, define their femininity in terms of their jobs. They did, of course, define themselves in terms of their work, but it was of a different nature. We shall elaborate this point in our discussion of male and female roles.)

This individualism coexisted on the frontier with cooperation. For example, the pioneers, of necessity, cooperated with their neighbors in a number of ways: raising barns, plowing fields for a sick farmer, helping with chores, and sharing equipment. These were not everyday activities, however. People lived in individual, often isolated family units, getting together with others generally only for recreational purposes or to help someone in need. There were, of course, some individuals who, because of religious or political values, chose to live in groups; they derived a sense of purpose and well-being from their contribution to the community. Such groups as the Amish and the Mennonites deliberately downplayed individualism in order to maintain the integrity of the group. Despite the differences between these groups and the more individualistic farmers, they were in many ways similar, as a result of the circumstances in which they both found themselves.

Morality   Robin Williams (1961:424) suggested that American society is characterized by a moral orientation. By this he did not mean people's conformity to the "detailed prescripts of a particular moral code" but, rather, "a systematic moral orientation by which conduct is *judged*." If so, then Americans think in terms of right, wrong, good, and evil. Why should this be the case?

Robertson (1981) noted that all societies have myths. We are familiar with the myths that played an integral part in Greek culture and those held by other peoples about the origin of the world and the birth of their gods. But modern men and women, too, have myths that explain and give order to their world. Robertson's myths are like values, in the sense that both are ordering mechanisms. There are many myths current in modern America, but we will concern ourselves here with one identified by Robinson: the myth of civilization.

The pilgrims, the frontiersmen, and the prairie settlers were all strangers who migrated to a hostile land and struggled to master it. They also sought to recreate the civilization that they had left behind. It was not that they sought to reinstitute the same state and religious systems but that they believed that their survival was linked with the maintenance of a certain type of social relations. "Civilized" meant settled, established, able to look beyond questions of mere subsistence. Thus, the farmers were more civilized than the "outsiders" such as the drifters, the squatters, or—according to the myth—the Indians.

The myths of civilization and morality joined hands: morality in early America literally meant being a God-fearing Christian. America's Puritan heritage contributed to the tendency to judge, to measure, and to weigh. In that sense, when Henry Martin added up his yearly expenditures, he was judging himself, but he was also implicitly comparing himself with others: those who did not save as much and those who may have saved more. From our discussion of work, it should be clear that a hard-working person was, by definition, a moral person. Anyone who did not work was either pitied or despised.

The links among morality, civilization, and outsiders (often simply defined as those who "are not like us") are more complicated. First, as we suggested, the outsider was seen as uncivilized, even savage. In the nineteenth century, Americans tried hard to develop a feeling of a community, a sense of belonging to a larger group. Anything or anyone who threatened this feeling of belonging, or threatened the emerging moral order, was feared and accordingly judged as immoral. The wilderness itself was something suspect; it needed to be tamed and conquered. The outsider, whether an Indian, a cowboy, or merely a drifter, was part of the wilderness and thus to be avoided.

One way to deal with these constant threats was to be a good Christian. To have a Christian education meant being armed against the unknown, the wilderness. Another way was to band together with others of like mind. Events that struck at this sense of community were particularly traumatic, for they caused people to feel their isolation even more powerfully. Knowing these things, we can better understand some of the events in the Martins' diaries.

Lucy Martin, for instance, talked about how hard it would have been for her to be among one of the first families on the prairie: "I don't know how I would have endured such loneliness. It seems to me that hard times...are so much more bearable if you can just know that others are there to help if they can and understand if they can't!" When her son Harold died, Lucy, in her grief, held onto her life by holding onto her baby, who provided the link with the living, with civilization. A death in a family raised the specter of isolation, of the constant threat of the wilderness. Thus, even the death of the Martins' cow has a certain poignancy: the cow had fallen down the well, and struggling alone with no one to witness its agonies, it died. Lucy remarked, "I thought about if off and on all day—how she suffered and how easy it is on these prairies to get lost or hurt or both if you are alone, man or beast, so it is certainly best not to be alone if you can manage that!"

The evening that Lucy spent with Flossie, waiting for Mary Turner to give birth, was passed recounting their early days in an unknown environment. They talked about children and childbirth, and Lucy recalled, "So we chatted on through the night, recalling this and that hard time and happy time and congratulating ourselves on our superior state of civilization." In short, they had managed to conquer the wilderness.

Both Lucy and Henry spoke of the need for a Christian education. But one of the most revealing statements was made by Lucy, who was furious with Jess Harper, a church member who criticized Henry for doing so many different things for the church. She described Harper as "a member of that motley trouble-making Farmers' Alliance and a known drinker who keeps whiskey in his house, though I know for a fact that Lizzie has begged him not to set such an example to their poor young ones." She went on to speak about the value of Henry's "organized Christian effort" on behalf of the community.

Henry was no less harsh in his judgments than Lucy was. He spoke ill of those who grumbled and complained instead of working hard, and he had no use for those who did not live a settled existence. "I found no class of people more reprehensible than the wretches calling themselves 'settlers' who merely made shift to live, hand to mouth, on their dubious claims—while waiting to be bought out at a profit and move on again." (As we will see in later chapters, this notion changed considerably, and geographic and social mobility came to be valued.) Another problem for Henry was the town council's decision to license two taverns, or "Devil's mantraps," as he called them. Thus we find Henry's values relating to abolition, the need for Kansas to be a free state, his Sunday school activities, his work, and his desire for temperance reform all linked in a general value complex of morality.

Efficiency and Practicality   As Williams (1961:428) defined it, efficiency is a standard against which Americans judge nearly all activities. In his autobiography, Benjamin Franklin (1771) talked constantly about the need to be engaged in useful work. He also stood as a model of efficiency, especially because of Poor Richard's sayings, such as "Industry need not wish, and he that lives upon hope will die fasting"; "Lost time is never found again"; "Plough deep while sluggards sleep"; and "God gives all things to industry." To Franklin, efficient work was the most rational means of accomplishing a task. Because our society has sanctioned the attainment of wealth, we devote much effort to finding more efficient ways of getting it. Williams noted (1961:429) that this results in technique being raised to the level of a value in its own right. Attention then shifts from one's goal, and its evaluation, to the means of achieving it. But for many years Americans did not seriously question the goal of attaining wealth or power or prestige. They simply accepted that anything that stood in the way of material progress was bad. Henry and Lucy accepted, as a matter of faith, that progress, which meant overcoming the wilderness, was a good thing. An efficient approach to one's goals was another mark of the civilized person, who engaged in rational, calculated, purposive activity.

The link between science and rationality in this country is well known. Henry Martin supported the Farmers' Institute and its programs because they offered a scientific-rationalistic approach to farming, which meant more efficient farming. (And the church programs offered more efficient means for saving souls.) Even today, there are few who question the worth of science, for it is accepted as the best means by which to solve a problem. Science, rationality, and efficiency are all valued in our society. This encourages a utilitarian approach to life, and so we judge an activity on the basis of whether it works.

The impractical person is often held up as an object for scorn, and so intellectuals are often ignored because they are seen as being impractical. United States Senator William Proxmire, for instance, has gained some notoriety by giving a "Golden Fleece Award" each year to the scientist or project that seemed to be the biggest waste of the taxpayers' money. Whether the project indeed was a waste of money was determined by whether Proxmire deemed it practical.

This emphasis on efficiency and practicality pervades the American culture and value system. If a society values activity/ work, achievement/success, and efficiency/practicality and also sanctions the attainment of wealth, then many people's activities will be channeled toward it. Our school system reflects our society's need to be practical, by teaching subjects that are useful. Henry was pleased with the curriculum at the state school because it was scientific and useful: "I was interested to find that the special course of study for young women (how to cook and sew and care for the home) was based on sound scientific principles."

Progress   Henry began his diary by explaining why he had decided to come to Kansas: "We would emigrate to Kansas and homestead there, beginning a new life in earnest hopes of better things for ourselves and our posterity." His statement exemplifies the value of effort/optimism or achievement/success as well as the dominant value of progress. The belief in progress, that things will be better tomorrow, has been dominant throughout American history and has resulted in what might be called a "booster mentality."

Consider the number of small towns throughout the United States today that claim that progress is coming in the form of a new shopping mall, factory, or industrial park. (There have also been battles to halt progress.) The settlement of the small towns on the Great Plains was based on this same mentality. People were encouraged to settle in a particular town because it had the best view or the best water, was the closest to the rail line, was growing the fastest, or had the best newspaper.

The idea of progress was believed to have a scientific basis, and Charles Darwin's work, *Origin of Species,* came to have far-reaching social consequences, known as Social Darwinism. As Richard Hofstadter (1965) showed, Darwin's theory of the survival of the fittest could be used to explain why some people were poor and others rich. The assumption was that those who survived were, by definition, the fittest and that because this was a law of nature, it could not be changed. Thus social reform, which was aimed at alleviating the problems of the poor, was bound to fail because it ran contrary to a law of nature. In its crudest form, Social Darwinism was also used to justify the existence of wide differences in wealth and position. The rich were rich because they were the fittest, and the poor were poor because they were not the fittest. Of course, all of these arguments ignored the fact that people might be rich because they inherited their wealth or poor because of limited educational and occupational opportunities.

Included in the theory of Social Darwinism was an evolutionary perspective which also was derived from Darwin's work. Social Darwinists saw society as inevitably progressing, especially if a system of laissez-faire dominated. The new social orders that replaced the old were "better," for they represented a higher and, again, inevitable stage. Progress was taken for granted, and any person or thing that blocked it was considered suspect.

There were two dominant schools of Social Darwinist thought in American culture: a reformist school and one characterized by laissez-faire, or the belief that one ought not to tamper with the natural order. Henry and Lucy Martin belonged to the first school. They believed that progress was coming, that it was inevitable, and that it was good. But they also believed that a good life for all could be hastened by active, organized, humanitarian efforts. This idea has been reflected at different times in our country's history in such things as the Social Gospel movement (around 1910) or the Moral Rearmament movement, which was dominant during President Dwight D. Eisenhower's administration. The laissez-faire side of Social Darwinism is still evident in movements and political parties that call for less government interference and in programs that try to put the poor to work instead of taking government handouts.

Social Darwinism and a belief in inevitable progress were also responsible for an antihistorical perspective. As Henry Ford said, "History is bunk." Apparently he meant that what has happened is not relevant to what may happen today or tomorrow; rather, we must turn our attention toward the future, as the past can provide little as a guide for our present or future behavior.

The development of a value complex is an intriguing process. Clearly, the Martins and thousands of other settlers turned their attention to the future. They needed to believe that things would get better, for their daily lives were grim. The idea of progress, that things would be better tomorrow—if not for oneself, at least for one's children—was appealing, and even better, it seemed scientific. And many of those who migrated west from Europe or the eastern seaboard actually did make progress. They saw it happen: they watched towns emerge where there had been none; rail lines snake across the entire country; and schools, colleges, and churches spring up around them. In short, there was, for a time, a link between an emerging idea and an actual experience. Had the day-to-day life of the settlers been different, it is unlikely that the idea of progress would have been so prominent.

Likewise, people had to work in order to survive, and so work became a positive achievement. As something to be valued, work also was reinforced by a religious system that emphasized individual effort. Religions that did not value work were not likely to flourish on the frontier. Therefore, the region's many different religious groups (e.g., Baptists, Methodists, Presbyterians, Episcopalians, and Congregationalists) had similar values regarding work, achievement, success, and progress. At any given moment, the existing value systems were a result of the unique historical experiences of a people struggling with their environment. Those values that did not explain this struggle and did not adequately reflect it simply were discarded.

Humanitarianism   A crusading vision has always characterized much of American activity. The tendency to engage in crusades, armed by Christianity against the wilderness or against drink, can have extremely negative consequences. For instance, the American Indians suffered mightily at the hands of white settlers who wanted a better life for themselves. Coupled with the crusading vision, however, is the notion that one ought to help fellow (white) human beings. There are many stories of barn raisings on the frontier or of people helping with the harvesting or planting because a farmer had fallen ill. Yet there was an element of self-interest in this altruism, for people hoped that if they fell on hard times, their friends and neighbors would, in turn, come to their aid. Immigrant groups that migrated together often helped one another build their homes and farms. Lucy and her friend assisted a neighbor in childbirth, just as they had been helped. Part of this humanitarian value orientation stemmed from the need to create a community: helping others established bonds.

There was a tension between the desire to help others and the values of freedom and democracy. In some of the communities described in Chapter 1, charitable organizations were founded to help those farmers who had been ruined by either the drought or the grasshoppers. Other communities, though, took a strong laissez-faire position, arguing that such problems were an individual's own responsibility. If such people could not cope, then they should return whence they came. These sentiments were not dominant, but some felt that giving aid was a voluntary, individual act, not something required of the state. Thus there were many arguments against state aid to the indigent and for any other individual problems. Remember that a lack of money was seen as something for which the individual was responsible, something that could be overcome by hard work.

Materialism   The next major value that we will consider is materialism—the emphasis placed on material well-being. Like the others, this value does not stand alone. Laski (1948:13) stated, "No church which urged the desirability of asceticism had any hope of influence or much hope of survival." In other words, the early American churches did not preach the virtues of consumption, although they did not argue against the accumulation of riches. In fact, as we have already seen, a mark of virtue might be one's material success.

The emphasis on consumption in American life is so pervasive that we sometimes overlook it. An evening of television is an evening filled with commercials advertising almost anything imaginable. Our newsstands are stocked with magazines such as *Us* and *People* which have as their main focus consumer idols—people whose claim to fame is their ability to maintain a life-style that others can only emulate. The advertising industry (Ewen, 1976) has been responsible for convincing many people that the only way to achieve happiness is through consumption. In a society of rapid mobility and change, purchased status symbols may be the only means by which people can find their place in the social hierarchy.

But for people such as Henry and Lucy Martin, production—not consumption—was the focus of their lives. The Martins were what we would consider primary commodity producers. They had a farm, grew much of their own food, and sold the surplus. Their consumption, such as it was, was often oriented toward obtaining goods that would fulfill such basic needs as food, shelter, and clothing. But consumption was not an end in itself. The Martins truly wanted a better life, and that life might come in the form of a piano in the parlor, good books, or a solid roof over their heads. But their vision of success centered on being good Christian people. Their lives were conducted in accordance with a general set of values that stressed respectability, hard work, discipline, and helping others. Their high status in the local community was attained because they were known as responsible people and successful producers.

During the Martins' time, strangers, upon meeting one another, often asked, "What church do you belong to?" They might later have asked where the person lived and what he or she did, but the first question often dealt with religion. Why? To be a good Christian meant that one was an acceptable member of the community, that one was, to use an earlier term, civilized. It was only later that people began to focus on other measures of status such as job, wealth, and clothing.

The values of early America, which stressed frugality and hard work and contributed to the growth of society, were ultimately eroded by a consumer-oriented society. Daniel Bell (1976) described this process as the "cultural contradiction of capitalism." Today people believe that they have a right to a certain level of consumption or material well-being. As Bell noted, the belief that one is entitled to more produces a great strain on the political-economic system. In short, materialism, which now threatens the integrity of our system, had its origin in values that were at one time adaptive.

Democracy   The value orientation of democracy has several parts. We cannot consider democracy without also examining attitudes toward freedom, independence, and equality. This country has always been dominated by egalitarianism, the belief that people are inherently equal and that no one should dominate. One reason for this strong belief in equality was that many early pioneers had come to the United States from countries in which a hereditary nobility existed, in which class lines were well drawn, and the political and economic systems were ruled by clearly identifiable elites. In short, as Reissman (1959) found, many of the first immigrants to this country had antiaristocratic feelings. Furthermore, according to Williams (1961:438):

> In this remarkable historical experience, through generation after generation the values of equality were crystallized and elaborated. People saw the disappearance of primogeniture, the abolition of indentured servitude, of imprisonment for debt, of slavery, of property qualifications for voting and public office; there was provision for the common man to acquire a stake in the land and to secure a free public education; women gained one legal right after another; and even discriminations against minorities were sharply challenged time after time.

One can, of course, disagree with Williams about the extent to which some of this has happened, but the average citizen did indeed see the amount of equality increase and the principle reinforced, if sometimes only in the breach.

America's religious traditions also reinforced its notion of equality. Everyone, theoretically, began life with equal opportunity, and everyone was "equal in the sight of the Lord." One could be a saint or a sinner, successful or unsuccessful; it was up to the individual to decide which. Yet the notion of equality conflicts with those values relating to freedom. Normally, freedom, another part of the value complex of contemporary democracy, means the absence of restraints. The ability or right to pursue one's interests without harming another is freedom. But the freedom to pursue one's interests in a society that emphasizes success, materialism, and progress can lead to great inequality. Economic freedom produces a society of haves and have-nots, which in turn prevents all people from beginning life on an equal footing, for if one is born into a wealthy family, one will have easier access to good schools, medical care, and jobs. Freedom cannot guarantee equality of outcome, which is quite different from equality of opportunity.

In the latter half of the nineteenth century, the focus was on equality of opportunity, with the assumption that equality of outcome would follow. Thus, both Lucy and Henry Martin believed that they were no different than anybody else, except that they might have worked even harder. They did not grumble like some but worked to overcome their economic misfortunes. Education was something that anybody could acquire if he or she wanted to. Hadn't Henry studied by himself in the evenings, reading the geography books and Latin grammars he had purchased? Didn't he go to reading groups and debate societies to improve himself, and weren't these opportunities available to others? Yes and no. Yes, in the sense that the frontier experience was a socially leveling experience. Many of the farmers began life on the same footing, and if anything distinguished them after a period of years, it was hard work and luck. (They may have escaped the plagues of grasshoppers.) No, in the sense that some people came to the frontier with considerable resources. Eastern money, for instance, allowed some to build hotels, to develop the shipping facilities for cattle and crops, or to control the banks that made the desperately needed loans. But even though there were clear class groupings, with distinctly different opportunities available to them, the myth of equality persisted.

And this myth persists to this day, although in a changed form. As we noted, there is a difference between equality of opportunity and equality of outcome. Given America's materialist orientation, more and more people believe that the outcome, as measured by one's ability to consume, should be guaranteed (Bell, 1976). But some would argue that such a situation, which could occur only through social legislation, contradicts the value of freedom. They are right, and that is another of the contradictions in the complex set of values that makes up our social heritage.

Freedom, equality, and democracy also reveal themselves in more mundane ways. Henry Martin continually talked about the need to be independent, that is, to pay off his debts. He did not want to be beholden to another person, did not want anyone controlling his life. Many people today still do not like to be controlled, and that is one reason that, for example, a large number of people go into business for themselves, even when the rate of failure is extremely high, and that executives of large corporations take courses on how to delegate work to others without offending them.

Dominant American Values   Before 1900, the United States was primarily a rural society. With agriculture as the major form of production, there was a strong emphasis on values such as activity/work, achievement/success, morality, efficiency/practicality, progress, freedom, and equality. But in time some of those have eroded; that is, they now have much less influence on us than they did previously. Materialism, which was once coupled with morality and achievement, has lost its link with morality, and we find consumption as a value replacing it. The belief in the inevitability of progress experienced a setback during World War I and the Great Depression. Like all other human creations, values change. Let us summarize them before we examine the next set of issues.

1. *Achievement/Success.* Linked with effort/optimism, achievement/success represents the desire for self-improvement, success, or achievement. It is often measured by quantity and is dominated by the belief that only one's own effort will obtain success.

2. *Activity/Work.* To be busy, to be useful, and to work are good in themselves, not just because they yield tangible results. Activity/work is closely linked with achievement/success. Americans' attitudes toward work reinforce their concept of individualism.

3. *Morality.* Americans tend to judge other people and other ways of life. Morality is an active stance toward a world viewed as needing to be changed in an organized and disciplined fashion. A moral person is one who has over-

come the wilderness and belongs to a community. Outsiders are, by definition, not moral.

4. *Efficiency/Practicality*. Americans value useful activity. Their emphasis on practicality, efficiency, and usefulness supports their emphasis on science and rationality. They accept rational activity and science without question.

5. *Progress*. No idea has more greatly dominated or characterized the American approach to life. The belief in progress is a belief that things will get better. It contains an evolutionary perspective and reinforces the concept of Social Darwinism. Social Darwinism and the idea of progress contribute to an antihistorical bias.

6. *Humanitarianism*. Americans believe in helping others. This value joins morality to produce progressive crusading visions and social movements designed to save others from their shortcomings.

7. *Materialism*. Materialism was originally an emphasis on material well-being, which was superseded by consumerism. From defining a person in terms of whether he or she was a "good Christian," Americans came to define a person in terms such as "clothes make the man."

8. *Democracy*. Democracy is a subset of values pertaining to freedom, independence, and equality, which described America at the turn of the century.

Elements of Culture

Cultures are designs for living that involve both abstract and concrete elements. We have discussed values, which are part of every culture, in some detail so that we can understand how a particular society evolves. American society, then, isn't just an abstraction or a geographical locality. It is also the values that comprise it at any given time. There are other dimensions to cultures which we should examine.

Abstract and Concrete Cultural Elements   Societies contain concrete and abstract cultural elements. For instance, the American flag is a cultural element. It is concrete in that it is a red, white, and blue oblong of cloth with a certain number of stripes and stars. It is abstract because it stands for something. In a parade, the flag may symbolize pride, patriotism, and a belief in the American way of life. Printed on the front of a T-shirt or appliquéd on the back of a pair of jeans, it can mean defiance of the larger cultural order. Flying over our embassies in foreign countries, it can stand for either tyranny and oppression or freedom and democracy. But the flag is clearly an *element* of American culture. Henry Martin's barn, the tools with which he harvested grain, and Lucy's caldron, used for boiling water, rendering fat, making soap, and boiling down jam, were all cultural elements. Today, these items hold little meaning for most Americans, except perhaps as antiques.

Cultural Complex   At a higher level of abstraction is a cultural complex, that is, a functionally related set of cultural elements. There are cultural complexes related to marriage and the family, others related to work, and still others related to religion. The set of cultural elements related to farming is part of a cultural complex.

The Martins were self-sufficient farmers; they purchased few commodities. They had a modest house because their scarce resources had to be devoted to developing their farm. As soon as they could, they built a substantial barn and a silo for fermenting fodder. They had dairy cows because they needed their products; moreover, they could sell the surplus butter or trade it for flour, cloth, or something they could not make themselves. They raised one or two pigs, feeding them partly on table scraps. They planted fruit trees so that Lucy would be able to can and dry fruit to supplement their diet through the long winters. And like most farm families, they had a few chickens for fresh eggs and an occasional Sunday dinner. All of these elements—chickens, cows, barn, silo, house, fruit trees, the butter churn, the grain reaper, and the plow, together with the Martins' values of independence and hard work— were part of the same cultural complex.

Cultural complexes change over time as their elements change. For instance, the turn-of-the-century economy was horse centered. It produced a cultural complex that had among its elements buggy manufacturers, harness makers, livery stables, blacksmiths, and horse-powered farm machinery. But horses gave way to cars and steam and gasoline engines, which in turn produced a new cultural complex made up of gas stations, gas station attendants, mechanics, automobile races and drivers, tire manufacturers, automobile manufacturers, parts stores and distributors, and so forth. In fact, this cultural complex is so important that it is possible to speak of the United States as having a car culture which has affected its family structure, dating patterns, and popular songs.

Determinants of Culture

The Environment   One's environment, or ecology, plays a major role in shaping the cultural system. This is obvious in the case of the traditional Eskimos, whose lives centered on hunting whales and seals, their major food sources. Because they needed the help of others to hunt large animals, they lived in villages that were organized around the hunt. The size of the village was determined by the available food supply, and so large, permanent villages did not develop.

In the South Seas, to take an extreme example, people do not have to organize their lives around hunting. Often they can gather food by means of a minimum of effort. Occasionally groups will join together in order to net fish in a bay, and the abundance of resources allows for the establishment of larger villages, although again there are natural limits to their size. Instead of the Eskimos' enclosed igloos, the South Sea people have open living quarters, encouraging the free flow of people throughout the village. The South Sea children are often treated as if they are the children of the community, with everyone taking responsibility for their socialization. But the Eskimos, again because of their environment, have a very different system of socialization.

The link between cultural practices and the environment is not always clear, though a cultural materialist perspective may help explain it. (A cultural materialist perspective assumes that people's beliefs, attitudes, and ideas—in short, their culture—are a response to a specific set of material conditions.) Using this perspective, Harris (1974) looked at the refusal of the natives of India to eat any of the nation's more than 100 million cows. The Indians venerate cows: they are sacred, and the people are forbidden to kill them. Most Westerners would believe this prohibition to be irrational: people are hungry, and the cows are everywhere—by the roadside, in houses, and even in busy downtown traffic.

The Indians' veneration of cows can be understood only by examining the relationship between Indian culture and the environment. Harris found that many Indian farmers are too poor to afford tractors. They use oxen to pull their plows, and if they were to kill them for food, they would ultimately be even worse off. According to Harris, cows provide India with 700 million tons of free fertilizer each year. Furthermore, the country is short of wood, and the people cannot afford to buy coal and oil for cooking fuel; they use well-dried cow dung instead. Finally, the cows scavenge for their food on unproductive land. As a result, the Indians are far better off not eating their cows.

How did the ecology of the Great Plains affect its culture? First, because the land did not have to be cleared of trees and stumps, as it did on the eastern seaboard, it was possible to cultivate larger tracts of land. Furthermore, the climate dictated certain crops for commercial exploitation, that is, wheat and corn. The size of the farm and the type of crop in turn contributed to the heavy capitalization of many early midwestern farms. In order to be a successful farmer, it was usually necessary to borrow in order to buy machinery, seed, and sometimes the farm itself. Early farmers, then, participated in a cash economy and were subject to the vicissitudes of the larger economy. When the price of grain dropped on the European markets, the farmers were immediately affected, because they had been raising their crops for export. The point that we want to emphasize here is that it was the ecology that restricted the type of farming that was commercially viable; it was not the larger economic order that determined what would be grown or what the size of the farms would be.

The size of the farms also affected the Great Plains' patterns of social organization, for people who were widely separated could not organize to deal with political and economic problems as readily as those living in towns could. The distances that separated neighbors made visiting an important activity. Lucy Martin's frustration when the minister arrived for dinner while she was still doing her chores was quickly offset by the realization that she would have others to talk to. The assistance that people gave one another through organized barn raisings or helping with the crops derived from their desire to see one another and to mitigate the loneliness of the prairies.

Drought and grasshoppers were also a part of the ecology and helped shape the culture. Farmers of the Great Plains were characterized by their fatalistic attitudes. They planted their crops, did the best they could, and then awaited the outcome. In the diaries and letters we examined, farmer after farmer noted, "Well, I've done my best, now it's up to the good Lord." Failure was not attributed to oneself but to events beyond one's control. Effort, optimism, and achievement were values that derived from a direct struggle with the environment, as was fatalism.

Technology   The way that technology influences culture can be explained if we take a broad historical perspective. During the Lower Paleolithic period, which began around 1,000,000 B.C. (Childe, 1942), people were using fire, stone and bone tools, and were trapping animals. They also formally buried their dead. During the Upper Paleolithic, which began about 50,000 B.C., people were using weapons: bows and arrows, sticks, and harpoons. Some painted the walls of their caves and wore clothing made from animal skins sewn together with bone needles. By the Neolithic, which began about 7000 B.C., people were living in permanent villages with populations of several hundred. They had domesticated plants and animals for food and made pottery and wove crude fabrics. During the Bronze Age, which began around 3000 B.C., people invented plows, canals for irrigation, sailboats, and wheeled carts and constructed large public buildings to house their priests and government officials. Some of the cities situated in river valleys had populations of several thousand. Finally, during the Iron Age, which began in 1400 B.C., people began to use alphabetic writing and coins.

Each stage of technological improvement provided different cultural possibilities. Childe (1942) argued, for example, that there were no priests, warriors, or government administrators until there was a surplus of food. In turn, this surplus was made possible by the cultivation of wild grains, the domestication of animals, and the invention of irrigation canals, hoes, plows, and other farming implements. Private property was not possible until people could mark goods with universally recognized symbols. The brands that ranchers put on their stock is a direct extension of the seal that Egyptians put on their property during the Bronze Age.

Banton (1965:45–47) described the impact of a new technology on the Yir Yurmont, aborigines of northern Australia. They originally possessed neither metals nor stone from which to make tools. The stone ax heads that the tribe later acquired came from four hundred miles to the south. The Yir Yurmont had an elaborate system of trade: "Up this chain came stones suitable for use as axheads and down it went spears tipped with the spines of the sting ray which were manufactured by aborigines living on the coast" (Banton, 1965:45). Trading took place during ceremonies initiating the male youth into the tribe. Only males could own stone axes, and borrowing of axes was rigidly controlled: a wife could borrow one from her husband, or a son from his father. Owning an ax was a sign of male superiority and dominance. In about 1915, a group of well-meaning missionaries came to the area, bringing a plentiful supply of steel axes with them (Banton, 1965). The older males in the tribe ignored the new axes, but the women and young men were eager to have them. No longer did the women have to go to their husbands, or sons to their fathers, to borrow an ax. The people thus lost interest in trading axes for flat stones, and the trade festivals disappeared. In addition, the religious system was altered because the traditional belief system associated distinct skills and objects with particular clans. And because the steel axes could not be categorized in this fashion, a significant part of the people's lives was no longer subject to religious definition. This in turn weakened the entire sacred system and its links with the past. In short, the Yir Yurmonts' traditional society collapsed, all because of steel axes.

We discussed in Chapter 1 the impact of technology on the culture of the Great Plains. The development of these lands was made possible by such inventions as the steel moldboard plow, which could cut through the dense sod of the prairie grasses. Barbed wire allowed farmers to enclose their lands, which prevented the ranchers' practice of open grazing and led them to adopt a system of feeding their cattle in enclosed pastures. The reaper, the thresher, and many other inventions made large-scale farming possible. Yet even in the same geographic environment, in which people use similar forms of technology, there can be wide differences in the type of cultural systems that develop.

Comparison of Plains Cultures

The Great Plains have had a rich and diverse history. Each group that settled in this area has had to confront the environment, adapt to it, and shape it to its needs. Traditional cultures were transformed over time, and the cultures we find today are a result of that long adaptive process. John Bennett (1969), in his classic study of Plains cultures, compared four groups in Saskatchewan, Canada: Native Americans, ranchers, farmers, and Hutterites. Saskatchewan is much like the Great Plains of the United States in that its climate is similar, it was settled at approximately the same time, its farming technology is similar, and it experienced struggles between farmers and ranchers and whites and Native Americans. The region of Saskatchewan that Bennett examined is called Jasper.

The Native Americans   Jasper's Native Americans were primarily Cree. By the nineteenth century, the Cree culture had already changed in response to the arrival of the white settlers. Originally a people of the forest, the Cree became heavily involved in the fur trade, which was one reason for their eventual movement to the Plains. As beavers and other fur-bearing animals became scarce, the Cree turned to hunting bison. For a time, they acted as intermediaries between the white fur traders and other Native American tribes. They were greatly influenced by white culture, and by the time they moved onto the Great Plains they were using the white settlers' firearms, tools, and food. They differed, however, from those groups that had totally adapted to a Plains culture. For example, the early Native Americans of the Great Plains organized their societies around the buffalo hunt, migrating as the herds migrated. During the fall, when the herds of buffalo were large, because they had gathered to breed, the hunts necessitated cooperation and social organization. The ensuing tribal ceremonies and sun dances that accompanied the fall hunt also provided a means for some common identification with a larger social unit. This unit, however, was loosely knit, based on kinship and loose bands, with informal chieftainship. When the fall hunt was over, the Cree would break down into smaller groups in order to follow the deer, elk, and bison, which also had broken down into smaller groups. The Cree were somewhat less organized, for they maintained some ties to the white fur traders; their migratory patterns were therefore influenced by things other than the horse and bison. But the Cree did adopt a form of social organization typical of that of other Native Americans of the Great Plains, and that was the Warrior Lodge—"a kind of men's club, police force, and planning council for hunts and raids" (Bennett, 1969:147). The Warrior Society organized the hunts, divided the spoils, and punished those who violated the rules of the hunt. This general form of social organization had resulted from the Crees' initial adaptation to hunting bison, riding horses, and moving onto the Plains. That adaptation was short-lived.

By around 1875, the bison was extinct in some areas. As the bison vanished and the integrity of the tribes weakened, the white settlers began to move rapidly into Jasper. But this area never experienced the destructive wars of rebellion that other areas did, because of the debilitation of the Crees by whiskey and smallpox and because the Canadian Mounties managed to maintain peace in a reasonably even-handed manner. The remaining Jasper Native Americans were herded off to a reservation north of the town. In 1960 about one hundred of them still lived on the reserve in shacks, tents, and plywood houses.

The Crees' economic adaptation to their reduced circumstances reveals the transformation of their own culture by the white culture. During the period of Bennett's study, the main sources of the Crees' income were monthly relief checks, the occasional sale of fence posts, part-time manual labor, fees from ranchers pasturing cattle, illegal sales of cows given to the Native Americans by the Indian Affairs office, and "borrowing and begging money; swindling of whites for gasoline or beer money; getting advances on wages or fenceposts and then not following through" (Bennett, 1969:163).

The Ranchers   The early history of the ranchers and farmers in Saskatchewan is like that of the ranchers and farmers in Kansas, Oklahoma, and Nebraska. The ranchers resented the farmers and saw themselves as independent; their original life-styles were similar to those of the Native Americans they were displacing. The Jasper rancher lived by himself until he could bring a wife "home" and prided himself on the fact that he did not need the town, going there for supplies but once a year. Even as late as the 1960s, Bennett found two families who still went into town only once a year. The ranchers highly valued skills such as roping, riding, and shooting, all of which were considered masculine pursuits. Their emphasis on masculinity and independence was tempered by a strong code of chivalry: an honorable man helped others. So, even though they believed the farmers were themselves responsible for many of their troubles, the ranchers often helped them when they were in need.

Ranching was difficult, and those who were not strong or could not endure hardship found other things to do. This reliance on one's physical abilities and strengths reinforced the individualist value system and also contributed to egalitarian sentiments, because people were measured by what they could do, not by who they were or had been.

The ranchers, like the Native Americans, lived in harmony with their environment. In other words, they used it as it was and did not transform it by means of the plow. The land was most suited to cattle ranching, and the early ranchers required a minimum of capital to be successful. They were able to acquire more land through leases and were considered good credit risks. Ranches were joined through intermarriage. All of this meant that the ranchers could reject a value system that emphasized cooperation and collective organization.

The Jasper ranchers of the 1860s maintained their economic dominance and their old life-styles. They were seen by themselves and the townspeople as guardians of the Western way of life, which was celebrated annually in the form of rodeos, in which Native American men would sometimes participate. Ranches were passed from father to son and seldom sold on the open market, thus tying the son to the local community. The daughters had wider options: they could marry ranchers or migrate to the city. Girls also were more likely to stay in school than boys were.

The Farmers   The farmers of the Canadian Great Plains came by wagon, train, or on foot from large and small towns throughout Canada, the American Midwest, and Europe. They arrived later than their counterparts in the United States, with the majority flowing in after 1910. The Canadians, too, could file a claim for 160 acres and preempt another 160 for $3.00 an acre. Some came simply to hold onto the land for a short period, hoping to turn a profit, but most planned to stay. Like their counterparts south of the border, they had to deal with drought and the ubiquitous grasshopper. The farmers were there to tame the prairie, not to live in harmony with it, as the ranchers did. Because of the difficulties of settling the land, a cooperative spirit dominated the farmers' efforts, and an active social life was part of their ideal.

In adapting to their economic difficulties, the farmers tended to use conservative strategies. Given the uncertainties of farming, as opposed to the relative stability of ranching, the farmers often had to consume their surplus, rather than putting it back into the farm, and so the productivity of many farms stayed low for a long time. In addition, the farmers often joined political associations in the hopes of influencing grain prices and government support. This led, eventually, to community grazing lands and crop support payments.

The farmers tended to band together and approach political issues in a fairly open fashion. They made full use of the political process: nominating their fellow farmers to positions, campaigning for them, and so forth. If they approached government officials, it was to request something on behalf of the community. On the other hand, the ranchers' political approach was secretive and individualistic. They generally ignored politics and tried to settle political issues in their favor by approaching a government official on a one-to-one basis.

The Jasper farmers maintained their conservative styles in both politics and land management until the 1960s. The experience of the droughts and the Great Depression had caused them to become cautious managers of their enterprises. Of course, as Bennett pointed out, those who had not acted conservatively were quickly put out of business, and so the group that survived tended to have similar values.

Unlike the ranches, the farms were not often kept in the family. On the other hand, it was possible for farmers' sons to secure their own land. In addition, there were many first-generation farmers, because of the devastating economic problems in the 1920s and 1930s that had caused many to leave. The ranchers had weathered these storms because of the lower cost of capitalizing their operations and because they were not so dependent on a ready source of water. The result of the turnover in farming operations and the increased options for farmers' children was that, unlike ranching, farming was not seen as a way of life.

The Hutterites   The group of farmers that best adapted to the Canadian Great Plains was the Hutterites, who did not buy land in the Jasper region until 1951. The Hutterites' culture allowed them to develop a successful, large-scale, diversified agriculture, and although their faith required them to withdraw from the secular world, at the same time it taught them how to use its rules in order to survive. Thus, it was perfectly legitimate for the Hutterites to use modern tractors and equipment, even though these were products of a secular society, because they helped them to prosper as a community.

The Hutterites came to Jasper to establish new colonies. (New colonies split off from older ones when they had grown to a given size.) They were able to pay cash for their farms and were able to capitalize them at a much higher rate than the average person could. For example, the Hutterites could afford trucks and tractors because, first, they had enough savings and, second, they shared their equipment. Whereas an individual farm family would probably have to have its own car or pickup, the colony needed only one for the group. Hutterite children went to school through the eighth grade only, providing the community early on with a large and willing number of workers. The children had no options other than farming or leaving, and most seemed to accept this. Furthermore, the Hutterites' beliefs stressed hard work, saving, and an ascetic lifestyle. All this meant that the colony saved more of its surplus than did the average farm family. These resources were then available to improve the farming operation, to allow the Hutterites to experiment with new modes of production, and to diversify their operations. These are some of the ways in which the Hutterites' religious values shaped their daily lives.

These, then, are four different cultures in the same geographic region, those of the Native Americans, ranchers, farmers, and Hutterites. The Native Americans moved from the forests and adapted to the presence of the whites, although the political and economic realities meant that their adaptation spelled their ultimate disintegration. The ranchers, farmers, and Hutterites, too, came to this area with different cultures, which were modified in the course of daily living. The Hutterites changed less than the other groups did, for their cultural style suited the existing conditions: they were already farmers, and their religious beliefs made possible large-scale farming.

The above descriptions illustrate our central theme that culture is the product of human action. It is a response to immediate circumstances, and it has a history and a future. Like all human creations, culture is not immutable; it is adaptive. Technology is part of culture, and as it changes, so do the ways in which people can respond to their environment. A society must always be seen as a complex, changing entity composed of people and their culture, history, ideas and beliefs, and environment.

Subcultures

Distinctive groups within a larger culture are usually known as *subcultures*. There are regional subcultures, occupational subcultures, youth subcultures, and religious subcultures, among others. In the case of Jasper, each of the four groups that we discussed would count as a subculture. Each had distinct values that set it apart from the others. The ethnic communities that dotted the Great Plains would also have been examples of subcultures, for they were distinct from what was regarded as the larger American culture. The members of these communities often spoke their native tongues, wore their native dress, and used traditional agricultural techniques. But often their values did not conflict deeply with those of the larger society.

At one time in this country's history it was possible to identify distinct regional subcultures: the Deep South, the Southwest, the Midwest, the industrial Northeast, and the West Coast. These regions might also have been distinguished by different language patterns—from the slow, smooth speech of the south to the New York accent. The Beach Boys capitalized on the myth of cultural variation in their song "California Girls." Today these distinctions are much less obvious because of the mass media, people's mobility, and mass consumption patterns. Nevertheless, there still are differences among those who have spent their lives on farms and in the small towns of the Middle West, those who have grown up in the South, and those who have been raised and socialized in large urban areas.

SOCIAL STRUCTURE

We learn a culture and we live in a society, which is a group of interacting individuals who share the same culture and live in the same area. The behavior of individuals in any given society is not random; it has a pattern. This does not mean that all people in a society do exactly the same thing all of the time but that, generally, people behave in predictable ways. For instance, in our society, people tend to stop at stop signs, get married, hold jobs, and respond when spoken to. Let us briefly examine some of a society's standard components and then look at ways in which societies as a whole can be categorized.

Status

Every individual in a society has a status, or a socially defined position, which allows us to locate that person in the social order. Status may refer to one's social position or it may, and usually does, refer to such things as race, age, sex, and birth order. A person's status in a society is important, and it carries with it certain expectations for that person's behavior. For example, "president of the university" is a status that determines how the person who holds that position will behave toward faculty, students, alumni, and government officials. The ranchers in Jasper had a social status and thereby a particular set of behavioral expectations: a rancher would, among other things, be hospitable and easygoing.

A person's status also defines how others behave toward him or her. "Child" is a status that defines the behavior of a mother and a father. A child is a dependent; a child is not responsible for its own care, and is thus entitled to food, shelter, clothing, and attention from others. Similarly, to be a black in our society means that others often respond to blackness and not to other qualities. In fact, minority members in a society are often treated as a social category, a status, and not as individuals.

Roles

A status is made up of a complex of roles, or customary ways of behaving. The statuses of husband, wife, mother, father, employee, son, and student all have responsibilities and customary behaviors associated with them. In our society, the status of male and female carries certain expectations for behavior. When people say that someone is not behaving like a woman, or not behaving like a man, they are judging the behavior of an individual against a set of role expectations. Some males, for instance, believe that women should assume the primary responsibility for child care, cooking, cleaning, and maintaining the home. They may also expect them to hold a job and "help" maintain the family's life-style. These same men may feel that it is "unmanly" to care for children or do housework. In short, they feel that the role of the male should not include such activities.

Role conflict occurs when there is a difference between what people think the behavior for a role is and what the occupant of that role actually does. The mother who holds a full-time job and in addition performs all of the roles associated with being a full-time housekeeper normally suffers. Her employers have one set of role expectations for her as an employee; her family has another that relates to her roles as wife/mother/housekeeper; and the two conflict. These role expectations are changing in our society, but slowly.

In the Martins' time, however, male and female role expectations were much more clearly defined than they are today, and neither Henry nor Lucy would have noticed any particular conflict among the roles that made up their particular statuses. We stated that the primary status for people like the Martins was to be a good Christian man or woman. Consider the multiple roles that combined to produce Henry Martin, a good Christian man. Henry was somewhat exceptional in that he was a true joiner. He was a farmer, husband, father, secretary of the local convention of the Republican party, land appraiser, Sunday school and church leader, part-time teacher of science, census examiner, president of the cemetery association, and county clerk. Furthermore, his neighbors expected him to be sober, hard working, and responsible.

Lucy's roles were quite different. Her first role—even before her children were born—was that of mother. This was more than just mothering in the biological sense; it also meant civilizing and providing shelter from the harsh environment. The home was, to use Lasch's (1977) term, "a haven in a heartless world." In describing Sarah's marriage, Lucy enumerated Sarah's duties: "Sarah will make Ben's home as dear and peaceful a spot as any weary man could desire." This meant providing a clean and orderly home, as well as baking, cooking, cleaning, churning butter, sewing, and caring for the children. It meant that the farm wife would be a true helpmate to her husband, shouldering part of the farm labor.

Women, then, had a double burden. They had to perform the physical tasks necessary for survival, and they had to maintain good Christian homes. Again commenting on the marriage of Sarah, Lucy stated, "I am so glad Sarah has grown to womanhood knowing how precious is any little service performed for the ones we love and what it is to share hardship and gladness and tears with a beloved companion." In other words, one of women's primary responsibilities was service to others. This service to others was actually an extension of mothering and hence meant civilizing the rest of the social order.

Women were more responsible than men for upholding their society's values. And on the frontier women also were responsible for seeing that their children attended school, in particular, Sunday school. The refinements in the home were the women's responsibility. This is still reflected in our culture today in a number of ways. First, women are much more likely to attend church than are men, and they are seen as responsible for encouraging the children to attend civilizing functions such as dance classes, Sunday schools, art classes, and, of course, school. If children misbehave, if they are "uncivilized," many people look to the mother to correct them. Second, women are much more likely than men to work in, and to express preference for, the "helping" professions, for example, social work, elementary school teaching, nursing, and occupational therapy.

Nonetheless, in the nineteenth century, some men did help with child care. Lucy proudly asserted that Sarah "won't have the husband I have for helping with the housework and baby-minding (though not the dreaded washing and ironing!)." Moreover, many women did "men's" work. Henry referred to Mrs. Perkins, whose husband had died in the late spring: "Sturdy pioneer that she was, she turned to and finished the planting that he had begun, with my help and that of the Mitchell boys. She farmed her own land for ten more years, with no more help than a hired man for planting and harvest, and found time enough beside for her usual visiting, churchwork, and care of new mothers." Henry admired her precisely because, besides everything else, she still was able to fulfill the primary role expectations for pioneer women, that is, helping others. But he, in any case, recognized her departure from traditional role behavior.

Today when we try to understand why males and females seem to be locked into certain forms of expected behavior, it is important to reexamine our history. Sexism, the belief that each of the sexes has distinct and unchangeable skills, talents, and forms of behavior, has sturdy roots, but historical change can alter its forms. Henry was expected to set out to find a homestead, break the sod, till the soil, and build a house. Yet, as Henry himself noted, there also were women who were physically capable of these tasks, and indeed, Lucy's daily tasks were not necessarily less onerous than Henry's. Before the early 1900s, women also contributed directly to the family's livelihood by raising chickens, gardening, milking the family cow, making butter, and sewing their clothing. They also augmented the household's cash income by selling surplus farm products. According to the farm diaries and daily records from between about 1850 and 1900, butter, eggs, and garden vegetables accounted for a considerable portion of the farm family's income.

As a percentage of the family's total cash income, however, the farm wife's contribution fell steadily as the production of crops for the national market rose. Many of the farms on the Great Plains were started with the hope of producing corn, wheat, other cereal grains, and beef and pork for the national market. By the time Lucy and Henry reminisced about their frontier experiences, the family no longer needed Lucy's help, such as the socks she knitted and sold to the cavalry. Of course, women continued to influence the level of the family's living, and a skilled housewife meant the difference between comfort and hardship.

Although women were no longer considered economic producers, their role in maintaining values and helping others continued. A successful farm wife had more time to devote to leisure activities. In his *Theory of the Leisure Class* (1912), Veblen described with bitter irony how success came to be defined. A successful man was one whose wives and daughters did not have to work; women worked at not working. Among the middle classes, productive economic activity for women was stigmatized, although many working-class women continued to toil. The developing educational system reinforced these stereotypes. Colleges, such as the one that Henry referred to, offered courses that taught women to be scientific housewives or teachers. Grade school texts described activities meant for girls: reading, sewing, singing, helping boys, and playing. Boys' books extolled the virtues of struggling, jumping, running, overcoming, and achieving.

Norms

In any social order there are numerous unstated rules that people use to guide their behavior. People are often unaware of a role until it is violated. In our society, for example, when someone gets on an elevator and another person is already there, they divide up the space. If another person gets on at the next floor, they divide it up again. They do not remain standing next to strangers if others have left the elevator but again divide up the space and move away. Men wear pants, not skirts. Most women do not sport crew cuts. We wear certain clothes in public places: we do not wear bathing suits to churches, museums, or courthouses. These generally accepted rules for everyday behavior are called *norms*, and they are based on a society's dominant value system.

Consider what it meant for someone like Henry to be a successful farmer. One of the norms pertaining to farming was that after harvesting, a "good" farmer would clean up his field. After the corn was out, the remaining stalks would be plowed under, and the field would be plowed, disked, and harrowed. A farmer who did not do this was regarded by his neighbors as unusual. This norm is so well ingrained that agriculture experts today have difficulty persuading farmers to leave their fields "rough" after harvesting them, as a means of reducing erosion and retaining soil moisture.

The violation of certain societal norms, such as that against murder, carries with it severe penalties. But the violations of other norms are not regarded as particularly serious. If someone dresses inappropriately for a particular occasion, such as a wedding or a job, people will either ignore the individual or make mild comments. *Folkways*, a concept associated with William Graham Sumner, are customary ways of acting. The violation of a folkway, such as that concerning dress, does not incur severe penalties. *Mores*, on the other hand, refer to ways of thinking and acting that a society believes are essential and, consequently, incur severe penalties when violated. In the nineteenth-century Great Plains, to steal someone's cattle or means of survival violated the trust that people depended on in order to survive, and the penalty often was death. Moving boundary stakes and questioning one's neighbor's claim were also severely punished. Friendliness, though, was a folkway. People were expected to assist friends and neighbors who were in need of help and to put strangers up for the night if they needed shelter; even so, the community did not punish those who did not. Instead, they defined such people as unfriendly and avoided them.

Each society represents a particular combination of roles, norms, folkways, mores, and values. If we look at social structures, or types of societies, from the broadest historical perspective, we can see what particular arrangements have existed in the past and thus begin to categorize them.

Types of Societies

Foraging Societies   Foraging societies, which dominated until about 7000 B.C., are to some extent the most primitive of all, in that they were the first human groupings. Even today, they still prevail in a few places in the world. Foragers, or hunter/gatherers, move from locale to locale, carrying few possessions, in search of food that is consumed in a relatively short period of time. They are simple societies organized around the distribution of food, with political, religious, and familial systems shaped by the quest for food and the present environment. For instance, the religious system of the Bushmen of Southwest Africa (Coon, 1971) centers on the hunt. The shaman, or holy man, enters a trance and makes predictions about whether the hunt will be successful and how the people will fare in coping with their harsh environment. There are severe penalties for violating the hunt's sacred mores.

There is little economic differentiation among foragers. They share their food, possessions, and resources equally, varying only in the short run according to the good or bad fortune that might befall a particular member or family of a foraging band. But even the unlucky do not starve, for others, realizing that someday they might be in a similar position, share some of their goods. Furthermore, as Leacock (1978) found, "The association of hunting, wars and masculine assertiveness is not found among hunter/gatherers except, in a limited way, in Australia" and in part because such societies do not separate private and public realms and their decision-making processes are quite flexible. The women in foraging societies have considerable control over their work conditions and the dispensation of the goods they produce.

Horticultural Societies   Horticultural societies (7000–3000 B.C.) vary from primitive systems whose members garden with Stone Age hand tools, to slash-and-burn methods of farming involving small numbers of people, to complex systems of farming such as those that existed among the Mayans in Latin America. What distinguishes horticultural societies from hunting and gathering societies is not what they eat but their degree of societal complexity and the often unequal means by which they share their resources. Unlike the Bushmen, those who live in horticultural societies have a number of possessions. The achievement of a food surplus meant that role specialization also increased. Priests, soldiers, well diggers, hunters, farmers, and pottery makers became numerous, and the wider split between the private and public realms laid the basis for the patriarchal family order. Sometimes the resource base was so great that populations as large as two to three thousand could be supported in one place. Horticultural societies require cooperation among the population and a collective agreement about the goals that they should pursue. The need to irrigate, for example, requires agreement about how it should be done, whose fields should receive the water first, what the ration should be, and so forth.

Agrarian Societies   The shift from a horticultural society to an agrarian one (3000 B.C.–A.D. 1800) is revolutionary, although the changes are slow and are probably unnoticeable to a person living through the transition. Childe (1942), writing about the changes in agriculture that occurred between 4000 and 3000 B.C. in the area in the Middle East known as the Fertile Crescent, pointed to such inventions as wheeled wagons, pottery, waterwheels, and plows, to say nothing of writing, numbers, and calendars. These inventions transformed religious, political, and economic institutions.

Hunters prayed to their gods that they would have a satisfying meal after the hunt. Horticulturists hoped to feed themselves daily and, if lucky, to save a little for difficult times. But the idea of working after basic needs had been met did not occur to them. With the rise of agrarian societies, this situation changed, and a religious ideology developed that encouraged the "farmers to produce more than they need[ed] to stay alive and productive and persuade[d] them to turn that surplus over to someone else" (Lenski and Lenski, 1978:181). The state also became more complex and gave rise to a warrior caste who protected the surplus, controlled the laborers, and sometimes made war on the neighbors. None of this is characteristic of a hunting and gathering society. The simple division of labor typical of the horticultural society deepens in agrarian ones, and there is a clear distinction between cities and rural areas, with the cities containing a number of occupational specialties. Although the small frontier town represents a very advanced form of agrarian society, we can use it as an example of occupational specialization: there were doctors, barbers, harness makers, blacksmiths, teachers, saloon keepers, grocers, livery stable operators, newspaper editors, ministers, sheriffs, deputies, cooks, and hotel owners, to name but a few.

The personal autonomy and authority of women have always been linked to their productive role. Women generally lose when a foraging society is transformed into a horticultural or agricultural one (Sanday, 1981); however, when the participation of women in the labor force increases in an industrial society, they may make some gains in status and power (Kelly, 1981).

Industrial Societies   Modern industrial societies are even more complex. Although historians and others disagree about when the Industrial Revolution began, it is probably safe to say that it was over by the turn of the century. We live today in an industrial society heavily influenced by science and technology. Industrialization deepened the distinction between rural and urban places and stimulated the growth of cities whose populations were sustained by food imported from the farms. The factory system, made possible in part by inventions such as the power-driven loom, was new to human history. Accompanying the rise of the factory system was the development of a distinct working class, a group of people who no longer worked for themselves but sold their labor power on the open market. The state continued to grow in power, balancing the needs of different social classes, collecting taxes, ensuring its own survival, and establishing means of social control.

Sociologists have used a number of terms to describe the shift from a rural to an urban way of life. As early as 1887, for instance, Tönnies distinguished between a *Gemeinschaft* and a *Gesellschaft:* those relations and attitudes characteristic of traditional, communal, and primary organizations and those that were secondary, impersonal, and bureaucratic. Robert Redfield (1941) expressed the same concerns and interests when he distinguished between *folk* and *urban* societies. A folk society was small, usually isolated, had a high degree of solidarity, used informal means of social control, and took into account the whole person. Urban societies, on the other hand, were characterized by opposing variables. They were large, impersonal, and had many competing value systems.

The society of Henry and Lucy Martin could be characterized as agrarian, and if we choose to use Tönnies's and Redfield's terms, they also lived in a *Gemeinschaft,* or a folk society. They treated, and were treated by, other people as distinct human beings, not as social categories. For example, the owner of the town's grocery store knew who Henry was, what he did, what his children's names were, and what church he belonged to. This man might have extended the Martins' credit solely because of his intimate knowledge of them. Their relationship was what we call *primary*. In a modern city store, a clerk deals with a customer not as a person but as a social category. That relationship is *secondary* and is entered into because it is the most efficient way to achieve a particular goal. The interaction has no intrinsic meaning, whereas the interaction between Henry or Lucy and the store owner would have a meaning that extended beyond the transaction itself. They also would probably have visited with both the owner and others in the store, as their relationship was much more than a simple exchange between the categories of customer and clerk. This sense of community, and its ultimate disintegration as industrialization progressed, is the focus of our next two chapters.

✳   ✳   ✳

The Wades and The Patchens 4

After their marriage in the early 1880s, Arthur Wade and Henrietta Thorn settled on a ranch in the Sandhills of western Nebraska. There they raised three sons—Lewis, Harlow, and Judson—and a daughter, Eleanor. The family's letters and diaries, written during the first two decades of the twentieth century, offer a firsthand account of the times in which they lived.

In the first passage, Eleanor ("Ellie") Wade Patchen tells the story of her life through 1920.

My father has a ranch in western Nebraska, in the Sandhills, where he settled in 1882. He's always done pretty well as a stockman, and during the War he did very well, buying and selling horses for them to use "over there." He's as strong and capable now as he ever was, but Mama and he are lonely these days because all three boys are gone. Harlow finally decided to join Lewis in his business, so now they are both in Omaha, partners in a dry goods and ready-made clothing store. Then we lost Jud in the War. So there's no son for Papa to hand the ranch on to. I think that's sad, and I hope either it doesn't happen that way to us, or else Tom and I don't build on it, on having your children follow your ways, as Papa once did.

I didn't have a hard—or even particularly exciting—childhood on the ranch, though I have heard from Mama about her hard times in the 'eighties. I wasn't born until 'ninety-one. I guess stories of the fence wars weren't considered suitable for a child's ears. What I *did* hear then only confused me. One month the cowboys would be cutting the settlers' fences, to give the cattle free range. Then the talk would be of how the homesteaders hated the fences, too, the ones on the big ranges, because they wanted the public lands. I know when I was a little girl Papa always carried a gun, but he never had to

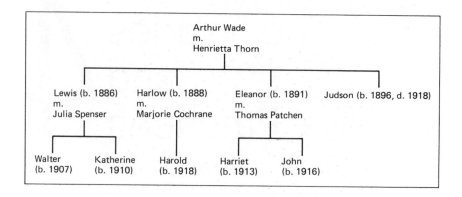

use it. After Teddy Roosevelt became President, and made the big ranchers stop their fencing of government land, I guess things cooled down. I remember talk about how to feed the cattle in the winter, after that, and about how the big feed and grain elevators were going up along the railroad.

A woman's life on even a small ranch, you know, isn't like life on a farm. By the time I was old enough to notice, we had four or more hands living in the bunkhouse always, and the first thing I learned about the real work was not to get in their way. Besides, it was Mama's idea to raise me to be a lady, like her mother back in Virginia. So mostly I was to stay inside the house! I don't mean to poke fun. I think it was very natural. She had hard and frightening times, herself, when they first came here, and then she just had the one daughter—me. So I was as ill prepared for my life as she was for hers—though I do feel I had more choice in my life. It's strange how these things happen.

Of course except when I was at school I helped her around the house, quite a lot. For one thing I was Little Mama to my brother Jud. (Mama wasn't ever a strong woman after my birth.) We only had one woman, ever, working for us, and Mama would say I was more to be trusted with Jud, or with special jobs. Nobody could clean lamps like Ellie! Or wash and dry the good china and glassware. Or iron our best shirtwaists without ever scorching a flounce. And what a lot of fine sewing we did! It wasn't till I went away to school, in 1906, that Mama finally got her sewing machine, a wonderful one, from the Sears, Roebuck catalogue. Thirty-five dollars, and it had a complete desk cabinet of walnut, you couldn't tell what it was when it was closed up. I believe I spent all my first summer home from school at that machine! I have my own little machine now, but do I ever have a whole day to sit at it? A whole night is more like it.

I didn't go to the public high school because Mama didn't want me boarding out in someone else's home. Instead I went to Mrs. Pinckney's Academy in Lincoln. I didn't mind boarding school; you can imagine how it was for me to have all the girl friends I wanted after being the only girl in our house all my life! But of course the public high schools teach more practical courses, and I surely could have used that.

When I was in my third year at the Academy, just starting to learn, of all things, the French language, I met Tom Patchen. He was driving for the livery stable which the school employed. Doesn't it sound like one of those trashy novels? Here is a fine young lady, dressed all in white, with a great blue bow in her yellow hair, and here is this handsome roughneck—but here the likeness stops. For Thomas Patchen was, after all, the son of the owner of the livery stable, which was also just beginning a very good business repairing motor cars and tires and the like. And Tom's father owned several farms outside Lincoln, besides the one Tom had grown up on. While Tom was handsome, all right (and still is), he was no roughneck, but

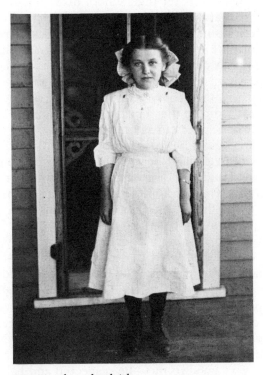

Portrait of a schoolgirl
Courtesy of the Kansas State Historical Society

a well-brought-up young man, four years older than I was, and—I supposed—with good prospects.

Yet we did carry on like people in a novel for months—letters, secret meetings—my, what fools we acted, when we might have made life simpler by finding a way to be properly introduced. We were certainly in trouble when we decided we knew our minds about each other and had to tell our parents. *His* parents wanted him to marry a girl *they* knew—and mine just didn't want me to marry someone they *didn't* know! and none of them liked the way we had met and carried on.

Such a lot of traveling back and forth across the state, and solemn conferences, and laws laid down. I was terribly unhappy when Mama told me I mustn't see Tom for a year, naturally, but I was convinced that we had brought it on our own heads, and I was willing to wait. I was pretty sure of us, you see. (I was right about that!)

But Tom wouldn't be dictated to. And—as I had no way of knowing then, for these were not our usual topics of conversation— he had no intention of staying on to take over his father's business, as his father expected. After high school he'd gone for a year and a half to the University, studying agricultural science, and his father had brought him home against his will when his older brother went out to California. Tom wanted more than anything to be a successful farmer. Moreover, he thought of me as suited to his plans because I'd grown up on a ranch—that will just show you how much we had talked together about real life.

So Tom got word to me that he had no intention of waiting a year for me. He had sufficient savings to take us where he wanted to be—the eastern edge of Nebraska, along the Missouri River, where the farmlands are rich and beautiful. He said he could farm as a tenant until we could buy our own place. You may imagine what I thought of all this. For two nights I scarcely slept. I wasn't so silly as to give him a blind "yes." It was no joking matter for us both to go against our parents' wishes, and I was having a little trouble imagining myself becoming a poor farmer's wife, even for Tom's sake. I had some idea of what that meant. It was just lucky for us both that I had felt for years that the life Mama wanted for me was a pretty dull life, for anybody with any energy. I was eighteen; at that age a woman is full of eagerness to show what strong stuff she's made of, and I thought there'd be no life-long break with our families once the Deed was Done. I was right about that, though it did take Mama some years to completely accept the fact; Papa, however, was very good to me—he respected and believed in Tom from the first, because he saw that I did.

Tom found a farm for us in the northeast part of the state, between the Elkhorn and Missouri rivers, about fifteen miles northwest of Fairview, which is right on the Missouri. Fairview is a town of 1,000 now. I believe it was smaller by some 200 people when we came to this part of the state in 1910, a little over a decade ago.

How we worked! We had a farm the bank owned. The family who lived there before us had owned the farm themselves until, I think, 1896. They had lost so much money in the dry years and couldn't borrow any, and finally the bank foreclosed on them—and then they stayed on for fourteen years, expecting all the time to get it back, somehow, until the man was just too old for the work. I don't know where they went. Tom didn't tell me that story at first— not until we began to see our way clear to getting off the place ourselves.

We did well. Tom had all these ideas about farming, and especially dairy farming, which were pretty new around Fairview; some of his methods are still not generally accepted, though he has been so successful. We began by leaving part of the fields fallow in the summers and rotating crops. We grew alfalfa and put in the new Turkey Red wheat. We began with just ten milking cows, and from the first, Tom bred our increase on the farm, rather than buying from drovers. He shares breeding stock with other farmers in the area. Every time he sells a bull, he buys a heifer. He already has a reputation for cows with a high yield and high butterfat, too, and some ribbons from the county and state fairs. I am saving them until there is enough to make a quilt with! Then he started a cooperative creamery and got two other dairymen in the county to invest with him in cream separators. That made a big difference in the women's work, I can tell you.

When we began with our ten cows, the rule was to have about 40 acres of land in feed for them, hay and corn. But we never had a hay field after the first two years. We bought hay and corn fodder from our neighbors and farmed wheat and alfalfa, with a man to help. For about four years it seemed as if Tom was milking half of every evening. I worked the dairy, and at threshing time, of course, I cooked for the crews, with only one woman to help.

We didn't go *anywhere* those first years, but church (and not always that) and the Farmer's Union meetings (at least Tom went) and to visit our families. We didn't know a soul here, of course, and it took a while to get to know our neighbors. Why, the closest friend I had the first year was Elizabeth Straub, who came to help with dinners for the threshing crews, though she could barely speak English then. And I would still be her friend if it weren't for her husband, Big Peter, as they call him! They were tenants, as we were—still are, farming over north of Fairview, amongst all these Germans from Russia; there must be a dozen families of them. I will never understand his disgraceful behavior about the War. I cannot see how a man could refuse for a minute to fight that monster the Kaiser, especially a man who never even lived in Germany. Such a stiff-necked, touchy person I never saw—but they are all like that. They went, finally, all these men and boys, but my, they had needed some encouraging.*

Of course Tom and I started here at just the right time. These last 10 years have been good years for farmers, and we got the benefit of the rise in prices, expecially wheat prices, during the War. Also we kept our health—and the cows kept their health—Fairview got a veterinary surgeon in 1912, and Tom learned a great deal from him.

Our children were born in 1913 and 1916, Harriet and John. I never had any trouble, either time, but after John was born we got Katy Rosenheim to work the dairy with me, though I had a fine old time teaching her about boiling everything. Harriet and John are strong, healthy children. Harriet has been in school for a year, and since our move here to our own farm, school is close enough for her to ride to.

Harriet's idea of a treat this year is for her Papa to drive her in to town in the Ford, which he will do if he has errands which don't require the wagon. We can go in and back in a few hours, now, in that automobile. *His* idea of a treat is the Saturday moving pictures. That's all right, but *I* still look forward most to the Chautauqua.† I always make time for that, and the last few years I have made time too for my Library Association work and for the Children's League.

This house we've bought doesn't look like much, yet. In fact the one on the old tenant farm was pleasanter in some ways; being stone, it was easier to heat in winter and much cooler in summer. Now we have this oil stove for heat, but I don't like it. And I miss the flowers at the old place—I was really fond of my lilacs and wisteria. I've started some here, and roses, too, but it'll take a while. Inside—well, I've got the kitchen and the washroom painted, but wallpaper will just have to wait; linoleum comes first. We have the telephone now. We all subscribed, around here, bought our own lines, and then we pay 25¢ a month into our own company. It is a real blessing in the winter to know you can call out if you can't get out easily. The roads are still no blessing, for the most part, though

---

*For Elizabeth Straub's viewpoint, see pp. 109–111.

†An institution that provided popular education combined with entertainment in the form of lectures, concerts, and plays often held outdoors or in a tent.

we did get our post road, so the mails supposedly can always get through. In good weather we can go out on the highway in the Ford and ride as much as fifty miles on a Sunday.

A new dairy barn comes before a new house, naturally, and Tom has designs for one without stanchions that he expects to be easier to keep clean. He is now also talking about—can you believe it?—milking machines. And a cheese factory to be run by the co-operative. I still worry where the money's to come from. My brothers in Omaha can get a business loan, when they expand, for so much less than we have to come up with! It isn't right. And a farmer really does need more and more machinery, all the time. And more help because he can't manage to do everything himself anymore. Tom, for example, will need to hire men to build the new barn. However, it looks like the market for milk isn't going to stop growing, as the market for wheat has, since the War.

I mean to put in a vegetable garden this year, but we shop in town every week now. Imagine! Well, you can't grow corn flakes, can you? and Hatty has decided she must have corn flakes, as the town girls do. It's funny. I knew every soul in the town near our ranch when I was a girl. We all knew each other. Here—since the War, especially, people always seem on the go, into the city or "back home" or else they up and leave for good. Not so many families own their land. And people are more different; I mean of different sorts. It's not just the Germans out east of town. There are all kinds of foreigners, and the railroad people don't mix much, and the people who own businesses in town, that little old town, seem to look down on farmers, some. Fairview has a Civic Improvement Association, started the year after we moved here. To beautify and clean up the town, and every spring they have a big cleanup campaign. I think that's fine but I do get a little put out hearing about the wonderful growing opportunities of wonderful Fairview. As if it didn't all depend, really, on us.

※ ※ ※

In 1919, a trip downtown in her father's Ford was a big event for six-year-old Harriet Patchen. This story, which comes from a letter written by her mother, is told from Harriet's point of view.

I do love it when I get to ride in the automobile. When Papa has a lot of errands, sometimes, he'll save them up for Saturday so I can come along and go downtown with him. I just love to walk down the street with Brother Jack and look in all the windows—the millinery shop, the furniture store, the barber's—that's always full of people on a Saturday. I like to say hello to people we know. This year Mama lets me do errands for her. Now that I am getting pretty good at reading, she gives me a list for the Gates Cash Merchandise Company when she can't come along.

Mr. Gates is an awfully kind man. He is never rude, and he gives me two pieces of hard candy, one for me, one for Jack, when we're all through with Mama's list. Sometimes he even lets me ring up my purchases on his beautiful new cash register. There's another general store in Fairview, the one that belongs to Mrs. Levin, but we don't go there. Mama says it's dirty.

Jack is still so little, he's only three, that I have to watch him, or he will get into things in the store. Besides food, there's dishes and combs and buttons and clothes and cloth, and ribbon and pens and blankets and medicine, and buckets and brooms and knives. Jack is just awful, the way he'll go right around a corner and start pulling things down. But Papa says he has to learn sometime, and I must learn to watch children, sometime. So we bring Jack along with us. He is *really* awful in the harness shop. Last Saturday we stopped there, after we went to the feed store. Papa was buying a work harness. I love the harness shop because it smells so good from all

Barbershop, circa 1912
Courtesy of the Kansas State Historical Society

the different tanned hides. They hang on a big pole which goes right across the whole shop. In the back is the workshop and shoeshop, and that smells even better, from soap and polish.

The work harness was awfully dear, sixty-five dollars, so Papa was talking like he might not buy it, and Mr. Rogers was going on about it.

"You see how heavy this is? And the traces, triple-stitched? You won't get all-brass trim like this for a penny less. And look at the width of these lines!"

I was over looking at all the things he puts on harnesses. He has a whole case full of open boxes of rings and buckles and rivets. I thought Jack was over behind the saddles, where there's a pile of lap robes he likes to climb on. But then! Then I heard a yell out back, and when I looked I couldn't see him anywhere, so I ran straight back past Billy in his leather apron, through the door into the yard. Sure enough. Mr. Walter and his boy were oiling a harness in the great big iron kettle. And they had just lifted the harness out of the oil with their iron hooks when Jack walked up with a fistful of blacksnake whips from the front of the shop and oiled *them!*

Papa was awfully angry. He said some words that Mama does not allow.

"Tom, Tom, the boy's all right. The oil's not that hot anyway, and the whips won't take no hurt, or not much."

Mr. Walters was as nice as could be, but it was no use, Papa made us stay in the Ford the whole time he was in the bank and the hardware store, and Jack just whined and snuffled the *whole* time because he didn't get to fish those stupid whips out of the linseed oil himself! I will *really* be glad when he grows up some.

✳   ✳   ✳

By the turn of the century, there were many communities of German immigrants in Nebraska. Some of these were "Volga Germans," a group that had settled in Russia for several generations but had maintained its ethnic identity. Elizabeth Straub, a Volga German who emigrated to Nebraska in 1910, had a close friendship with Eleanor Patchen, for a time. In letters written in 1917, Elizabeth Straub described the circumstances that led to their estrangement.

My Peter was not eager to go in the Army because all his life, all his father's life, that was the worst that could happen to a man. It is one of the great reasons our family have all left Russia, so the men would not be taken for the Russian Army. It is not that we want Germany to win this war. It is not that Peter does not honor his new country. They have not understood, because Peter and the others did not volunteer so soon, and because, also, we did not want to give up our children's school where they spoke the mother tongue, or to give up our names,* and because the priest went on with his sermons in German. They cannot forgive these things. He is not a coward. They are not traitors. When they came to shame us and painted the church and our doors with yellow and stopped the men when they went together in the street of the town, that day, they thought because the men and boys stood like stones that they did not care what they shouted. They cared. But in the old country, this was often the way a man or woman was punished for a bad thing. They cared. But they were *not* bad. They have pride. When they have nothing, they have pride.

But that was not the worst. Never have I thought it would be easy here, no matter what Peter said. Our family was right to come here and not to the city, that is true. So ugly a life, the factories. But it is lonely here. I knew. We are few, and we are the different ones. Our church is different. Our ways are different. When the newspaper began to tell lies, when people would not say "good day" to us in the town, I knew. What good, to explain? No good. But I had a friend—yes, a friend, here, in America, not of my family, my friend Ellie. Since the first year Peter and I came here. We came with nothing but our clothes, for Peter's father had taken all his money. It was his uncle who paid our passage. Peter would work on the farm and on threshing crews and as a trapper—that he had done before. I would go to work for the women in Fairview, but I liked best to do cooking, because American women do not clean their houses as I would. I cannot get a floor clean with only a mop, and I have known a woman angry, yes angry, when I brought my brushes. And laugh at me when I washed the porch. Also they always want the windows open, open. I learned. But I liked better to cook, and so at harvest time I was always out helping a woman to feed the threshers. That is how I met Ellie. Then I could not speak English. And Ellie was so good! She would speak very slowly, she would stop to say the words for things, she made it funny but did not laugh at me. Also she wanted me to cook the food I knew from my childhood—oh, not always, I understand hungry men must have what they know—but I gave them my dumplings and sausages and potatoes with good bits of bacon and onion in, and even I made red cabbage, cabbages from our own garden, that she paid me for. Yes, that was a good time.

*Many German settlers had changed their German-sounding names.

So I taught her some things, and she taught me. And we talked, always, much about our children, because we had our first babies the same summer, 1913, her little girl and my Little Peter. It is a bond between women, that. We were funny together and so happy with our good babies. Never did Ellie tell me my ways were wrong. Also she came to visit me, where we lived, by the family. And she praised our little house, which was nothing then, only clean, with its new paint and a bit of new lace on the cloths and sheets and only a little furniture Peter had made, he was working so hard for our bread. She said our summer kitchen was a sensible idea!* Oh, and one time—one day in her kitchen, Mrs. Treece was visiting her and said to me that my sister Gertrude was too young to marry, that we all had so many children we should wait a while to begin. And my dear Ellie said to her "mind your own business!"

So. That was for me the worst pain, that Ellie changed to me. When our men went away on the troop trains, and we all went together and stood crying on the platform, even then, I thought, I wish I could speak with Ellie, and when Peter came home safe to me, I wondered was Ellie a little glad.

✳   ✳   ✳

In 1914, Thomas Patchen described "three days in the life of Fairview, Nebraska, U.S.A." to a friend who had been away.

There's been more excitement in Fairview these last few days than the whole year before. That will tell you something about how quiet the town generally is, but here's the story, anyway.

Monday night got us off to a roaring start—no pun intended— when the oil stove in West and Son's hardware store caught fire and the brigade was called out. I happened to be in town that evening at a meeting of the Equity Union, and so I answered the call along with Jim Kellog and Harry Toliver. The Volunteer Fire Brigade has been in existence some eight or ten years but just last year raised sufficient funds for a firetruck, with hoses, retiring the old cart and horses. I tell you it got us there fast! the big bell clanging all the way and folks running after us into the street the way they will do.

Now Tuesday night I wish the weather had been unseasonably bad, bad enough to keep everybody indoors. A fire is a shocking thing, even if a man's insured, as West is—but there's no human malice in it, and the way folks help out—even folks in a mutual

---

*A small building, separate from the house, that was used as a kitchen in the summertime in order to keep the heat and the flies out of the house.

protection association, like the brigade—that leaves you with a good feeling. But there was nothing to feel good about in last night's excitement! On the contrary, it was a thoroughly disgusting business.

Young Arthur Hale and Dorothy Taylor were married yesterday afternoon and were supposed to go home to their new little bungalow on the edge of town after a wedding supper at her parents' house. Hale's a darn good carpenter and mason, too, and means to make his living from those skills, rather than from farming. Now, we don't know him nor his bride. They don't go to our church, and he votes the Democratic ticket—but that's beside the point. Although he has been unfortunate, to say the least, in his choice of friends in Fairview, that can happen to any young man without a family behind him, and if I'm right it wasn't just his so-called friends who disgraced themselves on this occasion.

The occasion was to be an old-style charivari,* and I guess it started out mild enough, with cowbells and dishpans and a general drunken caterwauling—until some enterprising youngster discovered the house and barn were empty. We found out later that the couple spent the night in Dakota City, Art having got wind of this celebration ahead of time. Well, that got the boys wild, apparently, and here I think some riffraff joined in, who were not of the original party. They dropped their cowbells and dishpans and went to work on the house. Darned if they didn't tear off all the screens and the lattice on the back porch and half the chimney before the neighbors were roused enough to chase 'em off. And that was a mistake, too, if you ask me—if I were Art, I'd want to see somebody called to account for the damage, but nobody's saying who they saw, and our stalwart police force arrived on the scene fifteen minutes after the fun was over. A real shame, and an ugly homecoming for the young woman.

Bringing us to Tuesday afternoon and the motor car wreck. I was present at this event also, having come into town with Ellie and the baby. Naturally the populace of Fairview has become accustomed to the sight of an automobile now and then, though horses don't seem to get used to them, and twice this spring the downtown's been treated to the sight of a runaway team or a buggy run off the road. But never before have we had a wreck involving two cars. Nobody knows exactly how it happened. Our local banker, E. W. Sills, was driving one car, and a salesman from out of town, another. Sills seems to have lost his grip on the steering wheel of the

---

*A *charivari*, or *shivaree*, was a noisy mock serenade to a newly married couple.

Automobile wreck
Courtesy of the Kansas State Historical Society

Studebaker when he saw the other motor car coming. The cars collided; Sills's turned completely over and righted itself, while the other fellow's plowed on into the ditch. This was about two in the afternoon, so luckily plenty of help was at hand. I made sure we got into the stranger's wallet so his family could be telegraphed immediately, and I heard that his wife was there at the hospital in Westpoint when he arrived.

So there you have three days in the life of Fairview, Nebraska, U.S.A.! I have to admit it seems pretty dim if you read the papers—small potatoes to what's happening in Belgium and France and any day now England, if the Kaiser's Zeppelins are what they're claimed to be. Ellie has simply quit reading the war news. I agree with her that some of the stories, about individuals, seem wrong to read—I can't be clearer than that about it. I have a pretty clear idea, however, that the war won't go away just because we ignore it. At the same time—Look. There is so much that is good in our lives, here and now. I would be wrong to slight that undeniable fact! My ideas for a dairy herd are paying off, the hay is selling at a good price through the co-op, I've got good credit and some savings, Ellie's folks have come round to accepting their only daughter's early and romantic marriage, we have a girl child who makes us smile a lot, and some time just lately to rest and read and draw up plans for dairy barns and houses in the evenings. That's peace. I can't see it any other way, I can't try to.

※   ※   ※

In 1904, Lewis Wade, the oldest of the Wade children, married Julia Spenser, a native of Missouri. The couple moved to Omaha, where Lewis worked in a dry goods store. At first, they lived in a boardinghouse, a situation that "Mother" Henrietta Wade referred to in the following letter.

November 13, 1904

Dear Julia,

I have taken somewhat longer to reply to your letter than usual because I have had the grippe this past week; however, I am much better now. We hope you and Lewis are keeping well and that you will soon succeed in finding the living accommodations you speak of in your last letter. I have never, as you know, experienced the life of a boardinghouse, although I stayed at summer hotels with my parents as a girl. I found that quite pleasant—but then I was a child, not a young wife wishing to make a home for my husband.

You will, I am certain, be very happy to find your *own* place. You must tell me everything about it. I well remember the time and trouble I took furnishing our first home here in Nebraska while doing everything else as well (in those days I was keeping chickens and a garden and doing all the cooking for the hands). Living in town will make it so much easier and more pleasant for you. You can go right to the big stores, find what you want, and see it delivered the next day. Yet do, dear Julia, let me know if there is any way in which I can be of help. Our mail carrier has bought a new automobile and now comes twice as frequently as he did before.

We are ready for the winter, with coal in the cellar and feed stored for the stock. Father Wade is still in a jubilant mood from the results of the general election. He says to tell Lewis that the country seems finally to have seen the daylight, even "old Missouri" going Republican for Teddy. (He asks to be excused from writing tonight, since he was out with the men repairing fences today and as usual made his hands sore on the wire.)

I must go presently and make sure the kitchen is put to rights. I fixed our chicken, for Sunday dinner, as I always do, but Vera has learned to make a respectable pie and good beaten biscuits—though usually I must remember to take them from the oven. I believe the poor girl to be very homesick if she is not in love! for it seems impossible for her to keep her mind on a task that takes more than thirty minutes to complete. She is a good, willing girl, but so dreamy. Her father and brothers are working on the Ellis ranch, which adjoins ours on the north. Mr. Ellis sent to have her whole family brought here straight from immigration in New York. They have scarcely seen the world—only their village in, I believe, Hungary, and our valley.

Please do write when time permits. You know you are always welcome here if you should want a visit "in the country," at any time, for any reason.

Yours truly,

Mother Wade

*   *   *

The year 1907 was an important one for Lewis and Julia Wade. Lewis was promoted to manager of the dry goods store, and Julia gave birth to their first child, Walter.

June 3, 1907

Dear Mother Wade,

Thank you so very much for all the beautiful things you've made for baby Walter. I do not know how you find the time for such exquisite work, but it is ever so much nicer than all my "store bought." I feel his Grandmother is here taking care of him.

Lewis is working long hours just now, because of his new position of responsibility at the store. I get lonesome, just the two of us in this house, much as I love it—but Walter keeps me pretty busy, and before too long I shall be able to take him out regularly in his fine new carriage. I wish you could see it, it is all of wicker in the most handsome design, and high, so I can talk with him as we stroll. One doesn't have so many visitors here as in the country, so I do look forward to getting out.

You ask about our new furniture. Of course, we had to have a rocking chair!—it is solid oak with a black leather seat and back set in with brass studs, very sturdy and sensible. Also, we have got a Grand Rapids upholstered chair for Lewis and hope to match it with a couch, in time. Then we have framed Father Wade's photographs of the ranch house and your-

Family portrait
Courtesy of the Kansas Collection, Kenneth Spencer Research Library, University of Kansas

selves and Ellie and Jud, and they are all in a row on the living room wall. The week before Walter was born I took down all the old curtains in the room and put up new hangings, a lovely deep blue shade. I wish you could visit before autumn.

I am getting my strength back fast; the doctor is pleased with me. Today I made custard pies, at Lewis's special request. We know rich pastry isn't good for him, but a new father deserves a special treat! Also I have a new washing machine and a new wringer for the tubs. I am sure you can imagine what a blessing this is, these days! You always ask me to tell you if I need anything, but just now I feel I have as much as is *good* for a person!

Lewis enjoyed his father's letter so much. He says to tell him that this legislature is outdoing the last. If Father Wade liked the regulation of the stockyards, he should be more than pleased with the new restrictions on the railroads. Lewis thinks, too, that the Department of Agriculture will get a big boost from the Progressives.

Walter is awake and hungry again, so I must close.

> Our love to you both,
>
> your daughter,
>
> Julia

✳   ✳   ✳

Three years later, Julia's second child, Katherine, was born.

April 7, 1910

Dear Julia,

I am writing to ask you if a visit with us would not do you and little Walter some good, after your difficult winter, with both a new baby girl and a sick child. I am sure that Lewis can spare you for a few weeks. Though he has become a big city businessman, I know he has not forgotten his boyhood here in the "wide-open spaces" and would not deny his wife and son the pure air and healthful outdoor pursuits and good nourishing meals which made *him* strong.

You know you can take the Burlington train right to Alliance, and now Father Wade will meet you with the automobile, so the last part of the journey will be in style as well. We do wish dearly for you to come, and we will do everything we can to make your stay a pleasant one. I know your ideas of child rearing are more informed than mine, but even an old lady can learn something new. Our Ladies' Guild has had several talks of late on the subjects of physical culture and nutrition, and I believe I may understand Walter's requirements, though it is true that when my boys were young, a mother's chief concern was to keep them filled up! I don't pretend to know as much as you young folk seem to about "vitamins," but we do not fry everything nor serve hot breads with every meal.

As for Walter's good times, his Uncle Jud is eager to show him around the ranch. Though Jud is only fourteen, he is a very responsible young man, and you can trust Walter to him. If Walter is strong enough, perhaps Jud can teach him to ride. Jud is good at making up all sorts of harmless games and fun and will be as gentle with your boy as you or I could be. So you see you will have some rest, yourself, while you stay with us. I think I know that will be welcome.

It is a busy time now for the men, getting the stock in and ready for shipping to Omaha. But we four can easily stay out of their way. Do come, Julia dear.

Love,

Mother Wade

*   *   *

When Eleanor Wade and Thomas Patchen were married in 1909, it was against their parents' wishes. Three years later, Henrietta Wade had still not visited her daughter's home. When Julia, on a trip to the Patchens' farm, learned that Eleanor was expecting her first child, she attempted to heal the rift.

November 12, 1912

Dear Mother Wade,

We have just got back from our visit to Tom and Ellie, and I know you will want to hear about it. We stayed three nights and were awfully glad we had made the trip. Lewis, of course, spent most of his time with his new brother, helping him out when he could and watching and learning when he could not. Tom has twenty cows to be milked morning and evening, though only about half of them are heavy milkers just now. Still, that takes a lot of his time, and Lewis could not help with that! He did make them a new mailbox and set it out on some new posts, seeming to enjoy himself. When I wasn't running after Walter or Kate, I did my best to keep up with Ellie in the house and the dairy. She flies around like two women, it is something to see.

So we never did get to bed early but stayed up after supper, when the children had been put to bed, talking and eating popcorn and apples, till we were sleepy, too. You musn't be worried about them, Mother Wade. They have so much get up and go that they are sure to succeed in their plans. Lewis is very impressed with Tom's knowledge of modern dairy farming and expanding markets and rates and prices and regulations and so forth. When they weren't talking politics, they were talking business.

Ellie sings all day long, I don't think she finds her life too hard, at all. Anyone can see how happy they are with each other. I know it isn't my place to give advice, Mother dear, but I wish you would visit them, too. (And I believe there may be a special reason that Ellie would like to see her mother before long!)

A neighbor came over one afternoon because his mule had got frightened and run through Tom's fence with the corn binder. So off we all went to help get the poor thing free. Then what should the man do but walk off with his animal with never a suggestion that he help mend the fence. I told Ellie that such behavior would not surprise me in Omaha but that back home in Missouri it could never happen. She replied that she and Tom are after all newcomers in the area. But I wonder: doesn't it seem sad to you that the more people there get to be in a place, the less interest they seem to take in each other.

We had fried rabbit one night, which we hadn't tasted in ages. Tom has this crazy young dog, I don't know what to call him, who catches rabbits in the alfalfa where they get lost and confused, it seems. The dog is quite a mighty hunter. He piled up five of them in the yard that morning, and so we had our feast.

I am sending you a clipping from our newspaper advertisements, about the tablecloths you were interested in, and the jacket for Father's birthday present. Just let me know of your choice, and we will send the things along. I wish we could be with you for the great occasion, but our visit will have to wait till spring as usual. Kate as forgotten Grandpa's ranch, I am afraid, but Walter remembers very well and looks forward to another good time with you. And so do Lewis and I.

Love,

Julia

*　　　*　　　*

Harlow, the Wades' second son, left the family ranch and went to Omaha to work with his brother Lewis. After a visit with Harlow, Arthur Wade felt compelled to tell his son exactly what he thought of his life-style.

April 10, 1915

Dear Harlow,

It is with considerable reluctance that I sit down to write you this letter. You are twenty-seven, a young man well past the age when you should need a father to lay down the law to you, and yet that is what I must do. I hope you will bear in mind that it is not my usual way, that I have supported all of my children in their life's choices, as many a man would not have done, when it went against his dearest dreams for them.

Be that as it may. You chose to leave the ranch, to be your brother's partner in business. I had no quarrel with that decision, and I have none. With your way of life in the city, however, I am sad to say, I am not at all in sympathy, and in the future, unless some changes are made, I shall refuse to support it in any way. Your expenses are outrageous for a single man, and I will not listen to any more stories of your debts. Lewis has a growing family to support, draws only a slightly larger salary from the firm, and has not applied to me for financial aid for the past eight years. When he did so, he paid me back promptly and with interest.

Our last visit to the city showed me pretty clearly what you are up to. For one thing you have no business driving that flashy roadster; for another your clothes are not suitable to your needs. A haberdasher is under no obligation to advertise on his person the top of every line in the store. Furthermore, your entertainments, by your own report, are excessive, particularly on the buying trips your brother unwisely allows you to make.

You will have gathered by now that I decline to assist you in moving to and furnishing an "apartment." You may do that for yourself if you are uncomfortable in your rooms. I saw nothing wrong with them.

There is a pernicious doctrine at work in this country of late: that a man shows his worth by what he owns, and the more fancy new things he can buy and exhibit to his neighbors, the more esteemed he will be. I can't understand how a son of mine comes to believe such fluff.

Enough of that. We have got beautiful spring weather here, and I was out riding about two hours longer than is usual for me yesterday, with no ill effects. We are going to bed later than we did in the winter and getting up earlier. Your Mother is as well and lively as I have seen her in a long time and sends her love. Your brother Judson would also, I am sure, if he were around, but he is off with the men getting the stock ready for shipment.

You wonder if your Mother and I ever contemplate selling the ranch and moving to the city. I know that such a move is becoming more and more the fashion, over our whole country, but it is not for us. We have put too much of ourselves into this land. Even if Jud were not here to take it over for me, I should hope to die on the place. It isn't that your Mother and I fail to take an interest in the rest of the world, as I am sure you realize. I do four times more reading and keeping up with national—and international—affairs than I did when I was your age. I don't object to travel, either. But this is home, and we are attached to our ways here and don't want them changed.

Think before you write to me again. I hope to find I have been harsher with you than I needed to be.

Your loving

Father

✻   ✻   ✻

Shortly after the birth of her son John in 1916, Eleanor Patchen received the following letter from her mother.

December 4, 1916

Dear Ellie,

I was extremely interested to hear of your Library Association. That seems to me a very useful idea to grow out of the Children's League.* (No, I will not write about the League work which I do *not* think useful—only that I am relieved to hear that you have not been persuaded to bottle-feed little John after all, whatever the advantages.) Not every mother has had your opportunities, and I am glad you have found a way to help provide them to others. Also I am in sympathy with the project for school lunches, a great boon for children who live outside of the town.

You and I between us brought up our dear Jud to be the fine young man he is, so I do not feel that learning the "rules of child development" is likely to do you or my grandchildren

---

*One of the many organizations and "Mothers' Clubs" that grew up during this period as a result of a new professional interest in child welfare. For example, the Children's Bureau, a governmental agency, was established in 1912.

any harm, but yes, indeed, I do believe that some matters may safely be left to a Mother's instincts.

You must write and tell me more about how the plans for the Library progress. You say you have made application to the state board and undertaken the task of raising funds. Have you asked any other local clubs or associations to join with you in the endeavor? I truly agree that no service to your children and community will be of more lasting importance, so don't let difficulties discourage you. But, my dear child, don't tire yourself out over it. I know how many responsibilities you have. You musn't exceed your strength, for no good will come of that in the long run.

Father says to tell you he got all the culture he needs for a year at our last Chautauqua, but you know him well enough to understand his joking. He is riding his hobbyhorse about "conservation" harder than ever these days, and to hear him go on about National Parks and public works and power sites being owned by the government is a real education. His desk is just piled high with papers and pamphlets.

Chautauqua week was extremely worthwhile this year. Despite the heat we spent four of the six days in and out of that big brown tent, regaling ourselves with lecture after lecture and performance after performance. I have heard speeches on prison reform, exploration in the South Seas (with a slide show), missionary work in Africa, a home course of Bible Study, the Teutonic Mind, irrigation—much to your Father's delight—and even nutrition. You would have appreciated that talk; the speaker was a woman, a Dr. Caroline Geiser, do you know of her?* There were many more women speakers and performers than I had ever seen before. Also, this will interest you—a children's tent was provided, at which young parents could leave their offspring while informing or entertaining themselves in the big tent.

Then, of course, we sat through the usual diet of political rhotomontade, sentiment, humorous talks, and rather indifferently chosen and performed music. A "musical humorist," Ellie, who did animal imitations on his violin! And Swiss bell ringers. Oh, my. Which reminds me—we have at last purchased a gramophone, and I have begun a collection of "records," which I shall take great pleasure in sharing with you on your next visit.

Father is talking about another trip to California for us in

*Caroline Geiser was a well-known nutritionist.

January if nothing happens to interfere with his plans. In a few more years, I shall insist that you and our grandchildren accompany us, before we are too old to make the trip. Don't you think that is a good idea? Perhaps Tom won't feel he can spare the time, and then, of course, you must do as you see fit, but I should dearly love your company. The ocean is so beautiful, Ellie, the children would love it so!

You should know that my sister Emily died last week. Of course you never met any of them, and you know that I did not maintain any real correspondence with them after we came out west. But she was my last living sister. Her husband wrote to me.

Now I must get busy and fry your Father's Sunday chicken. He is grumbling over the paper. He says he's ashamed of Nebraska for voting Wilson in and that it is time we got somebody in the Presidential chair who can do something a little more vigorous than write notes.* I am sure he doesn't think of the implications of this.

One more piece of news which slipped my mind until this moment. Your friend Martha Forrester Clark is home again with her parents in Alliance, having left her husband, whom she is divorcing, back in Illinois. I don't know much more than that about her situation. She has her little daughter with her. They are both quite frail appearing. Your Father jokes that the "call of the prairies" has brought her back. I hope the prairies are kinder to her than Illinois seems to have been.

This is not a good note to end on, but end I must,

As always,

your loving

Mother

❋   ❋   ❋

World War I was on the minds of all Americans, and Eleanor Patchen was no exception. The following excerpts from letters to her sister-in-law Julia reveal her concern.

1915 I know I couldn't let the war take Tom and all our boys and feel that it was all right. I don't know what the world's coming

---

*Wilson wrote "notes" to the belligerents, registering the disapproval of the United States.

to when civilized men revert to savagery and kill each other like so many beasts. I don't understand them. It seems as if human life was being treated more cheaply all the time. I've quit reading about the war, except headlines, for the incidents and personal experiences are too harrowing. We are hoping the U.S. will steer clear of entanglements.

1917 This war is beyond words. We just can't realize it, even when they are calling for more and more men. Jud is in France, and no one has heard from him since the day he sailed. Mother is nearly crazy from the suspense, you know. And there are thousands and thousands of other mothers who feel as bad as she and I do and who are trying to bear up and make home pleasant for those who remain.

Now they want to register all our boys who have turned 21 since last June. That will take in so many we know! It makes me boil to think of the whole world having to sacrifice the flower of its manhood for the egotism of a German fiend!

1918 Tom is in class four, with his occupational deferment, but may be called soon anyway. If he is needed, he may go with my blessing, and I wouldn't have him do otherwise. If I were a man, I'd be there or "bust." We've just got to lick the daylights out of every one of those Germans.

✳   ✳   ✳

Judson Wade, the youngest son of Henrietta and Arthur Wade, served in the United States Army during the war.

Somewhere in France

September 10, 1917

Dear Mother and Father,

Today marks the end of my second month here. We are still building cantonments.* I think they want me to fight this war with a shovel. I am billeted in a farmhouse with three other fellows, two from Nebraska and one from Oklahoma, all of us "country boys." The farm is in pretty bad shape, but you can tell the soil is good. Some wheat is ready to harvest, and you see all ages out with their scythes—old women, little boys. It is a beautiful country, and often I am reminded of home. There is one old woman here who brings us milk sometimes and treats us as, I suppose, she would treat her grandsons if they were here, a lot of laughing and scolding, most of which, of

---

Cantonments are groups of temporary structures for housing troops.

course, we can't follow, only the tone. But I have learned enough to "parley-voo" in the shops in town and mean to keep at it. What really gets me is the little children speaking French! There is one little "garson" who lives in the town, I don't know who he belongs to, who hangs around us but won't eat any of our rations except the chocolate. The other stuff is too strange to him. (That makes two of us!) When there is bread at the baker's we give him a loaf of that. It is good bread, but they don't bake it in pans—it comes in a sort of long thin stick.

In the town, the Germans crossed out the old French names of streets and painted German ones over. It makes me see red; that is just what the world can expect of the Huns if we don't beat them back.

We are awfully lucky in our commanding officer. Lieut. Wilson is not the kind of ambitious cynic some officers can be, but a man who cares about winning this war, and one concerned for his men. He is pretty young, I guess about 26 or 27, but there's no foolery about him.

I will write as often as I get the chance, but you mustn't worry if letters don't come. That doesn't mean a thing, the mail is impossible here. I have had just two of your letters and one from Sis, and I can tell from reading them that you've sent many more. Just keep trying!

Your loving son,

Jud

Paris

March 2, 1918

Dear Mother and Father,

They have got me patched up again, so I will be rejoining my company in a few days. You had a good idea when you got hold of the Red Cross to get mail to me! I got a whole packet of letters day before yesterday, and the socks too. I guess you know what a difference that makes. It's great news about Harlow and Marjorie's baby. And your description, Father, of Christmas with everybody together really made me feel I was there.

I haven't said much about this last six months. We're not supposed to, you can gather that from the holes the censor has cut out. But the main thing is that when I write home it's home I think of. What happens here is like another life. A lot of us feel, I guess, sort of superstitious about mixing the two of them up. It doesn't mean anything but that. I want to leave it all behind when I get home, if I can.

They've got to collect these, so I must close.

Love to all of you,

Jud

[Judson Wade died in the war.]

✳   ✳   ✳

In 1920, Thomas Patchen talked to a friend about his life as a dairy farmer.

No, it doesn't look to me like easier times ahead.* During the war, of course, prices were up because of the foreign market. Well, that's over with. *We'll* be all right because we've been fortunate. I don't see now where I got the optimism, back in '10, to believe we'd make it to ownership from tenant farming. And we couldn't have done it, without the possibility of a land mortgage, if the Farm Loan Act hadn't gone through in '16.† With our savings and a loan from the joint stock land bank, we just got over the hump in time. We won't be out of the woods for many another year, mind you. Long-term credit is still too damn expensive, excuse me, for a farmer. You have to go to Omaha, and *they* have to go to Chicago. A real change since I was a boy, and my father would go first to the local banker for credit—for his seed, for example—before he'd pick it up and load it and drive home with it. You knew where you were, at least. Now I have an account at Sills's bank in Fairview, and I just write a bank check for seed, chemical fertilizer, feed, a harvest crew's pay—but Sills can't handle credit for much more. For larger loans, stock

---

*As a result of World War I, there were rapid fluctuations in the value of farmland and the price of crops. By the middle of the war, for example, prices were double what they had been four years earlier, and in areas such as Iowa and Nebraska, the price of the best farmland had also doubled. When the war ended, prices began to drop. Wheat went from $2 a bushel in 1918 to $1 a bushel in 1920, and overall crop prices fell by a half. The effect was an economic depression in farming, which predated the Great Depression by at least nine years.

†The Farm Loan Act, passed by Congress in 1916, established a system of agricultural credit for the farmer. A cooperative system of federal land banks and joint stock land banks, which were organized with private capital, were established. The federal government provided the capital for the federal land banks and regulated interest rates in both systems.

transport, building, or even machines, I have to go to Omaha. No, life has not gotten simpler, don't think it.

I wouldn't like to imagine what it'd be like having to contract with wholesale dairies and go by their price lists, instead of dealing through the co-op. A dairy farmer can't hold onto his crop until the price goes up, you know! And in '16–'17, when the wheat crops were poor, I needed all that extra margin the milk brought in. Another advantage we have is the Farmer's Union, which runs a purchasing co-op and a retail store where we can stock up on some staples.* And I can get my natural disaster insurance at the same shop.

So far, you know, I haven't exactly been a joiner. I like making things work—building up the herd, designing a better barn, getting a higher yield. I've felt that it was sufficient for me to keep informed of where our own best interests were, without trying to change the world. But Ellie, now that she's looking forward to voting,[†] reads the papers through and asks questions. Why the farmers can't have a nation-wide co-op to control commodity prices, for example. I can't say she surprises me, it's just like her family. I don't know why I figured she would be mainly interested in local elections when, after all, most people around here seem to be paying them less and less attention.

No—she's got the right idea. It's a time to take a good long look around you, if you want to know where you are, that is.

✳   ✳   ✳

---

*A list of items that Tom Patchen bought at the Farmer's Union included:

Colorado potatoes, bushel, $0.75
Beans, all sorts, 10 lbs., $0.50
Onions, 50 lbs., $1.00
Cabbage, 100 lbs., $1.25

†The suffrage amendment was ratified in 1920.

5 Communities and Associations

THE years between 1900 and 1920 were prosperous ones for American farmers. Families such as the Patchens saw the price of wheat climb from about 60 cents a bushel in 1900 to a high of $2.15 in 1919, in the aftermath of World War I. Corn, which had been 20 cents a bushel, shot up to $1.51 by 1919, and the prices of eggs, cattle, pork, and chicken, as well as other farm products, all doubled and tripled between 1900 and 1920. Farmers used their new wealth to buy more land, purchase new machinery, and improve their overall life-style, even if this meant only larger orders from the Sears, Roebuck or Montgomery Ward catalogue.

During this period, the United States' population grew, and the country became more deeply involved in international politics and in various associations and organizations. Let us consider some of the main events that occurred between 1900 and 1920. As the century opened, the Spanish-American War had just come to a close.

In 1901, Queen Victoria of Great Britain died, and many believed that the Victorian era of conduct and morals had finally come to an end. In 1904, the St. Louis World's Fair opened, and 19 million people (close to one-fourth of the American population) found in it a confirmation of the wonders they expected from technology, science, and education. In 1902, American technology had produced the first moving picture theater, and in 1903, the first manned flight, at Kitty Hawk. In October 1904, the first subway began service in New York City. In 1908, the first Model T Ford rolled off the assembly line, and by 1914 a car was being produced every ninety-three minutes. In 1913, the Sixteenth Amendment, enacting the federal income tax, went into effect, and the zipper was patented.

In 1915, a German submarine sank the British ocean liner *Lusitania*, which had American citizens aboard. Nonetheless, President Woodrow Wilson continued to speak (as did the majority of Americans) for American neutrality in the "Great War." Anti-Semitism and racism increased. In October 1915, an estimated 25,000 women marched in New York, demanding the right to vote.

In 1917, restrictive immigration laws were passed; war was declared against Germany; and the Russian Revolution began. In 1919, President Wilson went to Versailles to sign a peace treaty with Germany and began his campaign to establish the League of Nations. In 1920, the Eighteenth (or Prohibition) Amendment was enacted, and the Nineteenth Amendment secured women the right to vote.

The face of America changed in many ways between 1900 and 1920. The events just listed illustrate the increasing impact of technology, the country's involvement in world politics, the continued growth of the federal government, and a change in consciousness. The United States was becoming more modern. Not all of the changes in technology directly influenced people living in rural areas, however. For instance, electricity did not reach most farms until the late 1940s, and indoor plumbing was a luxury that few of the Patchens' neighbors enjoyed. In this chapter, we will examine how much the lives of people in small towns were, in fact, affected by such changes.

The country changed in another way, which had far-reaching consequences: it became an urban society (see Table 5-1). In 1890, for example, 65 percent of the people lived in areas classified as rural, but by 1920, over half lived in cities, some of which had grown to immense proportions. By 1920, New York's population, swollen by waves of immigrants, was over 5.6 million. Chicago, a great trade center for the Midwest, had grown to 2.7 million, and a number of cities, which in the late 1800s would have hardly deserved to be

Table 5-1

URBAN GROWTH FOR THE CONTINENTAL UNITED STATES BY SIZE OF PLACE, 1890–1920

	1890	1900	1910	1920
Total population (in millions)	63	76	92.4	106.5
Percent urban	35	40	45	51
Percent of population in cities 100,000+	15	19	22	26
Percent of population in cities 500,000+	7	10.6	12.5	15.4

Sources: U.S. Department of Commerce. *Historical Statistics of the United States, 1789–1945* (Washington, D.C.: U.S. Government Printing Office, 1949); *Historical Statistics of the United States, Colonial Times to 1957* (Washington, D.C.: U.S. Government Printing Office, 1960).

called cities, had now emerged as large and important trade centers: Kansas City, Denver, Minneapolis–St. Paul, Omaha (where Lewis and Harlow Wade set up business), and Sioux City. Society was also becoming more complex, and the small community and the ways of life that it represented seemed to be passing away. This is what Father Wade had in mind when he chided Harlow about his "city way of life," in which a man's worth was determined by his possessions rather than his abilities. At least this is what many observers of the scene decided; their ideas of what was happening were shaped by their images of what a community was supposed to be.

COMMUNITY

In *The Sociological Tradition*, Robert Nisbet (1966) stated that a concern with community—its emergence, decay, revival—was central to the social sciences. According to Nisbet: "By community I mean something that goes far beyond mere local community. The word, as we find it in much nineteenth- and twentieth-century thought encompasses all forms of relationship which are characterized by a high degree of personal intimacy, emotional depth, moral commitment, social cohesion, and continuity in time. Community is founded on man conceived in his wholeness rather than in one or another of the roles, taken separately, that he may hold in a social order" (47). As such, the term *community* encompasses a vast range of behavior. Nisbet's definition emphasizes two variables: interaction or association and common values. We should also add another, *place*, for we often associate a community with a group of people who occupy a common territory and who also have a common set of values and interact with one another. But often, as Nisbet suggested, community stands for something.

Community as Metaphor

Community bespeaks security and familiarity. When we hear references to the loss of community or the erosion of community spirit, we know that something other than territory is involved. The rapid changes that were taking place in the early years of this century were a signal to many social scientists that the old way of life was being supplanted by another. Social scientists such as Tönnies, Durkheim, and Redfield were interested in the movement from one type of society to the next and in what would hold the new society together.

As we noted in Chapter 3, Tönnies (1887) distinguished between *Gemeinschaft* and *Gesellschaft,* whereas Redfield (1947) distinguished between folk and urban societies. Both of these men saw the *Gemeinschaft,* or folk society, which was fading from the scene, as a simpler one in which people could respond to the whole person, not just portions of the personality. In a folk society, or *Gemeinschaft,* people interacted with others on a daily basis and got to know them. They entered into relationships because the relationship was rewarding in itself, not because they thought they could gain something from the interaction.

The French sociologist Emile Durkheim tried to explain what held modern society together. In *The Division of Labor in Society* (1893) he distinguished between *mechanical* and *organic solidarity.* Mechanical solidarity was a characteristic of simpler societies. Because all of the people had the same values, their rules for behavior were clear. And if those rules were violated, the society responded, usually harshly, in a sort of Old Testament retribution, "an eye for an eye, and a tooth for a tooth." This was known as mechanical solidarity because the laws were applied mechanically; that is, for a specific violation of the rules there would be a specific punishment.

In modern society, however, such laws are applied differently. Durkheim noted that people do not hold the same things sacred; that is, they do not hold the same sets of values. There is a high division of labor, with people performing specialized tasks. Trade agreements, real estate law, tariff laws, and all other economic laws are characteristic of organic solidarity. People are bound to one another because of mutual interdependence. Their rights, obligations, and duties are specified by contract, and if they are violated, there is an attempt to see that the contract is honored, not an attempt to seek retribution.

Durkheim's modern people are above all economic actors who honor their laws, or social contracts, because it is in their best interest to do so. They cannot conduct their business unless there is trust, but this trust is grounded in the contract. It was precisely this shift that distressed many of those who lived through this period of rapid transition. "A man is as good as his word" and "A man's handshake is good enough for me" are statements about *Gemeinschaft* and about community. When a bank foreclosed on a loan to a drought-stricken farmer, it was the application of contract. In short, the contract-based relations of the marketplace were seen as replacing older forms of human relations grounded in ties that emphasized mutual respect and interaction.

Eleanor Patchen wrote in her diary that things were changing: "Many people are finding less time to go to church. That is a real shame." Although she used to know everybody in the area when she was a girl on the ranch, this changed after World War I. "You just don't know your neighbors." Furthermore: "Not so many families own their land. And people are more different; I mean of different sorts." This is clearly a moral judgment. That people do not farm or ranch, do not even own land, but instead earn their living working for others is somehow "just not right" to Eleanor. Clearly, she and others saw their way of life being challenged, and they responded. For example, they joined movements, such as Temperance, and attacked the outsiders' way of life. Another of their responses was to create new types of associations to replace those that no longer offered a sense of community.

We should emphasize that even though these people found themselves in a new social world, their bases of community had not completely disappeared; rather, they were moving from community to society. But even in a larger society, there still are communities—it is their bases that change. In order to understand this shift, let us look at what contributed to a sense of community on the frontier.

Bases of Community

We noted that community includes values, interaction, and place. Even though the settlers were widely scattered outside the small service centers, they still had a strong basis for community. Originally they were self-sufficient farmers who produced little for sale on the open market. (This was partly because there initially was no well-developed system to dispose of a surplus and partly because people needed what they produced.) But no family could easily meet all of its needs, whether for labor or food. We know from diaries and farm account books that the Great Plains settlers did a good deal of bartering. They traded work for corn or other work. One farmer might help another set fence posts, and that farmer would later help with the first one's threshing. They also shared their labor in major jobs—building houses and barns, butchering hogs, or haying. Sharing work over a period of time built up mutual obligations based on trust (Bender, 1978; Doyle, 1978; Russo, 1974).

In addition, the schools were often supported by subscription, which meant that a group of citizens had to band together to guarantee the support of a teacher. Usually they cooperated in either finding or building a schoolhouse. Churches were an even more important source for the spirit of community, for people gathered in churches not only to worship but also to attend bazaars, socials, camp meetings, and sometimes community revivals. Churches tied distinct groups of people more closely to one another.

Another source of community was ethnicity, although it was also sometimes a source of division. The fact that people in another town spoke another language made them unique and set them apart. One of the difficulties that the people on the Great Plains had was communicating with one another. Finding a person who spoke your own language meant that you had found "one of your own kind." Ethnicity was sometimes associated with different methods of farming, styles of dress, and religions and forms of worship. For the most part, the ethnicity of the early settlers was not a problem. The immigrants generally wanted to assimilate, to learn to speak English, and to adjust to their new homeland.

Nicodemus, a black colony that flourished in northwestern Kansas between 1877 and 1910, had its own special cohesiveness. As in many ethnic communities, its settlers had arrived in large groups from the same area; they also were often united by family ties. More than many communities, Nicodemus was united by common purposes—to be free of crime or violence and to acquire business, trade, and political skills free of white influence. In 1866 a local newspaper reported: "No whiskey shop, no billiard hall or other gambling hole; no drunkenness or rowdyism, no cursing or whooping disturbs the peace of the place." Moreover, those who could not abide by Nicodemus's standards were quietly asked to leave (Mould, 1980:31–32).

National and international events both heightened the sense of community and eroded it. The Patchens lived in an area of Nebraska that had been settled by mostly German immigrants. German communities were also found in large numbers in Minnesota, Iowa, and the Dakotas and in cities such as Milwaukee and St. Louis. The Germans, like the immigrant groups before them, seemed to have become assimilated; that is, they seemed to have lost their interest in and affection for their homeland and were on the road to becoming Americans.

When World War I began in 1914, there was a general feeling that it would have little effect on the United States. President Wilson seemed to speak for the nation when he declared that the United States would take a position of neutrality, stay out of the war, and, if possible, try to mediate the conflict. Few Americans expressed any enthusiasm for enlisting in "Europe's War," but this soon changed dramatically. As the war progressed, there was increasing unease and uncertainty about its outcome and about whether the United States could stay out of it. During the latter part of 1914 and into 1915, the German-American Alliance led a vigorous campaign on behalf of Germany. They sought to win sympathy for the German cause, raise funds to aid families in the old country, block attempts by the Allied powers to raise funds in the United States, and pressure President Wilson into imposing a trade embargo on munitions shipments to all of the warring powers (Clark et al., 1977:127).

The initial reaction to the German-American activities was decidedly unsympathetic. The *New York Times* labeled some of the efforts treasonous. The intensified activities of the German-American Alliance coincided with the sinking of the *Lusitania*, on May 7, 1915. Over 1,000 people, including 128 Americans, lost their lives as a result of a German torpedo. Although Germany had declared that it would blockade Great Britain and sink any ships entering the war zone, Americans saw this as an act of war directed against the United States. This heightened anti-German feelings, and rumors began to circulate that the problems in factories and shipyards were caused by German "traitors." By the time the United States entered the war in 1917, Germans throughout the country were subject to persecution. Their language, religion, and customs were all suspect. In some communities German-language newspapers were banned, and homes and churches were vandalized.

During this time, many people tried to define what it meant to be a "real" American. Newspapers, radio, ministers, and politicians all spoke of the need for patriotism. The "100 percent American" was in the process of being born. One was not supposed to be German, Irish, or British, but American. Elizabeth Straub wrote of how difficult it was to be a member of the German community. She grieved for her husband, who was subject to abuse because he did not want to join the army: "They have not understood, because Peter and the others did not volunteer so soon and because, also, we did not want to give up our children's school where they spoke the mother tongue or to give up our names and because the priest went on with his sermons in German. They cannot forgive these things."

Several events contributed to the anti-immigrant feelings. Immigrants were defined as outsiders who challenged the tradi tional American way of life—the values, attitudes, and patterns of interaction that contributed to America's sense of community. As Erikson (1966) pointed out, sometimes a society needs deviants to help it define itself. These deviants are created when the group is threatened, because the concept of deviance allows the group to refine its concepts of proper and improper behavior. This stress on the "American way of life" challenged ethnicity as a basis for community. Not until quite recently has ethnicity once again been generally acknowledged as a powerful force for unity.

Ironically, the wave of anti-immigrant feelings that swept the country prior to World War I made it easier for the United States to enter the war, even though most people were strict isolationists. The war, at least initially, forged a sense of purpose and a feeling of community and provided another chance for Americans to distinguish between "them" and "us." The effort of mobilization was extraordinary. When America declared war, it had almost no military force. The regular army and national guard forces numbered about 200,000 men, poorly trained and poorly equipped. It was estimated that at least 1 million men would be needed on the battlefront. The first troops arrived six months after war had been declared, and by May 1918 American troops had taken an offensive position and were fighting on their own front. In less than a year's time, over 2 million Americans had entered the war and fought in France. Barracks were built to house the trainees, and their equipment was manufactured in the United States and delivered on American ships built for the war. This effort was made possible only by close collaboration between the financial community and the government.

During World War I, the antiethnic movements strengthened their assault on that which they perceived to be anti-American values. In 1917, for instance, Congress passed a restrictive immigration bill almost halting the flow of immigrants from non-English-speaking countries. The bill restricted immigration to mostly white, middle-class citizens of northern Europe. It excluded alien radicals who could not read or write and a number of other "undesirables." The reasons for the bill's passage were many, but some stand out. First were the anti-German sentiments and prejudice against groups such as the Irish. The Bolsheviks had staged a successful revolution in Russia on November 7, 1917, and there was a "Red" scare in the United States. Revolutionaries and foreigners (often no distinction was made between the two) were suspect. In addition, the new industrial cities of America added a new dimension to the problem. Although by 1920 over half of America's population was classified as urban, the cities were still regarded by many as an evil to be avoided. If they had had a choice, many immigrants probably would have avoided the cities, but they were where jobs and housing were available. The cities were rightly regarded as dirty, noisy, and dangerous places to live in. They were seen by those in nonurban areas as centers of sin, decadence, and potential rebellion. How could the rebellion be stemmed and urban America civilized?

This was when the Temperance movement, which had its roots in rural, middle western America, came to the fore. The manifest purpose of the Temperance movement was to persuade people to stop drinking. As we saw in Chapter 2, the Martins were concerned with their neighbors' alcoholic habits, as people who drank were considered to be untrustworthy, poor providers, and un-Christian. Temperance was linked to reformist religion, which had deep roots in American culture. The Temperance movement was part of a larger movement aimed at improving American morals and civilizing the entire country. One's urban brothers and sisters needed to be reformed and saved from themselves, just as the "heathens" once did, which was why many middle-class religious organizations sent missionaries to urban areas. The Temperance movement was distinctly, although not wholly, anti-immigrant.

Temperance directly challenged the cultural values of such groups as the Germans and Irish, to whom drinking was a normal activity. Working men drinking together was regarded as a sociable activity, hardly something to be stamped out. The German Alliance, for instance, lobbied extensively against temperance, as did the Irish.

A number of German antitemperance groups also actively supported Germany before America entered World War I. This did little to calm the fears of other Americans, and it reinforced their belief that immigrants were revolutionaries at heart. Playing on the sympathies of a country mobilized for war, the temperance forces argued that the Prohibition Amendment ought to be passed so that everyone might give his or her full commitment to the war effort. A sober America would be an America safe for democracy. (Some temperance organizations argued, not too subtly, that immigrant soldiers trained in the art of war should be kept sober after the conflict, too.) Gusfield (1955) described the Prohibition movement as a last-ditch effort by white middle-class Protestants to impose their way of life on the country, and they temporarily succeeded when Prohibition became law in January 1920.

Another social movement that paralleled the Temperance movement and the anti-immigrant activities was the Women's Suffrage movement. The generation of suffragettes who dominated in this period differed from Elizabeth Cady Stanton and Susan B. Anthony, who wanted the vote as a way of gaining specific rights for women. The 25,000 women who marched in New York in October 1915 demonstrated in the interest of their class, not their sex. They were white, middle-class, native-born, Protestant women for whom "the vote was the crowning glory in solidifying the middle-class fortress of men and women against the potential onrush of the 'unqualified' voter" (Guettel, 1974:17). Many of them were also temperance minded, and they saw both of these activities as directed against the urban, immigrant East. In addition, many suffragettes were involved in the Settlement House movement, which was primarily an effort to instill middle-class values in urban immigrant families.

During this period, massive social changes signaled the loss of power in the rural sector. Economic and political decisions were shifted to urban areas, to Washington, and the forces of change were seen as beyond the control of many small towns. Before, they could link their destinies to their personal efforts, but now, their lives were determined by the forces of the marketplace. In addition, many urban dwellers seemed to reject the rural way of life. And thus to the rural inhabitants, the loss of community often meant that the rural community had lost its political and economic power.

Before we look at the kind of changes that were taking place in the lives of the Wades, the Patchens, and others in their communities, let us examine in more detail some of the ways in which people have tried to maintain a sense of community.

Maintenance of Community

Before something actually serves as a focus of community—a trait, behavior, activity, style of dress, or whatever—it must be seen as unique. People sometimes even create differences in order to enhance their feeling of community. During World War I, German immigrants saw themselves as different, in part because the larger community reacted against them. Those who settled on the Plains suffered considerably from their environment, and jokes abounded about the climate, grasshoppers, and the character of the people who endured them. These jokes and stories were told by the settlers about themselves, and they created a sense of being special. A Dakota farmer might tell about his friend who wanted to hang up his hat but could not find a peg, so he just put it up against the side of the barn and let the wind hold it there. You could never get good pumpkins in the Midwest because the vines grew so fast that they dragged the pumpkins along the ground and wore holes in them. One farmer lost three cows but finally heard them inside a pumpkin. The pumpkin had worn a hole in its side, and the cows had wandered in to get out of the sun. The weather in Kansas changed so fast that strange things could happen. A farmer saw his oxen fading fast because of the heat and ran to get a bucket of water. By the time he got to the ox on one side of the wagon, it had died of the heat, and so he ran to the other side of the wagon, but by the time he got to the other ox, the water in his bucket had turned to ice. One purpose of such stories was to reinforce what might be called the *insider-versus-the-outsider distinction*. To be an insider was to be part of the community.

At the national level, in order to create support for the war, the newspapers carried a number of exaggerated atrocity stories. Headlines described, for example, how the Germans used women as shields when they fought. Throughout the war the Germans and their allies were portrayed as beasts, whereas the Americans, French, and British were portrayed as heroes and saviors of civilization, another way to distinguish between "them" and "us." Such a distinction was often sufficient to explain the war. People often legitimate violence, whether it is directed against another country or their neighbors, by the assertion that "they aren't like us."

Rituals are also an important means by which the sense of community is maintained. Thomas Patchen complained about the charivari that became unruly and resulted in the real destruction of property. Nevertheless, the ritual had a purpose, albeit carried too far here. It let the bride and groom know that they had friends who cared about them. The charivari was originally a means of integrating a young couple into the community of married adults.

Many activities are rituals that reinforce the sense of community. Naturally, attending church has a religious meaning for many people, but it also serves to unite the faithful at set times in a common activity. Church rituals distinguish the community of Baptists from the community of Lutherans, often more clearly than their respective dogmas do. Curious about the religious difference between two Lutheran churches in a small town, the authors once asked one of the ministers to explain it. He looked puzzled and then said, "Oh, well, we hold a barbecue in the spring, and the other church holds a bake sale."

Eating is often associated with rituals that heighten the sense of community. The birthday cake, which marks the passage of years, is an obvious example. Part of the frontier hospitality was to feed anyone in need. To turn someone away from one's door was simply not done; it would have been un-Christian and uncivilized. Sharing meals was also a part of visiting. People shared their food because they shared experiences, which they wished to emphasize. Visiting, eating, and offering gifts of food were means of establishing bonds.

Letters from soldiers like Jud helped maintain the sense of continuity and membership in a social group, whether it be the family or a small community. These letters often contained little information about the war. Rather, the writers spoke about their health, knowing that their relatives would be concerned, and asked about the activities of the group: "How is father, mother, Jane, old Dr. Jones? How is the high school football team doing? the alfalfa crop?" The inquiry, of course, is about the familiar; it is the need for reassurance that there has not been any change, that one can come back, fit in, and belong.

The maintenance of a sense of community requires that its commonalities be identified. Going to church together, sharing work, and intermarrying all provide links that bind people together. Rural Americans tried to extend their way of life to their urban brethren but failed. In urban areas, new sources of group identification emerged. Immigrants, striving to be American, would buy American clothing so that they would look like everyone else. Consumerism was one of the ways in which people attempted to assimilate. The bonds of community were more tenuous in urban areas. For instance, a person might belong to a group that gathered after work to drink, though this group would have no kinship links, the usual network of support. The bases of community for both urban and rural America were changing, and new associations were arising to replace the bonds that had been severed. Let us look at some of the changes that were taking place in the Wades' and the Patchens' communities.

Changing Bases for Community

From 1900 through 1920, small towns were service centers for the Great Plains' farmers and their families. Even a town with a population of less than one thousand had a doctor, sometimes a dentist, a local newspaper, a general store, blacksmiths, churches, schools, and farm implement dealers. Those who grew up near these towns remember going into town on a Saturday afternoon and staying until late in the evening, visiting, shopping, and then going to a dance and returning home late at night by wagon. The small towns were like this for a remarkably short period of time in our history; that is, many of these towns lost their economic functions as the larger centers grew. People no longer shopped locally but went to Omaha or Kansas City where the selection of goods and services was better.

Eleanor Patchen referred to the consolidated school that Harriet attended: "The 'little old' schoolhouses around here have been closing for want of pupils these 20 years past. They say it is because more and more small farms have been put together to make big ones. I think myself it's as much people moving to the city." In order to continue their high school education, students would often move into town and live with a relative. Although the dropout rate in rural schools was high, especially at the high school level, a number of children completed high school and went on to college. The children of first-generation farmers had options that their parents did not have; for example, the oldest son did not necessarily take over his father's farm. Indeed, Eleanor Patchen began her account with the lament that children did not follow in their parents' footsteps anymore.

Children defied their parents in new ways. It is interesting to compare the rebellion of young Eleanor and Tom Patchen with that of Harlow Wade to see the changes that had taken place in one generation. Tom Patchen, not wanting to take over his father's livery business, migrated with his new bride, Eleanor, to the eastern edge of Nebraska. Eleanor's parents did not want her to marry someone that they did not know or become a poor farmer's wife. Tom's parents thought he was being foolhardy and was making a serious mistake. Yet they came to accept what their children did because the children were willing to work hard and long for their independence, values that their parents could accept and understand.

By 1915, Arthur Wade was lecturing his son, whose defiance carried with it a different set of values. Harlow wanted his father to help him furnish a new set of rooms in town. Arthur declined and asserted, "Your expenses are outrageous for a single man, and I will not listen to any more stories of your debts." He was further outraged because Harlow wore flashy clothes, drove a roadster, and spent his money foolishly. Arthur Wade still believed in thrift and believed that a man did not show his worth by what he owned. He associated the city with a leisurely, corrupting life-style. He still viewed self-improvement as learning and read a wide range of magazines and newspapers, whereas his son Harlow saw self-improvement as improved personal appearance. The point here is not that Arthur was right and Harlow wrong but that Harlow's life-style threatened Arthur's integrity, the old values, and the basis of community.

The elder Wades defined themselves and judged their worth by a set of standards that they saw as inapplicable to the new generation. Arthur Wade's objection to Harlow's clothes was an objection to the fact that people no longer dealt with the whole person and no longer entered relationships because they were intrinsically satisfying but because they were a means to an end. The world of things seemed to have come to dominate the world of people.

Letters written between 1900 and 1920 are full of stories about what one could buy. To a person who had lived on the frontier in a sod house and who now was confronted with automobiles, electricity, and store-bought clothes, the change was indeed worth commenting on. Rural delivery of the mail, telephones, and improved roads all made life easier, but they also extended the boundaries of one's existence. Little Harriet Patchen stated, "I just love to walk down the street with Brother Jack and look in all the windows—the millinery shop, the furniture store, the barber's—that's always full of men on a Saturday." The town and its amenities were attractive to a growing number of people. Writing to her daughter-in-law Julia, Mother Wade declared, "Living in town will make it so much easier and more pleasant for you. You can go right to the big stores, find what you want, and see it delivered the next day."

The inhabitants of farms and small towns eventually realized that their way of life was being devalued and that Puritanism and the work ethic that had helped settle the frontier were seen as outmoded. Van Wyck Brooks, in *America's Coming-of-Age* (1915), argued that culture had to confront a new reality and deal with actuality. According to sociologist Daniel Bell, a more inclusive culture was needed, one that pertained to the immigrants and freed people from the Puritan repression of sexuality, which continued to be identified with a rural culture (1976:62). People needed to grasp the new, which meant accepting the ideology of progress as defined by advertising agencies, and to be free. As Bell found (1976:63), American intellectuals attacking Puritanism preached an ethic of hedonism, pleasure, and play—in short, a consumption ethic.

American novelists such as Sinclair Lewis (*Main Street*, 1920), Sherwood Anderson (*Winesburg, Ohio*, 1919), and Willa Cather (*One of Ours*, 1922) criticized rural and small-town life. It was accepted, at least in places other than the small towns and farms of the Midwest, that this way of life was suffocating and should be allowed to die. In *America as a Civilization* (1957), Max Lerner noted that the small town was no longer a significant factor in national life: "What happened to the small town was not only that the big social changes undercut it and swirled around it, leaving it isolated, but they also drained it of its store of power. The power of America today is to be found largely with the business and community leaders of the city, who initiate policies for corporate empires, trade-unions, national pressure groups, and big-audience media" (Lerner, 1967:153). The farmer was no longer seen as the independent yeoman who formed the backbone of democracy: "His wife is peerless at baking pies and putting up preserves, which she now does in an electrically equipped kitchen; his children belong to the 4-H clubs...he is...a churchgoer, a moviegoer, a TV set owner....Yet he is not, as he was in Jefferson's or Jackson's time or even Bryan's, the bulwark of the American Community" (Lerner, 1957:142).

The small-town dweller was dismissed as irrelevant to national life and culture. The theme of modernity stressed that social change demanded new men and women. Society had replaced community, and the morality of the marketplace held sway. It was assumed that eventually the social forms of the city would completely replace those of rural America. Yet rural America is still with us, and the values and patterns of belief that many believed would pass into oblivion have been remarkably slow to change.

FORMS OF ASSOCIATION

All human beings are born into social groups. The social group of a child born on the frontier may not have extended beyond the boundaries of his or her immediate family. But the social group of a child born and raised in a town could have been extensive. Social groups affect behavior, because to be human means to interact with others and to learn culture. The level, size, and complexity of social groups vary greatly.

Primary and Secondary Groups

The term *primary group* was coined by Charles Horton Cooley:

> By primary groups I mean those characterized by intimate face-to-face association and cooperation. They are primary in several senses, but chiefly in that they are fundamental in forming the social nature and ideals of the individual. The result of intimate association, psychologically, is a certain fusion of individualities in a common whole...it involves the sort of sympathy and mutual identification for which "we" is the natural expression. (1907:23–24)

A family, then, is primary, because it comes first in an individual's life and is the initial source of that person's values and culture. Although a primary group is characterized by intimate, face-to-face interaction, primariness can also be maintained by other means. Jud's letters from the battlefield and hospital were a way of maintaining primariness, which, of course, is linked with a sense of community.

Sociologist Kingsley Davis (1949) extended Cooley's distinction between primary groups and secondary groups. Davis saw primary groups as close groups of a few people who engage in intensive interaction over a long time. The group's members have a common reason for interacting with one another and value both the interaction and the other members. For instance, the visits that Eleanor Patchen described fall into this category. People visited not to gain something material from their neighbors but because the interaction itself was pleasurable. Furthermore, the members of a primary group typically have extensive knowledge of one another's needs and desires and take this into account when dealing with them. When Mother Wade suggested to Julia that she come to the ranch for a rest after her illness, she was relating to Julia's needs and wishes as well as her own. She was telling Julia, I understand how you feel and what you want.

Finally, the primary group is conducive to warmth and spontaneity and controls behavior informally, through such mechanisms as shame, ridicule, laughter, and sometimes ostracism. Little Harriet, who at age seven tended her brother Jack, had only informal controls at her command. "Jack is still so little, he's only three, that I have to watch him, or he will get into things in the store....Jack is just awful, the way he'll go right around a corner and start pulling things down. But Papa says he has to learn sometime, and I must learn to watch children."

It is important to understand that an entire geographic community can be a primary group or a group in which primary relations dominate. Although the town that Harriet visited seemed large to her, it was small enough so that its people knew one another and so that visiting town on a Saturday afternoon and evening was a means of extending and reinforcing primary group ties and loyalties. It is an affront to the people in such a community when primariness does not operate. In writing to Mother Wade, Julia commented on a neighbor's rude behavior:

> A neighbor came over one afternoon because his mule had got frightened and run through Tom's fence with the corn binder. So off we all went to help get the poor thing free. Then what should the man do but walk off with his animal with never a suggestion that he help mend the fence. I told Ellie that such behavior would not surprise me in Omaha, but that back home in Missouri it could never happen. She replied that she and Tom are after all newcomers in the area. But I wonder: doesn't it seem sad to you that the more people there get to be in a place, the less interest they seem to take in each other?

According to Davis and Cooley, the characteristics of the secondary group are the opposite of those of the primary group. These characteristics also correspond to the differences that people believe existed between a rural and an urban way of life. In a secondary group, people enter a relationship for a specific purpose. They usually have a limited knowledge of the other members and generally restrain their feelings: people do not feel that they can "act like themselves." Finally, secondary relationships have formal controls. Business is no longer conducted on the basis of a handshake but on the basis of legal documents and formal requirements.

The farmer dealing with the grain merchant brought his grain to market; the buyer set the price for the grain; and the farmer, often unable to store the grain himself, sold it. The farmer's relationship with the buyer was of a secondary nature. Each entered the relationship for reasons that were irrelevant to their individual personalities, likes, or dislikes. In fact, primariness is usually avoided in business dealings, and people make great efforts not to reveal their personal needs or desires. For example, the price of grain would not be affected by whether the farmer was having trouble meeting his payments to the bank.

The increasing complexity of farming between 1900 and 1920 demanded greater involvement in secondary relationships. Farmers had to invest in more expensive machinery if they were to increase their productivity. This meant that they had to obtain credit from a local bank, and credit relationships were distinctly secondary. The prices for agricultural products, although increasing, were affected by national and international events and were not within the farmers' control. Farmers dealt more and more with intermediaries such as buyers, dealers, and agricultural agents. The inhabitants of small towns saw a rapid rise in the division of labor during this period. The jobs that people held and the tasks that they engaged in became more and more specialized. People's contacts with others lost much of the primary character they had had at the turn of the century. In short, instrumental or market relations, which are secondary in nature, grew in significance. To make up for the loss of primariness, people sometimes joined voluntary associations.

Voluntary Associations and Bureaucracies

The distinction between primary and secondary groups overlaps, to some extent, the distinction between voluntary associations and bureaucracies. A voluntary association, as the term implies, is one that people join because they want to. As in a primary group, they want to be with people who share some of their interests. On the other hand, we often have little choice in becoming part of bureaucracy. We do not join a state; we are born as citizens of a particular country. A bureaucracy is epitomized by distance; that is, its members attempt to eliminate primariness when making decisions. (Of course, primary groups can develop in bureaucracies, when members of a work team become friends, but that is not the distinguishing characteristic of a bureaucracy.)

Most prairie communities had a number of voluntary associations available to women such as Eleanor Patchen. In 1916, besides the church, there were at least nine different organizations in Fairview, Nebraska. Among them were the Daughters of the American Revolution, the Tuesday Night Reading Club, the Women's Christian Temperance Union (WCTU), a luncheon club, and the Child Welfare League. Tom Patchen could have joined the volunteer fire brigade, participated in one of the reading clubs, and belonged to a church, the Grange, the Republican party, and the Fairview Civic Improvement Association. Although there are many reasons for joining a voluntary association, there are some basic ones that we shall summarize below (McNall, 1974).

People join voluntary associations because they answer some basic social need. Belonging to a group may make people feel important or accepted. Joining the volunteer fire brigade, for instance, is a way of serving the larger community. And many of the activities of volunteer associations are pleasurable. To be a member of the volunteer fire brigade often meant playing on a ball team, going to picnics, and organizing fund-raising activities for new equipment, as well as fighting fires.

Associations offer their members ideologies that allow them to sustain their self-images. The ideology usually explains why the group's view of the world is correct and that of others is incorrect. The rural minister, for example, would not have chided his flock for their lack of a cosmopolitan style but would have pointed out that they were good, God-fearing Christian men and women, superior to those living in the cities. The Women's Christian Temperance Union gave its members a justification for their way of life and challenged them to do something about "Rum, Romanism, and Rebellion." (At one time, many members of the WCTU and other prohibition-minded groups believed that eastern Catholic immigrants would be led to rebellion by drinking and would establish a papacy in the United States.)

Group membership depends on the individual's willingness to support the group's self-image and ideology. A member of the German Lutheran church supports the group's dogma, just as a member of the Daughters of the American Revolution supports its ideology.

Groups maintain their distinctiveness and their primariness by establishing boundaries. In other words, if a voluntary association is to attract and keep members, it must explain why it is different from other groups. In some extreme cases, it may employ techniques of isolation to prevent contamination by other groups. For example, the different dress of the Mennonites who migrated to the Great Plains set them apart. Their clothes were a boundary. In most voluntary associations whose membership is fluid, the boundaries are not as rigid. The women who joined the Tuesday Reading Club may also have belonged to the WCTU and the Child Welfare League. But they also were different from other women. They could have viewed, and probably did view, themselves as the reform-minded members of their community, those who were educated, even "ladies." Ideology, then, became a boundary.

The voluntary associations on the Great Plains grew quickly. One of their first functions was to help to civilize the wilderness. People joined and formed groups as part of the process of transforming the wilderness, themselves, and other people. In time, some of these groups became extended primary groups.

A voluntary association may also become large and complex and acquire the characteristics of a *formal organization* or a *bureaucracy*. In a bureaucracy, business is conducted on a regular and continuous basis by officials whose duties, rights, and privileges are restricted by a set of rules (Weber, 1946). Corporations' organizational charts are typical of this division of labor, which simply did not exist during the Wades and the Patchens' time. The local owner of Gates Merchandise Company, for example, had to do many jobs. He swept the store, waited on the customers, stocked the shelves, made out the bills, kept the accounts, and closed the shop at the end of the day. This is not like a modern department store, with its many buyers for different types of clothing and separate divisions for advertising, display, community relations, personnel, credit, and so forth.

The second basic characteristic of a bureaucracy is that each position is part of a hierarchy of authority. Our modern court system is composed of separate layers, through which a person may appeal a decision all the way to the Supreme Court.

Bureaucratic offices tend to be self-perpetuating. Once an office is established, its life usually extends beyond that of its occupant. The office of the president of the United States is an example of this, for which there is an elaborate procedure to ensure that it is never vacant. Most voluntary associations are formed for some specific need. For instance, a group might be organized to solicit funds for a new schoolhouse, or a church might form a building committee to raise money. In each case, someone becomes the group's leader, perhaps even its "president." But once the task is accomplished— once the schoolhouse or church is built—the group and the office disappear. But this is not the case with most bureaucracies.

In a bureaucracy, business is conducted by means of written documents. Decisions and agreements are recorded, duplicated, filed, and enforced. Although Tom Patchen kept an account of his daily expenses, he did not draft letters of understanding to his wife. They did not put in writing their plans to build a barn or whether the barn would be built before the house.

Moreover, unlike the officials in a bureaucracy, the Patchens owned their resources, whereas bureaucrats manage theirs. A town manager, for example, is responsible for such things as the payrolls for public employees, making plans for growth, and securing financing for the town's expansion. Tom Patchen's responsibility was to himself; his success or failure was solely his own.

Finally, managing the resources of a bureaucracy assumes skills and talents. The bureaucrat holds an office by virtue of his or her knowledge and talent. The chairman of the board does not pass on the position to his or her incompetent child, at least not theoretically. Tom's father's livery stable, which had now taken on the task of repairing automobiles, was not a bureaucracy, and thus his father could legitimately hand over the business to him.

Changes at the national level—the growth of bureaucracies, the rise of instrumental or secondary relations, the increased complexity of everyday life—did not necessarily affect small towns in the way that many writers have portrayed. The sense of community— as place, as value, as interaction—did not just disappear. The form of community changed, and voluntary associations were, for example, one of the elements that forged new bonds. Yet, the community, or rather the idea of community, still is a powerful force.

Even though the United States is now an urban nation in which secondary relations dominate, the myth of community survives in people's desire for a simpler life and for communities in which people deal with and take into account the whole person. Some towns today exist in name only and are not communities in this sense. A turn off an interstate highway will often lead to an asphalt road pitted with holes, past a couple of boarded-up gas stations. If there is still a grocery store, it is usually dark, with plywood over its broken windows.

But some towns have fared better. They serve as centers for an entire county, and it is often the county courthouse and the related government services that keep the town alive. These towns also look different. They have, perhaps, a small cafe, open daily except Sunday, and usually at least one gas station—garage. Downtown is the courthouse and a well-kept park with a couple of picnic tables and a barbecue or two, a Woolworth's or a Ben Franklin store, a hardware store (now part of a franchise), and perhaps clothing and furniture stores, depending on the town's size. A drive up and down the town's streets, laid out on a perfect square, running from Washington to Monroe in one direction and Apple to Elm in another, takes one past modest, well-maintained homes. A Friday night football game will often draw the bulk of the town's population. People will walk around during halftime greeting friends and talking about common concerns (Peshkin, 1978).

Again, not every small town is like this. But whether the town is slowly disintegrating or still relatively prosperous, there is a distinct value system in operation. Peter Schrag (1970) returned to his hometown, Mason City, Iowa, to try to explain the political conservatism of middle America and the people's faith in the "system." Even though the people in Mason City watch the same television programs, read the same books, and listen to the same songs as those in the rest of the country do, they do not draw the same conclusions from them. "If the system works here, why doesn't it work everywhere else? Main Street's uniquely provincial vice lies in its excessive, unquestioning belief (in the Protestant ethic, hard work, honesty, and conventional politics)...if New York has come to doubt the values and the beliefs of tradition, it still hasn't invented anything to replace them" (Schrag, 1970:21). Schrag's answer to the title of his article "Is Main Street Still There?" is a resounding yes.

Mason City is like a great many other midwestern communities that have a distinct set of value patterns born of the experience of settling the frontier. The emphasis on hard work and individual initiative means that people often assume that if others do not have a job it is because they do not want one. But the value of work, family, and friends differs. The type of community that existed during the frontier period has taken new forms: different kinds of associations have sprung up to replace the kin-based work group and church.

The death of the community has been discussed again and again by both the social sciences and the popular press. In reviewing the literature on the collapse of the community, Bender (1978) asked, "How many times can community collapse in America?" Our answer would be, as many times as Americans need to redefine who they are. The decline of community, then, seems highly questionable. As Fisher and his colleagues (1977) concluded, there is reason to believe that community ties are stronger today than they were in the past. Yet we continue to believe in an arcadian myth (Williams, 1973), even when the facts dispute it, because we "*wish* to see an Arcadian past in order to make a statement about the present" (Fisher, 1977:197, emphasis in original).

The notion that the spirit of community has collapsed usually comes from urban writers who are seeking to understand the evolving forms of the city by comparing them with an idealized image of America's rural past. They forget that there was little to idealize, that rural life was difficult. These writers ignore the real sources of community on the frontier and fail to understand how they were reshaped.

In both rural and urban areas, people have been remarkably adept at maintaining the sense of community they need. Because their sense of community changes in response to historical pressures, people must constantly evaluate and test it. In times of economic or political crisis, people examine the boundary between friends and outsiders. During the Vietnam War, for example, the conflict in the United States led people to reexamine their notion of community. Some even formed new types of communities, such as communes (both urban and rural) and cooperative living arrangements. The search for community is perpetual.

✳   ✳   ✳

The Higbees and The Davises 6

The Higbee and Davis families lived outside Cooley, a small town in southwestern Kansas, close to the Oklahoma border. The Higbees, who owned their farm, had three children: Etta Sue, Ed, and Ruth Ann. William Davis, a tenant farmer, and his wife Caroline were the parents of Bill, Roy, Larry, and Darlene.

For American farmers like the Higbees and Davises, the Great Depression began after World War I and continued through the 1930s and the drought years. In the first account, drawn from interviews, Ed Higbee described growing up in Cooley during this period.

I was just eight years old when the stock market crashed, and nineteen when the Japs bombed Pearl Harbor. Took me quite a while to figure out what either event actually had to do with me. In fact I didn't know when the crash had happened. Two reasons. See, our parents always tried their best to make us kids feel safe. So I went through all those early years of the thirties, yes, right through half the dust bowl years, hearing my dad say "if it rains...if it rains" and being downright bored with the subject. I had my own headful of thoughts, being a hero in my own motion pictures, worrying about what the other kids thought of me—I just didn't listen when the talk turned to mortgages and rent. And nobody asked me to listen, not as long as I knew enough to do my chores and not ask for money. They were trying to protect us, see? And then in the second place, I'd never known anything *but* pretty hard times. They didn't begin for farmers in the thirties, you know, but just about the year I was born. My folks weren't tenant farmers, and they believed they'd earn enough to pay off the bank and own the land

151

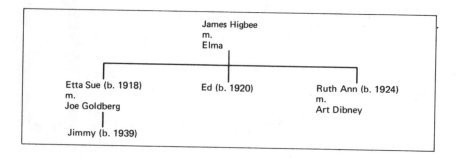

James Higbee
m.
Elma

Etta Sue (b. 1918)
m.
Joe Goldberg

Ed (b. 1920)

Ruth Ann (b. 1924)
m.
Art Dibney

Jimmy (b. 1939)

free and clear, one day—but that day just kept on refusing to arrive. So I'd been hearing "bank, interest, credit, next year, maybe next year" since before I could talk, myself. No wonder I didn't take much notice.

We had real happy times when we were kids, my sisters and I. Nothing meant more to my Dad than having his family happy. It's what his whole life was about. And farm families stick closer than others, just because you can't get away from each other, like the people in town can. You do everything together, work, play, church—it just seems natural that way, to a kid. Mind, when we got older we felt different about it.

Now Dad and Mother didn't put up with any fooling around. I can't remember when we didn't know what our chores were and know also when some extra work was going on, like plowing or building or butchering, that we were expected to pitch in and help in some way. It was just taken for granted. And we didn't ever imagine talking back to our parents. They laid down the law, and we listened. But see—we were good kids. I'm not kidding. That meant something. Dad and Mother didn't only love us, they were proud of us, and we always knew all that even if we weren't much for talking about it. I can remember just as clear my Dad saying to one of his friends, he knew I was listening, though I was pretending to read the paper, "Ed is the best worker I've got; he's worth two of any of the men I hire." Now that made me feel *good*. I was thirteen. And my sisters? That's a different story, of course, because it was held that there's more to being a good woman than just getting work done. You'd think there wasn't much opportunity for a girl to get into bad company out on the Oklahoma border in the dust? My Mother had different views! Mother was real strong on her daughters going to church and behaving themselves decently and staying away from girls and boys who weren't decent. And she had real clear views about who *they* were. Well. My little sister Ruthie has turned out a fine woman, a lot like Mother in some ways.

She is the original "cleanliness is next to godliness" woman, Mother is, her little house is as clean as working all day can keep it. I believe she must have suffered something extra during the dust storms. You know there were days, whole days, when not only all the things in the house but even the air was full of black grit. You couldn't eat clean, even. Some days we'd hang up wet sheets at the door and windows to keep the dust out and sit and listen to the wind because we still couldn't see to do a damn thing, even play Parcheesi.... Of course Mother couldn't do a wash, how could you get things dry? I never thought of it before, but that must have been pure torture for her. When the dust wasn't so bad, she'd try and keep ahead of it. I remember her taking down the curtains and shaking 'em every morning. And she'd keep Etta Sue and Ruthie sweeping and sweeping.... I remember—we had five cows, and I milked 'em—I'd strain that milk through three thicknesses of cheesecloth three times to get it clean.

It's hard to explain my folks during those years. I was all the way inside it, right until Etta Sue up and ran off—now, I'll get to that, it's a whole story. I was saying, I never once looked beyond my nose until 1939. All three of us kids stayed in school right through high school. Two reasons. Dad thought it would benefit us, which was maybe true, and there wasn't anything else for Etta Sue and me to do during those years anyway, off the farm I mean, no jobs for anyone, and especially kids and especially out there. So as I was saying, I was all wrapped up in my days at school, sports, I had this group of friends, I liked school pretty much. And I never questioned, I guess none of us questioned, our parents' position. We were all in the same damn boat, and some a little luckier or unluckier is all— yes, and I guess our family was on the lucky side. Dad was so determined to stay out of debt. I can't tell you how often I heard him use just those words—"stay out of debt." It's like debt was the worst that could happen. And yet—what else was he, ever, but *in* debt, to the bank and the machine companies and the men with the grain elevators? But see, for him that was all temporary. And a world

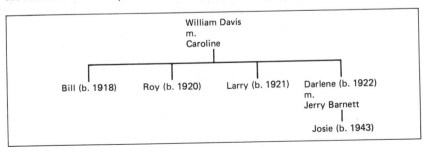

different from government programs, now those he had a real problem accepting. He really hated taking money for nothing and *not* farming land.* He hated us getting helped to finish school by the NYA.† "No one can not pay their debts and remain a Christian," he'd say about the idea of a moratorium, or cancellation. The only thing worse than debt was "relief." I wish I could say that word the way he said it. His independence, as he called it, meant as much to him as we did. I was brought up on that. I was taught to depend on no one.

Now school wasn't a place for me to learn questions about all that. The superintendent, for example, was a trustee in our church, and my American history teacher was the reverend's sister. And all the history we got was American history, which was mostly about how wonderful we are. Now don't get me wrong. I don't reckon I'd have fought a war for a country I didn't love. I don't mind saying it! But I learned a lot being out of the country. I met people who see the world in an entirely different manner. And there is room for some criticism here and there.

But I was about to tell you about my sister. See, she'd been graduated from high school about six months and was working as a clerk in the new dry goods store. This was in '39. People were beginning to really believe the dust bowl was over. There was rain and a real wheat crop. So Dad and Mother were feeling pretty good. Also, I forgot to mention we had the oil royalties since '37 when we put a well down on each of two sections. I don't believe Dad could've stuck it out without that extra, but I don't know, he wasn't telling.

Anyway, that was looking like a good year. Etta Sue was supposed to be going into town about one or two nights a week to stay with a friend—one which Mother approved of—and not a one of us imagined any different, not even Ruthie. (Dad wouldn't believe that, but I did because she was so furious.) But anyway Etta Sue eloped with a college-boy Jew from Chicago. Yeah. He'd been visiting family in town, the Goldbergs, they owned the furniture and appliance store. He said he was on his way to a job in California. They met each other in front of the motion picture house—we weren't supposed to go, but of course we all did—and Etta Sue and her friend Irene and this Joe and his cousin went walking after the

*A reference to government programs such as the Agricultural Adjustment Act, which paid farmers not to plant crops. See Chapter 7.

†National Youth Administration, originally a relief agency that was part of the Works Progress Administration. The NYA attempted to provide jobs for unemployed young people on various public projects and also administered a program of student work.

show, and he hung around town an extra week, and then they went off to California together. Got married someplace in between.

I never saw my Mother like that before or since, not even when she moved off the farm, and I hope I never do again. But that wasn't what hit me. See, Etta Sue came back again, three months later, stayed to have her baby, and took off again, leaving him behind. It was how she talked when she came back that made me start to see things. Here was Dad not speaking to her and Mother just grieving over her, and Etta Sue wouldn't talk to Mother or to Ruthie—who was real curious, too!—Etta Sue talked to me. And it was like I'd lived with a stranger all my life until then. My sister hated the farm, hated Cooley, hated Kansas. Hated Mother and Dad, is what it came down to, and especially Mother, for the very life they lived. She said there was never a day her last two years of high school she wasn't dead ashamed to look them in the face, they were so ignorant and stubborn. She called Dad a fool for believing things would ever get better for us, and Mother a worse one for leading the life of a slave for him for nothing. She just went on and on, and it seemed like I was fascinated. She never said what went wrong with Joe Goldberg, mind you, but I think it didn't matter a damn to her except he was a mistake, like. He wasn't her way out. She had to try another. I think myself *he* thought *he'd* made a mistake first.

But anyway. I saw the whole thing different then—not Etta Sue's way, but different. Things she said about—oh—how attitudes like our folks had, just feeding the rich, and being all wrong blaming the drought when it was stupid farming that ruined the land, I don't know what all; I suppose Joe taught her a lot of that. She said he was a Roosevelt democrat; I expect he was a little farther left than that. I didn't know what to call it, then. I barely knew what a Jew was before this war, let alone a Communist. Not that I believe he was that. All I knew was that she was saying you couldn't have faith in the future of that life anymore. It had gone all wrong. And though I didn't have a clear thought about it in my mind, I felt awful. When she left, I felt like I was left behind in a dumb trap. And when the war came—why, then—I enlisted the first chance I got, of course I did. Lots of us did. And at first—it was strange—it cleared up all my doubts. It was like being a kid again, taking orders, working so hard I hadn't time to think. Until the fun started. I was two and a half years in Europe, and I can tell you one thing. There aren't rules for everything.

Now I think, oh poor old Etta Sue, she didn't know half of what she was going on about. I hope she's made out o.k. Because I reckon, if anything, she underestimated how hard it can be to really get out of a trap you are born into. But you have to give it a try, you bet, there was no chance I would ever go back and pull in that old furrow. When Dad died, Mother expected I'd come back and take his place. And she owned the place, finally, because of the oil royalties and the wartime prices. So when I got home, well, it was real hard, and she is bitter towards me still, but I got her to sell up and move into town with Jimmy—that's Etta Sue's boy—where I fixed her up secure for the rest of her life. Now I've got my start with this truck company here. And I'll have my own company by the time I'm thirty—you can believe that.

Listen, I still say I was a happy kid. I mean to be a happy man. I don't carry the whole world on my back. I'm not trying to prove anything; it's enough for me if I can just be my own boss in a small way, I don't want more.

✳   ✳   ✳

The following are excerpts from letters written by William Davis to Mary Birdwell, the owner of the farm he worked. Birdwell, who lived in Indiana, had inherited the land, and so she owned it free and clear of the debts that ruined many farmers in this period.

1928   I believe you know how many important discoveries concerning methods of dry-farming have been made in this very state over the last thirty years. With deep fall plowing and soil mulching* and summer fallowing,[†] we can be sure our land out here will yield as abundant crops—of the kind suited to our own climate—as the richest land you see around you or indeed anywhere.

But there are other factors which must be taken into account when we decide what to plant. You will recall I advised you to get out of broom corn in 1919 when the market fell, and we never had cause to regret it, and similarly we were wise in ceasing to plant sorghum a few years later. Now, because we have invested in the tractor and combine, we can save so much labor and expense on the wheat crop (not least of which is my wife's labor in feeding harvesting crews!) that I strongly advise you to authorize me to put wheat in the new sections as well, after the deal is closed.

We have had a pretty successful decade here, if you compare our profits to those of farmers in general. Horse habits are no more use

---

*Soil mulch, a blanket of soil particles, was supposed to prevent evaporation. In a dry year, however, it increased it.

†Not planting a field in order to retain the soil's moisture. However, this often had the effect of exposing bare soil when it was most likely to erode.

out here, but I believe we have certainly found the way to get the most out of this land, and the value of your land itself, as you know, is on the rise again. The machinery is paying for itself, and the market in wheat is good. I think it possible it will go even higher than last year's $1.20 per bushel. I believe you should be as confident as ever of a successful year ahead.

1930   Money seems to be somewhat scarce in this part of the country this year, but I don't believe that anyone will go very hungry around here who is willing to work.

The local wheat price has been down to 50¢ a bushel, but it may improve. A good many farmers are feeding it to cows and hogs.

Now you must not be troubled that conditions the country over are not as good as we would like. There have been harder times, followed by better ones. Unfavorable conditions make us appreciate better ones when they come.

July 1931   The wheat price on this year's bumper crop is down to 25¢ now. Far more is being sold than people suppose, because so much is mortgaged. The same is true of cattle. The government comes in and pays for them at $20 a head, but the bank gets two-thirds of that.

It appears quite a few farms around here will have new owners. Some farmers working on too much borrowed capital are going to be in trouble, and merchants as well. I don't want you to worry, however, since we are in a relatively good position.

We have lived through worse and will probably be benefited by the experience.

November 1931   The wheat sown this fall needs rain very soon. There is too much wind, which evaporates what moisture remains. This year may be too rough even for the hoppers!

October 1932   No, our wheat crop was not a total failure but lacked quite a bit of coming up to expectations.

May 1933   The wheat has survived the dry winter, and the boys are home from school and being a great help.

Some parts of the state are completely blown up. All the water this side of the Pacific Ocean couldn't save them, for they have not seen rain since last June.

The wheat price is now 55¢.

July 1933   This has been the worst spring and summer since 1913. The wheat price is now 78¢.

November 1933   Those are some amazing stories you tell concerning the milk and egg dumping, and stopping trucks, in Iowa.* Now I have heard that people around here are burning their corn as fuel, since they see no future in even feeding up hogs on it.

*Davis is referring to acts of protest by farmers.

Dust storm, Morton County, Kansas, in the 1930s
Courtesy of the Kansas State Historical Society

But no one I know of in the vicinity has been dumping produce in the attempt to force the market higher. Those are extreme measures, and I think you would find that people around here are a little more conservative. I think you will find that [Henry A.] Wallace's AAA contracts* will see farmers through. We are eligible for pretty good allotments† and although it is not exactly how I would choose to get by, we can't be very choosy at present. I will send you your allotment check direct when I get it.

Roosevelt's pledge to raise farm prices encourages me not to sell your wheat at the present price. I have got an advance from the buyer which we are using to go on with.

March 1934 Don't worry about something that may never happen. We will look back on this and laugh when it is over.

The boys put their shoulders to the wheel and help. A decade ago the young people of this country headed for the city as soon as they could do so. The economic situation has certainly changed all that. There are no opportunities for them in the city, either. Bill Jr. also brings home some bacon from his WPA job,‡ 30 hrs. a week at 30¢ an hour. Of course, some of that is in commodities—I expect actual "bacon" any time now!

*The Agricultural Adjustment Act contracts were for land not planted. See p. 188.
†Allotments were determined on the basis of a farmer's previous three-years' production.
‡The Works Progress Administration (WPA), a relief agency formed in 1935, gave unemployed heads of families jobs on various public projects. In 1939, its name was changed to Works Project Administration.

September 1934 Since the rain we plowed the moisture into 165 acres in six days and nights, changing off on the tractor and running it over mealtimes. Rather strenuous. The heat has just about eliminated flies and hoppers as well as corn. Half the cattle have been sold out of this county to the government.

April 1935 Today we had the lamp lit from eight A.M. till noon and doors and windows shut tight. Caroline put damp sheets up over the windows and still the dust in the air made breathing uncomfortable. Our preacher had to give up halfway through the service Sunday because he could not talk any more due to throat trouble from the dust. My girl says they have to clean the classroom out at school three times a day, and that is all the physical activity they get as they cannot go outside.

July 1936 None of us are eligible for WPA work now, under the new regulations. In any case it has been a frustrating thing to depend on, considering the failed promises and long waits for projects to materialize. It is also a blow that the Supreme Court declared the AAA's financing unconstitutional but I have great hopes for what the Soil Conservation and Domestic Allotment Act can do.

We have been listing up the fields again.* It helps some, but we are still trading a considerable amount of soil around out here! The grass looks as if it were winter. The hoppers ate the trees to the bark.

Roy has gone to live at the CCC† camp where he is doing conservation work.

April 1937 We are all still healthy, despite the epidemic of dust pneumonia. The dirt storms are as bad as ever, but I believe we ought to stick it out. You know this is the greatest country in the world to come back, when it does rain. It always has rained again. I beg you not to lose heart but to carry on. We have hung on three years past so many others, even the Mennonites. I feel sure you will find a way.

I am sending your soil conservation checks to you direct.‡

✳   ✳   ✳

---

*"Listing up" created a ridged surface that supposedly slowed erosion. In 1936, the federal government paid 20 cents an acre to farmers who took this "emergency measure."

†The Civilian Conservation Corps (CCC) was established, in conjunction with the departments of Agriculture and the Interior, to provide work relief and to conserve and develop natural resources. The War Department built and administered camps to house enrollees who were between the ages of seventeen and twenty-three.

‡These checks were a provision of the Soil Conservation and Domestic Allotment Act.

Ruth Ann Higbee began keeping a diary in 1934, when she was ten years old. In the following excerpts from that diary, the original spelling and punctuation have been retained.

1934 I am sick to deth of Miss Wooster, and now we have the stupid hot lunches we never get away from her. Its bad enough her leaning over my sholder cheking my arithmetic or writing, brething her old moldy old breth on me and when shes ther telling me remember my napkin it is just too much. And she wont stay in the stupid teacherage* during girls recess even but has to come out and pretend to teach games. Ug. Why dont we have Miss Settel? She teaches such beatiful marching and drills. She can really play ball. Even the boys like to play with her. But no it is moldy oldy Wooster. Ug. How can I wait to be in junor high? If it wernt for Betty and Darlene I woud just die. She just hates us because we arnt town kids, but we dont care a bit. Why dont she go back where she came from?

1936 Today Darlene told me Roy has run off from CCC camp, which he wrote her was just like a prison. He wrote that he was going out to California to find work. I can hardly bear it I am so worried. It was the worst moment of my life when he left the farm. Now he may never return. Darlene and I cryed and cryed in the toilet, until the other girls asked us what was wrong. I feel so sorry for there mother. Darlene says she has stood up to everything till now. And I know they dont always have enough to eat, they eat that wheat mush all the time, and Darlene and Larry get there shoes from the board of education. And Mr. Davis lives in fear that the owner will sell the farm.

I know why Roy left. He thought he was doing the best thing. But o how I wish he coud understand how a woman left behind feels. If only he knew.

1937 Today the Davis family lost their farm. The owner sold all her farms up to someone with even more land, and Mr. Davis owed so much back rent they held an auction. Everyone went and bought things for a dime and put them back, but I wish it hadn't had to happen at all, it was awful being there. Mr. and Mrs. Davis were ashamed, though Darlene and the boys pretended they couldn't care less. The worst part was the city people, there were four of them, and they bought things and went off with them. That was real hateful. Now I don't know what will happen. They are planning to go back to Illinois to live with Mrs. Davis's sister for a while till Mr. Davis and the boys can get work. And Darlene says her uncle lost all his cows last spring; they got TB and the government took them,

---

*A teacherage was a residence provided for teachers.

and then they made him build a whole new cow barn and buy a new sterilizer. So they have awful debts, too. Maybe it will be all right.

Darlene showed me her last letter from Roy. It is from Oregon and dont say much, but he asked how I am, and says he is doing fine. I dont believe that, though, because he says tell Larry to stay home. I think he doesn't want us to worry. I wish I knew. But I dont know. Sometimes I think boys and men are really different. Dad and Ed never worry. They just do what comes next, and dont even talk about that. Maybe women can be like that if their life is hard enough.

Etta Sue and I snuck and saw a motion picture in Cooley on Saturday, *Mr. Deeds Goes to Town* with Gary Cooper, who I just love. It was awfully funny but it set me thinking too, because in the story you see real plain how ugly it is for a few people to own most everything.

I just hate that woman for selling her land.

1939 Well, Etta Sue sure has gone and done it now. I can hardly believe what a fool she's made of herself over that awful conceited Joe Goldberg. I suppose she thinks it's romantic. How she could. But then Etta Sue never has gotten along with the boys in school here; she's always held herself special, so they call her conceited behind her back. I hate to think what they'll call her now! Well *I* don't mind being friendly with nearly everyone, it doesn't hurt *me* to smile and say a kind word. *I* don't think I'm better than everyone else. I just hope she doesn't get her comeuppance too fast, but I'm afraid she will. Joe Goldberg is just as bad as she is, he thinks he's so wonderful. Mother is wild because he is a Hebrew, as she calls it. I wouldn't mind about that, I think it's pretty un-Christian to be so intolerant as that, though I don't say so. I expect there are as good and bad Jewish people as there are any other kind. But a big show-off is a big show-off, and that man with his six-cylinder Chevrolet and his lectures and long words and sophisticated ways certainly is. I pity them both. I'm glad one of us kids has got some sense. Mother is very glad to have me around just now. I can tell.

1939 I was right about Etta Sue and Joe; it didn't work out from the very beginning, I know, even if she won't discuss it. She is home again, and they are getting a divorce, even though she is going to have a baby. Mother and she think I don't know about that. Ha ha! as if I didn't listen to her throwing up in the commode nearly every morning. Mother is so old-fashioned that way. I will always tell my children about all those things. Poor Betty, she thought she was dying until I explained about periods. It was Etta Sue that told me about that, now I think of it. Well she's not telling anything now, but I do not blame her, I expect she has some terrible secrets. Maybe he beat her. Or maybe *he* just left *her*.

So the whole household is in an uproar over my prodigal sister. Even Ed is going around like he just noticed there is something else in the world besides Future Farmers of America and football. She talks to him, about what I cannot imagine. So I just go my own way and help out as best I can and get my schoolwork done. I really love typewriting and music, although I loathe Algebra and General Agriculture, what a waste of time. Next year I can be on the school paper and in the glee club. I think your interests are just as important as anything you do in school.

And, of course, I love my teaching at the Division of Education Nursery School. Mrs. Watson is so wonderful. I could listen all day to her talking about how important it is to raise your children properly to keep them happy and busy rather than being on at them all the time. I bet she never went around acting offended all day just because her daughter lost a sweater or dropped the cream. Of course, she wouldn't have as many chores as I do, and they have more money. But I understand about all that. I guess I get my work done around her, and good grades, and even make my own spending money, not that I usually spend it. Oh well, I don't care if nobody here pays much attention to me. A lot of good it's done my sister.

Betty talked me into seeing *Stagecoach* with her this week, though I thought it would be real boring, all cowboys and Indians. But the people were interesting. In the part where the old drunk doctor sobers up so he can deliver a baby, I was just holding onto my chair, hoping he would do it right. That is more interesting to me, how people act, than all the Indian chasing. That is why *Gone With the Wind* is the best motion picture ever made, because you can see how Scarlett ruins her own life with her vain, selfish ways.

1940 Jimmy doesn't seem to have much of his parents in him, but he does have a will of his own. Mother often says how much easier girls are, but I notice she thinks he's pretty cute when he's being "all boy," and of course, she is always thinking "poor motherless child," though he doesn't know the difference. After all Etta Sue left before he was old enough to recognize her. He just knows us, and I don't know which one of us he thinks is his mother. He'd be spoiled rotten if it weren't for me. You always hear how grandparents spoil their grandchildren, but you would think actually raising one would make you sensible. But no. So it was me that got him on a schedule and me that is firm about bedtime and thumbsucking and eating his meals. I sure don't recall that any of us was ever a problem about eating! But now Mother would like to give him just what he likes, which is so bad for him.

I wonder if I ever really will get to be a secretary. Next year I mean to take bookkeeping and office practice. I really love shorthand. But it looks like Mother is going to need me here until I get married, if I ever do. Ha ha. But there sure isn't anybody around now to dream about—except maybe Gary Cooper or Clark Gable. A lot of good that does.

1942 And now we don't even know what's become of Etta Sue. Mother and Dad never talk about it, of course. Neither will Ed; he appears to think he is protecting me from something. Ha. I bet I know as much as he does about what she is up to out in California. But I shouldn't make fun of him now when he is going off to fight for us. Especially since Dad is being so peculiar about it, acting as if it weren't happening. Sometimes I think he pretends the war isn't happening, he still talks about William Allen White* and FDR as agents of the devil. Ed has never done anything before without Dad's approval. Now in three days he will leave for Fort Leavenworth for training. Then we may see him one more time before he goes overseas. He will see things and suffer things I *can't* imagine. I can only pray he will come back safely.

Maybe I am a little crazy, because in a way I envy him. He is leaving here, but that isn't it. He is going to do something that is really big and important, that really means something. They can say all they like about how a woman contributes just as much by raising children. And I truly believe that we women are learning to do that better than ever and that our American children are going to make a better world. But well, it just isn't the same. I keep saving nearly all my salary with the idea I'll go to nursing school when Jimmy is in school and Mother can manage better. Even if she has started saying I am all she has left. Not just Ed but a whole lot of our friends are going. If it's true that a farmer is as important as a combat soldier, why are they all enlisting?

I could be an army nurse. Betty says that is just dreaming and that I just imagine I'll find Gary Cooper, like in *Sergeant York*. Well it's not true, I *will* do something.

❋   ❋   ❋

Ruth Ann Higbee graduated from high school in 1942 and went to work as a secretary. Thereafter, she met and married Art Dibney, a foreman in an aircraft factory. The couple, who lived in Wichita, were visiting Mrs. Higbee and Jimmy in Cooley when Ruth Ann made the following entry in her diary.

*William Allen White, the Pulitzer Prize–winning editor of the *Emporia Gazette*, was strongly in favor of American involvement in World War II.

1944 If it weren't for Art I would just go nuts. Mother is scaring Jimmy half to death the way she is acting, but she won't let me take him to stay with us: "He's all I have, you don't care, all you want is to get away" and so on and so on. It is really more than I can stand, Art says so too, that I shouldn't listen, that we have a perfect right to our own lives. But tomorrow he has to go back to the factory, they can't do without their best foreman. And I can't go with him, obviously I have got to stay here until she is better.

I guess I never realized how much she leaned on Dad. I know she was always the nervous one and the one who had trouble keeping her temper, with us girls anyway. Dad was a stern man, but he didn't go on and on about things, he just told us what he thought and punished us when we deserved it, and that was that. Now she is dragging up old stories I can't even remember—about him, too— and it is like she is angry all over again with Etta Sue, and Ed for enlisting when he did, and me for marrying Art and going to work with him in the aircraft industry in Wichita. What else could I do? He feels so bad about being 4F that he had to have a job that really made sense as part of the war effort. I love him for that, and he is good at it. She won't even listen but just goes on about how everyone leaves her.

Women on the assembly line at Beech Aircraft Corporation
Courtesy of Beech Aircraft Corporation, Wichita, Kansas

It is worst when she gets to Jimmy, accusing him of the same thing "as soon as he's big enough." Poor little guy, he doesn't know which end is up. He's old enough now to know she's not his real mother, and I bet he feels funny about that. But I couldn't have helped; when I left we were just fussing over him all the time, about what was right for him. That wasn't any good. Until this, he was probably better off with just her. And now—I've seen plenty of women trying to manage their jobs and their families too, and it is really rough! We won't start our own family until this war is over and I can stay home and devote all my time to my children, but I suppose we could take Jimmy, Art says so, and says he would help me. But she won't hear of it yet. So of course I can't talk to Jimmy about it, all I can do is spend as much time with him as possible. He *is* spoiled. But he's ok, too, he talks about wanting to be a soldier "like Ed and General Eisenhower"[*] and "kill the nasty Japs." And he has his little collections of tin foil.[†] He tries to comfort Mother, though he doesn't quite know what for; he's being on his best behavior around her, it's no wonder if he is stubborn with me sometimes.

At least there are good men working for Mother, and Mrs. Edmonds is wonderful, she sees just what's going on, and that is quite a help, but she can't be here all the time. I'll just have to wait and see.

✳ ✳ ✳

Etta Sue Higbee, Ruth Ann's sister, was quite close to her father's sister Lydia, who lived in Oklahoma City, and for many years they corresponded.

January 1929

Dear Aunt Lyddy,

Thank you very much for the book by Gene Stratton Porter.[‡] I love the part where Elnora's friend gets her a new outfit for school. Her friend reminds me a whole lot of you. I miss you to talk to, but your letters are fine. I think all you said was true about women going to school even if we do get married. I

[*]Eisenhower, a native son of Kansas, was held in special esteem by most Kansans during the war years.
[†]Tin foil was supposed to be saved for the war effort.
[‡]*The Girl of the Limberlost.*

don't mean to quit school, but I don't mean to be a teacher like you were, only I would like to be like you in other ways, because you have so many interesting thoughts and are kind.

Are you happy in Oklahoma City? I sure hope you aren't lonesome, but if you are, I will write more letters. I don't care much for my other aunt, but don't you tell. (I know you won't.) They came down from Wichita after Christmas and stayed for dinner when we didn't know they were coming. So then we all had to go for a ride in their new Plymouth, and when we got back, they went to the hotel, and we still had to take care of the animals.

I would rather read my books than listen to them talk. Wichita is not so wonderful. I bet Oklahoma City is much nicer. Maybe I will visit you there someday, but don't you look out for me until I say so.

Please write me back soon.

Love from your niece,

Etta Sue Higbee

January 1930

Dear Aunt Lyddy,

Thank you very much for the books by Mr. George Barr McCutcheon. They are my very favorite presents this Christmas. *Graustark* is a beautiful book. Don't you wonder if there are any princes just waiting for an American princess to save them? I will keep my eyes open.

I am glad you are settled in your new house. Mother and Dad are surprised to hear you could buy a house for some money every month, like renting. It seems a good idea to me and awfully lucky you could be so close to Uncle Emmett's job. I am praying he will stay well, now he is better.

No we don't have a radio, but I have a friend Wilma Lewis who does, and sometimes I go there and listen. We just love "Amos 'n Andy."

I hoped so hard I could come visit when you asked, but Dad says we just can't afford the money. He is renting two new quarter-sections, and we got a truck to pull the combine so he can get to them in an hour and a half. He says next year it will all pay for itself, and then maybe I can come see you. I guess you know how it is.

You ask if I am doing better in school now I go to the junior high. I guess not. I try, Aunt Lyddy, but English and

Social Studies are so boring, and I am just no good at Mathematics at all. The only thing I hate worse is Home Economics. You said school would get more interesting, well, maybe if you were one of my teachers.

Write me real soon now.

Your loving niece,

Etta Sue Higbee

June 1932

Dear Aunt Lyddy,

If you thought I would be mad at you because there wasn't a birthday present this year, you should of thought twice. You know how I enjoy every word of your letters. They are a real help to me, and that is what is important. We are all of us having a hard time of it. I am sure Uncle Emmett will find another job soon, but I wish you wouldn't have the worry. I know you will help him keep his spirits up and be a real help besides. If I know you, you won't sit around.

Here in Kansas we see some real sad cases of men who want to work for anything, food or clothes. This week a man cleaned the chicken house and barn out, and Dad paid him with eggs and a dozen jars of our peaches. And Mother sold off the Coleman to pay for our school clothes and books. We were praying for rain in family prayers every night, and then the thunderstorms flooded the creeks and Prairie River, and hail killed a third of the wheat. I guess it will be a while before I visit you.

Meanwhile you keep on writing to me.

Your loving niece,

Etta Sue

P.S. I promised I would tell you how eighth grade has turned out for me. Well it was better. I got *B*s in English and General Science, and nothing worse than a *C* this time. But it is not more interesting.

January 1933

Dear Aunt Lyddy,

It was wonderful of you to send me some of your own books for Christmas. So far I haven't found one that is too hard for me, although *The Homemaker** makes you think a lot. I would like to be like Eva is, I mean after she goes to work. Were you thinking of that? Because I am not a terrific student and don't have any idea about what I will do when I graduate?

I admire you for going back to teach after dear Uncle Emmett died, but I admired you all along. I mean you would do what you wanted to even if you didn't have to.

I like to think I am the daughter you didn't have. We better not tell anyone. But for myself I don't care if I have any real babies, either. Eva is so miserable trying to do right by hers and no good at it, I think I would be like that. And husbands like hers don't grow on trees.

Yes, I will write what I think of *Alice Adams.* Mother gets annoyed at me for reading "all the time" and wonders why I can't just work harder on my studies. But that is so different. It isn't about *life.* I only like school because my friends are there, and sometimes I think we learn as much from talking to each other as listening to our teachers. Except for you and your letters, so don't stop writing even if you are ever too busy to.

Your loving

Etta Sue

✳   ✳   ✳

In high school, Etta Sue's good friend Wilma Lewis moved to Texas. Wilma's father had given up farming and taken a job on the railroad.

October 1935

Darlin Wilma,

I can't bear you not being here for our senior year. I miss you every morning waiting for George Kramer in his old coupe. Wouldn't you think it would be fun to be one girl riding with two boys? Well it ain't, kiddo, and that is a fact. Even if the Kramer boys were our kinda guys! I am just going to live through this year somehow. My folks are harder to live with than ever, I guess you know something about that, but at least your father had the sense to know when he was licked and try something better. I hope every day that his job on the railroad will hold out and that your mom will get to feeling better. You ought not to be at home like that but having some fun.

The Homemaker by Dorothy Canfield is a novel in which the wife, Eva, goes to work while the husband keeps house and takes care of the children.

Mother is as full of beans as ever, but you know she is just set against our having fun. I don't mind the work around here, but then I do want to go out a bit, if only I could get a job after school, but you know there aren't any. The kids don't have to worry about that. Eddie is happy as a clam to be in high school, he is going to be real popular, in spite of being a farm kid, because he is athletic and has a big gorgeous smile and is always cheerful. I think I am just the opposite lately, I get so awfully blue and can't see the point to anything. It is funny how people in the same family turn out so different. Ruthie, though, is a lot like I was at her age, she has always got her nose in a book and daydreams over her chores and catches it all the time from Mother. Oh well, she will wise up in a year or so.

All the dances are to be cancelled this year, the student council decided (of course, Mother approves), because so many can't afford it. Of course, the ones who can will have their own parties as usual. I don't know if I'll go on being in 4-H this year. Of course I have to go to the Youth Fellowship meetings or Mother will have a cat, but the 4-H projects are like Home Economics class all over again, and you know me, Wilma ol' girl, I don't get all dreamy eyed over such things. I *really* can't see the point of prize biscuits.

Well, this is a long enough letter, isn't it? I will try and spare you next time. Write soon and let me know how you are doing down there. I will be real glad if I hear your mom is well and you can get out some.

Your friend,

E. S.

June 1938

Dear Wilma,

You know if there was any way in the world I could come to be at your wedding, I would do it. I am very happy for you. Gordon sounds like a wonderful person, and if anybody deserves the best, it is you.

I am sure you are right about leaving school. I went to our "vocational teacher" about three times my senior year, and it was just about as much help as getting my palm read or praying for rain. I haven't used one thing I learned in school on this job except some arithmetic, and you know what a whiz kid I was at that! I think the main thing I learned in school was when to sit quiet, what do you think?

The job is ok. I thought I would hate having to be sweet to people all day long, but it is not so bad because we don't have all that many customers. The only hitch is that Mr. Markham hired me to look good in the store, and he takes a personal interest in my looks, if you get my meaning. Oh well, I have seen worse old goats, and young ones too, and I think I can handle him. Meanwhile I have one-fourth of my salary to have a good time with, at least as much of a good time as a girl can find in Cooley. The high school movies continue on Fri. nights (with the eternal fudge for sale), and the Roxy changes twice a week. Every so often there is even a picture worth watching, that isn't some story about a girl marrying her gorgeous young boss or one of those high society things. The drugstore has put in a little fountain and stays open after the shows. Pretty exciting??? The other possibility is driving, if you have a car, across the border to have a few beers. You can just imagine what would happen if I got caught at that.

Remember Irene Thomas? We didn't think so much of her when we were sophomores because she was always hanging on that drip Billy Hollis. Well, his family sold up and left town about a year and a half ago, and she has improved a lot. (Although she still spends more time in front of the mirror than two of you and me put together.) Anyway, they have a radio, and several girls spend the evenings there one or two nights a week, and sometimes some guys too. In fact we are allowed to dance in the living room, although on the porch is sometimes more interesting—but no, not me, kiddo, nothing doing there.

Of course, we do a lot of just walking around and talking. No, I wouldn't say that I am in a better frame of mind than last year if I stop to think about it. After you two get settled in Fort Worth, I will really think seriously about visiting. If there are jobs available there, like you say, I might give it a try. It would sure be great to see you again.

You just imagine I am there at that wedding—but hey, don't you pitch any bouquets in my direction!

Your friend always,

E. S.

*　　　*　　　*

*After her short-lived marriage and the birth of her son, Etta
Sue left Cooley and headed west. In San Diego, she found
work as a clerk in an airplane factory and roomed for a
while with a woman named Anne Kettle. When Anne later
moved to Portland to take a job in the shipyards, the two
women kept in touch by letter.*

March 1941

Dear Anne,

Yes I am still right here in San Diego and likely to stay here
for the duration. I'm not clerking anymore either—I've got a
job making airplanes. Right now I'm on the swing shift again,
which suits me fine, though it is mostly a lot of fresh kids
who want to start a party at the end of the shift when I just
want to get back to my little room and rinse off the surface
dirt and *sleep*. (I can take a real bath in the A.M. when I won't
wake the neighbors up.)

They are good kids though, all sizes and colors and some
from college who are just as friendly and helpful as the rest. In
fact I am getting to be friends with a couple of them. We have
been swapping books. Have you read *Look Homeward Angel* by
Thomas Wolfe? He is pretty wonderful.

It is, of course, the men who have been here a while who
will drive you nuts. Here we are doing the same work, getting
paid the same, dressing the same (and you can bet nobody
bothers with makeup or hairdos. A funny thing is that all the
day-shift guys wash up before they leave, but the women don't
bother. You should see our hands. A quart of Ponds wouldn't
make this girl lovely—*if* I wanted it to!) and still you would
think every one of us was a bathing beauty or chorus girl at
least, to go by the way the men hoot and whistle and yell
"Woman in the yard!" and get their hands misplaced pretending
to show us our jobs. A girl on the line complained to the
foreman, who informed her he wouldn't have *his* daughter
working here for anything. Terrific?

No, it is not as glamorous as the magazines!

No, I haven't written "home." I know you mean well,
Anne, but unless Mother were to come out and see me here,
which she will never do, she wouldn't believe I haven't become
a prostitute. She simply doesn't know the facts of life, how can
I explain myself to her? I'm divorced, and I didn't want my
baby. That's all she knows. And besides, back there I *was* pret-

ty useless, which was as bad in Dad's book as my "sinful" behavior. It's really hopeless, Anne. I still don't think I can let another man get close to me. I told you about that, and you understand it, in fact I don't know how I would have gotten through last year without you to talk to. But the folks at home could never understand, I couldn't tell them, and they would think Joe was a bad man, and he wasn't, really.

Write soon and tell me how it is in the shipyard—do the men give you trouble? Does it really rain all the time in Oregon? Are you as sick of sandwiches as I am?

Yours,

Sue

January 1943

Dear Anne,

It's good to hear from you again, and I am thrilled by your news, although your new address is not so thrilling, Des Moines, *Iowa*, migosh, well, that is bound to change. A WAAC!* I expect you will do well, you couldn't have gotten picked for training otherwise. So congratulations.

But you are not the only woman with a new job. I am still in the same old plant all right, but they now call your friend a forelady (ugh) in the training room. It seems I have gotten a reputation for being listened to by the young kids who come on the job here, but actually I don't do much laying down the law. (I had enough of that as a kid to last a lifetime.) I don't need to. There is no lack of responsibility and determination in my girls. They really want to get the work done and understand the meaning of cooperation and being on a team. So many of them now have fellows in combat somewhere, and that gives them an extra reason if one is needed to get these machines in the sky. *I* think we are winning a war.

I know you won't have much time for letters, but try and keep in touch; I will be interested to hear about your career in the Air Force, ok?

Yours,

Sue

✳   ✳   ✳

*A member of the Women's Army Auxiliary Corps.

After their farm was sold in 1937, the Davises moved to Illinois to live with Caroline Davis's sister Gloria and her family. From her new home, Darlene corresponded regularly with her friend Ruth Ann Higbee.

September 1937 Here we are in my aunt's house. It is real nice, but I don't think we will stay very long. Not because they wouldn't have us, only my dad and uncle don't get along. Dad doesn't act like himself at all since we came here.

Bill has got work as a farm hand, but it is not regular. Mom wants to look for a job like Aunt Gloria has, but Dad won't hear of it. I think if he could find work, he might feel different, but then folks resent it when there is two jobs to a family. Aunt Gloria says she has to put up with a lot of smart remarks, but it doesn't bother her if she can go on taking care of her own. She is really a wonderful woman. She cooks for the hot lunch program at the consolidated school. I go to school with my cousins Myra and Ken. It is not a bad school, only a lot larger than I am used to and a lot more activities. There are clubs you have to be invited to, not honor societies, just for having fun. There are kids here who don't seem to know there has been a depression or a dust bowl.

December 1937 Well, I guess we didn't have a very merry Christmas. Two days before, Dad took off one afternoon in Uncle Fred's pickup and hasn't come home yet, that is a whole week now. We found the pickup parked by the bus depot, and we all think the same thing. I know it has happened like this to other families, but I never thought it would happen to mine. What made him do it? What will Mother do? If only Roy were here, because he was her favorite, I don't seem to be any help at all.

I am sorry for sending you news like this during the holidays.

March 1937 Mother is just a different woman since she got her job at the bakery. It is pretty hard work, but she says she was always used to that. She says what was driving her crazy, and Dad too, was not having any work to do. She says he was too ashamed to face us is why he left. I think she is too forgiving. I don't think much of that sort of pride if it makes you leave everybody depending on you.

Besides I don't see what is so great about working. Work isn't worth anything; only money is worth anything. If we were rich, I would sit around listening to the radio and reading magazines all day and not care a hoot. You tell me if you don't think so.

No, I don't like school here any better, it is not much fun if you don't belong to any crowd. Still I am better off than the bohunks who the other kids treat like dirt, and you should see how they try to dress and act like them anyway, it is really pathetic.

February 1939 I am sorry for your news about Etta Sue. She and I never got along, but I wouldn't wish her problems on anyone. I can just imagine how your mother and dad are keeping an eye on you now.

I have written you some about how kids in Chicago have different ideas about dating and all that than they do in Cooley. I was shocked at first when I saw how some of these girls would be out every night with a different boy and talking at school the next day about how far they let them go. A girl can play the field and get pretty friendly, and no one thinks anything of it. Nobody says they are loose, like they would back home. So maybe what is sad about Etta Sue is not that she was sneaking to see him like that but that she married him. Because that is a serious decision, and it sounds to me like she wasn't doing much serious thinking.

I agree with you 100 percent that your folks are wrong to make such a noise about his being a Jew. There are a lot of Jews at my school, and mostly you can't tell them from anyone else. Yes, I know you say Joe is a pain in the neck, but what I mean is that could just be Joe. Anyway, Etta Sue will have a hard enough time without your mother going on about that. Not that you could convince her. I still can't get Mother to read a letter from Roy, and of course she really wants to, it is so stupid.

September 1939 I am going to be real frank and say right out that I do not agree with you about what Etta Sue did, and then you can have the whole rest of this letter, I hope, to cool off in. If I had come to hate a child's father, I don't think I would be a good mother. And that would be the worst thing for the child. Anyway Etta Sue sounds in so bad a shape, she shouldn't have the responsibility. And maybe she knows that.

There, I have had my say. I guess it is hard on your mother and you, but your mother will probably end up being glad it turned out this way.

July 1941 Hold your breath and sit down. Your old friend has some news. Jerry has asked me to marry him, and I guess you know what I answered. You see he is accepted for OTS* and will be leaving for St. Louis in two weeks. It seems like a big rush to get everything ready but isn't really because we will have a tiny wedding, and I don't have to worry about setting up housekeeping because we will rent furnished when we get there.

Are you surprised? I have been wondering and wondering if he would come to this decision. For a while I thought he was going to be noble, because it is a difficult life being a pilot's wife and he

*Officer's Training School.

believes we will be in this war soon and I agree, so he has talked a lot
about how unfair it is to leave a wife under such circumstances. But
I guess we will cross that bridge when we come to it!

Mother is pleased because she likes Jerry a lot. She is working
hard at the restaurant now she is manager. She has opened a savings
account and says her boss, Mr. Dorsey, is considering letting her
into the business. *My* impression is that there will be *two* weddings
in the family this year.

I told Jerry I would like to go on doing my work for the Red
Cross at least part time after we were married, and he said we would
see. I don't intend to work if it will keep me away from him, so a
factory job is out of the question. But if I can get Red Cross work
that is, eight to five, I can do morning's work in the morning before I
leave and be home in plenty of time to fix myself up nice and get
dinner ready for him.

April 1942 Yes, I am staying in St. Louis. Now that Jerry is
overseas, I have to fill up a lot of empty time, and the idea of
changing cities and jobs just does not appeal to me. Mother wrote to
say that she understands how I feel. She is fine and happy married to
Mr. Dorsey and busy—certainly too busy to do any "baby-sitting" if
I should need it. Now, shhh. Don't say a word, I am not sure yet. But
I will be so glad if it is true! We could live quite easily on Jerry's pay,
and to tell you the truth, I would not mind staying home. The
happiest I have ever been was our first two months here when all I
did was fix our place up as nice as it could be and take care of Jerry.

Now I have a terrific idea. You are about to graduate, and I have
a little extra money now, and I would just love to make you a
present of a trip to St. Louis to visit me for a week or so this June.
Will your folks let you do it? You tell them I am dying of
lonesomeness, it won't be far off the mark.

September 1943 Can you stand another letter of me going on
and on about my wonder child? If I read everything you write to me
about Art, I guess so!

Josie is truly a sweetie pie, and I would be a perfectly happy
woman these days if only her daddy were here with us.

She is sitting up now and trying to feed herself with a spoon,
and she is such a happy healthy baby she almost never cries. She has
got enough hair on the top of her head now for me to put a bow in
and has ribbons in four colors. I have just bought myself a Brownie
camera so I can send Jerry pictures, and I will send you some. I
believe she is as cute as any baby in the magazines and cuter than
most!

No, I still haven't heard from Roy. He is in a POW camp all
right, they even know which one. But no one can tell if letters and

packages get to him. Still, I keep sending them. I don't know which is worse. *He* is not in danger every day of having his plane shot down, but if the stories are true, he could be tortured and starved to death. I look at Josie, and I just thank God she has no idea what terrible things are going on in the world, and I pray she will never know.

✳   ✳   ✳

After Roy Davis ran away from the CCC camp in 1936, his only contact with his family was an occasional letter home. Five years later, as he was waiting to be shipped to the Philippines, he wrote to Darlene to explain why he had left.

August 1941

Dear Darlene,

Here I am in San Francisco, waiting for transport. It is some city, but we are not getting to see much of it this trip.

No I don't mind telling you about all that now. I couldn't write home about it at the time, first, because I plain didn't have paper, let alone a stamp, and, second, because I figured it would just have worried Mother. Worrying about me now is different, if she does. A son in the army is not like a son on the bum.

When I ran off, it wasn't for any real good reason. They kept us busy in the fields all day and then in classes at night, where they shut up anybody pretty fast that wanted to discuss politics. And the discipline was strict, but after a couple of weeks of boot camp, that looks like a vacation, I can tell you. I think now I was just mad at everyone there because I was nearly the youngest kid at the camp and got picked on, when I had thought I was a big shot because I had left home. Live and learn.

I ran off expecting to find some swell job in Calif. and come back with a pile of dough. And I thought, well, at least they won't have me to feed at home. It wasn't as if I was any help any more after the government was paying Dad not to plant. We were just hanging around waiting for the axe to fall, which it did, and I still don't think I could have been any more help than Bill or Larry was. Back in Illinois, they made it seem worse for him probably. Well, this isn't what you asked to hear. I am talking to myself, but you know it isn't easy to stop wondering about a situation like that. He sure did his best for us. And I wish he would of known I think that. But we never could of said so then.

Well, ok then. I hopped a freight, and there the fun began. Probably you think most hobies are older guys, but not so. I landed in a car with eight kids in it, only one older than me, six guys and—this will really get you—two girls. They had mostly been together for about four or five months. Sometimes one or two would leave. I joined up sort of, and so did some others in Texas, till we were about twelve. I found out there are thousands of kids on the road like this. Mostly they live in gangs, sort of taking care of each other, working some or begging or stealing—in a small way—food, clothes. Mostly they left home because it broke up, like ours did, only sometimes, and specially the girls, because they were being given a rough time. Or just kicked out.

The reason for the begging and stealing is not that it is easier, because it ain't, it is because the relief stations keep you moving on "so you will go back home." What a hope. They give an old guy six meals and two nights' lodging, and a kid one meal, one bed, and the girls they just throw in jail.

So there are no end of tricks to get up to. For instance, if you ask for just a little you are likely to get more. Ask a woman for leftovers, she'll cook you a meal, where if you ask for a meal she will slam the door. And the best house to hit is one with laundry on the line, she'll be home, and a lot of men's clothes, she'll be a good cook. Some kids would fake being crippled or blind. And around a Catholic church is good, and you do better if you can stay clean. I learned more in two weeks with those kids than a year in school.

I expect you want to know how bad the girls are. Well they ain't angels. They say either they like the guy or they get cash. Just like that. But I didn't meet a one that didn't have a dream of getting to settle down and marry and have kids, and I never would of thought this before I knew them, but I think some of those girls would of made fine wives and mothers if they ever got the chance. They mostly fixed our food and kept our clothes mended, which is a real problem on the road.

I wasn't the only "deserter" from a "Roosevelt roost"* by a long shot. Nobody on the bum has a good word for any government program; most have been burned by them. They don't see stealing as wrong. They kind of admire the big-time gangsters. They think that most rich men are big-time gangsters who are

*"Roosevelt roost" was slang for a CCC camp.

getting away with it. Some of them call themselves Communists, I don't know about that, but I went along with the idea that we could of had a revolution if this war hadn't turned things around.

To make a long story short, I didn't make it to California that year but hung on with the kids, some of them had been on the road for three, four years. We traveled back up through Iowa and Minn. and back down to Chicago and around again, anywhere to keep moving, and all pretty much the same. The best times were in small towns. But after about four months I got sick of it all of a sudden, and also I got in a fight with the "leader." So I just stayed behind one morning and hopped a car by myself and made it out to the coast to Oregon on my own. I did picking and packing up and down the coast for a year before I signed up for the Army, and there's not much of a story in that time, just hard work and rough company. The company is as different here as you can imagine. I was pretty tough when I first enlisted. I listened to some of the guys complain about the food and wished they'd been some of the places I had. It was worst for me to get used to having every minute planned out, mess, cleanup, drill, mess, detail—you don't mind the discipline, that is necessary, but the routine was hard at first.

That's over now. Next time I write you will be from the Philippines. I wanted to get assigned to duty in Europe, I had an idea it would be great to be under Eisenhower's command, the boy from Abilene and the boy from Cooley. But it looks like it will be General Douglas MacArthur instead. It makes no difference really because the war will get there too, as the Japs favor Germany.

Keep the letters coming, kid. It is good to hear from you.

Your brother,

Roy

Roy Davis was taken prisoner by the Japanese army. For more than three years, Darlene heard nothing from her brother, although she continued to write to him faithfully. Finally, in October 1945, she received the following letter.

Dear Darlene,

Here I am again all right, the proverbial bad penny. I am looking forward to meeting my gorgeous niece I didn't even know

World War II veteran, 1945
Courtesy of Lauraine Mulally

about until your letter came after armistice. Yes, you are very lucky to have Jerry's baby. I am sure he was a fine man, and I know how hard a time you are having without him. But believe me, you can be grateful you had some time with him, as he said in the letter you copied for me; no man can be sorry he took his part in this conflict. He did what he had to do and he did it well, and you know that is a great cause for satisfaction. Little Josie will always be proud of her daddy.

I am in Yokohama on my way to San Francisco, and if you mean it, I will come straight on to St. Louis. I don't want you two to have to make that trip. I am sure I can get this okayed with the doctors. I am not supposed to work for a while yet, but I am in a whole lot better shape than most of these guys. And there is a lot of back pay, so don't you worry about that.

This is the first letter I can be sure you will get in more than three years. I got two from you myself and one package. The Japs were not very good about that. Most of what you will hear about POW conditions is true. (But this kid could take it.) The worst part is that they try to make you feel stupid and low; for instance, you had to salute every member of the Japa-

nese Army, no matter who you were. I have seen our own
Colonels slapped in the face by a little yellow sergeant. Our
guards were trained to despise us and shout at us, and they had
tricks for getting us to break rules or pretending we had or just
inventing new ones so they could "punish" us. Other cute
tricks were roll calls several times a night and not letting us
sit down or lie down all day and a guard who sat and counted
every time we used the latrine. If you fought back, you got
your whole group, sometimes twenty men, in trouble. If you
could not stay angry, this sort of thing would wear you down,
you had to stay angry. I don't regret what happened to me a
bit, for I believe we have to make sure people understand *it
must never happen again.*

Yes, you will get to do some feeding up. Like most of us, I
have been about forty pounds underweight for the last couple of
years. I have gained back ten here at the hospital, and I tell
you it is like heaven, the steaks and the ice cream and the Red
Cross nurses being angels. I sure do look forward to eating
home food again. I used to dream, in camp, of the chicken and
biscuits we used to have when we were real little. And the
cherry pies. That is an order!

During part of our second year, on Formosa, we were supposed to farm for ourselves, although the Japs always lied about
that and would harvest all or nearly all the crops at night or
when we were in the stockade. It took a while to get used to
some of their farming methods, too, for instance, human fertilizer. They have no shame about this. The women will squat
down and relieve themselves in public, and they don't care
about seeing or being seen naked, either.

We planted peanuts, of course we could eat some of those
while we went down the rows away from the guards, and sweet
potatoes. Mostly we lived on rice and broth, which sometimes
would have beans or a kind of cheese made from beans in it.
We would share the beans out so each of us got maybe four or
six. The Japs took most of the Red Cross Spam and tuna, and
then they would say Americans were disgusting savages because
we eat so much meat at home. I could tell you a few stories
about savages, but they would not be about Americans. In all
three years and four months, I never saw an American betray
another American, we kept each other going.

In Manchuria we had very little to eat, but neither did our
guards, because by that time we were winning and food was
scarce. We were not supposed to know what was going on in

the outside world, but word got through, mostly through the Chinese prisoners. That is how we heard of VE Day. Some of the senior officers knew Eisenhower personally. I was proud to be a Kansas boy that day!

I worked in an industrial plant in Mukden.* It was cold up there, but not so bad for those of us who could still work. A lot better than the mining camps. When the Russians joined, the Chinese said it was over, and they were right. I tell you that Red army looked good, but not as good as our own air force helicopters flying over. *That* is when we knew we were white men again.

It still feels like a miracle to sleep on a bed, but I am getting used to it. And to talk English all the time and to see how strong and clean everyone looks.

But you will see me the picture of health too in no time. I saw a lot of homeless kids on the way here. I think of Josie safe and happy and healthy with you, and it makes me feel real good.

Your brother,

Roy

✳   ✳   ✳

*Located in northeast China, Mukden is the chief city of Manchuria.

7 Socialization and Sex Roles

THE preceding chapter traced the lives of the Higbee and Davis families from the 1920s through the early 1940s. We saw each of the children begin an adventure shaped by unpredictable events: the crash of the stock market, the Dust Bowl, World War II. Their lives and personalities were the result of a continuous interaction between their biological selves and the cultural context. They were each born with specific talents, which would be molded by what was going on in the larger society. As the Higbee and Davis children grew up, they learned to be members of a larger social order. They discovered what it meant to be a man, a woman, a farmer, a factory worker, or a volunteer in the army. That is what socialization is about: learning to be a functioning member of society. What is it, though, that is learned? It is culture. Culture is not something fixed; rather, it is a creative response to the physical, social, or economic environment (Bauman, 1973). Culture is situational: it is specific to time and place. It is the result of historical events, which are also the product of human effort. Human beings are created by, and create, the larger social order.

People are never completely constrained by their culture. For example, because socialization is a learning process, not everyone learns the rules in precisely the same way. Unique life experiences cause people to interpret the world in different ways. Moreover, the cultural context changes; there are always new historical events to respond to. In addition, socialization does not have time limits; people are socialized and resocialized throughout their lives. In order to put these ideas in perspective, let us look at the changing cultural context of the Higbee and Davis children.

THE CULTURAL SETTING

America's response to the end of World War I was to retreat into its own affairs. People had grown tired of almost everything related to internationalism: the draft, rationing, the struggle over the League of Nations, and the "Red" scare that followed the Russian Revolution of 1917. President Warren G. Harding best described this mood when he called for a "return to normalcy." For many, normalcy meant getting back to the business of business, because they identified America with capitalism and laissez-faire individualism. If the government had any purpose at all, it was to facilitate growth and prosperity by creating a suitable climate for investment.

On a wave of sentiment directed against foreign involvement, labor, and liberals, Harding had been elected president in 1920. The progressive movement suffered, and both the farmers and the laborers lost their political champions. But even before Harding's election, the divisions among the progressives had become evident.

During the war the federal government had instituted progressive taxation and established labor boards. Such reforms were sufficient to satisfy those progressives who saw no further need for separate movements and drifted away from reform-minded political groups. Many of the progressives were also deeply divided over the legitimacy of the Russian Revolution and the Bolsheviks' activities. Organizers operating in the United States in the name of Communism and Bolshevism did little to allay the fears of conservatives and of those who thought political reform ought to be confined to such issues as higher wages or the establishment of government regulatory agencies. There were attempts in states such as Minnesota to form alliances between urban workers and farmers, but for the most part these efforts failed.

At the end of the war years farmers were hard pressed to make ends meet. Overall farm prices had increased steadily during the early part of the century, but in 1919, they took a sharp downturn and did not recover until World War II. Many farmers had expanded their operations, buying more land and equipment in anticipation of growth and prosperity, and so many were heavily in debt when farm prices began to slide. In states such as North Dakota, where the Farmers' Non-Partisan League controlled the state government, the farmers tried to organize cooperative elevators and credit associations. The farmers lobbied Congress for relief, with little success. During President Calvin Coolidge's administration, which began in 1924, the first arguments for "parity" were heard. Under the McNary-Haugen bill, the government would buy selected products from farmers and sell them at a lower price in the world market.

The farmers would be paid at a rate such that the prices they received for their crops would be directly related to the prices of goods they had bought before World War I. This meant, for example, that if in 1915 wheat sold for 50 cents a bushel and gas cost 25 cents a gallon, then if gas cost $1.00 in 1925, wheat would sell for $2.00. President Coolidge vetoed the proposed bill.

Working people did not fare much better than the farmers during these years. Returning veterans put tremendous pressure on the economy, which had gone into a downturn after the war. In 1919, there were strikes in all of the major industries (steel, coal, the railroads). The most violent confrontations occurred in the steel industry, where the average workweek was sixty-eight hours (Morison et al., 1980:420). In almost every case involving a struggle between labor and management, the federal and state governments supported management, thus allowing strike breakers to be used, condoning violence, and ignoring management efforts to destroy the unions. Business saw Calvin Coolidge as its man, and his victory in the 1924 presidential election was "a ratification of the policies of the 'New Era' in which a benevolent capitalism would develop the American economy in the national interest" (Morison et al., 1980:424).

The "New Era" was to be ushered in by great alliances of capitalists. Manufacturing firms, banks, and utilities were merging into a few giant corporations. "In 1933, some 594 corporations, each capitalized at $50 million or more, owned 53 percent of all corporate wealth in the country; the other 387,970 owned the remaining 47 percent" (Morison et al., 1980:427). There was nothing unusual in the idea of a close tie between government and business, with both working to provide prosperity for the nation. Indeed, real wealth did increase during Coolidge's administration, but there was also a continued concentration of wealth. As Table 7-1 indicates, in 1918 one percent of the population received almost 13 percent of the total income, and still did in 1937. There was a steady growth in income in the middle class, but not at the expense of those in top brackets.

Another major change taking place in the United States was the continued growth of the urban sector, often swelled by immigrants whose ways of life were unfamiliar to most of the population. By 1920, a total of 51.2 percent of the population lived in urban areas, ending almost three centuries of rural

Table 7-1

CONCENTRATION OF WEALTH IN THE UNITED STATES

Percentage of National Income Received by Selected
Portions of the Population, 1910–1937

Year	Top 1%	Top 10%	Lowest 10%
1937	12.8	34.4	1.0
1934	12.5	33.6	2.1
1929	14.6	39.9	1.8
1921	13.5	38.2	2.0
1918	12.7	34.5	2.4
1910	–	33.9	3.4

Sources: U.S. Department of Commerce, *Historical Statistics of the United States,
1789–1945* (Washington, D.C.: U.S. Government Printing Office, 1949), p. 15;
Historical Statistics of the United States, Colonial Times to 1957 (Washington, D.C.:
U.S. Government Printing Office, 1960), p. 167.

dominance, both in culture and number. Throughout the 1920s, rural America saw its values scorned by a new generation of writers, including Sinclair Lewis, who described the deadening provincialism of small-town life in *Main Street* (1920), and H. L. Mencken, who mocked the "boobacracy" of middle America. There seemed to be a revolution in morals in the cities, and in the minds of many, urbanism and corruption were synonymous. That is one reason why, when Etta Sue Higbee left Cooley for the West Coast, her mother assumed the worst. If Etta Sue was not at home, then she was no better than a common prostitute.

One issue that pointed up the difference in urban-rural values was the Eighteenth Amendment, which prohibited the sale of liquor. As we said in Chapter 5, the Prohibition movement was a symbolic crusade, a last-ditch attempt by rural America to impose its values on its urban brothers and sisters. Drinking symbolized urbanism, a lack of morality, and the potential for revolutionary change.

Religion became increasingly conservative, and Protestant fundamentalists tried to impose their will on the public through the school systems. Some of the southern states passed laws prohibiting the teaching of evolution, and in 1925 William Jennings Bryan, at one time a champion of Populism, was pitted against the famous criminal lawyer Clarence Darrow in the Scopes Trial, in which John Scopes was found guilty of teaching evolution. (There is a strong parallel here, of course, with recent conservative movements which would make America more "moral" through such means as teaching creationism instead of evolutionary theory.)

There was a growing tendency to use laws, the courts, the schools, the churches, and whatever else might be necessary in order to guarantee the survival of older American values. In order to keep America "pure," the Ku Klux Klan directed its hostility toward Catholics, blacks, and Jews. Racism was on the rise, and restrictive immigration laws were passed during the 1920s.

Etta Sue violated the values of her society when, in the words of her brother, she "married a college-boy Jew from Chicago." Her friends were also quick to note that she had married someone different. The point is not just that Etta Sue's friends were anti-Semitic but also that Jews were considered different, something that they didn't understand, something that they saw as urban and cosmopolitan.

Despite these movements and the clash between rural and urban values, there was an atmosphere of optimism and prosperity. Herbert Hoover took office and looked forward to a period of unequaled growth.

In a six-month period, between December 1928 and September 1929, the value of common stocks almost doubled. Bank borrowings increased, and billions of dollars of new securities were floated. Dreaming of instant riches, almost everyone who could borrow the money to do so invested in the stock market. The crash of October 1929, which ushered in the Great Depression, affected all social classes and groups in the United States. The Depression lasted for at least thirteen years, broke the grip of Republicans on the presidency—after Hoover there was not a Republican in the White House until Dwight D. Eisenhower was elected in 1952—and changed the function of government and its relationship with business.

The Depression hit the farmers particularly hard, as they were already suffering from the postwar drop in prices. Before the crash of 1929, market prices had started up, the value of land was increasing, and William Davis, the tenant farmer whom we read about in Chapter 6, had received $1.20 a bushel for wheat. The next year wheat dropped to 50 cents a bushel on the local market, and then plummeted to 25 cents in 1931. At the same time, many areas of the Plains were affected by a severe drought, which culminated in the Dust Bowl years of the middle 1930s: "Today we had the lamp lit from eight A.M. till noon and doors and windows shut tight. Caroline put damp sheets up over the windows, and still the dust in the air made breathing uncomfortable. Our preacher had to give up halfway through the service Sunday because he could not talk any more due to throat trouble from the dust."

Eventually, in an effort to maintain prices and to dramatize their plight, farmers began dumping eggs and milk and tried to stop the trucks of those taking their products to market. Davis noted that some people were burning their corn for fuel rather than trying to sell it. The farmers' economic problems were not linked to their ability to produce; rather, they had no buyers, at least not at prices that would permit the farmers to break even. Calves and pigs were destroyed along with crops, while at the same time the children of urban laborers suffered from malnutrition.

The response of farmers and laborers to the Depression caused a shift in values and changed people's beliefs regarding the meaning of work. The Higbee children had been raised by parents who stressed the need to work; yet now work seemed to have little reward. People lost their farms, their homes, and their jobs, and many came to depend on government support in order to survive. Accepting relief payments contradicted the values that had been established during the settling of the Great Plains. Ed Higbee, in reference to his father's desire to stay out of debt and to keep working, stated, "He really hated taking money for nothing and *not* farming land. He hated us getting helped to finish school by the NYA. 'No one can not pay their debts and remain a Christian,' he'd say about the idea of a moratorium, or cancellation."

By the early thirties, over two million people were simply wandering the roads, crossing and recrossing the country, looking for a job and a meal. Etta Sue told her Aunt Lydia that she had seen "real sad cases of men who want to work for anything, food or clothes. This week a man cleaned the chicken house and barn out, and Dad paid him with eggs and a dozen jars of our peaches." It wasn't only men who were on the road, wrote Roy Davis to his sister: "Probably you think most hobies are older guys, but not so. I landed in a car with eight kids in it, only one older than me, six guys and—this will really get you—two girls."

The Depression was blamed on Hoover, the Republicans, and business. According to Roy Davis, the people on the road thought that most rich men were "big-time gangsters" who were "getting away with it." Hoover believed that volunteerism, that is, the response of private charities and local governments, would be sufficient to solve the problems of the Depression. Of course, they were not. The low point in his administration came in June 1932 when a "bonus army," made up of veterans of World War I, marched on the Capitol Building to demand early payment of their bonuses. Hoover called out the national guard, which rode down on the men, and on their wives and children, who were camped out on the Anacostia flats, within sight of the Capitol Building. One political commentator declared: "Never before in this country has the government fallen to so low a place in popular estimation, or been so universally an object of contempt. Never before has the chief magistrate given his name so liberally to latrines and offal dumps, or had his face banished from the screen to avoid the hoots and jeers of children" (cited in Morison et al., 1980:480).

In 1932, Franklin Delano Roosevelt, promising a "New Deal" for "the forgotten man," was elected to the presidency by an overwhelming margin. But not everyone was confident about the election; on the eve of Roosevelt's inauguration, the banks closed their doors and the stock exchange suspended trading. The country waited for a response from the White House. It was not to be disappointed; Roosevelt argued for emergency measures and warned Congress that if it did not go along, he would use the broad powers of the executive branch.

It is important to emphasize that the New Deal was not a revolutionary change in American political values. The government had previously regulated business by means of tariffs and legislation aimed at preventing monopolies. Rather, Roosevelt had to focus all of these diverse functions of government toward one end: ending the Depression. But the economy did not immediately recover.

As noted previously, the farmers were squeezed by debt and a lack of markets. Foreclosures and bankruptcy auctions became so common that about one out of every ten farmers lost what he had worked for between 1927 and 1932. In the early thirties, almost half of all the farms sold were subject to foreclosure (U.S. Department of Commerce, 1949:95). Farmers often banded together in order to prevent such sales. For example, a group of farmers would appear at an auction of the kind described by Ruth Ann Higbee, purchase goods for a bid of 10 cents, and then return the items to the family. Outsiders were strongly discouraged from participating in these auctions: "The worst part [of the auction] was the city people, there were four of them, and they bought things and went off with them. That was real hateful."

Roosevelt introduced a variety of programs to alleviate the farmers' plight. The Agricultural Adjustment Act (AAA) resulted in higher prices for farm goods, partly by regularly paying farmers not to grow certain staples; it also eased farm credit. Because of the prolonged drought, farmers were compensated for taking soil-conserving measures. Millions of dollars were spent to help tenant farmers become owners, and the government subsidized coopera- tives, built camps for migratory workers, provided health care for farmers, and increased the amount of technical assistance available to help farmers make improvements. Many of the principles established during the New Deal are with us today—for example, subsidies for crops such as cotton, tobacco, and peanuts, as well as the idea that the government ought to help farmers achieve a living wage by acting as a buyer of last resort.

The young men in the Civilian Conservation Corps (CCC) camps built forest trails, campgrounds, and lodges, and fought forest fires and erected dams. The Public Works Administration (PWA) and the Works Progress Administration (WPA) gave the country new municipal and university buildings, hospitals, army posts, highways, parks, airports, and power plants. The Federal Arts Project under the WPA put artists to work producing plays; the Federal Writers' Project hired scores of writers to produce social histories and state guidebooks; and the Federal Music Project employed musicians and formed orchestras. Finally, the National Youth Administration (NYA) tackled the difficult problem of helping young men and women who were out of school and without a job.

Although the various projects of the New Deal helped a broad spectrum of Americans, Roosevelt was supported mainly by urban laborers and immigrants. Both the Davis and the Higbee children made disparaging remarks about the president's programs, despite having benefited from them. Even when people found it impossible to find work and even when they could not survive without the support of the federal government, they were still reluctant to accept that assistance.

Business people and established members of the community were often critical of the New Deal. They saw it as a form of socialism, a system in which one class was pitted against another. In addition, they denied that the Depression was the result of the structure of American society. For an example, let us turn to the town of Muncie, Indiana.

Helen and Robert Lynd first visited Muncie in the 1920s and in 1929 wrote the classic *Middletown*. In 1935 they returned to Muncie and eventually wrote *Middletown in Transition* (1937). Muncie's business leaders argued that the Depression was just an aberration, a one-time event that would cure itself. They tended to be laissez-faire economists who believed that "the best government was the one that governed least." Muncie's business leaders believed that "because of 'poor, weak human nature' there will always be some people too lazy to work, too shortsighted to plan." Welfare only "'undermines a man's character' for him to get what he doesn't earn" (Lynd and Lynd, 1937:415). On the subject of

Roosevelt, they were more vehement. There was "an insane man in the White House" being advised by mindless thinkers (499). A local banker asserted, "We businessmen here aren't just a bunch of tories, but we're scared to death that a lot of reckless political wild men will take everything away from us....We've no faith in Roosevelt....He isn't fit to be President and can't hold a candle to Hoover" (499). Many voters, of course, disagreed; in fact, a growing number of Americans were coming to see the present political and economic system as a problem in itself. There was a growing distrust of business and increasing disbelief in the inevitability of progress and prosperity.

The impact of the New Deal was significant and long lasting. It established the principle of government intervention in the economy. It oversaw a massive growth in government employment, as well as an increase in government agencies responsible for the health and welfare of all citizens. Yet, although the New Deal did stabilize the economy, it did not end the Great Depression, which continued until the United States entered World War II.

Promising jobs, full employment, and the destruction of Germany's enemies, Adolf Hitler became chancellor of Germany in 1933 and its chief of state, *Führer*, in 1934. Although many writers and politicians warned that Hitler and his National Socialism (Nazism) meant war, most Americans wanted to ignore them. The isolationism that had developed as a result of World War I still prevailed. Many feared that America's involvement in the war would be a victory for so-called urbanism, and they were correct: World War II forever changed American politics and consolidated the triumph of urban over rural values.

The United States was slow to become involved in the war, though, for Roosevelt had extreme difficulty persuading Congress to aid the Allies. In 1939, Hitler moved into Czechoslovakia and by May 1940 occupied all of Western Europe except Great Britain, which was subjected to merciless bombing raids. But the United States still did not enter the war, although it did vote credits for aid and arms for the Allied forces.

Two of America's most influential journalists, William Allen White of Emporia, Kansas, and Walter Lippman, who wrote a nationally syndicated column, argued for the country's involvement in the war. White formed the Committee to Defend America by Aiding the Allies, but the "opposition organization, the America First Committee, top-billing Charles Lindbergh, paraded, picketed, protested, and preached an amalgam of isolationism and pacifism. Most Americans wanted both to halt Hitler and to stay out of war, but in pursuing the first aim it was not clear that they could fill the second" (Morison et al., 1980:543).

In 1940 Roosevelt was elected to an unprecedented fourth term, although his share of the popular vote fell to 55 percent. The election clearly revealed what until that time had only been a trend: a solid, urban, working-class vote for the Democrats and a middle- and upper-class vote for the Republicans. Although Roosevelt held an overwhelming electoral advantage, it did not help him to convince Congress to join in the war effort. Debates over whether to enter the war on the side of the Allies ended, however, when Japanese fighter planes attacked the American naval base at Pearl Harbor on the morning of December 7, 1941. The next day, Congress declared war with Japan, and on December 11, 1941, Germany and Italy declared war on the United States.

As we stated in Chapter 5, the impact of World War II on the United States cannot be underestimated. To the American farmers, it meant a tripling of cash income between 1940 and 1945; moreover, the wages of workers in manufacturing firms more than tripled (U.S. Department of Commerce, 1960:283). The war also brought about a massive shift in population, as people moved to work in plants outside their hometowns. The port cities of both the East and West coasts saw a rapid rise in population that was not reversed after the war. Like Etta Sue Higbee, who left home and went to work in an aircraft assembly plant, others left to work in shipyards, munitions factories, and plants manufacturing tanks, personnel carriers, and rifles.

The war also reinforced racism. Japanese Americans were sent to "relocation" camps. American soldiers were shown training films that denigrated the Japanese character. *Life* magazine (1941) ran an illustrated article, "How to Tell Japs from Chinese," designed to help people distinguish between our Chinese friends, fighting the invading Imperial army, and the Japanese. Schoolchildren were given pencils emblazoned with the slogan "Full of Lead to Shoot a Jap in the Head."

By the end of World War II, the Higbee and Davis children had been exposed to new values, which emphasized urbanism and cosmopolitanism and challenged those of the small town and rural America. In fact, the country had become urban during this period and had elected a president, senators, and congressional representatives who represented those values. The mass media had become a reality. There were nationally syndicated radio shows, and the movie theaters in every small town showed films depicting new ways of life and new moral standards. In 1945, 26 million people owned automobiles, once the prized possessions of only a few. Mobility was the new way of life. The values of work, industry, and thrift, which the Higbee and Davis children's parents had accepted without question, had been put to a hard test by the experiences of the Great Depression. The values of a Puritan sexual morality and a settled, homogeneous community life had been tested by the war and its aftermath.

As noted earlier, who and what people are is the result of socialization, the interaction between biological being and social and historical context. People must learn culture and become socialized in order to become fully functioning human beings. How were the Higbee and Davis children socialized between 1920 and 1945?

THEORIES OF SOCIALIZATION

Science fiction stories about cloning present an incorrect view of how people are "produced." Theoretically, cloning could produce an exact physical replica of Hitler's body. However, that is all one would have: a physical replica. For, in order for two human beings to be exactly alike, they would have to have identical experiences, which is impossible.

The way in which we develop as separate and unique members of our society is complicated, as indicated by the number of theories that trace this process. The four theories that we will discuss here, however, recognize that the self or personality that ultimately develops is the result of actual historical conditions.

Theories of the Self

Charles Horton Cooley   Charles Horton Cooley's (1902) theory of the *looking-glass self* is an early and fairly simple interpretation of how the self develops. Cooley saw the self as a social product, the result of interactions between the self and others. The looking-glass self is our image of others' responses to us; for example, if people are continually told that they are intelligent, attractive, and energetic, they will believe that they are. But if they are told they are useless, unintelligent, and lazy, they may come to act that way, whatever their natural endowments might be. Generally, people seek out those who reinforce their positive self-images and avoid those who do not. The theory of the looking-glass self does not imply that the self or personality that develops is unrelated to one's corporeal being; it simply recognizes that how we see ourselves is the result of constant interaction with others.

Consider Etta Sue Higbee. Etta Sue was not defined as a good student and, from what we can infer, was not particularly appreciated by her family. She was "different." She then embarked on a series of actions that her family disapproved: "she married a college-boy Jew," left her baby with her mother, moved away from her hometown, got a divorce, and went to work. Etta Sue's letters indicate that she was struggling with her family's negative evaluation of her and found it difficult to develop a positive self-image. Even though she knew that her behavior was acceptable to the people she was working with, she also knew that her mother disapproved of her. Etta Sue's self-image reflected this interplay between herself, her family, and the larger world.

Parents often say to their children, "You are being naughty; you are misbehaving; your behavior is unacceptable." The children, because of a combination of guilt and shame, often try to modify their behavior so that it conforms to adult expectations. Children see themselves as others see them and will conform to win the others' approval. These "others" play a major role in the theories of George Herbert Mead (1934).

George Herbert Mead   George Herbert Mead's work was a direct extension of Cooley's. Mead recognized that much of the interaction between people is symbolic, not physical. That is, they use symbols, signs, gestures, and, above all, language. Language is social; it is learned; through it, children learn the accepted rules of society and come to respond to the *generalized other*. The generalized other is not a specific individual but refers to the generalized sentiments, wishes, desires, and expectations for role behavior that are held by the larger society. These expectations might, of course, be embodied in one person such as a parent who draws on them in socializing the child. The parents, or the *particular other* as Mead calls them, are the primary influence in their children's lives. Children are socialized by learning to predict what others will expect of them—by *role taking* or *role playing*. Of course, children play roles by acting like mothers or fathers or fire fighters or doctors.

In Mead's framework, unlike Cooley's, the self is more than the others' attitudes. The self has two components: the *I* and the *Me*. To Mead, the *I* represented the spontaneous and free element of the individual personality. Pure *I* would theoretically be a self that acted only on impulse without social direction or without consideration of the generalized other. The *Me* is the conforming part of the self and represents society's demands. The balance between the *I* and the *Me* varies with the social situation. For example, in playing a game with one's close friends, the *I* may dominate, but in appearing for a job interview, the *Me* may be more sensitive. An individual's personality is the balance between the *I* and the *Me*, which changes over time. Mead saw personality as constantly changing; as people mature, they become more capable of playing roles and more sensitive to the expectations of others.

People sometimes have different expectations. Consider the auction described by Ruth Ann Higbee. The farmers went to the auction intending to buy the goods being sold for a fixed price of 10 cents and to return them. But the people from the city came to buy the goods cheaply and to take them home. Sometimes there was violence at these auctions when the outsiders refused to "play" by the established rules. In another example, Etta Sue Higbee made a fool of herself, according to Ruth Ann, because she married Joe Goldberg. "I suppose she thinks it's romantic. How she could. But then Etta Sue never has gotten along with the boys in school here; she's always held herself special, so they call her conceited behind her back....Well, *I* don't mind being friendly with nearly everyone....*I* don't think I'm better than everyone else....Joe Goldberg is just as bad as she is, he thinks he's so wonderful....[A] big show-off is a big show-off, and that man with his six-cylinder Chevrolet and his lectures and long words and sophisticated ways certainly is." What Ruth Ann was complaining about, among other things, was her sister's violation of expected *role behavior*. The expectations of Etta Sue's schoolmates were clearly not sufficient to cause her to conform, but she was aware that she stood outside the group and that the generalized other disapproved of her. She knew what the expectations for her behavior were, but she chose to ignore them, although she was aware of the social costs. Mead did not suggest that a person's self was the result of dominance by the generalized other but believed that who one is is a result of the interchange between the *I* and the *Me*.

Another way of interpreting what happened to Etta Sue is by means of *labeling theory*, in which human behavior is considered deviant "*to the extent that* it comes to be viewed as involving *a personally discreditable* departure from a group's normative expectations, *and it elicits* interpersonal or collective reactions that serve to 'isolate,' 'treat,' 'correct,' or 'punish' *individuals* engaged in such behavior" (Schur, 1971:21, emphasis in original). When using labeling theory, it is important to remember that some people (for example, parents or psychiatrists) have far more power to assign a label and make it stick than others do (see Scheff, 1968:3–17).

Psychoanalytic Theories

Sigmund Freud   Sigmund Freud's theories of personality development are somewhat similar to Mead's in that they both view the personality as being composed of major systems. To Mead, the system is the *I* and the *Me*; whereas to Freud, the system is the *id*, *ego*, and *superego*. (For a more complete discussion of Freud's theory of personality, see Hall and Lindzey, 1957.) The id is composed of one's inherited capacities and abilities as well as bodily drives, instincts, and needs. According to Freud, although there is always a tension between the organism and its environment, the id cannot tolerate tension and so operates at the most basic level to maximize pleasure and minimize pain. Freud called this the *pleasure principle.*

The needs of the organism, however, require mediation with the real world, which is the function of the ego. Whereas the id knows only the internal world of the mind whose reality is subjective, the ego distinguishes between what is in the mind and what is in the world. It operates on the basis of the *reality principle.* The ego, then, is like a scout for the body, in charge of all its functions. It says to the body, "this is food, this is not; this is an acceptable form of release, this is not." The ego becomes the body's decision maker, mediating the demands of the id, the real world, and, finally, the superego.

Freud's superego is much like Mead's generalized other, representing the moral demands and expectations of the larger society. But unlike the generalized other, which stands outside the individual, the superego is an integral part of the personality. "The superego is the moral arm of personality; it represents the ideal rather than the real and it strives for perfection rather than pleasure" (Hall and Lindzey, 1957:35).

Freud believed that a given personality developed in response to four major sources of tension: (1) the growth process, (2) frustrations, (3) conflicts, and (4) threats, whether real or imaginary. Furthermore, he believed that one's basic personality, or self, was formed by the end of the fifth year. At first, the infant is preoccupied with obtaining food and is not involved with the family as a whole, but only with the mother. In the words of Mead and Cooley, the child has no generalized others, no societal mirror in which its personality is reflected. The child-mother bond does not provide for this separation.

With toilet training, socialization—as we defined it—begins in earnest, and children begin to internalize different roles. They distinguish between themselves and those who make regulatory demands, such as going to the toilet in a proper place and time. During this stage, children are slowly integrated into the larger social world, and the mother-child bond begins to loosen.

Between the third and fifth years, children deal with their sexual and aggressive feelings. The *Oedipus complex* makes its appearance in this stage. Freud believed that the Oedipus complex represented the son's wanting to possess his mother and resenting his father because he stood in the way. In the Electra complex, the daughter wants to possess her father and displace her mother in his affections. These feelings, Freud argued, are present throughout life, and so children's rebellious feelings for their parents alternate with love for them, and these feelings are reflected in their adult lives in their relationships with authority figures, who might not love them enough or who might hurt them by rejecting them. Despite later criticisms of Freud's theories, early patterns of socialization do, as he claimed, have long-lasting consequences.

More recent students have found that gender identity is established far earlier than Freud supposed. It seems to be assigned (it is not the biological fact but the assignment that matters) by the age of three. All infants identify first with their mother. For girls, this first identification need never be shifted. Of course, this greater security of gender identity creates its own problems for women, who may not have the sort of identity crises experienced by males as they become adolescents and then young adults. In fact, women's identity crises may be postponed until middle age, after they have fulfilled the assigned role to marry and have children. Or they may, as adolescents, consciously use their mothers as negative role models, in greater or lesser conflict with their assigned gender. (Freud's emphasis on biological factors undoubtedly led him to give too little weight to the social consequences of gender identity. If his ideas are seen as metaphors for the very real fact of male power in society, they are more useful to the student of society. For a discussion of these issues see Chodorow [1978], Person [1974], Schafer [1974], and Stoller [1968].)

Children form emotional bonds with others only insofar as they give pleasure. These bonds are narcissistic. When mature love is directed toward others, "sexual attraction, socialization, group activities, vocational planning, and preparations for marrying and raising a family begin to manifest themselves" (Hall and Lindzey, 1957:55). Some people remain arrested in the narcissistic phase.

Christopher Lasch (1979) suggested that because current permissive child-rearing patterns do not allow children to rebel against their parents and form autonomous personalities, our entire society can be labeled narcissistic.

Erik H. Erikson   Like Freud, Erik Erikson sees life as fraught with crises, and each stage of the development as relating to a particular crisis. His first five stages constitute childhood, and the later three phases, adulthood. To Erikson, an "individual never *has* a personality, he always is redeveloping his personality" (Maier, 1965:28). Individuals progress from one stage to the next with an occasional lapse back into a previous phase of development.

In the first phase, children acquire a sense of trust. (In each of Erikson's eight phases, there is a potential dichotomy unique to that stage. For instance, in the first phase, this dichotomy is between trust and mistrust. In the second phase, it is between autonomy and shame; in the third between initiative and guilt; and so on to the eighth phase, in which it is between integrity and disgust or despair.) In the second phase, children establish a sense of autonomy and become aware of themselves as separate beings. They substitute regulation of self for regulation by others. During this stage of development, children must master the difficult task of being able to control themselves without a loss of esteem. They must challenge parental authority in order to learn autonomy. In the third stage, children develop a sense of initiative and overcome their sense of guilt. During this phase, children actively fantasize about the type of person they wish to become and experiment with roles. Children's ability to play, indeed their need to play, facilitates their development of initiative. The tension in this phase arises from children's desire to experiment with the guilt from feeling that they have gone too far, or not far enough, to realize their potential.

Erikson "desexualizes" the tension between a son and his mother and a daughter and her father. When a mother accepts and encourages her son's attachment to her, it affirms his maleness as a social role. At the same time, the larger society encourages an identification between the boy and his father. The situation differs for the girl, who desires the most trusted man in her environment— her father. (Later, she will transfer this love to another man.) Though she is attached to her father, her identification may continue to be with her mother, the female role model, because her mother "stands for all that is embodied in her own strivings for femaleness" (Maier, 1965:47). In Erikson's model, the parent of the same sex serves as the superego—the ideal against which the individual's behavior is judged. Sex-role identification takes place during this phase, when the child, in order to escape being a child, says, "I want to be more like this person *in order to be autonomous.*"

Although Erikson failed to mention it, this is also a stage in which most girls must establish some identification with their father or father figure if they are to live successfully in the world outside the family. For boys, this break with the private family world is facilitated by their identification with the father's (usual) separation from it by means of an outside job. It is more difficult for girls to separate from a nonworking mother's confinement to that private world.

In the fourth phase, children acquire a sense of industry and shed their sense of inferiority by determining to master whatever they are doing. As adolescents in the fifth stage, they establish an identity separate from that provided by the family and become committed to a specific sexual and occupational identity. By the time they reach the sixth phase, in which they achieve intimacy, they are young adults seeking full participation in society. In fact, establishing an intimate relationship with another person is one of the keys to further growth and development. In the seventh phase, people acquire a sense of generativity, the feeling that they are growing and changing and being productive, which is often characteristic of the middle years. Finally, in the eighth phase, people develop a sense of integrity and overcome despair by understanding that they are part of the human life-cycle.

Having briefly examined Freud's and Erikson's models of personality, let us see how they might help us understand the personality development of the Higbee and Davis children. We do not, or course, have the children's reports of how they felt or what they were doing in the earliest stages of their development, nor do we have their parents' accounts of how they raised the children. But we do have statements such as Ed Higbee's: "See, our parents always tried their best to make us kids feel safe." It is likely that this attempt to make their children feel safe and trust in their environment was characteristic of both their infancy and their childhood. Parents often make considerable sacrifices to shelter their children from the harsh physical and psychic environments. For instance, even during the height of the Great Depression, many parents tried to put the best face on things by either not telling their children about the family's pressing debts or by reassuring them that things were going to get better. In infancy, then, the children learned to trust their parents and began the explorations that would take them into early childhood, which is the second phase of Erikson's model.

Children must learn to control their bodily functions and respond to the needs and demands of others. Ruth Ann Higbee, talking about Jimmy, the child left by her sister, stated, "So it was me that got him on a schedule and me that is firm about bedtime and thumb-sucking and eating his meals." It is through such activities that children develop a sense of autonomy and learn to challenge their environment. This continues until the early kindergarten years. The development of autonomy is encouraged if the children also are given activities that they can control. For example, many farm children are given simple tasks, and they begin to imitate their parents. They might help carry wood, weed the garden, pick berries, pick up eggs from the hen house, or fill the mangers with hay. Normally, parents respond to such activities with approval, which helps the children become independent.

In the third stage, which Erikson sometimes called the play stage, the children's dream and play world dominates. In the play stage, children experiment with new roles, both real and imagined. Sometimes these roles reflect the current prejudices. Etta Sue's son, Jimmy, talked about wanting to be a soldier "like Ed and General Eisenhower" and to "kill the nasty Japs."

In both Erikson's and Freud's models, sex-role identification takes place in the third stage. Identification with the same-sex parent is made easier if the parent of the opposite sex supports the same-sex identification. For instance, Grandmother Higbee, who was raising Jimmy, supported his male behavior. Ruth Ann said, "Mother often says how much easier girls are but thinks he's pretty cute when he's being 'all boy.'" The implication is also that girls must behave in a particular way—to be easier or less aggressive—which is supported by their parents. Identifying with the same-sex parent, though, does not mean that children will necessarily grow up to be like them. For example, Etta Sue did not want to be like her mother. As her brother said, "My sister hated the farm, hated Cooley, hated Kansas. Hated Mother and Dad, is what it came down to, especially Mother, for the very life they lived. She said there was never a day her last two years of high school she wasn't ashamed to look them in the face, they were so ignorant and stubborn. She called Dad a fool for believing things would ever get better for us, and Mother a worse one for leading the life of a slave for him for nothing."

The key to Etta Sue's rejection of both her parents may lie in the patterns of development characteristic of Erikson's fourth and fifth stages. In the fourth stage, when children have begun school, they continue to drive toward autonomy, initiative, and industry, which are represented by their mastery of specific tasks. For Ed Higbee, this came when his father declared, "Ed is the best worker I've got, he's worth two of any of the men I hire." As Ed noted, "Now that made me feel *good*." Etta Sue, on the other hand, indicated in her letters to her Aunt Lydia that she was not particularly fond of school and not doing well. "You ask if I am doing better in school now [that] I go to the junior high. I guess not. I try, Aunt Lyddy, but English and Social Studies are so boring and I am just no good at Mathematics at all. The only thing I hate worse is Home Economics." In order to master their environment, children must feel useful, not inferior. When Etta Sue wrote to her friend Anne Kettle, explaining her new life and why she left home, she stated, "And besides, back there I *was* pretty useless, which was as bad in Dad's book as my 'sinful' behavior." Etta Sue's parents equated being a good man or woman with working, paying one's debts, and doing one's share in the world, yet the Depression made that impossible for some people. Etta Sue saw her own and her friends' parents as unable to live the kind of lives they had regarded as moral and sometimes unable to deal with the contradiction. One such person, William Davis, simply left home.

Erikson's and Freud's theories imply that for development to proceed normally, children must be in a nonthreatening environment. That does not mean one without conflicts or firm or even autocratic methods of child rearing, but one that assures some security. The Great Depression removed that security and introduced debt, loss of family and friends, and, for some people, loss of home. But psychoanalytic theories often do not adequately incorporate the real world, insofar as they assume that development proceeds in a uniform fashion. To reiterate, socialization is learning the rules—the culture—of a specific social order. But the rules may be in flux.

When the stock market crashed in October 1929, the Higbee children were approximatly eleven, nine, and five years old, and the Davis children were nine and seven years old. They grew up, as Ed Higbee said, constantly hearing about disaster: "So I'd been hearing 'bank, interest, credit, next year, maybe next year' since before I could talk myself." The opportunities for work, for school, and for becoming an autonomous person were limited. Many children blamed their elders for the Depression, and many adults blamed the financiers, the politicians, and big business. An atmosphere of distrust was generated. Then, World War II pulled young people away from their homes and neighborhoods. Some, of course, seized the opportunity because it provided a job or because it meant that they could demonstrate their ability to act as functioning adults, which is how Etta Sue described her work in the aircraft factory.

For those who were adolescents during the Depression, it was not easy to establish a separate identity and make a commitment to specific sexual and occupational identities. Maxine Davis, in *The Lost Generation* (1936), referred to the adolescents of this period as betrayed and bewildered. They had been brought up to believe in prosperity, education, and hard work:

About three million of our young people who are out of school today have no work, through no fault of their own. Many others are engaged in slim part-time jobs so trifling in the time they fill and the money they produce as to have little or no meaning to the young workmen. Bleakly our youth has been marking time while the clock ticks away its bright years, the good years of plowing and sowing and sweating. (Davis, 1936:4)

Davis's solution, and that of many others, was to send American adolescents back to school. The state, which Davis referred to as "The Wise Father" in one chapter title, was to provide "service" stations for youth (CCC camps, schools). It was to provide recreational facilities, so that they would not spend their time hanging out on street corners, and juvenile courts, which would apply laws different from those for adults. The idea that the state should guarantee children's welfare and assume an important role in their socialization grew during the Depression and after.

Adolescence, as Coleman pointed out, was discovered in the early twentieth century. It was no longer seen as a dangerous period in which impulses needed to be controlled but as a period of "development which had to be allowed full scope to play itself out" (1974:23). The crusade against child labor and the drive for compulsory education began to level out the age differences in schools, too. During the late 1800s, it was not unusual for one grade to have an age difference of five or more years between the youngest and the oldest pupil. Children entered and left schools at their convenience or that of their parents. The 1920s changed that pattern, for by then school was seen as economically valuable; a diploma had market value: "The percentage of the population 17 years old to graduate from high school rose from 6.4% in 1900 to 50.8% in 1940..." (Coleman, 1974:26). The Depression affected the pattern of enrollment because more and more students stayed in school when they could not find jobs.

The response to the problems of youth and education during the Depression was to make education more useful. Lynd and Lynd (1937) cited a 1933 report issued by the Department of Educational Research in Muncie, Illinois, that noted:

> [Our philosophy]...advocates that the aim of education
> should be to enable every child to become a useful citizen, to
> develop his individual powers to the fullest extent of which he
> is capable, while at the same time engaged in useful and
> lifelike activities....We believe in the doctrine of equal
> educational opportunity for every child to develop according to
> his abilities, interests, and aptitudes. (Lynd and Lynd,
> 1937:221)

The message was that education was good and that adolescents
belonged in school. The mass media, educators, and reformers all
echoed this message:

> Education is the cantrap that opens the gates to the Promised
> Land. This generation feels sure of that. Though they see their
> brothers and sisters, their cousins and their friends, frame their
> sheepskins, and then apply their learning to the complicated
> business of mixing "lemon cokes"—selling shoes—taking
> movie tickets, increasing numbers of boys and girls want more
> and more education; their confidence in the magic of book-
> learning is undaunted. It's the answer to everything. (Davis,
> 1936:114)

From then on, an entire category of individuals—school-aged
children—would have no meaningful economic function. The ways
in which children could develop a sense of initiative and identity
shifted away from the family to the school and peers. The children
of the pioneers had demonstrated industry on a daily basis by
performing tasks that contributed to the economic welfare of the
entire family. They could identify with their parents and against
their control; that is, they could become their parents' peers in the
world of work—indeed, their survival on the frontier depended on
it. But children of the Depression often did not have this option, and
so their identities came to be established in peer groups. As
adolescence became a separate status, affirming one's identity
meant becoming like other adolescents, rebelling against parental
norms and authority.

Etta Sue "snuck and saw a motion picture in Cooley on
Saturday." She told her friend Wilma, "Of course I have to go to the
Youth Fellowship meetings or Mother will have a cat, but the 4-H
projects are like Home Economics class all over again, and you
know me...I don't get all dreamy eyed over such things. I *really*
can't see the point of prize biscuits." Etta Sue's identity, her sense of

self-worth, was established by reacting against her parents and the values of many of those around her. When she reached the sixth stage, that of young adult, Etta Sue tried, and failed, to develop further by establishing an intimate relationship with Joe Goldberg.

Her failure in marriage also made it difficult for her to become intimate with another man, at least by her own account: "It's really hopeless, Anne. I still don't think I can let another man get close to me." Etta Sue's life experiences were such that she had difficulty trusting other people, which meant, according to Erikson and Freud, that her development was arrested, that is, fixed at one level. Instead of developing intimacy in the sixth stage, she became isolated; in the seventh, self-absorbed. In short, development through the life-cycle does not necessarily mean "full" development.

The feeling of generativity, which should come in the seventh stage, is the notion that one is growing and changing and making in one's own terms a meaningful contribution to the social world. But in the Depression, many adults were unable to reach this stage. Those who lost their farms—their life's work—and left home, like William Davis, did not develop a sense of generativity, but instead a feeling of self-absorption and failure. Finally, during the eighth stage, instead of integrity, they often generated despair and disgust. Etta Sue's mother complained about her children's leaving her and worried about her grandchild's doing the same thing, because her value system defined her worth in terms of being a good wife and mother. Her son left home, and her daughter married someone she did not approve of, left her baby with her, and went off to work on the west coast. So by her own standards, she felt she had failed, and so she probably did not develop what Erikson called integrity.

Socialization is a lifelong process. Personality is not fixed but changes in response to the prevailing circumstances. Sociologists speak of *resocialization* to describe those extreme forms of socialization in which a person must abandon one role and take up another. For example, brainwashing is an extreme form of resocialization. The ease or extent of resocialization depends on such factors as (1) the individual's control of the situation, (2) the individual's ability to suppress previous statuses, (3) the individual's denial of the worth of his or her old self, (4) the degree of group pressures and pressures from significant others, and (5) the degree of individual participation in resocialization (Broom and Selznick, 1963:119–123). If the individual is in a prison camp, his or her control by others is almost total. Previous statuses can be suppressed by simply denying them. Roy Davis, in describing his prison camp experiences to his sister Darlene, noted, "You had to salute every member of the

Japanese army, no matter who you were. I have seen our own colonels slapped in the face by a little yellow sergeant." In short, all prisoners were treated alike, which meant they could not reaffirm a previous identity. This is also a means of denying the worth of the old self. Sometimes group pressure was used to bring into line the person who would not conform, by punishing everyone. "Other cute tricks were roll calls several times a night and not letting us sit down or lie down all day and a guard who sat and counted every time we used the latrine. If you fought back, you got your whole group, sometimes 20 men, in trouble." Finally, if the individual gives up, his or her resocialization becomes easier. Roy pointed out that "if you could not stay angry, this sort of thing would wear you down, you had to stay angry." In short, one had to work actively against being resocialized. Our social selves, then, are plastic and subject to change, although under normal circumstances people's response to life crises does not bring about a radical alteration of their personality.

We have not yet explored what kind of social self people are likely to develop but have simply determined that change does occur in response to the material conditions of one's culture. In the next section, we will consider social learning theories.

SOCIAL LEARNING THEORY AND SEX-ROLE SOCIALIZATION

Behaviorism

Instead of emphasizing internal states, the behavioral school argues that one should look at observable traits and their consequences: "Behaviorists believe that all learning, including how we learn to be masculine or feminine, can be explained with the same basic rules" (Tavris and Offir, 1977:164). This school assumes that all behavior is controlled by its consequences. For instance, if a pigeon is hungry, pecks a spot, and is rewarded with a pellet of food, it is likely to peck the spot again. If people burn their hands when they put them on a hot burner, they are not likely to touch a hot burner again. Similarly, if a boy is told, with a smile and a nod of encouragement from his mother, that he is acting just like his daddy, then he is likely to go on behaving that way. But if he puts on a dress and lipstick and his father makes cruel jokes about it, he is not likely to do it again. If a little girl is given a doll, a buggy, and a tea set for Christmas, accompanied by smiles and compliments, she will probably enjoy playing with them. From this perspective, the role of the actor in the learning process is passive (Frieze et al., 1978:117), for he or she is simply responding to external reinforcements and/or expected reinforcements. One might decide to avoid the pain of parental ridicule or to win parental approval by acting in a specific way. The little boy behaves like his daddy in anticipation of a reward from either parent, and the little girl behaves like her mommy with the same expectations. But as many critics have pointed out, there are limitations to this approach. For example, children appear to engage in a great deal of spontaneous imitative behavior that is not immediately reinforced or punished. Finally, if one follows this theory to its logical conclusion, that is, that all learned behavior is the result of being rewarded or punished, then one would have to conclude that "parents would be kept busy twenty-four hours a day rewarding and punishing, rewarding and punishing" (Tavris and Offir, 1977:165). Approaches that take into account both social context and biology seem more appropriate.

Cognitive Development Theories

Jean Piaget   Piaget assumed that all social realities, whether values or actual cognitive processes, are human creations (Maier, 1965:90). Our mental images of ourselves are the result of our interactions with the social world. Once these images are formed, they shape future interactions. According to Piaget, all children in all societies go through a set of basic phases, or stages, in their cognitive development, although the content of each differs from one society to another (Frieze et al., 1978:114).

The first phase, the *sensorimotor*, starts at birth and ends at age two. It is called sensorimotor because children respond to their environment physically. During the latter part of this phase, children come to recognize that there are external objects with their own meanings (Piaget, 1950).

The second phase, which runs from about age two to age seven, is the *preoperational* phase. (This phase of cognitive thought represents a collapse of the preconceptual and the intuitive thought phases.) The phase is called preoperational because children are not yet capable of mature intellectual thought. Rather, their thinking is egocentric (self-centered) and perception bound, which means that they cannot understand such concepts as quantity, cause, or even difference. A child may kick a table or chair in order to "hurt" it, because it caused pain when the child bumped into it. Although the children's increasing command of language allows them to deal with concrete objects and to externalize, they are still not able to assume the role of the other. A child may be coached to respond correctly to the question "Who is mommy's little boy?" but when asked if he is Mrs. Jones's son, he probably will not be able to answer correctly.

When the third phase, the *concrete operational*—from about age seven to age twelve—is completed, children are able to apply concepts such as cause and quantity. Their response to the world is still concrete, however, and so they interpret abstract concepts such as God, truth, justice, liberty, and freedom by means of their immediate experiences. For example, they usually define freedom in terms of being able to do "whatever they want" all day long.

In the *formal operational stage,* which begins in adolescence, young people develop full use of their cognitive power, in particular, the ability to take the role of the other. The rules of society are internalized and are generally unquestioned. As they relate to moral development, these rules move from a stage of simple injunction for behavior that may or may not be observed, to a stage at which people come to recognize that rules are necessary for the operation of the social order and ought to be followed by mutual consent (Piaget, 1948). Not everyone reaches this final stage, however. The main reason for arrested social development, in Piaget's scheme, is a lack of exposure to formal thinking or to relevant social experience. In short, in order to develop mentally, people must interact with their physical and social environments.

Lawrence Kohlberg   Lawrence Kohlberg (1966, 1969) extended Piaget's theories of moral and cognitive development and applied them to the way that children acquire their gender identities. He distinguished the three theoretical perspectives (Freudian, learning theory, and cognitive developmental theory) in terms of how they account for gender identity. Freud's theory suggested that children "incorporate. . . large chunks of the same-sex parent's personality into their own, mainly as a way of reducing the anxiety and conflict caused by Oedipal desires" (Tavris and Offir, 1977:168). Social learning theorists, or behaviorists, assume that girls learn to be feminine and boys masculine because they are rewarded for doing so and are punished when they do not. Cognitive development theory, on the other hand, assumes that children are always trying to bring the world into balance. Beliefs, values, and actions must be congruent in order to reduce tension or frustration. According to Kohlberg, children "know" which gender they are, realize that it is permanent, and model their behavior accordingly. Thus children behave like boys or girls because they find that behavior rewarding.

Kohlberg (1966, 1969) identified three stages, or cognitive steps, that children pass through in acquiring the appropriate sex-role behaviors. In the first stage, children discover that they are a member of one sex and can correctly and consistently distinguish between boys and girls. In this stage, gender distinctions are concrete. For instance, preschool children rely on features such as dress and hairstyle to decide who is a boy and who is a girl. Once a stable gender identity is established, it becomes the organizer for information about the social world. This concrete thinking becomes a factor in *sex-role stereotyping*—the belief that only certain types of activities, occupations, or behaviors are appropriate to boys or girls. For example, if long hair is associated with girls, then getting all of one's hair cut off might make one a "boy," and little boys with ringlets are teased by their playmates for looking like girls.

In the second stage, children develop a specific set of values for various behaviors associated with their gender identity. This is an extension of the first phase, as children imitate sex-appropriate behavior and avoid what their friends and parents regard as inappropriate. During this phase there is considerable pressure by the members of one's own sex to conform. That does not mean that little girls never play football but that somehow, and children are not quite sure why, girls' playing football and boys' playing house are just not "right." Etta Sue Higbee was expected to make biscuits, and Roy Davis was expected to work alongside his father in the field.

Finally, "as a result of this differential valuing and differential modeling, each child develops an emotional attachment (identification, with the same-sex parent)" (Frieze et al., 1978:125). This attachment leads to further imitative behavior if it is supported, that is, if significant others and the local community support this behavior. For instance, in a small town between 1920 and 1945, people's opportunities to experiment with different role behaviors for their gender were limited. Women were expected to "stay home and raise a family." Ed Higbee described his mother as the "cleanliness is next to godliness" type, implying that a "good" woman stayed home and kept a clean house. Thus, gender identity is a result of the complex interaction between an individual's biology and the world at large. Let us now examine some of the processes and forces involved in sex-role socialization.

AGENTS OF SOCIALIZATION AND SEXUAL STEREOTYPING

The agents of socialization both shape and filter the cultural material from which people are formed. For example, the parents interpret the children's political and economic realm. Some families might have explained the Depression as an aberration, something that would pass quickly, whereas other families might have seen it as the result of rich people's speculation in the stock market. The mass media also reflect and influence society's general values and holds up ideal images—the real man, the real woman. These ideals, especially sexual stereotypes, are often reinforced by the family and the schools. In short, each of the agents of socialization is situated within a larger cultural context, shaping, and being shaped by, one another.

The Family

One of the earliest and most important influences on a child's socialization is the family. Parents begin the process of sexual stereotyping: Darlene Davis writes to her friend about her new baby that "Josie is truly a sweetie pie....She has got enough hair on the top of her head now for me to put a bow in and has ribbons in four colors." The parents have a distinct set of expectations for the different sexes in the family. Ruth Ann and Etta Sue's mother felt that young women should be brought up to be moral. As Ed Higbee said, "Mother was real strong on her daughters going to Church and behaving themselves decently and staying away from girls and boys who weren't decent." After moving to Illinois, the Davis's son Bill found work as a farmhand, but when Mrs. Davis wanted to go to work, her husband would not hear of it.

The process of sexual stereotyping continues throughout a child's life as the parents express their preferences for "correct" role behavior. And as Kohlberg's theories suggest, the child actively strives to adjust to these role expectations. Mrs. Higbee wanted her daughters to go to 4-H meetings and make biscuits, and when Etta Sue did not conform, there was no doubt about how both of her parents felt. Ed and Ruth Ann knew that their parents disapproved of Etta Sue's marriage, her leaving home, and her abandonment of her baby. As a result, Ruth Ann knew full well what was expected of a good woman: to stay home, have children, and take care of a husband.

The School

Parents are not the only major influence in determining sex roles. Formal education also plays a part. Ruth Ann and Etta

Sue took courses in typing and home economics, whereas their brothers studied science, mathematics, shop, and agriculture. Of course, as Kohlberg noted, most children come to like acting feminine or masculine. Ruth Ann asserted, "I really love typewriting and music, although I loathe Algebra and General Agriculture, what a waste of time. Next year I can be on the school paper and in the glee club....And, of course, I love my teaching at the Division of Education Nursery School....I could listen all day to [Mrs. Watson] talking about how important it is to raise your children properly." The school helped channel young men and women into jobs considered appropriate to their sex: girls became nurses, social workers, teachers, and helpers of all kinds, whereas boys became farmers, soldiers, truck drivers, and businessmen. These stereotypes are slow to change.

Several studies of elementary school textbooks have found that they reinforced what children learned from their parents and teachers. Florence Howe (1971), who examined the reading material available to school-aged children, concluded that young girls were being taught to be helpers, whereas boys were being taught to be innovators. A group called Women on Words and Images (1972) examined a total of 2,750 stories in over one hundred children's readers and found the same patterns. The readers presented boys as more active and as having a much wider range of career options. When all of the occupations illustrated in the stories were categorized, a definite stereotypical pattern emerged. The top eight occupations for men were airplane builder, animal trainer, architect, artist, astronaut, astronomer, athlete, and author; the first eight occupations for women were acrobat, author, babysitter, baker, cafeteria worker, cashier, cleaning woman, and cook. Schools were, of course, attempting to train children for the available jobs.

Between 1920 and 1945, the number of role models available to young women was limited. They could be housewives/mothers, nurses, teachers, or social workers. World War II, of course, provided some of them with new models and new opportunities. But even though many women entered the labor force during the war, they left it when they were forced out of their positions by returning veterans. Many left quite willingly. They had entered in order to do their part for the war effort, and they left, as did Darlene Davis, because they wanted to return to being wives and mothers, which is what they had been socialized by parents and teachers to believe they should be.

Often teachers themselves served as *negative role models* for young women. For instance, in Middletown, described by Lynd and

Lynd (1937), female teachers were paid less than male teachers "because they didn't have families to support," or at least that was the assumption. During the Depression, many school boards passed resolutions stating that "no female teacher may be married," and so those who got married lost their jobs (Lynd and Lynd, 1937:227, 229). Working women were second-class citizens.

The Media

The mass media played an important role in creating sexual stereotypes. Note that Etta Sue Higbee joked to her friend Anne Kettle: "You should see our hands. A quart of Ponds wouldn't make this girl lovely." One of the most popular movies of all time, *Gone With the Wind*, was seen by Ruth Ann Higbee to have the moral that women ought to be humble and serve their men: "That is why *Gone With the Wind* is the best motion picture ever made, because you can see how Scarlett ruins her own life with her vain, selfish ways." Today, of course, some viewers might see Scarlett as the only one in the film with any strength of character. The media of 1920 to 1945 bombarded women with images of what a good housewife and mother was, or should be. A woman's role was portrayed as helping her man, as well as getting one. Men were portrayed in equally stereotypical fashion: returning home from the office, briefcase in hand, being met by their wives, children, and family dogs. During World War II, posters appeared showing women ministering to the needs of the sick and weary, while men were depicted as conquering, achieving, and overcoming incredible odds.

The Peer Group

A *peer group* is a group of people of approximately the same age and social background who share a set of values and norms. One's high-school friends often constitute a peer group and provide a set of socialization experiences. The Higbee and Davis children and their friends went to the movies, sat around and talked after school, and organized parties. Ed Higbee's high school football team supported his sense of self-esteem. As an athlete, he was admired by his classmates, which reaffirmed his gender identity. Etta Sue's friends supported one another: "Remember Irene Thomas?...Anyway, they have a radio, and several girls spend the evenings there one or two nights a week, and sometimes some guys, too. In fact we are allowed to dance in the living room, although on the porch is sometimes more interesting." The peer group offers an opportunity to challenge, although not necessarily reject, the values of the larger community or those of another peer group. Darlene Davis told one of her friends: "I have written you about how kids in Chicago have different ideas about dating and all that than they do in Cooley. I was shocked at first when I saw how some of these girls would be out every night with a different boy and talking at school the next day about how far they let them go. A girl can play the field and get pretty friendly and no one thinks anything of it. Nobody says they are loose, like they would back home."

Family, schools, the mass media, and peer groups operate together, and so sexual stereotyping becomes a powerful force. It is this conjunction that caused the adult Ruth Ann to say, "We won't start our own family until this war is over and I can stay home and devote all my time to my children." It is also what causes agencies to treat boys and girls differently. In describing his experience as a hobo, Roy Davis noted, "They give an old guy six meals and two nights' lodging, and a kid one meal, one bed, and the girls they just throw in jail." Also, while on the road, though the women might be tough, they were still expected to be "little wives." "(S)ome of those girls would of made fine wives and mothers if they ever got the chance. They mostly fixed our food and kept our clothes mended, which is a real problem on the road."

Finally, sexual stereotyping contributes to sexual harassment. Women, especially working women, often are treated as sexual objects. Describing her work, Etta Sue pointed out, "The men hoot and whistle and yell 'Woman in the yard!' and get their hands misplaced pretending to show us our jobs. A girl on the line complained to the foreman, who informed her he wouldn't have *his* daughter working here for anything. Terrific?" It should not surprise people, then, that stereotypes of men and women raised during this time are quite different from those of today's children.

The war and the Great Depression were a watershed in American history. Although we cannot capture all of the changes, let us note some of the main ones we've referred to in this chapter. The federal government's involvement in the economy became a reality, the power of the executive branch grew, and government assumed a greater responsibility for social welfare. There was a shift in population from rural to urban, which was also reflected in a value shift. Children moved out of rural areas in response to the growth of the manufacturing sector, and to war-related jobs that were concentrated in urban areas. The class structure became more rigid, a phenomenon that was reflected in the voting patterns as more and more laborers, urban dwellers, and black Americans voted the Democratic ticket. Adolescence came to be seen as a period of growth and expansion, which was reflected in a child-centered curriculum, stressing the need to develop useful citizens.

As we've seen, the children of the Great Depression were bewildered by what had happened to them and felt betrayed because the promised prosperity never materialized. Many people responded to the Depression and the war years by becoming increasingly conservative. The "gray-flannel" fifties grew directly out of these experiences (see Chapters 8 and 9). Caution became a watchword in politics and economics.

*   *   *

The People of Baker

8

"Baker, South Dakota" is a composite of three small midwestern college towns. The documents presented in this chapter are based on the words and reports of residents of those towns.

When World War II ended, veterans began to flood American colleges. State College in Baker was no exception. In the following letter, Leona Johnson, a student in Baker, described the influx to her friend Gertrude Wiersma, who lived in Potter County.

November 11, 1946

Dear Gert,

How are you doing out there in the West? You are missing something not being in Baker this fall. They say there are almost a thousand freshmen at the college this fall, and more veterans than you will ever see in one place again. I have got my same old room with Mrs. Schlomer and that is lucky, because there isn't enough room in town for all the college students, let alone us high school kids from out of town. I wouldn't mind sharing my room with some of the college men! (joke) That is what it would take for me to get their attention, but I don't think Mrs. S. would care for it.

I sure wish your father hadn't sent you to live with your grandmother. Mine would do just the same, though, never mind what the rest of us wanted. There is just one way to do things as far as they are concerned, and the world can change all around them and they won't see it, they just go up to the Grange and complain at each other. Raymond just goes off his

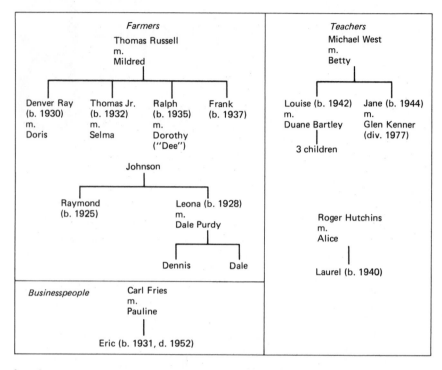

head sometimes. He is full of ideas how to improve the farm, and he is saving money himself (of course this is still a secret from Father) to put a heater in the barn for his FFA* prize hogs in the winter. But there will be a fight; you know how we had fights over me finishing high school even with the free tuition.

There is one guy at the high school who is as cute as any college man and, I guess, thinks I am cute enough too because he took me to a movie over in Elkton last weekend. (Mrs. S. is super about this, she says she doesn't see any harm. If I get my work done and get in early, she doesn't see why she'd discuss it with my folks.) Anyway, do you remember Denver Ray Russell? He is a senior, too. If you know who the Russells are, you know his dad is not at all like ours, and I don't just mean the money. Denver plans to go into business as soon as he is out of college, and his father is behind that all the way. Denver Ray will be a success, everybody says so, in fact I bet you he's Most Likely to Succeed in the yearbook, besides all the other things.

The Russells have a truly beautiful house, they have their own electric and water system and bathroom. The reason I

*Future Farmers of America.

know all this is he took me out there with him after school when he was doing an errand. I was pretty nervous. Mrs. Russell was awfully nice to me though, just as kind. She has a whole modern kitchen with a gas stove and a toaster and an electric mixer. Denver just worships her, all the family does, and no wonder. She does everything for those four boys because she hasn't got any daughters and has her own apple orchard and keeps remodeling the house herself. Denver says when he was little, he didn't think she ever rested, and I can believe it. He says she organized the first home demonstration club in the county and has been county president three times, and she's been secretary of the school board as long as he can remember.

I guess I sound like I have a crush on her as much as on Denver Ray, and maybe that is true, because no matter how I love my mother, she is not the sort of person I want to be. I want to do things. All she will do is go to church and pray for endurance. I don't want to pray for that!

Well, there isn't much other news. There is a big Homecoming at the college this year, all sorts of celebrations in honor of our returning heroes. One really silly thing, a "Hobo Day" which a whole lot of men and boys are growing whiskers for, they all look ridiculous to me.

Write me soon and let me know how you are doing.

Your friend,

Leona

November 29, 1946

Dear Gert,

You're a good friend. No, I'm not angry with you, because you were right about Denver Ray. I figured it out at about the same time your letter came. "Why doesn't this guy ever take me anyplace in Baker???" I thought the cool way he acts at school was just his way, so I didn't mind if he never hung around my locker or anything. But then something else happened, and I'll tell you because you are my dearest friend and can keep secrets. I heard him talking about me, I guess I don't have to tell you what he was implying. If he'd actually been saying it, I think I would have been angry enough to go up to them and ask him to repeat it. I was *angry*. But what he said, which I can't repeat even to you, I just couldn't ask anybody to say, again.

So. So much for that "romance." You were right about who

you date in high school, and I have learned that lesson the hard way. Now I just pray none of our friends believe the filth he is trying to spread. I believe they won't because they know I am not that sort of person, even if I did act like a moron.

But this doesn't mean I think I have to give up my ideas of having a life as good or better than the Russells someday, only I hope I raise my sons better in some ways!

I am glad to hear you have found friends in school there and that your grandmother is feeling better and letting you go out. I'm taking Clothes Design, too, and my suit is going so well that I may enter it at the fair, like Mrs. Schroder is always after us to do. The only thing is, then I wouldn't have it to wear for four weeks and I will want it for church. I got new heels to match it especially, and they don't go nearly as well with my old dress.

Your history teacher sounds horrible, like Miss Taylor in sixth grade only worse. Remember how she used to unbutton her blouse in front of the class? Preserve me from getting like that! Do you think married women ever get that way? (joke)

I miss you a lot and look forward to your letters.

Your friend,

Leona

Leona Johnson married Dale Purdy, who came from a farm family outside Baker. They had two sons, Dennis and Dale. When Dale senior was killed in the Korean war, Leona went to live and work in Rapid City, South Dakota. Shortly after moving, she wrote the following letter to her mother.

Dear Mother,

Thank you for the dishtowels, they will come in very handy. Both of the boys are doing well, I wish you wouldn't worry. They go straight from school together to Mrs. Arthur's, and she gives them their snack, and I come by and pick them up right after I get off work. Rapid City is not a bit dangerous, it's just as safe as Baker would be, and I have a good job here, Mrs. Boone says I can get to be a buyer if I go on as I am going. So I believe I am doing the right thing. If Dale had lived, of course, it would be different, I have told you that before. But the days are over when a woman could farm alone, that was clear as soon as Dale's father passed on. Here the boys are in a good school, we have a nice garden apartment, I can afford all the good clothes they need and even those bikes at Christmas!

No, I haven't met anybody yet. I am too busy right now, but I don't mean to say I have set my mind against it. I meet more people here than I did there, you know, but I am just not ready. I am not the same silly girl I was before I met Dale, after all. A mother has to feel differently. I feel as if I couldn't even look at a man that I wouldn't pick as a father for Dennis and Dale, and I am sure you agree about that. The boys are so proud of their father. His picture in his uniform is in their room, and they always say good night to it, and when they are older I will read them his letters from Korea and when he went on leave to Japan. I don't want him forgotten.

Of course I get lonely, but the people at church are very friendly. We never miss, and the boys like Sunday School.

Now you take better care of your back. I don't want to hear anymore that you have hurt it moving furniture or in the garden. What good does that do? If Father wants it clean behind the couch, you tell him do it himself, and he can use a hoe, *he's* got *his* health, and that is that. It's no use for you to be laid up a week out there. You be a good girl now and do as I say, or I will come up and bring a doctor out myself, I don't care what Father does. I mean it.

Well, it is my bedtime. Only two months till Christmas, and we will be with you.

Love,

Leona

And a big kiss from both your grandsons.

✳   ✳   ✳

Denver Ray Russell, whom Leona Johnson had dated in high school, graduated from State University in 1952 and married Doris, the daughter of a local doctor, a year later. They settled in Baker. In 1956, Russell was working for Arthur Bates, the owner of a large construction firm, and wrote him the following memo.

I have got to pick up the lumber myself if we want it here by Monday, so I'm taking two trucks (Jim Ahrens is driving the other one) to the Black Hills first thing in the A.M. Hannum backed out on the plumbing when he heard our new schedule, but I got Neyens to come in under his original bid. I think he was under the impression we had another bidder somewhere. I figure on saving us some by the trip. I'll call when I get in.

Russell wrote the following letter to his wife Doris while attending a convention in Pierre, the capital of South Dakota. Doris was expecting their first child.

May 3, 1956

Hi honey, I sure miss you, but Dad is right about the contacts I make at conventions. I know you want me home with you now, and I want to be there, but you have got to be my brave girl and remember what I told you. Mr. Bates is a fine boss, as far as learning about homebuilding goes. And he is forward looking enough to see that it is not just in the town additions that the money is, right now, but also in barns and new houses for farmers, who want houses like anybody else now the REA* is in. He depends on me for that market, just like I said. But I have my sights set on more, only I want this to be kept pretty quiet, ok, sweetheart? There is an even bigger market in office buildings, and here's where the stock growers can really be of use to me, because the big ones aren't just sitting out on the farm anymore, they are like Dad, leaders in their communities, on the board of this, the committee for that, and director of other things. When I get ready to start my own company, I'll know folks all over the state and know where the need is for more space, who is expanding what and even be ready to contract for public buildings; I'd like to see our name on the schools and libraries this state will be needing in the years to come. So you just sit tight; I plan for you to be sitting pretty.

I hope you are feeling a lot better in the mornings. I don't want you to overdo or worry about a thing. I have got my hands on something really good here, you'll see. By the time our kids(!!) are in school I will buy you a fur coat and build you a house that will be the envy of all the girls in Baker, and that's just a start. I want the best of everything for my sweet wife, and I'll see she gets it.

Your D. R.

✳   ✳   ✳

*The Rural Electricity Administration.

---

*The Department of Agriculture salutes
Walter Meester, 1952 South Dakota Eminent Farmer*

Walter B. Meester doesn't mind calling himself a "swivel-chair farmer." "Lately I have to spend just about full-time in the office, to keep up with the paperwork and off-the-farm activities," he says.

He was born in 1886, in Minnesota, and came to Hamlin County with his parents, who homesteaded here, a year later. His father died when he was 10 and by the time he was 12 he was managing the farm for his mother and two younger sisters. At 25 he married Anna Rice, a farm girl from nearby, and the young couple relocated on an unimproved half-section which is a part of their present 1200 acres "balanced" farm. Over the years Walter had kept enough livestock to feed up the crops he raises, some years buying feeder pigs so he wouldn't have to sell the grain. "This lets me return the manure to the soil. Besides, it pays better than selling grain as a cash crop."

He says the milk cows and silage kept the family going during the drought years, but he left the milking business in 1944, and now keeps breeding cows and heifers, of which quite a few are registered.

For six years he has been chairman of the livestock-crop improvement association, and is an active member of the weed board. He has several fields, which he contoured before the AAA was recommending the practice. His eldest daughter, Vivian, helped him lay out some of the first contoured fields in the county.

Walter and Anna have raised four children, Vivian, Susan, Joe, and Ray. Mrs. Meester has always contributed to the farm income by keeping a big vegetable garden. Even during the drought years hardy varieties were planted in April and a program of moisture conservation provided mature vegetables. "The same principle applies to children," she says. "They have to absorb the principles of honesty and industry, if they are to grow up useful."

All of the children have been graduated from State College. Vivian is now Mrs. Harold Kellog, living on a farm near Watertown. Susan is Mrs. John Clark of Sacramento,

California. Joe is in partnership with his father, and Ray is a veterinarian in practice in Aberdeen, South Dakota.

Last fall, Mr. Meester's neighbors elected him county commissioner for a four-year term and he is finding it time-consuming. He has been on the board of directors of the Western Calf Show from its inception till recently. He is still an active member of the Boy Scouts and Izaak Walton League, and has been active in Methodist Church work for over forty years.

He is held in high esteem by all who know him well. No important action affecting the livestock interests of the area would be taken without his counsel.

He claims he has retired on his farm, and is enjoying it.

———————————— ✳ ————————————

Adapted from press releases of South Dakota State University.

Michael West, a professor of agronomy in the school of agriculture at State College, became well known for his research on plant diseases. Shortly after receiving his Ph.D. in 1947, West, his wife Betty, and their daughters, Louise and Jane, left Pacific Grove, California, and moved to Baker. The following are excerpts from West's letters to his parents.

December 28, 1947

Dear Mother and Dad,

We're very grateful for the Christmas check, which you know we can use in a number of ways. Life in Baker is not very hard on the poor professor's pocketbook, as a general thing, but of course the move has strained it a bit.

We are absolutely delighted that we no longer occupy space in the "Barracks." All three of my girls need more room, badly, and now we have got it: a pleasant little frame house eight blocks west of the campus. This is fortunate for us all, since Betty can walk to town and I can walk to my classes on the days when I am teaching. The house isn't new, but it has a good deal of charm.

We are doing some needed painting and papering, but the major project before the new semester is the bookshelves which I am building for both sides of our fireplace. I look forward to

the new year and the extension work.* It is no hardship to
leave the departmental paperwork and the survey courses to my
colleague, and even the traveling hasn't been a difficult adjustment. I am unceasingly fascinated by how much I learn, where
I am supposed to be teaching. I am also finding my work with
the experimental station valuable not only in itself, but in
teaching my class in plant pathology. Betty says she doesn't see
enough of me—but she is as proud as I am of the important
work that is being done here. I arrived at the beginning of an
era, I believe, and every year since has confirmed that
conviction.

I should add that Betty really hasn't much time to miss
me, with our two lively daughters to look after. I will turn this
over to her now so that she can give a few words about them.

Your son,

Michael

September 11, 1950

Dear Mother and Dad,

We are all back into the swing of things in Baker again, after
our good visit with you in the land of sunshine. Jane is over-
joyed to be going off to school with her sister at last, and I
believe their mother is pleased to have some time to herself,
for a change. She will have no difficulty in keeping busy. She
has just been invited to join one of the local women's book
clubs—this is no small thing, for even in Baker, some social
activities are traditionally "town," and not every wife of a faculty member is likely to be included. Betty's work for the Historical Society, her membership in the garden club, and her
work in the League of Women Voters, which was organized
here last year, have apparently given her the necessary entrée
with the old residents.

No, as a matter of fact I don't talk politics much here,
although there's one like-minded man, our rector, Frank Bentley. Father Bentley comes here from the East—as we came
from the West—and is registered as an Independent voter, a bit
of ecclesiastical diplomacy insufficiently appreciated, I suspect,
by many in his Republican congregation. We share some opinions which don't get to the pulpit, I assure you. South Dakota

*Like many professors in agricultural colleges, West took an active part in the
educational work of the county extension program.

Tuesday Literary Club
April 1952

The April 1952 meeting of the Tuesday Literary Club was held on the twelfth at the home of Ethel Kelly. Refreshments of angelfood cake and sherbet were served by the hostess, after which the program was presented. The hostess introduced Grace Robbins, a State College student and winner of the Speech Contest of Native Sons and Daughters. She gave her winning speech, "A Garden Grows in South Dakota." Lois Sprague gave an interesting review of *Jubilee Trail*, by Gwen Bristow.

Fourteen members answered Roll Call. Mary Barker was a guest. The minutes of the February and March meetings were read and approved. Lois Wells, Treasurer, reported a balance of $16.85.

A birthday card was signed by all present, to be sent to our absent member, Ida Reid, who is in the hospital with a heart condition.

The President, Madelaine Ericson, announced that there would be election of officers at the May meeting. It will be held May tenth, with Carrie Edwards as hostess, at the Polka Dot Pantry.

Republicans (are there other South Dakotans?) regard President Truman with deep suspicion simply because he is a Democrat and still has some New Deal ideas, but they rather like his decisiveness over this war and seem to accept his estimate of the threat to world peace which the North Koreans present. On the other hand, I have overheard some of my neighbors accepting Joe McCarthy's estimate of the threat of Communism in our government. No, I stay out of such discussions. There are the times when a pipe is most useful. Betty is the member of our family who can negotiate the political waters with tact and serenity, though I believe our Louise has inherited her gift. Jane, no; we wonder who she does take after.

Being away for a month has opened my eyes to the amount of building and development that is going on in South Dakota. Of course, the way things are moving in Pacific Grove is considerably more dramatic, but Baker is doing all right—new houses, dormitories, trailer housing for the G.I.s (Nothing, still, for married students—as one esteemed colleague put it to me, "if they're married, they should be working.") The college can afford it, due to new legislative appropriations and endowments. The state has also authorized a bonus for veterans, which may affect G.I. enrollments. I hope it does; they are by and large the best students we get. When the dams that are being built in the Missouri River Basin are completed, the S.D. economy will be further stabilized.

The extension service has begun a new program of traveling exhibits, which set up booths for specialists from each agricultural department. It is being very well received; I took the family to the fair in Clark County the week we returned, and the girls had a fine time while I did my job. Jane had her first experience with a Ferris wheel, and she would have stayed on it all afternoon if Louise could have been persuaded to do likewise. I am told that this has been "the best summer of her whole entire life." Of course that is due mostly to the efforts of her grandparents—successful, I may add, with all four of us.

Your son,

Michael

✳

The Department of Agriculture salutes
Mrs. W. B. Kneip, 1948 South Dakota Eminent Homemaker

Mrs. Kneip is a lady who can always be counted on to do more than her share in helping out with any community activity.

She was born Ethel Weiler at Riverside, South Dakota, in 1888. She attended high school in Alexandria, and taught rural schools for five years. She then clerked in general stores for three years. She married William Kneip March 3, 1918, and came to live on the old Kneip homestead four miles north of Elkton.

Three sons and three daughters were born to them, Herbert, Charles, Edward, Helen, Ferne, and Janice. All of the boys have attended Baker High School and Herbert and Charles have attended State College, majoring in agriculture. Herbert holds two degrees from State and is an assistant professor of agricultural engineering at State.

Charles works with the soil conservation service of the U.S. Department of Agriculture and Ed, a senior at Baker High, plans to attend State and become an agronomist. He is president of his 4-H club.

Helen was graduated from State in 1944 in general science and is now Mrs. Robert Maxwell, of Atlanta, Georgia, where her husband is a chemist with the Standard Oil Company. The young folks met when he was in the army training program at State College.

"He is certainly a nice boy," says his mother-in-law fondly.

The young couple have one daughter, Cory.

Ferne is a sophomore at State in home economics. She is an assistant 4-H leader. Janice is a sophomore at Baker High School and is also an active 4-H club member, active in GAA, band, orchestra and pep band, student council representative, and vice president of her class.

Mrs. Kneip has been very active in church work in Elkton, and is a past president of the Ladies and Mission Society. She has also been a member of the Elkton Jolly Bunch Extension Club for over twenty years.

When neighbors are in need of help, she is there. She is often referred to as the "mother of the community." One friend put it this way, "Her six children and their success best prove her success."

The Kneips live on a 320-acre diversified farm with beef cattle and purebred Poland China hogs. Some of Mrs. Kneip's hobbies are knitting, sewing, embroidery, rug making, reading, and television.

———————————— ✳ ————————————

Adapted from press releases of South Dakota State University.

October 20, 1955

Dear Mother and Dad,

Indeed the girls are happy with their new school building. It is quite an edifice, lots of light and space, and what the girls call "green boards," an innovation I would like to introduce in my own classrooms. But we are all even happier with our plans for an addition to this house, so each girl can have her own room. Yes, we have ended our year's debate on the subject. As you know, I came back from the Paris conference last year fired with the idea of a family trip to Europe, and it does look as if we could do it now. However, we have decided to wait until the girls are a few years older. Betty feels they will appreciate it more, and of course she is right about that. Meanwhile, we will be able to offer you guest room accommodations on your visit, and some good music as well; we have invested in the long-awaited hi-fi system, and Betty is already sending away to Chicago and New York.

Meanwhile, the extension service has been able to work up a new program for training personnel—we've even hired a new man to handle it. As a result I expect to be doing more experimental work, on forage legume diseases in particular. The opportunity to go to professional conferences has made a good deal of difference in my work, both as an encouragement and in terms of what can be learned. You can never predict where the new breed of alfalfa or new chemical treatment will show up. You remember my stories about the breakthroughs concerning rust-resistant wheat?

So the important things go on, despite human pettiness. I will give this over now to my elder daughter, who wishes to give you her full description of our plans for the house, backyard barbecue, and garden this year. Jane has disappeared, as

Agricultural Hall laboratory, South Dakota State University, circa 1953
Courtesy of South Dakota State University Photo Lab

usual, on the birthday bike—but I will see she has a few words for you next time.

Your son,

Michael

*   *   *

Danny Berry and Gary Coover grew up together in Baker. Just before their senior year in high school, Gary moved to Minneapolis.

October 6, 1955

Dear Gary,

I really still can't believe you're not here for our senior year. What a crummy time for your dad to decide to move to Minneapolis.

This year is going to be busy—it already is, but I'll get to that in a minute. I've got to take these exams if I want to get into any decent schools. And you know I want out of here just as fast as possible. Not just out of the town and down the road, but out of the *state*! It also means that I've got to behave in my classes this fall. I found out that the colleges don't care about your spring grades. After all, they accepted you, or rejected you, by that time, right? Anyhow, I got this book about the exams at the library, and it's sort of scary. How am I supposed to learn all of what they want to know before the exams are given? Even worse, because I need their recommendations, I'm going to have to behave in that jerk Sheerer's class and in my English class and in my math class, though actually I like Goettle pretty well.

Anyhow, if things go O.K. with my grades this fall, I should be able to get into a fairly decent school, though what my parents can afford is another matter. It's really hard to get them to talk about me going away to school. They made noises about me going to the college here, but I said "no way!" I told them that if I was going to be a doctor, I needed to go to a good school so that I could get into medical school. But they still keep telling me to try and get a scholarship, and then they'll help me out, whatever that's supposed to mean.

It doesn't seem like there's going to be many of us going on to school or who will be leaving town to go to school. I sort of thought Marlene, Ray, Dave and Jim would go, but even they are making noises about staying in town and going to the

College for a couple of years. If they do, they'll never get out of here, because they'll still be living at home, seeing the same people on weekends. You know the old story.

Oh, guess what. That jerk Daryl, who got the big head just because he had been named all "county"—big deal—has already flunked out, he says dropped out, of school. He was supposed to play on the team as end but couldn't make it in the classroom. He's back working with his dad and hanging around the A&W on Friday and Saturday nights. It's incredible, the number of people who just can't ever seem to leave. All of the greaseballs are still around. You remember the guys who spent all of their time in the shop classes working on their projects and their cars? I still can't believe the school started auto mechanics. Jim Denny went the whole hog. He customized a 1950 Merc, chopped it, channeled it, dropped the front end, reversed the shocks, and the thing rides about four inches off the ground. That whole crowd has cornered the market on 1942 and 1932 Fords. They got a lot of their ideas from *Hot Rod Magazine*, and are sending away for parts to Chicago. The big thing is to bore the block out, shave the heads, put on dual carbs and exhausts, and smoke. Do you know what a 1946 Ford with all the chrome removed and the holes leaded up is called? A lead sled. Cute? Me, I still got my 1949 Plymouth. I thought about bull-nosing it and taking off the junk on the trunk lid, but I'd have to do it when my father wasn't watching. I guess I'll settle for a new paint job and some Naugahyde.

I don't know where guys like Denny get the money for their cars, either. Some of us suspect that there is some midnight auto supply work going on. I know that Marvin Flory ripped an Olds generator out of a car that was in his neighborhood and stuck it on his Chev. Oh, well, the car belonged to one of the college kids.

More later, write about the big city.

Your pal,

Danny

Dec. 4, 1955

Dear Gary,

Don't be a creep. Yes, I'm still going with Judy, and Christmas is coming. I kept telling myself that I was going to break up with her. I keep telling myself that every week. I told you I tried at the beginning of the school year, and she got sick and threw up. I'd feel too crummy if I did it right before Christmas. She keeps talking about the shirt she bought me and about what she wants. She wants one of these fuzzy angora (?) sweaters that she's seen some of the college girls wear. Well, they do feel nice. However, dear mother says it isn't right to give girls clothes. You can't win.

Maybe I'll just be a coward and break up when I leave for school. I sure wish I could go out with Diane, though. I really like her, and I just don't even feel as though I even like Judy anymore. Maybe after Christmas. Pray for me.

I've still got my job at the new clothing store. It makes dad happy, even though I spend half the money I earn there on clothes, which they give me at one-third off. Dad says I need to learn to work, to be responsible, etc., etc., etc. He's right, I guess.

By the way, you read weird stuff, Coover. I can't even pronounce the names of some of the people you're telling me to read. I haven't got time either, with practice after school and debate and one thing and another. I'll read more next year when I get to college—I'll have to. I did read Steinbeck's *Grapes of Wrath*. I'll try *Cannery Row* next.

I got all my applications off, and now all I can do is sit around and wait to hear. That's going to make me nervous for a while. I sure hope we end up at one of the same places we applied.

Remember Joanne Darby? Well, she's going out with one of the College guys, and you can guess how we feel about that. Maybe people shouldn't assume the worst, but they do. I doubt if anybody we know will ask her out again.

You're being awfully quiet about your love life. Stop reading weird books and ask somebody out.

Your pal,

Danny

*　　　*　　　*

Teenagers Norma Clark of Baker and Joyce Anderson of Rapid City, South Dakota, became friends at a summer music camp held on the campus of the local college.

Sept. 11, 1956

Dear Joyce,

What a date! Never again—unless I don't have anything else to do on a Friday or Saturday night. No, not even then. I'd rather actually wash my hair. What am I talking about?

Well, Wayne Hooley, one of the gear heads and a big Future Farmer, had been after me to go out with him. It was no big thing, just a coke date. Anyhow, he got this 1942 Ford, at least that's what I think it is, and that's all he talked about all night. Somehow it made Steve's talking about the football team seem interesting.

It really was worse than *Latin* class! Dual carbs, chopped and channeled, leaded, and so on. I couldn't imagine what he was talking about. I suppose it could have been worse; he could have talked about his 4-H project. And guess what we did for the evening?

I thought we'd go and get a hamburger and coke down at Brian's Cafe and talk, and I'd see some of my friends. No, we rode up and down Main Street for two hours, and then I had him take me home. That's his and his friends' idea of fun, not mine. His friends with their hot rods were either cruising up and down like Wayne or sitting on the hoods of their cars, which were parked in the Supershop lot. I really did not want to hang around there. A couple of the other girls who were sitting around just aren't my friends. So I kept saying, "Oh let's just ride around, it's really neat." Sincerely.

Really nothing much is happening with me right now. The same classes, the same people. I've still got to do some shopping for school clothes. I saved my clothing allowance for 2 months, and I got Mom and Dad, and even Grandma, to give me money for my birthday, so I'm looking forward to a big day of shopping. I'll never find what I want in this town, though, so Mom's going to take me shopping in Sioux Falls. There's a Jonathan Logan dress in this month's *Seventeen* which I *love*. And I want a charcoal gray straight skirt to go with my pink sweater set. It will be a ball. I wish you were still here so that you could come along with us.

Write and tell me about school, what kind of outfits you bought for this year, what the kids in your school are wearing, what the guys are like and how much your mom lets you get away with.

Love,

Norma

*   *   *

*Carl Fries, whose Norwegian ancestors came to this coun-
try in the 1870s, had a successful furniture and appliance
business in Baker. His wife, Pauline, and Mildred Russell,
the mother of Denver Ray, were sisters. After his son Eric
died in Korea, Fries wrote the following letter to his sister
Inge in Hamlin County, South Dakota.*

1955

Dear Sis,

I am surprising you with a letter because I need a woman's
advice. I have been to our pastor about this, but he hasn't been
able to help, although he has tried, and I have talked to
Pauline's sister Mildred Russell, who is a good woman but always busy and inclined to expect problems to go away if you
ignore them. Well, that isn't working for us.

Ever since our boy was taken, the home doesn't appear to
mean much at all to Pauline. All her energy is going into the
Women's Auxiliary and canvassing for the building fund, and
the suppers and bazaars, and so forth. Now those are all good
things, good for the church and for the community, mind you,
and I don't mean to say she isn't doing a fine job and an
important job. I'm not complaining that she isn't taking care of
the home all right, either. Only she's wearing herself out. You
know we could afford now to have a woman in to clean—even
cook, if we wanted. We could afford vacations. We could go
anywhere, to Hawaii in January if she'd do it, or go to see the
family in the old country. She won't get someone to help out,
and she won't consider a trip. I got her to go to the doctor, and
he prescribed these pills, but she threw them out. I got her her
own car, but she only uses it to run errands in.

You know, Sis, that it hasn't been easy for me either, losing our only son in Korea. There's been three generations of us
in business in Baker, and now that's over. I hung on to the
business through the Depression and built it up and expanded,
and now it just doesn't mean so much to me. I never blamed
Pauline that she couldn't have any more children after Eric, but
I think she doesn't know what a grief it's been to me, too.

But that's not what I set out to tell you. I am pretty upset,
as you can see. She comes home, fixes some kind of supper,
cleans up before I'm finished, and starts cleaning house. Now
what kind of life is that? It's wearing us both out. She never
used to be this way. She always kept things nice, but she was
no fanatic, and she used to give dinner parties for our friends I

would have been proud to invite anyone to, and luncheon parties for her friends, too.

So what I'm asking is if you will write us and get her up
there to visit you for a while. I'm afraid you'll have to make
up some story that you're ill, or she won't do it. I have talked
myself blue about this. She just won't slow down. She says if I
give up the hunting and if I quit minding the store and the
business bureau and I don't know what all, the hospital board,
the Sons of Norway. She uses all that against me. I can't turn
around without her saying, see, I'm just as bad. You can see
how she can make it sound. But I would, if she would. Only
you understand I can't walk away from all that for nothing; I'm
needed, the work's there, I need to know it's for something.
She deserves some good times. We both do, only I can't convince her on my own without some help. I know what a favor
I'm asking, but I can't see any other way at the moment. I
know I can count on your understanding and goodness, and I
will do whatever you advise about the whole thing. Better write
me at the downtown store, or phone there during business
hours if you'd rather. Thanks a million.

I hope all you folks are ok.

Love,

Carl

✳   ✳   ✳

*Laurel Hutchins was the only child of Alice and Roger
Hutchins. Roger Hutchins taught history at Baker High
School. Laurel was ten when she began a diary, from which
the following excerpts were taken. Her original spelling and
punctuation have been retained.*

September 13, 1950   Today I walked over past the Sherburn
mansion again on my way home from school. If I pretend Im going
to the library, the girls don't care when I dont walk with them. So I
can do both, I get some books and I go very slow all around the
whole block the house stands in the middle of, using my imagination. It is like she is a princess in a tower. The way she is old and
alone is the evil spell. If I were a prince, I could save her.

October 5, 1950   She is out in the flower garden again today, in
her disgize. I dont beleive she is at all crazy like they say. If I were
that rich, I wouldn't act like anybody else. So what if nobodies
mother gardens in a big hat? it looks mysterius to me. Maybe she

likes to be. Besides she was just out there with a trowel putting in bulbs, what is crazy about that? I know she saw me, I went around twice but she pretended she didnt. I wish I was brave enough to speak.

October 21, 1950   I did it!! I said hello Mrs. Scherburne (that is how it is spelled). And she smiled and said hello back. Next time I will think up a conversation.

November 15, 1950   Now it's cold she is never outside, I will have to do something.

December 10, 1950   We all have tickets for the Christmas program, 10 of them to sell before the fifteenth. I am going to try to sell her one.

December 12, 1950   I did it!! It was not at all like I expected. She was sad I think but she asked me in. All the way to the kitchen. I was right about the evil spell, it is on the house, too. There is a whole lot of old furniture and old rugs and pictures and china cabinets and two pianos and hundreds maybe thousands of books, it is all old and dark and I don't think very clean. But the kitchen is warm, with lamps in it and plants and the radio on, playing music. She made me sit down and we had tea and I told her all about my father and school and the Christmas program. She bought a ticket but she may not feel well enough to come. I never asked her a single question! But she said I should come back.

Family portrait
Courtesy of Kay Stewart

April 14, 1951   This afternoon Mrs. Scherburne was really sad. She was telling me about the things she and her brother brought back from their trips to China and Japan and she nearly cried and had to stop for a while, I was somewhat frightened. She told me about the rugs, they are called Oriental, but that doesn't mean they came from China or Japan, they are from Persia. Only now it isn't Persia anymore, but Iran, we learned that in Geography. She said it isn't Japan anymore either. I wonder if she meant about the bombs. I wonder if she dreams about them too. I wish I hadn't told Daddy about it. He gets angry, not sad. Like about Korea.

I was glad to get home today, to our kitchen. Everything is where it goes, and clean, like everybody else's. I made mustard sandwiches. Yum!!

October 11, 1953   Today while we were doing American history I really got in trouble. I said my father said the book didn't say nearly enough about the Indians. Mrs Stirling got furious as if she wrote the book herself, and was going to send me to the principal only then I said I probably made a mistake. I wish I hadnt said that!!! but I don't want to get Daddy involved. Mrs. Stirling went on and on about how sorry we are about Wounded Knee and all that. That is not what Daddy was talking about.

Joyce and Davetta came up at lunch and said Mrs. Stirling doesn't like you to show off. She doesn't like Joyce either because she has two professors for parents, that is even worse than one high school teacher. But Joyce is so smooth! I just hate her for it sometimes. Her with her paperdolls she makes with all *her* clothes and the ones she *wants*. She can't draw anyway! So I went home with Davetta after school which I never did before, although she is always hanging around. At least she is not always putting on lotion and looking in her purse. But now I wish I hadn't because it was embarsing. Her grandmother had just gotten back from the hospital where she cleans and was sitting on this old broken-down couch in the living room with her shoes off, and their breakfast was still all over the table. Davetta doesn't have her own room. I feel really sorry for her. It must be awful to have your mother run off. I invited her to our house tomorrow, but I bet she doesn't come. This was a fairly awful day.

June 2, 1954   My present for graduating from eighth grade is to decorate my room myself, of course I can't go to Fries furniture and pick out a whole new suite like Norma Clark did, but we will paint the room white like I want and made new striped curtains and a bedspread and a ruffle for the vanity to match and buy a rug—maybe even shag carpet if we can afford it—oh, I would love a blue shag carpet. Joyce is wild with envy, her parents refuse to let her decorate her room herself because they say her taste is sure to change. Ha, Mother says I have good taste now. I can't wait to tell Mrs. Scherburne. She is always interested about pretty things, honestly I think she has taught me more about art than any of the teachers. She told me last week that amateur really means—lover. "I have been an amateur of life," she said, and laughed. I said there is nothing wrong with that but all the same she knows I mean to be more than an amateur artist. So many of the girls in Baker have no ambition at all. I think that doesn't matter if your husband doesn't, if he is just going to stay in the family business or farm—but I will never marry *that* sort of man.

✳   ✳   ✳

Jane West Kenner, the younger daughter of Betty and Michael West, left Baker in 1962. In the following interview, Kenner described her youth in Baker.

I go back to Baker, now, at Christmas, and of course I'd go if Mother or Father were ill or anything. But when I left for college, *I left.* I was born there, and I went to grade school and high school there, you know? If you've never lived in a small town like that you cannot imagine—You'd think the sixties would have made some changes? Not really, not in Baker. My parents are proud of that, but I go mad. It's as if I were in high school again; oh God, a freshman in high school in 1958 and NOT POPULAR!! and no idea what the problem was, really, me? Baker? the entire world? no, really, I can't stand it.

Listen, my father is okay. I admire him, I have to. He's given his life to the university and with, well I think, really high motives. I mean, you cannot complain about wanting to grow more and better food for the world, can you? He came to Baker as a young man with a brand new degree. He could have gone to places with much more prestige, but they had just organized an experimental station, and he's not only been responsible himself for ways of controlling I don't know how many plant diseases, he's an international expert, he teaches and does extension work, sometimes, still, you know, on committees with farmers introducing new developments, although he's an emeritus now. All right. But it's important. If he didn't have time for me, I've always had to accept that *his* work was *special*, you know?

Mother—and my sister, my older sister. She is much more like mother, more—that's what I mean about Baker not changing. I can understand that Mother never wanted to work outside the home, and I don't mean she hasn't always been busy. The women in that town, for one thing, are so house proud—it's absolutely scary. I knew droves of women who waxed their kitchen floors every other day! But she was—is—into community work too, all the clubs a faculty wife can be in, League of Women Voters, and I don't think we ought to just put that down. For her generation. Although when I look back on the work she was doing for the league in about I guess it was '56, about integration, I simply cringe. The superficiality. The *ignorance.* Still, that was Baker. My sister, oh, well, never mind— Well. All right. I suppose it's a case of "but for the grace of God."

She got married right after high school because she was pregnant. And. And we all had to pretend *we didn't know.* Three years older than me. She never did anything *else* wrong! But that's why my parents were delighted to send me away to college; it's what they had wanted for Louise. Although, of course, I haven't exactly fulfilled the old expectations. . . . So she has three kids now, and they and her husband, who is a sort of farmer, I'll get to that, they're her life. She doesn't even do the sorts of community work Mother does, except church and PTA. But "she will when the kids are older." My god, they're in *high* school! Yes, it could have been me, I think. If that big gorgeous blond guy had wanted me when I was seventeen. I was desperate. Louise was desperate, and she was popular. Still. Duane could make you desperate. Incredible. He had everything, you know? President of the student body, of FFA, he played football *and* basketball, debate, Demolay,* editor of the paper, in the glee club. I can't even think of half of it now, but of course I heard and heard and *heard* about it for two solid years, just when I truly believed in all that crap, and he was gorgeous. Of course I did! Madly!!

And it was a good thing he had all that energy because his parents were not at all happy with the marriage; he was supposed to go to State; he'd been there a year when they got married. So they had to live with his parents, Louise learned everything-a-farm-wife-needs-to-know at her mother-in-law's knee while Duane went on and finished college and helped his Dad out too. He still works their farm part of the time—they have their new house about twenty yards from the old one—but he also works at the big feed and grain plant and sells all over the Middle West and belongs to Jaycees and all that. Louise, Louise cans and freezes. What can I tell you? She has a garden, my father likes that a lot. She doesn't know there's been a women's movement.

Right. Me. Obviously I would have given anything to be like her

*An organization for the young male relatives of Masons.

*

Baker League of Women Voters
March 13, 1956

The Annual Meeting of the Baker League of Women Voters met the evening of March 13, 1956, at the home of Mrs. Frank Patten.

The Secretary's report was read and accepted. Mrs. H. A. Rauth, the newly appointed Treasurer, reported a balance of $209.59.

Miss Rude reported the various activities of the Voters Service Committee. A discussion of the film on voting which was sent by the Ford Foundation followed, and several suggestions were made for its use. Mrs. Wallace planned to contact the Supt. of Schools to see if some recognition could be given the room bringing back the most "I Have Voted" cards.

Mrs. Grulke reported on the work done by the Resource Chairman and their attendance at workshops as well as the hours each has spent on her item. Credit goes to:

Mrs. R. V. Atkinson, Chairman of state item on "Water and Water Rights"
Mrs. Ralph Gunderson, Chairman of the national item on "Water Conservation"
Mrs. Charles Starksen on "Problems in the Mid-East"
Mrs. Michael West on "Desegregation of Our Schools"

There was a discussion on the allowance made for the President's expense to the National Convention, and it was agreed that $100 was inadequate. Mrs. Harnly moved to allow an additional $100. The motion was seconded and the vote was unanimous in favor.

There was a discussion of the rummage sale to be held April 30th. All members were asked to save rummage for this sale. Other means of raising money were discussed, and referred to the Finance Committee.

Meeting was adjourned.

*

until *it* happened. And even then I was confused for a couple of years, by all the pretense. I didn't see, for example, or—or know that I saw, that for my parents the worst thing was Louise had married a farmer. No, I have to explain this, it's an important part of the whole thing for me. Because in Baker, it's not like most universities, it never was. It's the agricultural college, and it exists to help the farmers, and the farmers care about it, support it. There's very little resentment of professors, the idea they aren't really working. And it was supposed to go both ways. Daddy was always talking about how much he learned from the farmers. But I came to see that it's—it's like you don't want your daughter to marry one. Oh, nothing *obvious*, all very polite, lots of good will, big dinners, little compliments. God. Of course, now the great family unmentionable secret is that poor dear Jane is divorced, right?

So, anyway, when I got that sorted out in my mind was when I began to think, well, what else is there besides this? Because Baker *is* the university and the farming community and services for all that. And that's when I thought, hey, what if I'm not a cheerleader or anybody's steady, what if I don't win a Kiwanis scholarship or whatever? *There is really a world out there.* Let me at it. But it wasn't easy. Because Baker people think Baker is the world. Oh, it's true, my father took us all to Europe, a six-week tour when we were sixteen and fourteen. Louise moped for Duane the whole trip. Me? My father's slide shows of it, when we got back, are what I remember. I never got *close*, I never felt it was real, that time. Only Baker. For example. Remember short shorts? Nobody in Baker wore

League of Women Voters panel discussion, 1952
Photo courtesy of *Brookings Daily Register*

short shorts. And as for Elvis Presley—the girls who liked him were outcasts. When I was a junior I decided I really could not belong to the church choir anymore. You notice I couldn't decide I didn't want to belong to the *church* anymore? Not a possibility, the West family simply went to the Episcopal services. Well, of course, Louise was a Lutheran-by-marriage by then, but we tried not to think about that, either. I couldn't even say that the choir director made awful selections and was too sentimental; it was that I needed more time for my studies. I couldn't say I wouldn't take communion anymore, no one would have believed I *meant* it. This is hard to explain. Of course we knew that part of being Episcopalians was being better than Lutherans, who were better than Baptists, still—all of us, everyone was supposed to be like everyone else, anyway. It was like—okay, for example, I read a lot of books nobody else was reading, that year. And my English teacher, my *English* teacher, had a little talk with me about it. I couldn't possibly understand Camus, you know? Because not everyone could. So there had to be some *insincerity* there. *Calling attention* to yourself. Especially if you were a girl! So I saw, eventually, that no one was pitying me for not being like Louise; on the contrary, they were resenting me for being "conceited." I found I preferred that. Of course— I *was* conceited. I was also reading books I didn't understand, but—that's how I got into academia, after all. And how I stay there!

✳   ✳   ✳

The following account is based on an interview with Ralph Russell, one of Denver Ray's brothers, in which he described Thanksgiving 1957 at the family farm in Baker.

Mother doesn't feel right about it unless she can set at least twenty down to Thanksgiving dinner. We all bring something. This year my wife Dee contributed the pumpkin pies, three of them, and Denver Ray's wife roasted four of his pheasants to "supplement" the turkey and the ham. Denver Ray's been out hunting every season for years now and got pretty good at it, though he doesn't really enjoy it, just goes because of who he can go with. Better that than golf for business reasons. I guess—at least you get something out of it.

Selma, that's my brother Tom's wife, brought rolls and a frozen fruit salad, and Aunt Pauline [Fries] brought two church-supper–sized pans of baked sweet potato. Well, I won't go on, I will just leave the fixings to your imagination, except for the fact that there were two bottles of wine on the table this year. I guess we are going to get used to liquor being legal in Baker County at last, after all the ruckus. Counting kids, we made up twenty-one to table, because Uncle Herman from Dad's side of the family brought his wife and two youngest all the way from Sleepy Eye, Minnesota. He brought wine, and she brought and unpacked a dozen wine glasses her mother brought from the old country, beautiful things with a sort of pink-gold shine on them. There wasn't any room on the table for other decoration, I can tell you, just food. But the house was perfect as usual. Mother had flower arrangements in the living room and paper decorations on the windows and shelves—the kid's turkeys and pilgrims and the like. It looked comfortable. The new carpets and couch, the good smells—and outside a good hard November frost, about an inch of snow, the bare trees against the white sky. If you can't get sentimental about a day like that, what's the use in it?

We were supposed to be watching the kids in the living room—and the television was on as well—but after a while voices began to be raised, as usual. When the family is all together, it is just regular for Dad to take to preaching, things wouldn't seem right without it.

"This country's going soft, I tell you. And we better realize it before it's too late. Look at this Sputnik. Did we put it up? No, by God, the Russians put it up; sometimes I wonder if we've forgotten how to get a job done in this country anymore."

"Now, Tom, there isn't anyone can say that about the college here, it's always pulled its weight in science education, not to speak of experimental science...."

"That's not the same thing that...."

"Dammit, it is the same thing, and have you forgotten how in the war this school had more military trainees than students and programs in everything from aviation to aeronautical engineering? What we did once, we can do again. What it is, we're slower because we're not just dancing to the tune of some damn dictator."

"I'm not arguing that, Carl. Everybody knows the Russians are going hungry, their five-year plans are taking ten, they haven't got a tenth of our farming knowhow. I'm not arguing comparisons, I'm talking about drive, we've lost momentum."

"But Dad, is a space program really that important, then?"

"You better believe it will be when they start putting missiles in the satellites."

"Listen, they don't want war any more than we do."

"There you're wrong. We're not talking common human sense, nice as that would be to contemplate, we're talking about world domination, we're...."

"Maybe so, maybe so, but that's not the way they'll go about it."

"The hell it isn't. Oh, they've got their spies all right, and agitators, but what I mean look how they handled the situation in Hungary last year."

"Right, right, were those tanks and guns, or weren't they? I say...."

"What do you want, then? Want to see our colleges turned over to the army again? You want to join up?"

"You bet I do, if...."

"The point is the *point is.* If the Democrats, if that McGovern...."*

"Gentlemen." Mother, arms folded across her new calico apron. I'm watching because she is too good to miss, in this mood. When I was little I didn't enjoy it much, but now....

"Take leisure to observe that Leo is on my coffee table eating one of my purple mums, and Stevie and Carrie are nowhere in sight. Six grown men, and that's the best you can do?"

Faces go slowly back to their normal color. The kids are found in the downstairs bathroom, and before the basin overflows. By the time dinner is on the table, Dad is holding forth on the new arts center and the two or three families who headed the fund drive, all of whom had, according to him and Uncle Carl [Fries], ulterior motives. Carl's family has been here "as long as any, but without any such need," says he, "to memorialize themselves."

So we all troop in to dinner, and Dad says the blessing, short and sweet, before the carving and serving begins. Herman pours all the grownups a little wine and toasts "the ladies, who have done us so proud."

So then they had to be encouraged to drink "to themselves," and of course, Aunt Pauline had refused any wine anyway, and Mother too, claiming one mouthful would make her feel dizzy, and she still had dinner to see to. But none of the rest of us refused, though Dee doesn't really care for it—still, this was an occasion. Of course, it is something else altogether to get the habit, like poor old Tod Wheeler. And I don't know that I think it's cool to have cocktails before dinner like some do. But this was a celebration.

✳   ✳   ✳

Doris Russell, Denver Ray's wife, described the same Thanksgiving.

It's hardly my idea of the way to spend a holiday, but I tell myself that's because I've never been part of a large family myself. Before I married into this one, I mean. My father's parents, of course I knew

*George McGovern, United States Senator from South Dakota, 1963–1981.

them, Grandpa was a physician in Baker before Dad was. We used to have dinner with them on Christmas day, just a usual sort of Sunday dinner, as I recall. I was brought up to prefer keeping things simple, and this...!

Four or five or six women working all day (and maybe half the day before) to make a dinner for so many people that no one can really talk to anyone and then cleaning up and dividing up leftovers the rest of the day.... Well, it isn't the work so much, I guess, as all the people. Five women in a kitchen is four too many. And there are always arguments. Mother and Father Russell always find something to lecture about, and it is not the family way to listen meekly. Or my way, for that matter. I don't know what the men were going on about this time, but in the kitchen we were discussing, of all things, the sex education classes at the high school. At least that reduced the number of women in the kitchen. After about two minutes Aunt Pauline dried her hands, removed her apron, and marched upstairs. And Uncle Herman's wife shooed her thirteen-year-old off "to mind the little ones" at the first mention of "it."

"Well, Mother Russell, there isn't a thing to be done about it now, in any case. They're going to teach the classes whatever anyone says."

"I know that, Selma, but I will never give my approval."

"I guess most parents approve."

"Now that's just it, Doris. I don't believe for a minute that most parents know what they think! They're positively led astray, that's all it is. They don't know what's right anymore, they're afraid of their own children. Well, I know what's what. If a girl's properly raised, she doesn't need to know all those things. 'Birth control!' That's for the sort of woman who is too selfish and frivolous to be a mother! I suppose there are rich people and movie stars who have nothing better to do with their time than get divorced and remarried every other year, like that Liz Taylor. Let them teach that stuff to girls in those fancy colleges back east if they want to—a decent high school girl in Baker, South Dakota, has no business looking at pictures—pictures of, of...."

"Male and female anatomy?"

"Well, do you see the good in it? Oh, I'm not a complete old fool, I know there are poor women, too, who really shouldn't have more children. But that's married women, with husbands who can't support them, not...."

"Not girls? What about that poor child last year who had her baby 'unassisted,' as the paper put it, and was charged with killing it?"

"Now, Doris, those charges were dismissed."

"Oh, Mother Russell. That's not the issue. The pathetic thing shouldn't have had to go through any of that, and if...."

"If she'd been properly brought up...."

"If she'd been properly *informed*...."

"Well."

"Well."

"If you had a daughter, Doris...."

"If I did, I'd tell her exactly how a woman can protect herself, as soon as she could understand about it."

"Hm! And I suppose the boys...."

"Denver will tell the boys. Ignorance is ignorance, that's all, and people always suffer for it."

"I think she's right, Mother Russell."

"It's easy to say, Selma, but you can get to know too much, too. It seems like there isn't any *childhood* anymore."

"It's going to be their world; they'll have to live in it."

"Like Laurel Hutchins, I suppose? Off to New York to live with a bunch of crazy artists and I don't know what? Now I *do* hope *she* knows how to protect herself."

"Oh, Mother Russell. Well, I expect she does; Alice Hutchins has good sense."

"My mother would no more have raised the subject with me than, than...."

"Nor would mine, but...."

"No, now you listen to me, Selma. And you too, Doris. I'm quite serious—and I'm not trying to change the subject now. My mother didn't like being a woman much, that's why she wouldn't talk about those things. That wasn't good, really, and I know it. I didn't want to be a girl. I followed my father all day long, every chance I got. I teased him into teaching me how to do nearly everything he could do, or nearly. But I don't regret that now. And moreover, I picked up a good bit of what you call information along the way, just from observation, so I wasn't completely ignorant! And if I've suffered for any of that, I don't know how."

"That's fine for a farm child. But hardly a tenth of the children in the Baker schools are farm children anymore, and besides they want different lives, they want...."

"A lot of nonsense."

"Maybe, but they do want travel and new experiences and getting to know different kinds of people, they won't just settle down and raise families as soon as they can."

"Well, I wish them luck. But I daresay human nature won't be changed by 'information.'"

"Oh, Mother Russell."

"Listen to them in the living room. I wonder if anyone's watching those children."

Of course no one was, and so we got that straightened out and dinner on the table, and then everyone was too busy passing things and eating them to get a conversation started again, and a good thing, too. I know we'll be coming back to Baker for the holidays, even after we have our own place in Sioux Falls, but it will be easier, then, I'm sure. It is just too much, now, in every way.

*　　　*　　　*

The following interview with Ed Atwood, managing editor of the Baker Record, took place in 1981.

Q: When did you start working on the paper?
A: In 1974. I'd just finished my degree in journalism at Vermillion* on the GI bill. When I came back home here, the job was waiting for me.
Q: And was the town different after the war?
A: Not the town so much as the college; that's where the growth was, at first—and mostly, in fact, right along.
Q: Did you feel you knew the town when you got back?
A: Well, I was a young man. I didn't know everybody *well*, but, yes, I knew who everyone was, if that's what you mean. It was a small town—still is, but it doubled in size by the sixties.
Q: Do you still know everyone?
A: I do, it's been my business too. And in Baker the personal touch counts for a lot. Always has.
Q: Have you ever been in politics?
A: Held any office, you mean? No, but I've supported some candidates and issues.
Q: Did you usually know the people in local offices personally, in the fifties?
A: Sure—there was usually a mix on the city commission, for example, professionals, local farmers, pretty often somebody from the college. I knew them.
Q: Businessmen?
A: Sure—for example, the developer, Art Bates, Sam Byrne, the implement dealer; his family's owned the International Harvester franchise since the year one and the Ford dealership since early in the war, let's see, Carl Fries owns the big furniture and appliance store, he was on for several terms, want me to go on?
Q: You'd say, then, the wealthier businessmen?
A: No, not necessarily.

*Town in which the University of South Dakota is located.

Q: Do you—have you generally—known who had the money in Baker?

A: I guess everybody knows. It'd be hard to hide in Baker, even if you wanted to, and mostly folks don't—the personal touch again. I don't mean that people who are well off in Baker got to throwing their weight around, making a show of it. They were interested in the town is what I mean.

Q: Some have made a show?

A: Oh, there's some big fancy houses, especially back at the turn of the century, banking money—the Scherburne place—feed and grain money, railroad money. After the war, the whole town prospered. Moreover, you got to take into account, this wasn't a town where the "haves" sat around wondering when the "have nots" were going to rise up against them. There weren't "have nots," in that sense. The farmers represent one solid interest, whether they are well off or not—and some definitely are. But they all had the same view of Ike's farm policies, for example.* The Farm Bureau was, and is, very powerful in the country. And in town, the families with money genuinely attempted to better things for the town as a whole, over and over again. It wasn't often a case of money trying to swing a deal to make more money.

Q: Not ever?

A: I could tell you of more cases where land or properties were sold under value or donated for civic improvement, a lot of fund raising, clean dealing all the way—take the Industrial Development Corporation, now that didn't hurt the owners, but it was a good thing for the town.

Q: No other kind of story?

A: I tell you. You'd have to have been a magician to fool this town for long—a fool to try it. I'm not saying nobody's ever looked out for number one, but if scandal's what you're after, I can't oblige. Now it's not moral purity I'm talking about, but the feeling people had, the postwar feeling, that we'd been through it, *been* through the Depression and the way, and we knew we'd pulled together and made it, and so there was the feeling we could work together for a common goal. You get events like all the labor volunteered for the new county agricultural building. There are dozens of service organizations in town—for example, the Elks ran medical clinics. Want me to go on?

Q: So there's no distrust?

A: People work together, I'm saying. It's that people figured these men were financially sound; if they were into politics or

*For example, flexible price supports, which the farmers wanted fixed.

development or whatever, it wasn't for the dollars, they didn't need that. Nobody much thought "there's gotta be an angle, they've gotta be out to get us."

Q: Why was Baker like this?

A: Size, mostly. Conservatism, of course—you haven't missed that? Actual prosperity, as I said.

Q: There were no poor people in Baker?

A: Damn few, damn few. It's still that way. Can you find 'em? There's no place that's "the other side of the tracks." There's no race problem, because they aren't here. Fred Lawrence came home from Korea with a Japanese wife. That poor girl must've wanted to hide plenty of times, her first few months in town. The first and only Oriental in town. Our kids don't get in big trouble, they mostly take jobs, don't "hang out" like kids in bigger towns. There haven't been hard drugs available here, even at the college. Crime? You look at our old crime reports some time. The largest number of arrests is for drinking. Something like ten felonies a year, in the fifties.

Q: And the people who aren't either poor or wealthy, they're in the majority, the *large* majority?

A: Sure they are.

Q: Did any special group of people go to the country club? Belong to any of the clubs?

A: No, at the country club it has always been the whole mix; it is the best place there is to go, in town. Everybody goes there. It's close to downtown.

Q: And for other entertainment? Each other's homes? I mean, I know there were cultural activities, I'm talking about social gatherings.

A: Yes, I'd say so. Parties, and the like. The most exclusive groups in town would be among the college professors, but that's just common interests, and even there, there's always been a lot of mixing.

Q: So the clubs in town, like the Riding Club, were just common interest groups?

A: I'd say so, yes. Now, of course, there are old friendships, older families. But the influential people haven't acted exclusive. It's no secret in Baker who can pick up the phone and get things done, what's getting done.

Q: So you really would say there are almost no class distinctions made in Baker?

A: I would!

*　　　*　　　*

9 Social Class and Stratification

ENJAMIN Franklin noted how lucky he had been to marry a woman who was "as much disposed to industry and frugality as myself" (1730/1944). They lived simply; Franklin's breakfast for a long time consisted of bread and milk, which was eaten "out of a twopenny earthen porringer, with a pewter spoon" (90). But things were soon to change.

> But mark how luxury will enter families, and make a progress, in spite of principle: being call'd one morning to breakfast, I found it in a China bowl, with a spoon of silver! They had been bought for me without my knowledge by my wife, and had cost her the enormous sum of three-and-twenty shillings, for which she had no other excuse or apology to make, but that she thought *her* husband deserv'd a silver spoon and China bowl as well as any of his neighbors. (90)

Franklin advocated a life-style of hard work, thrift, and temperance, not primarily as a means of obtaining material goods (although that might happen), but as a way of acquiring grace. Today, a person who behaved like Franklin would be considered unusual. For many people, consumption has become an end in itself; they work in order to acquire things. As a result, our society judges people on the basis of their possessions. Exactly how this is done varies considerably from community to community. As we saw in previous chapters, at one time a person's worth or standing in the community depended on such things as whether he or she behaved like a good Christian or worked hard. But today's criteria are different. This chapter will discuss some of the changes that have taken place. First, however, we will examine the issue of stratification and social class by analyzing the people of Baker.

To begin, let us examine some of the social and economic changes that occurred between 1940 and 1960. One of the most obvious was the shift from rural to urban, which was similar to that occurring on a national level. For instance, as shown in the following list, in 1940 only 32 percent of the people in the country lived in towns, but by 1960 over 53 percent of them did; at the same time, the rural-farm population dropped from 51 percent to 31 percent.

YEAR	URBAN	RURAL NONFARM	RURAL FARM
1940	32%	17%	51%
1950	44	16	40
1960	53	16	31

There were two reasons for the gains in urban population: first, a few people moved from their farms to the cities, and, second, the natural increase in population was concentrated in the cities. In 1940, for instance, the population of Baker County was 16,560 people, but by 1960 it had grown to 20,046. This was due mainly to the growth of State College, which had a small enrollment before World War II but had 2,669 students by 1960. Professors such as Michael West moved to town in order to work at the college. So although Baker's population did grow, the increase can be traced mostly to the growth of the college rather than the flight from the farms.

From 1940 through 1960, the total number of farms in Baker County remained relatively stable. In 1945, there were 1,880 farms, which averaged 275 acres in size. By 1959, the number of farms had fallen to 1,692, but they averaged 295 acres; only 33 were smaller than 10 acres, and 14 farms exceeded 1,000 acres in size. In an effort to expand their operations, some farmers were able to purchase land from older farmers who did not have sons to take their place or from the few who sold out and moved on to something else. Most of the nation's farms were working farms; that is, they were the principal source of income for the family, not part-time ventures. Even Raymond Johnson, whose father's farming venture was not successful, wanted to keep the farm and improve farming methods rather than get outside work.

The condition of the farmers improved markedly between 1940 and 1960. In 1940, only 14.8 percent of all farmhouses had electric lighting, and only 6.2 percent had running water. But only ten years later, 90 percent of the farms had electricity, and about half had complete plumbing facilities.

Baker's work force also grew in size and complexity. A total of 52 percent of the workers were employed in agriculture in 1940, but by 1960 this figure had dropped to 30 percent. In 1940, about 3 percent of the urban labor force was employed in construction; 1.5 percent in manufacturing; 3 percent in transportation, communications, and utilities; 14 percent in wholesale and retail trade; 18 percent in business and personal services (for example, doctors, lawyers, insurance agents, barbers); and the remaining approximately 8 percent were scattered in numerous other activities. In 1960, a total of 19 percent of the work force was employed in wholesale and retail trade; close to 20 percent of all those working were teachers; and there were increases in the number of people working in finance, insurance, real estate, and city, county, and state government. In fact, by 1960, it was possible to classify 37.8 percent of Baker's labor force as white collar.

The actual number of restaurants, furniture stores, machinery dealers, clothing stores, bakeries, drugstores, hardware stores, and other enterprises in Baker increased somewhat between 1940 and 1960, and they also became larger. In 1940, for instance, the average store employed two people, and service establishments (repairmen) had only one employee. In 1960, the average store had 4.5 employees. The average employee's income also rose. The yearly income of those in retail trade jumped from an average of $1,510 in 1940 to about $2,300 in 1960.

Although it is difficult to get an accurate picture of income concentration in Baker, several details are clear. First, the number of wealthy farmers, such as the Russells, grew. For many, farming had become a business to be conducted like any other. Capitalization and cash flow concerned commercial farmers as much as they did the town's business community. Between 1940 and 1960, all indices showed a growth in the farmers' real income and an improvement in their standard of living. Just as there was a concentration of income and wealth among farmers, so there was among the town's businesspeople. Between 1940 and 1960, Baker's professional sector grew, with a number of people working at the college. Between 1950 and 1960, however, there was not a dramatic improvement in the living standard of many of Baker's citizens. In 1950, a total of 32 percent of the families had incomes of under $2,000 a year. A decade later, 35 percent still had incomes of under $3,000 a year, even though the national economy was growing. There also was a substantial middle-income group: 53 percent of the families' incomes fell between $2,000 and $5,000 in 1950, and ten years later,

60 percent fell between $3,000 and $10,000. In 1950, a total of 15 percent of the families had incomes over $5,000. Finally, 5 percent had incomes over $10,000 in 1960. Thus, even though a few families were considered well-to-do, fully one-third were not. And what was happening in Baker was not unlike what was happening in the country as a whole. (See U.S. Department of Commerce, 1947:334–339; 1949:267–271; 1952:346–353; 1962:322–331.)

THE NATIONAL SCENE, 1945–1960

The Rise of a Working Class

A working class usually refers to those people who do not own their own means of production and who sell their labor power on the open market in competition with other workers. In this sense, a working class has been a feature of modern society since the end of feudalism and was already well established in the United States by the beginning of the twentieth century. Cities such as Chicago, Omaha, Kansas City, and Minneapolis had large working-class populations long before 1945. A continued shift in the country's occupational structure saw fewer people working on farms and more becoming white-collar workers (see Table 9-1). Many white-collar workers, however, like blue-collar workers, worked for somebody else.

Table 9-1

MAJOR OCCUPATIONS OF AMERICAN WORKERS, 1940–1976

(in percentages)

	Total Labor Force (in 1000s)			
	51,742	*58,999*	*66,681*	*87,485*
	1940	*1950*	*1960*	*1976*
White-collar workers	31.1	36.6	43.1	50.0
Professional and technical workers	7.4	8.6	11.2	15.2
Managers, officials, and proprietors	7.2	8.7	10.5	10.6
Clerical workers	9.6	12.3	14.7	17.8
Sales workers	6.6	7.0	6.6	6.3
Blue-collar workers	39.8	41.1	36.3	33.1
Craftsmen and foremen	11.9	14.2	12.8	12.9
Operatives	18.4	20.4	18.0	15.2
Nonfarm laborers	9.4	6.6	5.5	4.9
Service workers	11.7	10.5	12.5	13.7
Private household workers	4.6	2.6	3.3	–
Other service workers	7.1	7.8	9.2	–
Farmworkers	17.4	11.8	8.1	3.2

Sources: U.S. Bureau of the Census, *Historical Statistics of the United States, Colonial Times to 1957* (Washington, D.C.: U.S. Government Printing Office, 1960), p. 74; *Statistical Abstract of the United States, 1977* (Washington, D.C.: U.S. Government Printing Office, 1977), p. 406.

One of the patterns that became more entrenched during World War II was the routinization of work. The move toward bureaucratization and systematization occurred because the developing industrial system required a work force capable of "pacing its toil and its very life cycle to the requirements of the machine and the clock, respectful of property and orderly in its demeanor" (Montgomery, 1972:411). As a result, the laborers' control over the work process lessened. Until about the nineteenth century in Europe and the early twentieth century in the United States, even though artisans might have been working for someone else, they often set their own work pace and determined their own hours (Calhoun, 1981). By the mid-1940s, however, such standards were almost entirely imposed by the employers.

Why did workers lose control? Some claim that the loss was due to the increase in the division of labor, the need for accuracy and precision, and the bureaucratization of work. Many argue, for example, that the standardization of products made it necessary for control to be vested in one person—a supervisor. Workers could not be left to their own devices because the products they turned out might differ. If they were making parts to be assembled into an automobile, for example, then someone other than the workers had to oversee the entire process. Slowly, then, in the name of efficiency and scientific rationality, workers were reduced to automatons. But a number of studies have suggested that workers lost control of the work process because they lost a political or class struggle (see especially Braverman, 1974). Owners wanted to maximize output and profit, and thus they needed to take control of the work process, which they did in the name of progress and efficiency. But there is evidence that neither the quality of product nor worker efficiency improved once labor became bureaucratized. Nevertheless, the nature of work changed: it lost its meaning as the workers lost their control of the process. The result was a new type of working class. (It should be noted that today a number of tasks—sewing, finishing clothing, computer work, machine tooling—are being returned to the home because it is cheaper for employers. The quality of the work has not suffered and, in some cases, has improved. [See Buck, 1979; Green and Weiner, 1981; and Koeppel, 1978.])

The developing industrial system, which grew rapidly with World War II, transformed society: "For the working population, this transformation manifests itself, first, as a continuous change in the labor processes of each branch of industry, and second, as a redistribution of labor among occupations and industries" (Braverman, 1974:9). We have already emphasized the growth of white-collar positions (see Table 9-1). Many people assume that white-collar workers are from the middle class, whereas blue-collar workers are not. And they believe that the United States has become a middle-class society. It is important to understand, however, that many white-collar jobs are unskilled or semiskilled positions; for example, the positions of store clerk, salesperson, or bank clerk require very little training. Moreover, many so-called professional workers do not make decisions about the work process. The manager of a fast-food restaurant or a large chain store has a given set of rules and regulations to enforce. The job is not supposed to include innovation or extra responsibility. Depending on the criteria used, such as control over the labor process or the lack thereof, many Americans can be categorized as workers (see Wright, 1978, for a discussion of modern society's class structure).

But people who work under the control of others do not always see themselves as members of the working class. When we speak of *class consciousness*, we mean the recognition by a specific group of people that they stand in the same relationship to the economy (or means of production) as do another group of people, and act accordingly. For instance, class-conscious workers understand that they are members of the category of people who sell their labor power, and their political activity reflects this understanding. Striking workers are an example of a class-conscious group of people. The evidence we have from Baker and from other studies of the United States between 1945 and 1960 shows that most people who sold their labor power did not see themselves as members of the working class. Most people tended not to make rigid class distinctions and, in fact, had the general impression that the entire country was becoming middle-class.

Images of the Middle Class, 1945–1960

C. Wright Mills (1951) was one of the first social scientists to recognize the emergence of a white-collar class. Mills, though, was not sanguine about its arrival: "The white-collar people slipped quietly into modern society. Whatever history they have had is a history without events; whatever common interests they have do not lead to unity; whatever future they have will not be of their own making" (1951:ix). In Mills's view, the white-collar worker was always somebody else's man—be it the corporation's, the government's, or the army's—locked into place with little hope of improvement. Unlike those who sold their labor power, these people had nothing to sell but their personalities. For Mills and others, the political and social consequences were particularly frightening. Mills had always believed that the small farmer shouldered the burden of democracy and that working with one's hands, for oneself, guaranteed the survival of those values on which the nation was founded. Not so with the white-collar employees, whom he saw as frightened and conservative.

In *Class in Suburbia* (1963:33), Dobriner argued that what distinguished this frightened group was respectability: "The lower-middle-class...[have] jobs [which] lead into peculiar niches having no future. Lack of a college degree from the right sort of school holds them back....Boxed off and turned back into the main stream of the middle strata, they cling...to the value of 'respectability.'"

In writing to her friend about Denver Ray Russell, Leona Johnson emphasized the importance of respectability in a small town: a girl must be careful "about who [she] date[s] in high school, and I have learned that lesson the hard way." The line between morality and status is narrow. In a small town, the standards of respectability prohibited sexual activity outside marriage, drunkenness, not providing for one's family, and not being clean and orderly. Laurel Hutchins commented on visiting another girl's home: "It was [embarrassing]. Her grandmother had just gotten back from the hospital where she cleans and was sitting on this old broken-down couch in the living room with her shoes off, and their breakfast was still all over the table." In "proper" homes, it is implied, these things do not happen.

William H. Whyte, Jr. announced the end of the Protestant ethic and the rise of a new social type in his book *The Organization Man* (1957). In Whyte's view, the organization ground down genius, demanded conformity, and emphasized belongingness and togetherness, along with a "well-rounded" personality. The Protestant ethic, which emphasized individuality, initiative, and achievement, was being replaced by a social ethic. In the future, people would learn to get along in order to get ahead. Their values were being redefined in line with the bureaucracy's needs.

This theme of changing character is the subject of David Riesman's *The Lonely Crowd* (1953). Instead of a nation of *inner-directed* personality types, Americans were becoming *other-directed*. Inner-directed individuals can rely on their firm belief in a consistent set of values, usually learned from parents and close associates, to guide them through life's ambiguities. External conformity is not the end for inner-directed persons, only consistency with this set of principles. Not so with other-directed persons, who conduct their lives according to their need for approval. Riesman stated:

> What is common to all the other-directed people is that their contemporaries are the source of direction for the individual— either those known to him or those with whom he is indirectly acquainted, through friends and through the mass media. This source is of course "internalized" in the sense that dependence on it for guidance in life is implanted early. The goals toward which the other-directed person strives shift with that guidance: it is only the process of striving itself and the process of paying close attention to the signals from others that remain unaltered throughout life. (1953:37)

This suggests, among other things, that the mass media and children's peer groups have assumed major roles in socialization. Other-directed children are extremely sensitive to what others think of them and adjust their behavior accordingly. One must consume the right things in order to belong to the right group. Norma Clark pointed out in her letter to her friend Joyce, "I'll never find what I want in this town, though, so Mom's going to take me shopping in Sioux Falls. There's a Jonathan Logan dress in this month's *Seventeen* which I *love*. And I want a charcoal gray straight skirt to go with my pink sweater set. It will be a ball....Write and tell me about school, what kind of outfits you bought for this year, [and] what the kids in your school are wearing."

During the 1950s, a homogenization of culture, through mass advertising, and the standardization of clothing, music, reading material, movies, and so forth became a reality. The good life, imagined in material terms, was the American Dream. To some extent, consumption destroyed distinctive life-styles. Aronowitz (1973:16) suggested that even leisure time became commercialized and that the burgeoning capitalist order reached all levels: "The colonization of private life by the structures of industrial society is revealed most directly in the overwhelming role played by consumption activity in leisure or unbounded time. The distinctions between the private and public realm that constitute the real basis for the cultural autonomy of the working class are constantly being undermined."

A number of voices were raised against the apostles of progress and prosperity: Mills, Riesman, and Whyte all had their reservations about the values of the new middle class. Sloan Wilson's 1955 best-seller, *The Man in the Gray Flannel Suit,* was about a man who felt as though he lived in two different worlds, "the matter-of-fact, opaque-glass-brick-partitioned world of places like the United Broadcasting Company and the Schanenhauser Foundation," in which he learned how to "package" himself as a valuable employee, and the world of his immediate family. "There must be some way in which the...worlds were related, he thought, but it was easier to think of them as entirely divorced from one another" (22).

It has been argued that much of this change took place in the urban centers, bypassing rural and small-town America. Yet the forces shaping the occupational structure of the country as a whole also affected small towns such as Baker, in which there was a rise in the number of clerks and shopkeepers and in which adolescents as well as their parents resonated to the cultural tunes being played elsewhere. Of course, individual values determined to some extent how a person would respond to, for example, the pressure for consumerism; but, however consumption took place, it was of the standardized products now available.

The Power Elite

By 1945, power and authority in the United States had assumed a national character, with major political and economic decisions being made in Washington or financial centers such as New York and Chicago. According to C. Wright Mills (1959), a national class system had emerged, with a small and powerful group of people—the power elite—who were in a position to affect political, economic, and military decisions. Those belonging to it knew one another, joined the same clubs, went to the same schools, saw their children marry one another, and as a result shared a set of interests distinct from those of the larger public. Several of Mills's assumptions have been challenged, but his principal argument, that the United States' political and economic system operates in the interests of the corporate rich, seems valid. The American political system is a capitalist one, and the federal government guarantees a favorable climate for investment and acts to check the rival interests of distinct class groups.

At the national level, then, we can discern a variety of trends. The work force was restructured, with laborers' losing control over the work process. The number of white-collar positions grew, and the national wealth increased. There was not, however, a significant redistribution of wealth in the country (see Table 9-2). For instance, in 1947, the lowest fifth of the population received only 5.1 percent of the national income, whereas the highest fifth received 43.3 percent, more than eight times what the lowest received. And this situation has not changed appreciably, for in 1978 the lowest fifth only received 5.2 percent and the highest received 41.5 percent. The position of the middle class, too, has remained relatively unchanged since 1941. Thus, the growth of the middle class has involved more of an occupational shift than a shift in wealth, which remains concentrated in the upper class.

THEORIES OF SOCIAL STRATIFICATION

The Functionalist Theory

The classic statement on the functional theory of stratification was made by Kingsley Davis and Wilbert Moore (1945), who stated that all societies are faced with the problem of motivation. In order to survive, a society, no matter what its size, must persuade people to fill certain positions and to perform the duties required of those positions. The number of positions and their associated duties depend on the size of the society and its degree of development. The United States is a highly industrialized society with a complex division of labor, and the positions it has to fill (e.g., dishwasher, dentist, lathe operator) are almost too numerous to count.

Some jobs are difficult, or require long training, or are unpleasant; people must be motivated to accept such jobs. According to Davis and Moore, societies motivate people by offering them at least one of the following rewards: sustenance and comfort, amusement,

Table 9-2

CONCENTRATION OF FAMILY INCOME IN THE UNITED STATES, 1941–1978

Year	Lowest Fifth	Second Fifth	Third Fifth	Fourth Fifth	Highest Fifth	Highest 5%
1941	4.1	9.5	15.3	22.3	48.8	24.0
1947	5.1	11.8	16.7	23.2	43.3	17.5
1950	4.5	11.9	17.4	23.6	42.7	17.3
1955	4.8	12.2	17.7	23.4	41.8	16.8
1960	4.8	12.2	17.8	24.0	41.3	15.9
1970	5.4	12.2	17.6	23.8	40.9	15.6
1978	5.2	11.6	17.5	24.1	41.5	15.6

Sources: U.S. Bureau of the Census, *Statistical Abstract of the United States* (Washington, D.C.: U.S. Government Printing Office, 1964), p. 337; 1969, p. 322; and 1980, p. 454.

and respect. In short, people can be enticed to work at a task if it allows them to purchase comfort. They will also work at jobs that are particularly interesting (i.e., for amusement) or that command a great deal of respect, such as the position of judge or doctor.

A position's rank is based on its importance to society and on the scarcity of personnel qualified to fill that position. Because necessary skills are unevenly distributed, only a few people can fill the most important positions. Thus, these positions and those who occupy them are accorded a differential status, which in turn means differential access to society's scarce and most desired goods. Physicians, for instance, usually earn a high income, enabling them to purchase what society deems valuable, be it a house, a car, a vacation, or leisure time. From this perspective, social stratification is both functional and inevitable. It is functional because it allows society to fill important positions, and it is inevitable because knowledge, skills, and talent are not evenly distributed and people must be rewarded for their highly developed talents. This theory of stratification has been vigorously challenged. Tumin (1953) argued that a stratification system breeds historical inequities, that people do not really have to make sacrifices by undergoing long periods of training because they are paid back, and that a different value system might reward people more equitably. But this argument ignores the fact that whether a society's reward is money, power, status, or honor, the society still will be stratified.

If we applied the functional theory of stratification to a community such as Baker, we would not question whether the existing system was acceptable but, rather, try to understand how it relates to what the community considers as functionally important. For example, the college professors in Baker were usually held in high esteem. This fact is in accord with a theory that predicted that positions requiring extensive training will have a higher status than those that do not. And because society as a whole values education, it is more likely to honor people who have more of it. Another reason that the professors at State College in Baker were respected was that most of them were involved in agriculture, in a heavily agricultural state. Michael West, for instance, specialized in the study of plant diseases, and his work was directly related to the livelihood of many of the people in the county. Farmers, too, though not particularly well rewarded for their labors, were held in high esteem by most of the population. In fact, the State Department of Agriculture presented a Citation of Eminence to outstanding and successful farmers (see pp. 219–220). But this is nearly all that the functional perspective allows us to say about the people of Baker.

Useful as it may be for understanding the status accorded to a specific position at a specific time, it does not explain how systems of hierarchy evolve over time or how rigid such systems might be. To understand these issues, we must use another perspective.

The Marxian Theory

Karl Marx's theory was initially a reaction to German philosophers, particularly the Hegelians, who proposed that ideas had a reality of their own, which moved through history and affected human consciousness. Marx objected to this perspective because it ignored the fact that all ideas and concepts are the result of human beings who think, act, and feel. In addition, he argued that men and women are creative, laboring beings who realize themselves by transforming nature. The first historical act is, therefore, a material act; quite simply, people must work in order to eat. Material forces shape social factors—ideology and human consciousness.

Human history is an economic history. The various stages in the development of the division of labor determine the relationship of individuals to one another. As Marx asserted in the *Poverty of Philosophy* (1847/1966), "The hand-mill gives you society with the feudal lord; the steam-mill society with the industrial capitalist (95). Ideas do not have an independent reality; they flow from one's relationship to the material world. If societies differ in terms of their idea systems, it is because they have different material bases or different divisions of labor. Marx and Frederick Engels explained their position in *The Communist Manifesto* (1848/1948):

> The history of all hitherto existing society is the history of class struggles.
>
> Freeman and slave, patrician and plebian, lord and serf, guild-master and journeyman, in a word, oppressor and oppressed, stood in constant opposition to one another....
>
> In the earlier epochs of history, we find almost everywhere a complicated arrangement of society into various orders....
> In ancient Rome we have patricians, knights, plebians, slaves; in the Middle Ages, feudal lords, vassals, guild-masters, journeymen, apprentices, serfs....
>
> Our epoch, the epoch of the bourgeoisie, possesses, however, this distinctive feature: it has simplified the class

antagonisms. Society as a whole is more and more splitting up into two great hostile camps, into two great classes directly facing each other—bourgeoisie and proletariat. (9)

In Marx and Engels's view, society would break down into a situation in which the bourgeoisie and the proletariat, two distinct classes, each with a distinct ideology, were pitted against one another. People could stand in only two relationships to the means of production: they would either own them (the bourgeoisie) or they would not (the proletariat). Thus, the economic system determines individual behavior by compelling those who do not own the means of production to work and so provide the labor for others.

Because the proletariat must sell their labor power to the capitalists (bourgeoisie), they will lose control of the productive process and of the fruits of their own labor. They therefore will become alienated from their own labor and from one another. To Marx, only nonalienated labor will allow people to realize their social natures. Thus, the fact that capitalism causes alienation enables the workers to identify the source of their misery and to take action. In the Marxian sense, to be *class conscious* means to recognize that one stands in a specific relationship to the means of production and to take action on that basis.

The class-conscious actions of the bourgeoisie were seen by Marx as *reactionary*. The capitalists take more than their share of the means of production: they use the labor power of the workers to realize a profit that is not returned to the workers. The real source of wealth in capitalism, or any other economic system, is derived from human labor power. Therefore, in the Marxian schema, the emancipation of the workers will lead to the emancipation of all.

In the case of the United States, the class system is much more complex than this and has a number of characteristics that have inhibited the development of class consciousness. Reissman (1959) summarized those characteristics: feelings of antiaristocracy, a frontier psychology, the Protestant ethic, antiradical attitudes, urbanization, and industrialization. The ideology of the Great Plains settlers was certainly antiestablishment in its egalitarianism: one was what he or she achieved, not what one was born to. A frontier mentality—the notion of unlimited opportunities and optimism— was fostered by free land and the ability to move physically and socially. The Protestant ethic undermined class consciousness, because it implied that if a person amassed considerable wealth, it was through hard work and virtue. Antiradicalism is reflected in America's reluctance to blame the political and economic system for major crises such as the Depression. During the 1930s, most people tended to believe that things would get better and that change was just around the corner, rather than to analyze the problems of capitalism. Finally, urbanization and industrialization prevented the creation of two distinct classes. Reissman (1959) and others argued that the United States has consumption classes rather than political classes.

Even though Marx incorrectly predicted the imminent demise of capitalism, his materialist theories remain useful. For example, let us examine Marx's idea that people's beliefs and values are related to their material circumstances. A person's social class, which in the United States is largely related to his or her material possessions, is the best predictor of that person's values, attitudes, and behavior. We can generally predict from a person's social class which political party he or she is likely to belong to or his or her attitudes toward social welfare programs.

It is difficult to divide Baker's population into the proletariat and the bourgeoisie. As we pointed out earlier, farming poses a special problem. Farmers are independent entrepreneurs who own their own businesses. Yet often they have worked only for themselves and their families; they have not hired other people on a regular basis. The family farmer is engaged in what is called simple commodity production; that is, the family consumes a portion of what is produced and sells the surplus. The surplus, however, has the family's labor power invested in it, not that of a hired worker. In *The Communist Manifesto*, Marx and Engels also recognized the problem of categorizing farmers, for they seemed to be neither members of the bourgeoisie nor the proletariat. Marx and Engels felt that they were a particularly reactionary group.

The farmers in Baker, like farmers elsewhere, also had a distinct value set. These values varied according to religious affiliation, political party, and even size of farm. But they all seem to agree on certain things. For example, when we interviewed several independent family farmers in Kansas in 1980, we asked them what made them angry. They responded without hesitation: "A person who doesn't tell the truth"; "Someone who isn't a straight shooter"; "Anybody that lies"; "A person you can't trust." Farmers often pride themselves on keeping their word as well as on being able to count on their neighbors to help them out in times of trouble. There is a clear relationship between their material conditions and their social attitudes.

Unfortunately, the Marxian model cannot be usefully applied to Baker. First, we do not have the materials that would allow us to distinguish the attitudes of the affluent farmers, those who are at the margin, and the various groups in the town. Second, the issues that are likely to cause people to analyze events in terms of class were not raised in Baker between 1945 and 1960. There was no crisis leading to a struggle between a group that saw itself as the working class and one that saw itself as the bourgeoisie. Finally, in small towns there is a conscious attempt to avoid using class terms to describe people.

The Weberian Theory

To Max Weber (1864–1920), a society's system of stratification was the result of the complex relationship of class, status, and party. Weber (1946) started with the assumption that laws exist when there is a probability that given social orders will be supported by given groups of people. The legal system influences power, or the probability that a person, or group of persons, will be able to realize his or her will. Economic power, then, is not identical with political power, but it may result from it. The relationship among these variables supports the legal order, which legitimizes power or honor. Stratification is the result of the distribution of this social honor. Although the social, legal, and economic orders are closely related, they are not identical. Classes, status groups, and parties are a phenomenon of this distribution of power. The Weberian system, then, contains three components of power: classes, status groups, and parties. Each is based on a separate element or variable, which the society ranks.

Weber's *class groups*, which are similar to Marx's classes, are groups of people who are in the same class situation and have the same economic life chances. One's class position is based on wealth, which can be property or a salary. Many wealthy people do not draw a salary but, rather, own stocks, bonds, real estate, or precious goods such as gold and silver. This is why income concentration does not accurately reflect the concentration of resources in our society (see Table 9-2). In Weber's system, a class is not necessarily a conscious political group, for it simply refers to people who have the same kind of usable property.

Status groups are loosely organized communities, and whereas class groups are economically determined, status groups are determined by prestige. Since property is not the only qualifier of status, both the propertied and the propertyless can belong to the same status group, although property will, of course, influence which status group one belongs to. In small towns, the old rich, who may no longer have much money, are often seen as being on the same level, if not above, those who have recently acquired their money. Mrs. Scherburne, for example, was held in awe because of her style of life: "There is a whole lot of old furniture and old rugs and pictures and china cabinets and two pianos and hundreds, maybe thousands of books, it is all old and dark....She told me about the rugs, they are called Oriental."

Weber noted that status groups maintain their character through such things as style of life, lineage, marriage, and social intercourse. People with the same tastes and level of participation in art, literature, music, and recreation are members of the same status group. Lineage and in-group marriage also limit access to the status group. Forms of address, titles, and so forth are kinds of social intercourse that act as controls. Status groups monopolize the society's goods and services and set the patterns for the rest of society in clothes, art, literature, and sports. Because status groups withdraw scarce goods from the society and inhibit their exchange, they hinder the free development of the market principle.

It is easy to see how status groups operated in Baker High School. There were divisions between those who were from farms, those who were in the college track courses, those who were interested in Future Farmers of America, those who were interested in cars, and so forth. Sometimes the status groups overlapped, such as when a person was defined as both a "gearhead" and a member of the Future Farmers. Danny Berry, in relating events at the local high school to his friend Gary Coover, who had moved away, emphasized this: "All of the greaseballs are still around. You remember the guys who spent all of their time in the shop classes working on their projects and their cars? I still can't believe the school started auto mechanics." Danny then went on to describe the kinds of cars they drove and what they were doing to modify them—that is, their lifestyle, or the characteristics of their status group. There was also, even for adolescents, a conscious decision not to mix the status groups. In a letter to her friend Joyce, Norma told her about a bad date, when she was taken for a ride in Wayne Hooley's car: "I thought we'd go and get a hamburger and coke down at Brian's Cafe and talk, and I'd see some of my friends. No, we rode up and down Main Street for two hours, and then I had him take me home. That's his and his friends' idea of fun, not mine."

Clothes are symbols of identification with a particular clique or status group. Norma was also concerned with the type of clothing she was going to wear to school, as the wrong clothing could identify her with the wrong status group.

As Weber suggested, control of marriage is one of the ways in which status groups preserve their character. To be a member of the State College faculty meant that one belonged not only to an occupational group but also a status group. This can be seen in the recollections of Jane West Kenner, one of the women who left town. She talked about her sister's marriage to a farmer and her parents' reaction: "for my parents the worst thing was Louise had married a farmer....Daddy was always talking about how much he learned from the farmers. But I came to see that it's—it's like you don't want your daughter to marry one. Oh, nothing *obvious*, all very polite, lot of good will, big dinners, little compliments." Which church the West family attended was also important: "The West family simply went to the Episcopal services. Well, of course, Louise was a Lutheran-by-marriage by then, but we tried not to think about that, either....Of course we knew that part of being Episcopalians was being better than Lutherans, who were better than Baptists."

Finally, in the Weberian schema are *parties* that are stratified according to their consumption of power. Members of specific economic classes often belong to specific parties. In Baker, however, party membership cut across class lines. Many were traditional Republicans who vigorously opposed Roosevelt's policies, which they saw as benefiting the urban working classes. Sometimes, the Democrats suppressed their enthusiasm for Roosevelt or Truman in order to be accepted by the local community, that is, to be able to join the status groups to which they aspired.

Finally, let us examine how this tripartite system of class, status, and power can help us understand one family.

The Kneip family belonged to the class of successful farmers, for they "live on a 320-acre diversified farm with beef cattle and purebred Poland China hogs." They were also members of a status group with a distinctive style of life. First, Ethel Kneip was listed as a 1948 South Dakota Eminent Homemaker. While doing all that was expected of a farm wife and mother, Mrs. Kneip was also "a lady who can always be counted on to do more than her share in helping out with any community activity....She is often referred to as the 'mother of the community.'" In short, Mrs. Kneip fulfilled her community's definition of a good farm wife. She was seen as guarding the family's welfare and working for its improvement. The success of her children was her success, and her two daughters were continuing in the same tradition: "Ferne is a sophomore at State in

Home Economics. ᴐne is an assistant 4-H leader. Janice is a sophomore at Baker High School and is also an active 4-H club member, active in GAA, band, orchestra and pep band, student council representative and vice president of her class." It is often the women who maintain the boundaries of the status group, through the mechanisms already identified, for example, control of marriage, social intercourse, and associational activities. The activities of Ethel Kneip and her children guaranteed the continuity of their status group.

Following Weber, one would suppose that, because of their relative wealth and because they were members of a respected status group, the Kneips were probably able to exercise power through a political party, even though the options available to them were somewhat limited. Many of their neighbors were Republicans, and the Kneips probably were too. In order to be politically effective, then, they would have had to work within the framework of the existing party structure, and the party, be it Democrat or Republican, would have had interests that cut across class lines. On local issues pertaining to agricultural interests, however, Mr. Kneip and those like him probably had some influence.

We have talked in general terms about class, status, and power without examining the kinds of divisions that people in Baker and other small communities were likely to make. Did they speak of the lower class and of the rich? Did they make any class distinctions at all? As we try to answer these questions, we will also look at some of the other concepts that social scientists use when considering inequality.

CLASS AND STATUS GROUPS IN THE COMMUNITY

There have been many studies of small towns in the United States and the ways in which the people in these communities distinguished one another. Vidich and Bensman's classic study, *Small Town in Mass Society* (1960), shows how carefully the issue of class can be ignored in a small town. In the 1950s in Springdale, New York, Vidich and Bensman talked to people who made it clear that it was "a social *faux pas* to act as if economic inequalities make a difference" (4). They spoke as though there were just two social categories, "good folks and bad folks." This, of course, is similar to the emphasis on respectability in Baker. And it signals the importance of status groups rather than class groups.

The farming community in Springdale judged people according to whether they were good workers. Farmers were often suspicious of those who took vacations or even felt a need for them. They believed that people should work hard, accumulate but not waste money, and get ahead: "Through the judicious manipulation and exercise of a combination of hard work and self-improvement a man improves his social position" (Vidich and Bensman, 1960:51). The emphasis on equality and the belief that everyone could get ahead did not, however, prevent people from distinguishing among one another and acting on the basis of those distinctions. Vidich and Bensman sketched out a broad class scheme with five major categories:

1. *The Middle Class*
   A. Independent entrepreneurs such as grocery store owners.
   B. Rational farmers who approached farming as a business and used their profits to expand their operations.
   C. Professionals and skilled industrial workers.

2. *The Marginal Middle Class*
   A. Aspiring investors, people on their way up, and part-time farmers who had additional jobs in town.
   B. Hard-working consumers, wage workers, and people who had more than one job.

3. *The Old Aristocracy* was composed of a group of former business and financial leaders.

4. *The Traditional Farmers* were those who were not interested in expanding their operations, who wished to avoid debt, and who stressed independence.

5. *The Shack People* were "the object of universal derision in Springdale, a declassed group. By their style of their dwelling—the jerry-built shack, the converted barn, the abandoned tenant house—they implicitly reject the whole complex of middle-class life styles" (69).

In Baker there were similar categories. For instance, the town and the county could be broken down into the following categories:

1. *The Big Farmers* were those who had farms averaging around one thousand acres in size and who saw themselves as businesspersons.

2. *The Traditional Farmers* were those who still saw farming

as a way of life rather than a business and who avoided going into debt.

3. *The Old Aristocracy* included people like Mrs. Scherburne, the banker's widow, and those who had been major merchants and/or professionals in the town for a long time.

4. *The Professionals* were the professors at the local college, as well as the town's doctors and lawyers.

5. *The Part-time Farmers and Workers* aspired to the middle class but were not owners of their own businesses, and/or their farms were too small to derive a full-time living from.

6. *The Entrepreneurs* were the owners of the numerous small businesses, such as grocery stores, barber shops, service stations, and restaurants.

7. *The Workers* were those who worked full time at manual tasks at the college, the service stations, the grain elevators, or the local stores.

We could also group these categories according to whether they were upper, middle, and lower class. But although the people of Baker recognized such categories, they did not go out of their way to emphasize them. According to Ed Atwood, managing editor of the *Baker Record*, the townspeople tried to smooth over their differences, rather than start conflicts. On whether everyone knew who did and did not have money, he said, "I guess everybody knows. It'd be hard to hide in Baker, even if you wanted to, and mostly folks don't—the personal touch again. . . . Oh, there's some big fancy houses, especially back at the turn of the century, banking money—the Scherburne place—feed and grain money, railroad money. . . . Moreover, you got to take into account, this wasn't a town where the 'haves' sat around wondering when the 'have nots' were going to rise up against them. There weren't 'have nots,' in that sense." Despite his assertion, in 1950, a total of 32 percent of the families in Baker had a cash income of less than $2,000. The idea that Baker was a society of just "plain folks" clearly dominated their thinking and inhibited the development of class consciousness.

In *Elmtown's Youth,* based on interviews conducted in the early 1940s, Hollingshead (1949) discusses the relationship between social class and behavior. The people of Elmtown made distinctions not unlike those that Vidich and Bensman found in Springfield, New York. When asked if there were classes in Elmtown, the townspeople used such terms as "society," "the top group," "the middle," "those with money," "riffraff," "people just as good as anybody else," and "the right family." It is important to note that the Elmtowners assumed that class and behavior were linked and carried these expectations into the high school. For example, the children who came from the bottom of the class ladder were expected to do poorly in school and to be less gifted than the children of the elite. Hollingshead found (1949:172) that a direct relationship existed between a student's grades and class position even when intelligence was taken into account. That is, a student from an upper-class family was more likely to get good grades than was an equally or more intelligent child from the lower classes. The children from the lower classes were channeled into the vocational tracks in high school, whereas the children from the upper classes were put into the college preparatory curriculum. The schools, then, reinforced the community's class system. The schools, instead of fostering equality, came to sponsor inequality.

The schools in Baker also reinforced the existing class or status group relations. First, as we've already noted, there were distinct cliques in the high school. Some students were involved in Future Farmers of America. Others, who took auto mechanics and customized their automobiles, overlapped with the FFA group and with the children of those best described as workers. The children of professionals, on the other hand, were concentrated in the college preparatory courses and pursued other extracurricular activities. Students' backgrounds were clearly taken into account; Laurel Hutchins noted, "Joyce and Davetta came up at lunch and said Mrs. Stirling doesn't like you to show off. She doesn't like Joyce either because she has two professors for parents, that is even worse than one high school teacher." Showing off to these teachers often meant displaying knowledge and sophistication that the teacher did not possess.

Leona Johnson, who moved into town from her family's farm to attend high school, took classes that would lock her into her status group. For instance, she noted, "I'm taking Clothes Design, too, and my suit is going so well that I may enter it at the fair, like Mrs. Schroder is always after us to do." Leona also found out that the boy with whom she was infatuated, Denver Ray Russell, had been saying unkind things about her. She thus withdrew from the relationship in order to maintain her respectability: "So much for that 'romance.' You were right about who you date in high school, and I have learned that lesson the hard way. Now I just pray none of our friends believe the filth he is trying to spread."

Class boundaries were maintained by dating, and it was easy for Denver Ray to imply that because he was dating "down," it was for sex. But one could also breach the boundaries of the status group on the basis of personal characteristics, as Hollingshead (1949) found. For example, an exceptional male athlete with a pleasant personality would be accepted in higher-status groups. The same was true for the attractive, personable, and well-behaved young woman. Intelligence alone was insufficient and could often have a negative effect. For example, in recalling her high school days in Baker, Jane West Kenner pointed out that her interest in literature only isolated her, that it was perceived as inappropriate: "So there had to be some *insincerity* there. *Calling attention* to yourself. Especially if you were a girl! So I saw, eventually, that no one was pitying me for not being like [my older sister]; on the contrary, they were resenting me for being 'conceited.'" The pressure to conform to the traditional roles of both sex and class was powerful.

MEASURING SOCIAL CLASS

W. Lloyd Warner (1960), one of the foremost students of the American stratification system, saw social classes as concrete entities: "To belong to a particular level in the social-class system of America means that a family or individual has gained acceptance as an equal by those who belong in the class. The behavior...must be rated by the rest of the community as being at a particular place in the social scale" (23). To measure a person's location in the class order, Warner used two techniques: *Evaluated Participation* (E.P.) and the *Index of Status Characteristics* (I.S.C.). Evaluated Participation, the more complicated method, has six techniques for rating an individual's class position:

1. Rating by *matched agreement* of community informants. In this method, one selects a group of people who are supposedly well informed about the community and then asks them to rate the social class of specific people. A person's status would be the average of the ratings.

2. Rating by *symbolic placement,* or identifying someone by means of status symbols, for example, possession of material objects. Mrs. Scherburne, who had Oriental carpets, dark wood walls, and solid furniture, would be symbolically

placed because of these objects. Likewise, someone who had linoleum floors, wore overalls to town, and went around in the house with slippers on when guests were present would be symbolically ranked.

3. Rating by *status reputation,* or placing a person in a class because he or she engages in certain status activities. A community might consider golf to be a higher-status activity than bowling.

4. Rating by *comparison,* or stating that a person is equal to, inferior to, or superior to someone.

5. Rating by *simple assignment,* as when an informant states that someone is a member of a particular class: "Oh, they're old money," or "They're just part of the riffraff."

6. Rating by *institutional membership* or participation in some organizations. In Baker, for example, the college faculty was seen as distinct from the town's old families. Betty West, the wife of a professor, scored a social coup when she was invited to join the town's book club.

The difficulties of using this procedure should be obvious. First, it is hard to locate respondents who are sufficiently knowledgeable and sufficiently dispassionate to rank all the members of a community. This is theoretically easier in a small town (although in practice, the smaller the town is, the less willing the informants are to make such statements), but it is almost impossible to do in a large town.

Warner, recognizing the limits of Evaluated Participation, devised the Index of Status Characteristics. He realized that much of what went into rating people could be summarized by occupation, source of income, house type, and dwelling area. Thus, he scored each of these elements and compiled a total. A professional who made a lot of money and lived in a substantial dwelling in the best part of town would be classified as a member of the top status group. Although designed to overcome the limits of Evaluated Participation, the index also has its limitations. For example, in a town like Baker, the dwelling areas are not clearly distinguished; the old stately homes often are next to much more modest ones.

Using the index, Warner and Lunt (1941) divided Yankee City, the fictional name of the town they were studying, into upper-upper, lower-upper, upper-middle, lower-middle, upper-lower, and lower-lower classes. Only 1.4 percent of the people were classified as being in the upper-upper class, and 25 percent of them fell in the lower-lower category—which reveals something about Warner and Lunt's view of the class system. How we look at the class system, whether from the bottom up or the top down, determines how many classes we see, as well as the behavior we attribute to the people in the different groups.

This was clearly demonstrated by Davis, Gardner, and Gardner (1941) in *Deep South*. They separated the class system into six categories, and their respondents defined each. The upper-upper class were the "old aristocracy," the lower-upper class were "aristocracy, but not old," the upper-middle class were "nice, respectable people," the lower-middle class were "good people, but 'nobody,'" and the two lower classes were simply lumped together as "po' whites." But the classes were seen quite differently from the perspective of those on the bottom (the lower-lowers) looking up. They viewed themselves as "people just as good as anybody," the upper-lower class as "snobs trying to push up," the lower-middle class as "way-high-ups, but not 'Society,'" and for the lower classes the upper-upper, lower-upper, and upper-middle classes all were categorized as "Society, or the folks with the money" (65). If one is at the bottom of the class ladder, one defines class on the basis of money. But if one is at the top, one defines class on the basis of family background and symbols of status.

Depending on the criteria used, a town's class or status system can be broken up into several different categories. If the criterion is status variables, that is, life-style, then the resulting distribution is different than if the criterion is occupation. When sociologists systematically rank large numbers of people, they usually rely on just occupation and education, because residential area, type of house, income, values, and so forth are closely tied to a family's profession and amount of education. Jane West Kenner's father, a college professor, was well educated. Because of both his education and occupational position, he maintained a distinctive life-style. The family decided, for instance, to wait until the girls were older to visit Europe so that the girls would receive maximum benefit from the trip.

Even though occupation and education can be used to classify large populations, they do not include behavioral elements. In towns such as Baker, people tend to rely more on status variables. They are interested in lineage and in whether a person upholds the values of the larger community. They consciously try to downplay economic differences and to treat everybody in the same way. Many voluntary associations cut across class groups, for example, the

Baker country club. According to the newspaper editor, Ed Atwood, "The country club...has always been the whole mix, it is the best place there is to go, in town. Everybody goes there." (Of course, not everybody could afford it.) But if people did act exclusively, according to Atwood, it was on the basis of common interest: "The most exclusive groups in town would be among the college professors, but that's just common interest, and even there, there's been a lot of mixing." Nevertheless, we still find class related to behavior.

CORRELATES OF SOCIAL CLASS

We have already discussed a number of the behavioral elements that relate to class, especially in high school. For instance, regardless of their intelligence, students from the upper end of the social scale are more likely to be found in the college preparatory courses, and students from the lower end usually are in vocational classes such as auto mechanics. The Wests always went to the Episcopal church, which had a higher status than the Lutheran church or the Baptist church did. These are patterns that tend to hold across the country: that is, upper-status families are more likely to be found in the Episcopal church than they are in a Southern Baptist church, just as upper-class high school students, regardless of their intelligence, are more likely than lower-class children to be in college preparatory courses.

A person's social class is one of the best variables for predicting other values and beliefs. Social class also relates to attitudes toward child rearing, sex, and sex education. In Chapter 8, the discussion on Thanksgiving Day was among women who not only were from different generations but also had different class values. Mother Russell objected to sex education at the local high school: "Now that's just it....I don't believe for a minute that most parents know what they think! They're positively led astray, that's all it is. They don't know what's right anymore, they're afraid of their own children. Well, I know what's what. If a girl's properly raised, she doesn't need to know all those things. 'Birth control!' That's for the sort of woman who is too selfish and frivolous to be a mother! I suppose there are rich people and movie stars who have nothing better to do with their time than get divorced and remarried every other year." Thus the lower one's class position is, the more conservative that person is likely to be in regard to such issues as birth control, abortion, and women's rights. Also in regard to the Thanksgiving dinner, Doris Russell, whose father and grandfather were physicians, commented that it was hardly her "idea of the way to spend a holiday....I was brought up to prefer keeping things simple, and this...! Four or five or six women working all day...to make a dinner for so many people that no one can really talk to anyone and then cleaning up and dividing up leftovers the rest of the day."

What a family regards as a necessity varies by class. Michael West, writing home to his mother and father, talked about the plans for the house, "so each girl can have her own room." Laurel Hutchins commented on her visit to another child's home: "Davetta doesn't have her own room. I feel really sorry for her. It must be awful to have your mother run off." There is little doubt about Davetta's social standing in comparison with Laurel's. To have one's own room—to have privacy— was a value that varied by class.

MOBILITY

Historical conditions, such as differential fertility, technological innovations, or migration, can affect people's mobility. People in the upper classes generally have fewer children than is necessary to replace themselves, and this creates opportunities, of a sort, for the children of the lower classes to move up. Technological innovations can open new realms of employment, such as the computer industry, or can expand the number of white-collar positions. Finally, because immigrants often take the less skilled and desirable jobs, they can push up those at the bottom of the class ladder. This, however, changed after the early 1900s, for many immigrants to the United States came with skills and talents that placed them high on the class ladder.

There are also individual factors that affect mobility. For example, if a boy is born into a white-collar family, a blue-collar family, or a farm family, he will probably take up the same general occupation that his father has. But there may be mobility within that category; that is, if his father is a clerk, he might be an insurance salesman, or if his father is a mechanic, he might be a lathe operator. Interestingly, the sons of farmers tend to stay in that category, eventually taking over the family farm, or, when it is economically feasible, starting one of their own (see Blau and Duncan, 1967, for a discussion of movement within categories).

Education is another factor. There is a consistent relationship between educational level and lifetime income. The farmer's sons who attended State College in Baker and became farmers themselves were more successful than those farmers who did not attend college. Social class, however, is a better predictor of lifetime income than education is (Jencks et al., 1972). (One's social class, of course, influences greatly the amount of one's education.)

Baker's growth in the late 1940s and early 1950s was due in large part to the townspeople's belief that education was the road to mobility. Veterans, using the GI bill, swelled enrollments in the college during this time. Danny Berry, writing to his friend Gary Coover, talked about the need to get out of town and to get into a good school in order to be mobile. Jane West Kenner and a number of other students moved to urban areas and experienced upward social mobility as a result. Blau and Duncan (1967) found that those who migrate are occupationally more upwardly mobile than are those who remain in the town in which they were born and that those who move to urban areas are occupationally more upwardly mobile than are those who move elsewhere.

Sociologists distinguish between the status that one is born into and the status that one achieves. *Ascribed status* is inherited status: one is born the son or daughter of a wealthy banker or a poor farmer and consequently inherits his or her parents' status. Carl Fries, whose son was lost in Korea, did not know what to do when his son could not inherit his business, an ascribed status: "There's been three generations of us in business in Baker, and now that's over."

Conversely, the children of the eminent farmer Walter Meester had *achieved status*: "All of the children have been graduated from State College. Vivian is now Mrs. Harold Kellogg....Susan is Mrs. John Clark of Sacramento, California....Ray is a veterinarian in practice in Aberdeen, South Dakota." It is assumed here that women take on the status of their husbands.

STRATIFICATION OF THE FAMILY

So far we have treated class and stratification as though they are outside the family. But there is also a hierarchy within the family. In most families, the women are considered subordinate to the men. This is evident in Baker, though most Baker women would not have considered it a problem during the time of which we are writing.

In Chapter 7, we discussed the subtle processes whereby people come to accept particular behavior patterns as normal. Many people assume, for example, that women work in the home, cook the food, and clean the house, whereas men work outside the home, earning the family's income. This pattern is seen as normal because it has been common; however, it is not inevitable and has not been characteristic of all societies. (It is, of course, no longer characteristic of our own, in which only 7 percent of all American families fit the pattern of housewife, breadwinner, and children at home.) Women who work in the home "producing" their family's meals, doing the laundry, cleaning the house, doing the shopping, driving the children to lessons, mending socks, and ironing shirts are usually unpaid laborers. Their labor power is exploited, and women who are dependent on their husband's wages are in a subordinate economic position. This situation does not usually change substantially when a woman works outside the home, for her wages will be smaller than her husband's, her job will be less secure, and she will still do most of the housework (U.S. Department of Labor, 1979). The family, then, must be seen as an arena in which gender and class struggles occur (Hartmann, 1981).

An argument refuting the notion that the women in a family are oppressed is that the husband is simply earning the wages for both him and his wife and that his wages are shared between them. Yet there is no evidence that a husband's wages are a just compensation for both the husband's and the wife's work. In fact, a woman's labor is usually appropriated by her husband's wages. Most men could not do the work they do if their wives did not prepare their meals, clean their clothes and home, and so send them back to do another day's work (Dalla Costa, 1972). This division of labor, then, represents a hierarchy in which the man controls the woman's labor.

The evolution of the sexual division of labor is a long one. According to Faragher (1980), the stereotypical view of the frontier woman is as the helpmate of her husband, working at his side to build a better life for themselves and their children. It is true that women did help on the farm, and in some cases, especially in the 1800s, they produced many of the goods for cash sale—butter, eggs, and vegetables. But the women did not have control of the money that they made, for it was often needed to pay off debts, invest in machinery and livestock, and meet additional needs. This pattern of male dominance, or patriarchy, was reinforced as the farms became more commercial and/or as men held second jobs. By the 1940s, for instance, the men were the farm managers, and the women were the farm wives, who continued to contribute to the success of the farm and the well-being of their families but whose economic power was diminished. Women spent less time directly working on the farm and more time taking care of their families. Leona Johnson particularly admired Denver Ray Russell's mother: "The Russells have a truly beautiful house....Mrs. Russell... has a whole modern kitchen with a gas stove and a toaster and an electric mixer. Denver just worships her, all the family does, and no wonder. She does everything for those four boys because she hasn't got any daughters and has her own apple orchard and keeps remodeling the house herself."

Anna Meester, whose husband was cited by the Department of Agriculture as one of South Dakota's eminent farmers, was in a similar situation. The citation stated that "Walter and Anna have raised four children....Mrs. Meester has always contributed to the farm income by keeping a big vegetable garden. Even during the drought years hardy varieties were planted in April and a program of moisture conservation provided mature vegetables." According to Mrs. Meester, the same principle applied to raising both children and vegetables: "They have to absorb the principle of honesty and industry, if they are to grow up useful."

Even when women's labor time shifted from the fields to the home, the amount of work they did did not decrease. This was also true in the town, where the women who stayed home worked long hours, too, usually longer than men did. This pattern still holds true. Though it varies with both the number of hours that women work outside the home and the age of their children, a study of Syracuse, New York, families found that the total amount of work that women did in a week was far above that of men (Walker and Woods, 1976).

Women are supposed to be the passive recipients of men's largess. In fact, many men see their success in the local community as being tied to their ability to provide for their women. Denver Ray Russell was proud that he could write to his pregnant wife, "I don't want you to overdo or worry about a thing....By the time our kids(!!) are in school I will buy you a fur coat and build you a house that will be the envy of all the girls in Baker, and that's just a start. I want the best of everything for my sweet wife, and I'll see she gets it."

Men's work is seen as real work, and women's work is not. Carl Fries wrote a long letter to his sister complaining that his wife, Pauline, would not slow down and was ruining her health. We could also interpret this to mean that she was not taking care of him: "All her energy is going into the Women's Auxiliary and canvassing for the building fund, and the suppers and bazaars, and so forth. Now those are all good things, good for the church and for the community, mind you. . . . I'm not complaining that she isn't taking care of the home all right, either. Only she's wearing herself out." He went on to list what his wife was doing and then grumbled that when he complained to her, she told him to take it easy and to cut out the things he did: "She says if I give up the hunting and if I quit minding the store and the business bureau and I don't know what all, the hospital board, the Sons of Norway. She uses all that against me." But, Carl claimed that he could not give up what he was doing because "I'm needed, the work's there." Apparently he considered her work less important.

Yet, women's volunteer work in the community needs to be seen as just that, work. Women often do what we call *face work*. They act on behalf of their family, integrating it into the community's larger social network. by putting its best "face" forward. Women are often seen as responsible for the upward or downward mobility of their family. Michael West, a professor at the local college, was proud of his wife: "She has just been invited to join one of the local women's book clubs—this is no small thing, for even in Baker, some social activities are traditionally 'town,' and not every wife of a faculty member is likely to be included. Betty's work for the Historical Society, her membership in. . .the garden club, and her work in the League of Women voters. . .have apparently given her the necessary entrée with the old residents." The value of women's volunteer work is measured partly in terms of how it affects her family's social status.

After World War II, wage labor moved away from the home and off the farm. Men sold their labor power, and women labored to maintain their family, without being economically rewarded for doing so. Men's wages came to obscure women's contributions, while at the same time justified the women's being confined to the household. Although women still worked outside the home, sex-role stereotyping continued to encourage them to stay home, take care of the house, and raise the children. The house-proud women of Baker were just that—proud that they were successfully fulfilling a traditional role. The Thanksgiving table was filled with more food than anyone could possibly eat, and the men's toast to the women's labor was "[to] the ladies, who have done us so proud."

SUMMARY

As Americans moved to the prosperity that began to unfold in the 1950s, there was also a shift in values. The frugality which Benjamin Franklin had preached in the eighteenth century gave way almost completely to a consumption ethic. Writers, both popular and academic, pointed to the rise of white-collar workers, the organization man, and changes in the overall occupational structure. Dramatic as these changes were, at least in the imagination, a number of things remained the same.

Income concentration did not really change very much between 1945 and 1960. In fact, it is about the same today as it was in 1940. There was a growth in real wealth in the country, but there were also many people who were locked into poverty. The concentration of wealth and power, which had begun before World War II, deepened. And, even though there were more white-collar workers and fewer farmers, more people—both in terms of absolute numbers as well as percentages—were working for somebody else. They were selling their labor power on the open market, and they had lost control over the work process itself.

The concentration of wealth, power, and loss of control over work still did not cause people to think and act in terms of class, at least not most of them. Class consciousness took a back seat to status consciousness, which fit with Americans' overall value patterns. People were what they could buy, and mass consumption made more and more of them seem to be the same. The active struggle for power, for prestige, and wealth was something that many people in Baker believed happened elsewhere—the cities, Washington, D.C.—and they were not entirely wrong. Though their economy and well-being were shaped by national factors, in Baker, there was a continued emphasis on personal effort, optimism, and hard work, even if it was geared to purchasing nationally advertised and marketed goods. Status consciousness, not class consciousness, was the reality of the day.

✻   ✻   ✻

Vi Mercer 10

Born in 1892, Vi Mercer lived on farms in Minnesota for eighty-six years. In 1978, she moved to a nursing home in a small town in the southeastern corner of the state. In 1980, Vi met with a sociology major who was collecting information about the rural poor. Their conversation follows.

Q: Can you tell me something about what it was like for you to be a child on a farm?

A: I can tell you most anything. We had a farm in Brown County, five miles from town. Well, I don't know that you'd call it a town, when I was a child it was never larger than about seventy-five people. My father had a dairy herd and farmed sweet and feed corn and hay, mostly. I was one of five children, though one of my little sisters died of infantile paralysis, they didn't know what it was then. They are all of them dead now, but me, the oldest. I was the oldest girl, so of course I had a lot to do. From when I was about nine I guess, I was used to getting supper while Mother helped with the milking. She didn't want me to learn milking, she wanted something different for me.

We had a yellow stone house, two stories, two bedrooms upstairs. Those rooms were like ice in the winters; we just piled the quilts on and slept spoon fashion. Downstairs was a kitchen and a parlor which we mostly left alone. Folks lived in the kitchens in those days, for the warmth, except in the summer—then we lived outside. On the porch or under the trees. We would do everything out there on hot summer days, eat, wash, all under those big trees. We didn't have any other way to keep cool, only swimming in the lake. I didn't like that because of the leeches. That never bothered the boys. They used to think it was

277

humorous to come out with those ugly suckers on their legs, just to make us girls scream. And naturally we screamed.

My mother and father were good parents, wonderful parents. I don't only mean church going and hard working, for near everybody we knew was those things. I mean they had time for us, they knew us. Now I believe that's hard for a parent anymore. How can you keep track of your children, teach them what's what, if you're in one place and they're in another all the time? And you don't know who their friends are? We didn't go to school above four months of the year, any of us, except my sister Flo. She got to be a teacher, she was the one of us who went past eighth grade.

These days, even on a farm, you only need one man to do the work of what used to be four people. And the same for the women, you can't think how much easier. So even on farms, people don't work together like they did. I believe it is a lonelier life everywhere for everybody. My granddaughter, she always

Portrait of a farm woman
Courtesy of Viola Mason

tries her best to come and see me, but she's up there in Minneapolis, and she's a high school teacher. Besides she has her husband and two little boys to take care of, too. She wants to do both. It isn't that her husband doesn't make good money. He does. Shirley wanted to go on teaching. I could've went up there, but I wouldn't. I have lived here for twenty-five years, since my second marriage, and I have no ambitions to live in the city. Besides it would have cost us a packet more, and I'm a long-lived one you know, I'll see one hundred yet. Well, I am rambling on— this surely is not what you want to hear. Just stop me, why don't you? Where was I?

Q: You were telling me about your childhood. Can you tell me what was the worst part of living on the farm in those days?

A: Now, do you mean the worst part or the worst time of it?

Q: Oh—either one.

A: Well, I can tell you both. The worst part was the hard *work*. We had to all of us *work* to make that farm go. My grandfather bought the land, and my father just went on working it. My grandfather died when I was two, I think; my grandmother had died before I was born. After my grandfather was gone, my father could make some changes, that was when he went over to the milk herd, and that was a lot of work while he went on building it up. And you know, we had to have horses to take care of. And water didn't come out of faucets, nor did we have the rural electric, not till after my *own* children were born, so there was always lamps to fill and clean, all winter, and the stove, and we had to cook food the day we ate it. Only in the winter you could freeze some things, we could just bury meat in the snow. And we cooked *large*—there was at one time nine of us, counting my cousins who lived with us after their folks died. Washing was a whole day's work, and we girls did a lot of mending and sewing. All of us were busy all day long from when we were quite small, except in the winter, and even then there was the animals to see to, and that meant early hours and late ones. When I was a big girl and wanting to go out and have me some fun, evenings, I would get up at 4:30, 5:00, to do the churning or the baking before breakfast. Then I was allowed to go out, later.

But I worked harder after I was married. That is another story. You were asking....

Q: The worst time?

A: Yes. All right. That would be when my mother died. That was in 1921, of a cancer. Now doctors didn't operate so much in those days. And anyway she left it too late, she was a modest woman, her generation didn't talk about female ailments. I knew something was making her feel bad a year before she went, but she wouldn't admit it until the pain was too bad. She hung on and hung on, I think that must run in the family. But now *she* was quite a young women, not yet fifty, and strong to begin with. She died in August, at home naturally, and it was in the midst of a heat wave. Well, we couldn't get ice out there before it melted. It was only delivered in town three days of the week, and it seemed like those days was always when the horses was being used for harvesting. Sometimes I could get one hundred pounds, which was a terrible expense, you know, and it would last a day, and then I would just keep sponging her down with witch hazel and water and fanning her. She didn't want nobody else near her, the last week, she was ashamed. Like I said, she was a *young* woman. No, I've got past that. Of course, a person would have to, being here. So many of 'em would have something wrong, you can't hide it if you care to. I'm grateful for this place, I truly am. They keep us real comfortable and clean. I wish I'd had these air conditioners and refrigerators and such for her.

Q: And what was the *best* thing about those days?

A: Now, that is an easy one. The best thing was when we were all together entertaining ourselves. We didn't have TV or toys, like kids do now, or go to the stores. We had visitors or went visiting, and we played games or just talked. I wasn't allowed to go hunting, but I could go fishing, and I sure loved that. Ice fishing, even, I loved it. Still do. Evenings, Mother or Flo would read to us, or my cousin Irene, she made up games, too. Flo would make up school games, question and answer, like she was already a teacher, geography and arithmetic. I remember just as clear. Of course it isn't the least bit like what the children learn now, it is all different. Or maybe we would fix some treat we didn't usually take the time for, we'd make cream caramels, my, I can taste them now, though I couldn't eat them if I had them—not with these plates.

Q: I understand you were still farming when—until right before you came here?

A: That's right.

Q: Can you tell me something about how that was different, say these last twenty years, from how it was when you were a girl?

A: Oh, in simply every way you can think up—except the weather don't change. Or rather it still does. My. Well, first off, all the machines, the tractor and so on, although this farm I had out here wasn't a big one, and we didn't invest in the machinery like some do. And in the house, it was like a city house, we tore that old one down, my second husband and I, when we got the place in '54, right after we was married, and he built me that new ranch-style house. It was beautiful, I had *everything* in that kitchen, and he went right along buying me gadgets till the day he died. He was set on spoiling me, Ben was. Course I spoiled him too. One thing—a big clothes dryer. Well I never cared for that, the clothes don't smell right, out of a machine. I'd rather hang 'em, I kinda like to get out and do that. He pestered me and pestered me to use that thing, and I wouldn't, only for some of his work clothes or if it was raining or down below freezing.

Q: So you see that as the main difference? An easier time because of the technological developments?

A: You could say so. Of course I was happiest in my life after I married Ben, even if we were such old folks, we were awfully happy. We had good times. We'd go to the movies all the time, or we'd go dancing. Ben didn't only take me fishing, he took me hunting with him. We took fishing trips up in the North Woods, it's real beautiful up there. My first husband couldn't do any of that, he couldn't take care of me, you see, he was hurt when the boys was just babies. So that was a hard time in every way. It seemed it soured his disposition, too—he never learned to accept that he was a cripple, not ever, and he always would reproach himself that I was bearing the burdens. Yes, that was a hard time. Well. There is another thing different for farmers nowadays—especially us old ones, it's a lonesomer life than it used to be. Neighbors don't mean so much to each other, and families have got so spread out; a woman feels that most, I think. My granddaughter and her boys is all I've got. My boys both died in Italy in the war, eight months apart, in 1944. Floyd's wife was pregnant with Shirley when he went overseas. She's all I have, Shirley and her boys. But she's real good to me. She phones every week and comes down every month. Why there are old people here, people who aren't sick and who are still real sharp, mind you, who don't see family from one year's end to the other. Now *that* is *lonely*. And not everyone makes friends as easy as me. There's a woman here who cries herself to sleep every night, just like a child. But she won't let you give her comfort, she'd be ashamed of that. Now where was I? You don't want to hear this old stuff.

Q: The farm you had with your second husband. Was it successful?

A: Well no. No, no—up until 1960 or so we did just fine. See, it was mostly soybeans and a truck garden. And Ben kept some bees,

Cooper's farm, Russell County, Kansas
Courtesy of the Kansas State Historical Society

till about '68, I think it was, and we had the apple orchard. Prices were real good at first. And I had my chickens—I have always had my chickens. And we never expected to get our entire living off of it, it was a small operation, we both had other work. Ben was a real fine carpenter, and he used to go two, three days a week, more in winter, doing repairs and cabinet work and remodeling. He'd build whole sets of furniture for people, refinish things. He could do most anything and had a real good reputation. But then the arthritis began to get him, and he just got so he could do less and less that way, and we had to replace the tractor, and though our prices went up, so did everything else. It just cost more and more, that's all, and we never quite got ahead. We couldn't put enough money *in* to get enough *out*— like the big farmers could. We had expected to put by some savings, and we just never did.

And I guess now—I think I waited too long to sell the place. Why back in '73 we was offered six times what we paid for it, and then when it did go up for sale, my debts took most of that. That was his last illness and my medical expenses, you see. But anyway, you were asking—I worked out, myself, I worked part time in the laundry for Mr. Lindberg, for twelve years, and I worked in people's houses too. Right up until my stroke I had four ladies depending on me. Two of 'em sends me cards and come to visit, to this day. But that is the only way a person can make it on a small farm anymore is with some other income. It's all the big farms, big business, really, the way they are run, that are successful now. But we just could not seem to decide to let it go. I loved that place, it had all my things in it, and after Ben passed on, it was like—well, I tell you, I could still talk to him sometimes, just as if he was still there. Now if I did that in *this* place, they would think I had gone senile for sure—but he wouldn't be here, anyway. Just where we were together, on that farm.

Q: Did you have help on the farm then?

A: Oh certainly. I mean to say, I rented it, I had two men working it, for two-fifths of their crops. I only worked part of the garden anymore and kept those chickens. Till I got to worrying about my high blood pressure, I mean. Then I sold 'em off and had a man to tear the chicken house down, I didn't want it around. I had no desire to be talking to my departed chickens!

Q: So then you went on working out?

A: Long as I could, but then I had my stroke, and I couldn't get around anymore.

Q: Did you try to keep the farm then?

A: I did. For about six months I did. But you see, we hadn't had enough medical insurance, either of us, and the Medicaid wasn't so much help, except for the hospital. I couldn't pay the bills and keep it; it was that simple, no matter what. If I would've lived on dog food, like you hear of old people doing in the cities. Shirley came down all the time after I was back home, and she would see I had what I needed, nobody could have done better, and I had my good neighbors too, doing my shopping and such. The men that was working the land would stop in, why one of 'em, Leonard it was, took over working my garden for me and wouldn't let me pay him. But it was plain I couldn't meet the bills without I sold it. And it was getting real hard to get my work done decent anymore, see, I really can't reach down or up easy. And I got tired so fast. So one evening I just called Shirley on the phone and I told her, and she was so glad, she was afraid she was going to have to tell *me*, you see, she was just dreading that. "I'll be right down, Grandma, we'll all come, and we'll figure everything out, just what you want to do." That's Shirley. Well. I knew what was best. This place hadn't been here long. The planning commission was against it for the longest time, because it is part state-subsidized—like they didn't want federal programs, back in the sixties. We are so independent out here! But you know, there isn't enough young people in these towns anymore to pay for us old ones. They built this place finally in '78, and I knew all about it because my friend Velma Dodge brought her husband here after his accident, he was hurt bad in an accident on the highway and just never came back somehow, he was unconscious for five days and his mind just wasn't right after, and he was crippled up, too. Like my Ralph was, only worse. He's gone now.

But so I knew this was a decent place. It is. They try real hard. It is a good, decent staff, kind people. And it is in my town. There isn't much to do in here, that is the real problem, but at least here I can have my visitors. And I have made me some good friends here, too. You ought to talk to Phyllis Johnson, that lady over there in the blue housedress. She can tell you more than I can about farming. She raised six children on a farm, and two of her boys are still farming, went to school up in St. Paul and learned to do it right, like young people have to these days.

Q: Can you tell me something about the years when you were raising your two boys and farming on your own?

A: Now what sort of something?

Q: It must have been very difficult. What made you stay with it?

A: Oh my. I didn't have a *choice*. My husband, Ralph that was, wouldn't have let me give up that land, not for anything. It was for the boys, you see, and especially after he was hurt, he felt that was all he *could* give them. You may well say difficult. I learned to milk cows and butcher hogs after I was thirty-five years old, not to speak of disking the fields—all of that. I had a man to help, but not to depend on. There is a difference.

Q: So you did all that for—how long? Fifteen years?

A: Twenty-six, young lady—twenty-six. From '27 till 1950 when he died. Then I sold that old place, you can be sure. It was no use to me, and I never liked that western part of the state. I just sold it and moved back here, where I felt it was home, and got me an egg farm. I just raised chickens for three years, '50 to '53, till I met my present—second husband. After we decided to take the big step, I sold that farm and put my money in our new place, except what I helped to send Shirley to college on.

Q: But while you were working the other farm—you said that was a hard time. What was hardest about it?

A: Like I say, working all the time. That's all. That's *enough*. Now, I got to like working the fields. I got away by myself that way. But I just worked morning, noon, and night getting everything done and everybody taken care of, making sure Ralph wasn't feeling left out and the boys wasn't getting in trouble. Oh, but they were good boys, don't mistake me, wonderful boys. They were so proud of getting big enough to be a help to me. Wonderful boys. Of course, it is better for children on a farm. No, I never had complaints about my boys, but a woman alone—you worry. You do worry. When they come to leave me, they just felt that they had to be in that war, you see. Young Ralph, he cried about leaving me alone like that, but I told him I understood. I told him I was proud of 'em.

Q: And after...

A: But I didn't understand. I don't yet. But it was how it had to be.

Q: And afterwards—you were alone, that is—with your husband, did you have trouble keeping the farm going?

A: I did like I did here, I rented out part, for part of the crops. Ralph still wouldn't sell, but he—most days he just wouldn't talk about it. That was a bad time, and I don't really care to talk of it.

Q: No, all right. It would have been easier for you, do you think, if you could have arranged for Ralph to be someplace like this?

A: I can't answer you that. He would not have wanted it. Not even towards the last. I can't tell.

Q: But for yourself...

A: For me to be here myself, you mean? I am doing fine, young lady, just like I told you. I am a lucky one. I have family and friends and I also have my *wits*. If there was any one thing....

Q: Yes?

A: Well it can't be helped, but like I was saying before, there isn't much to *do*. What they call their activities. We never were much for watching the TV. And I'm—well I'm not used to—I always worked so hard, and I also played hard, you see. I don't really take to all this *retiring*. But it's how it has to be. I'm luckier than most, and I surely had my good times. I did.

Q: Yes. Well, I certainly thank you....

A: No, it's me should thank you for listening to me go on. I don't know what you got out of it. What do you want with all this old stuff anyway?

Q: Oh, why, it's very valuable, this sort of personal historical account....

A: You taking up farming?

Q: No, no, I'm—I will probably be a teacher.

A: That's a fine career for a woman. Like my Shirley. But you won't teach about me? Will you put me in a book?

Q: Oh—I hope so, yes.

A: Now what kind of a book would *that* be?

Q: Oh—about, about how people make up our—society.

A: Oh my. That's quite an order. In a book. Oh my.

* * *

Social Change and Stability 11

L IKE many Americans of her generation, Vi Mercer grew up on a farm, which meant a childhood of hard work with few amenities. Houses were cold in the winter and hot and stuffy in the summer; there were no fans, no refrigerators, and no electric light. Vi Mercer now lives in a nursing home with comforts she never had when she was a girl. When she was asked to recount some of the major changes she had experienced, she pointed to technological changes: bigger tractors, electricity, air conditioning, better medical care. When we look at things this way, as we often do, we tend to see ourselves and Vi Mercer caught up in these changes rather than being responsible for them. It is true that we live our lives in structured situations—in families, in social institutions— but it is also true that as we live those lives, we change these structures.

THE STRUCTURE OF HISTORY

To paraphrase anthropologist Marshall Sahlins, history has a structure, and all structures have a history (1981). Structures are found and realized only in their practice. The family would be only an abstraction if people did not live in families, practicing the behavior of husbands, mothers, breadwinners. It is through action that we recreate, or reproduce as the Marxists say, the social order. And in recreating the social order, we change it. In the course of our daily lives, living out our routines, we do not often worry about change. Yet the very acting out of the routine automatically causes change to occur—slowly but inevitably.

In *Historical Metaphors and Mythical Realities* (1981), Sahlins explained how the Sandwich Islanders (Hawaiians), in reproducing their social order, transformed it. The voyages of Captain James Cook and a ritual ceremony in the late 1700s provide the key to his analysis. Each year, with the appearance of the Pleiades on the horizon, the islanders began a four-month celebration, with the new god, Lono, displacing the old god, Ku, who was associated with the ruling chief and human sacrifice. The ceremony commenced with a symbol of Lono being carried in a clockwise circuit around the island, marking Lono's appropriation of the land. The king and the high priest, who represented another god, then went into hiding for a short period. When the circuit was finally complete, Lono returned to the temple from which he started, and the king came ashore. There was a ritual battle between the followers of the king and the god, and at its end the king went into the temple to offer a pig to Lono and welcome him to their temporarily shared land. Then Lono suffered a ritual death, and the celebration ended.

How did Captain Cook figure in this? He visited the islands in 1778, and nothing remarkable happened; however, on his second voyage, his ship sailed into view just as this ceremony to install Lono was beginning. Cook did not dock immediately but began a clockwise circuit of the island, just as the image of Lono was being carried around the island. The islanders also noticed that the symbol of Lono, which was a cross with white cloths hanging down from its arms, resembled the sails of the ship circling with them. When the islanders got back to their starting place and it was time for Lono to assume his place in the temple, Cook finally came ashore. By all accounts, he was treated as though he were the god Lono, and he made little effort to convince the natives that they had made a mistake. The ceremony progressed according to the tradition, but as the time drew nearer for the old god and the king to assume power, the islanders grew worried and asked Cook when he would be leaving. Again, somewhat incredibly, Cook set sail on the day that Lono was supposed to leave. But unlike Lono and unluckily for Cook, he came back to repair the ship's mast. Thereupon the Hawaiians killed Cook, and the manner of his death both reproduced the Hawaiians' whole value complex and changed it; they used their new values to elevate the political status of the Hawaiian kings, who then increased their trade with the British, whom they favored because of their mythic connection with Cook. As the trade increased, so did the Hawaiians' contact with the Europeans. In order to cope with these new events, the old taboos were used. In the new situation, the chiefs continued to act for the king, using the old taboos. This divided the people and the chiefs, led the people to violate the taboos, and eventually destroyed the chiefs' base of power. Thus, following the old routines caused a radical social change.

In the same way, the farmers in the Great Plains who failed to adapt their methods to the needs of the area helped create the Dust Bowl and necessitated a number of new economic relationships between the farmers and the federal government. Likewise, those who exhibited especially old-fashioned or conservative values and whose behavior often caused their children (for example, Etta Sue Higbee and Jane West) to react against these values began the process of creating a new set of values.

Vi Mercer, too, changed the social order by reproducing it. As a farm wife, she was not expected to have full responsibility for running the farm, but when her husband was incapacitated, she had to raise their two children alone. She did what a responsible parent of her generation did—she kept doing the job she had been trained to do. As a farmer, and not just as a farmer's wife, she contributed to the slow change in this country that has made alternative careers for women more acceptable and that has enhanced the amount of status and power that women do have.

We have talked about the role of the individual in transforming social structures and have noted that social change is not simply a haphazard process. We speak of change easily and just as easily recognize it. But what does it actually mean? We need to see what changes and how.

THEORIES OF SOCIAL CHANGE

One way to explain social change is through social stability. We need to imagine a complete picture of a society with all its details, frozen in time. We could thus examine its separate institutions—the family, religious groups, the economy, the political and educational systems—as well as its level of technology and all the manifestations of its value system. Then we could examine the same society at another point in time and compare and contrast all of the items for which we had information. The problem with this approach is that societies are not static entities. Trying to explain a society is a bit like trying to explain an atom, which is never stable. The atom's very "stability" comes from its internal motion. The same is also true of a society. Anthony Giddens (1981) explained the difficulty of trying to separate stability and change: "A stable social order is one in which there is close similarity between how things are, and how they used to be. This indicates how misleading it is to suppose that one can take a 'timeless snapshot' of a social system as one can, say, take a real snapshot of the architecture of a building. For social systems exist *as* systems only in and through their 'functioning'...over time" (1981:17, emphasis in original). A society is a process, and this process has a structure. Theories of social change have sought to explain this though some theories are quite inadequate. We will look at some of these theories and then devise our own general theory of social change.

Evolutionary Theories

On the surface, simple evolutionary theories make sense. They assume that societies move gradually from simple states to more complex ones. This certainly is the case with the history of the United States. The world we described in the first chapters, that of the Martins, was not complicated by overpopulation or bureaucracies. Today, however, most people's entire lives are shaped by enormously complex institutions, and the number of each person's possible interconnections with the more than 200 million other people in the country is beyond imagination.

Early sociologists tended to believe that there was a definite pattern of progress to which all societies adhered. Auguste Comte (1853) believed that human thought could be divided into three stages, through which both individuals and societies passed. Societies moved from a primitive state, in which spirits were thought to guide natural events, to a modern scientific period, in which people explained events in terms of cause and effect. For example, the Hawaiians considered their gods Lono and Ku to be responsible for much of what happened in their daily lives. Vi Mercer, on the other hand, understood that unless she planted crops suitable for the climate, applied the right proportion of chemicals, and harvested a crop that had a good market value, she would not get a return on her investment.

Hard work, scientific farming, and the economy, rather than God's will, were her explanation for her experience. Herbert Spencer (1898) also believed that societies evolved in a distinct pattern. Using the model of Darwinian evolution, he viewed societies as organisms and claimed that the present societies were more fit than those of the past were.

These unilinear theories of evolution were generally repudiated when it became clear that they contradicted observable facts. There was no reason, for instance, to assume that contemporary societies were necessarily more complex than earlier ones were. Ancient China or the Byzantine Empire had bureaucracies that would rival those of today. There were large cities with a high division of labor in ancient Peru, Africa, and elsewhere. Nor did social development always follow a distinct pattern; one society, for instance, might skip a period that another passed through. Tribes in many Middle Eastern countries have progressed directly from a nomadic life-style to an industrial culture because of their oil wealth.

Recognizing that change does not necessarily mean progress, that it is not inevitable, and that it does not always follow the same pattern, theorists (see, for example, Lenski and Lenski, 1978) now refer to *multilinear evolution.* The shift from simple to more complex is seen as a tendency based on a variety of processes. The United States moved from simple to complex, but not all at once. Many of the regions we discussed in this book maintain life-styles and value patterns that have been unusually stable for over a century. We would argue that one of the reasons for the stability in the agricultural areas of the Great Plains is that the way in which people earn their living there has not basically changed. They may use modern equipment, but they are still private capitalists working for themselves. The mode of production, then, has remained stable. Too, even though radical change came to the Hawaiians, some elements of their system remained stable for longer periods. In fact, it was because the system of taboos continued to be used that change occurred.

Cyclical Theories

Among the earliest theories of social change are the cyclical ones, which saw an inevitable rise and fall in civilizations. The Greeks considered themselves as having descended from a golden age. Many of those who have lived through the tragedy of a world war speak of the decline of Western civilization. The death of Judson Wade (in Chapter 4) caused his parents to question whether they lived in a civilized world.

Sorokin (1947) viewed all societies as swinging back and forth between two poles, the sensate and the ideational. In the sensate period, people emphasize materialism, obtaining things and pleasure, whereas in the ideational periods they concentrate on ideals and spiritual concerns. We can find both of these tendencies in any society. We can see the 1960s antiwar demonstrations and experiments with drugs and alternative life-styles as reflecting the ideational, but they were also caused, in large part, by the affluence of the American bourgeoisie—the sensate. Sorokin's ideas fail because they do not account for overlaps.

In *The Decline of the West* (1918), Oswald Spengler portrayed the life-cycle of civilizations as similar to that of humans: birth, maturation, old age, and finally death. Yet the processes that Spengler described were too general and were wrong in the sense that although all societies change, not all follow the rigid pattern he outlined. In *A Study of History* (1934–1954), Arnold Toynbee examined twenty-one civilizations and concluded that decline was not inevitable. Rather, each society went through a period of growth and decay but could respond to challenges to begin a new, and higher, cycle. But again, this approach is limited, for all societies do not pass through the stages defined by Spengler, nor do all respond to the challenges mentioned by Toynbee.

The major problem with both cyclical and unilinear evolutionary theories is that they see societies as subject to inexorable universal laws. In fact, the pattern of change in any society is unique to its place and time. A particular conjunction of values, institutions, and economic base determines whether change will occur and in what direction. Finally, the idea of laws of change overlooks the role of individual actors. Those who moved their families and possessions over the unfamiliar frontier into the "great inland sea" of grass were not just in the grip of inevitable historical forces; they came for their own reasons. Any theory of change that seeks to explain change by means of only one factor is inadequate.

Functional Theories

Durkheim (see Chapter 5) set the stage for functionalism by asking, "What is the role of a social institution in the maintenance of the society as a whole?" How does a particular social unit, for example, the family or a religious institution, contribute to the stability of the social system? The assumption here is that the institutions in question have positive functions for the society, that social stability is good. The families we examined in this book provided for the integration of the individual into the larger society. Families like the Martins, Patchens, Higbees, and Davises wanted their children to grow up and become "good citizens, useful members of the community." A family functions to guarantee the survival of the society by passing along values and culture and raising and replacing members of the larger society. To the extent that it does so, it is successful. But functional theories have been criticized *ad nauseam* for neglecting conflict within and between institutions and for seeing societies as integrated wholes. Nevertheless, functional theories show us that most societies are remarkably stable and that they exist over extended periods of time and beyond the individual.

Marxian Theories

"The history of all hitherto existing society is the history of class struggles" (Karl Marx and Frederick Engels, *The Communist Manifesto*, 1848/1948:9). The Marxian approach locates the source of change in the class struggle, which is determined by the mode of production. In a capitalist society, people are paid a wage, which disguises the fact that they are paid for only a portion of the wealth they produce, whereas the profit goes to those who own the means of production. Nonetheless, Marx took extreme care to point out that a historical materialist analysis did not mean that noneconomic phenomena could not shape economic systems nor that there was a direct, one-to-one relationship between the economic and the noneconomic system (sometimes referred to as the superstructure but here as the ideological sphere). Marx did, however, tend to view the technological system, or the mode of production that depended on it, as the determining factor (McMurtry, 1978).

What does this mean in our historical context? From a strict materialist perspective, we would have to argue that the value complex that developed—effort/optimism and the belief in progress—was the result of the material base and/or that changes in values were the result of changes in technology. The settlement of the Great Plains would be seen as based on the introduction of machines and on the markets on the East Coast and in Europe. The style of family life—nuclear families organized around the production of cash crops—would also be seen as determined by the level of technology or the mode of production.

The materialist would probably also argue that the Great Plains were developed because of the needs of capitalism. Capital (both as money and as a system of social relations) would be seen as needing to expand into the new frontier, just as capitalism today "must" penetrate the Third World. Individual decisions to move and to farm would be seen as the result of the expansion of capital rather than as the result of human values. Furthermore, the materialist would argue that the Great Plains became free rather than slave states, because wage labor was a much more efficient form of exploiting the land and accumulating surplus products than slavery. In short, the level of technology, the needs of capitalism, and the way in which the land was exploited—all material factors—would be seen as determining the institutions and values that developed. But this explanation would be distinctly one-sided.

Toward a General Theory of Change

The writings of Louis Althusser (1969, 1970), the French Marxist, help us understand social structure and change. Althusser (1970) believed that a society is composed of separate and relatively autonomous spheres. For instance, a society has political, economic, and ideological spheres. Together they constitute the system, or a society at a given historical moment. The uniqueness of a given society depends on the relationship among these different spheres. To say that they are relatively autonomous means that none is independent of the whole, but this says nothing about their relative importance. At one time the polity can be the driving force in a society, as when the state decides to stimulate the economy by cutting taxes. At another time the economy can be the driving force. For example, the interests of the railroad owners influenced government policy to drive the Native Americans from their lands and to open those lands to the white settlers and the railroads. Ideology may also be the principal force, for example, in regard to the founding of the Republic or the way in which the Puritans organized the Massachusetts Bay Colony. For the Hawaiians, their religious, economic, and political systems which constituted the complex whole were changed with the death of Captain Cook. At one moment, the Hawaiians' religious system dominated and changed the chiefs' political power. But as trade with the Europeans increased, the economic system brought about changes in their religious (ideological) and political systems.

Each sphere determines how the other spheres will change. That was Max Weber's thesis in *The Protestant Ethic and the Spirit of Capitalism* (1904/1958) when he argued that a Calvinist religious ethic influenced the development of capitalism. As we said in Chapters 1 and 3, a religious ethic that preaches activism, asceticism, and individual effort helps the development of capitalism. Those elements of a sphere that do not support the other spheres are eliminated. Capitalism cannot exist without a compatible ideology. But capitalism did not create the ideology, and the ideology did not create capitalism.

In the settlement of the Great Plains, this meant that technology enabled the successful cultivation of Russian red winter wheat. The political system made it possible for people to own large portions of land, which enabled them to earn a living by growing crops for markets in the East and Europe. The economic interests of the land speculators, especially the railroad owners, contributed to the development of the Great Plains by opening up the land and enabling the people to move their crops to market. The settlers were independent, which influenced their politics and, when hard times came, pushed many of them into active class movements, such as Populism, in their attempt to change both the economy and the polity. We can, then, identify the Great Plains' polity, economy, and ideology and see the interplay among them. This is what is meant by history's having a structure. The spheres provide us with a framework. We speak of links and tendencies, not cause and effect. We understand that if sphere A changes, then B and C also will, as part of the complex whole.

We have still not studied how change takes place within one sphere. Change occurs because of fundamental contradictions within the sphere. These contradictions are called *dialectical contradictions*, in order to distinguish them from mere conflict, which may have little or nothing to do with change. The Hawaiians' religion changed because it eventually conflicted with the other spheres and became internally contradictory. As well, women's roles and status have changed and will continue to change because of contradictions within the family and the economy.

The idea of dialectical contradictions gives us a particular image of change. In discussing Marx's use of a dialectical framework, Rader (1979:xviii) noted that Heraclitus gave us an excellent image of what is involved: "War is the father and king of all things.... Opposition is good; the fairest harmony comes out of differences; everything originates in strife.... We enter and do not enter the same rivers, we are and are not.... The way up and the way down are one and the same." In the opening pages of this chapter, we reiterated what Heraclitus stated: a simple cause-and-effect language cannot capture the nature of a society that exists both in and through space and time (Giddens, 1981). Novack (1971:70) explained how dialectics differs from ordinary logic:

> Dialectics bases itself upon an entirely different standpoint [than formal logic does] and has a different outlook upon reality and its changing forms. Dialectics is the logic of movement, or evolution, of change. Reality is too full of contradictions, too elusive, too manifold, too mutable to be shared in any single formula or set of formulas. Each particular phase of reality has its own laws and its own peculiar categories and constellation of categories which are interwoven with those it shares with other phases of reality.

The world and the separate spheres must be seen as a structured totality, one that is in constant tension. Dialectics shows us that a change in one sphere brings about changes in the others. Yet cause and effect are difficult to isolate, for change is constant and multidimensional.

Gouldner saw the source of change and ideology in modern society as the tension between the part and the whole. Contradictions within the ideological sphere cause change. For example, in regard to socialist societies, Gouldner (1976:289) stated that they all have a basic, ideology-generating contradiction: "Their culture is egalitarian but their social structure is hierarchical; their ideology calls for workers' control of the forces of production, but these are actually controlled by the state." This tension between ideas and reality was constant in early America, as it is today, though the sources of tension have changed. In the colonies, there was a tension between the ideals preached by Great Britain and its treatment of the colonies. These disparities between ideals and practice brought about change.

J. Hector St. John De Crevecoeur, a French nobleman, became a naturalized citizen of New York in 1764. He wrote a series of letters and essays about his experiences on the American frontier, the most famous of which was published in Europe as *Letters from an American Farmer* (1782/1925). In one of these letters he described a visit to the South, commenting on the wretched life of the slaves and the indifference of the planters to their suffering: "Their ears by habit are become deaf, their hearts are hardened; they neither see, hear, nor feel for the woes of their poor slaves, from whose painful labours all their wealth proceeds. Here the horrors of slavery, the hardship of incessant toil, are unseen....The cracks of the whip urging these miserable beings to excessive labour, are far too distant from the gay Capital to be heard" (225–226).

Harriet Martineau, a foreign traveler in the nineteenth century, commented on two problems that particularly troubled her: slavery and the role of women in the American society. In *Society in America* (1837), in a chapter entitled "Morals of Slavery," she began: "This title is not written down in a spirit of mockery; though there appears to be a mockery somewhere, when we contrast slavery with the principles and the rule which are the test of all American institutions—the principles that all men are born free and equal ....This discrepancy between principles and practice needs no more words" (Vol. 2:312–313). She applied the same logic to the position of women: "One of the fundamental principles announced in the Declaration of Independence is, that governments derive their just powers from the consent of the governed. How can the political condition of women be reconciled with this?" (Vol. 1:199). She noted that only children and slaves have fewer rights than women.

The moral outrage experienced by Crevecoeur and Martineau was shared by many Americans and clearly contributed to the Civil War. States were designated as free by those who condemned slavery, not just because they wanted a state free for wage laborers. The underground railway to help slaves escape was created by people who believed in what they were doing, just as the town of Nicodemus, Kansas, was settled by former slaves who sought freedom (see Chapter 5).

The model that we have sketched is multicausal, having three relatively autonomous spheres (economy, polity, and ideology). At any given historical moment, one sphere will be dominant, and its movement will determine the direction of the other spheres, primarily by eliminating those elements that do not support the dominant sphere. There also are tensions within the spheres themselves, which bring about change and movement. Our model recognizes that societies evolve but makes no assumptions about higher or lower forms and does not try to see change as progressive. It also acknowledges that change does not occur at the same rate and level throughout a society. In one area of the Midwest, for instance, simple commodity production may dominate, whereas in another area, manufacturing is the prevailing mode.

SOURCES OF CHANGE

We have said that a major source of change is the contradictions within the spheres, and we now will discuss some of the standard sources: technology, population, and the environment.

Technology

As the telephone company tells us, the phone can help us keep in touch with friends and family, over long distances and on the spur of the moment. None of this was possible at other times in our nation's history, and families depended on letter writing instead. The automobile made the suburbs possible, though streetcars would have worked as well. It is unlikely, though, that we would have had drive-in movie theaters with only trolleys and not cars. But now that the cost of using an automobile is increasing, a number of television stations have a special "drive-in movie" evening on which they show low-budget films. Technology, the economy, and the culture are tightly woven together.

Vi Mercer singled out technological change when she spoke of change in her life—air conditioning, refrigeration, and better medical care. In our early chapters, we showed how inventions shaped the lives of the people on the Great Plains. Barbed wire enabled them to enclose land for farming and also to confine cattle so that they could be fed for market. At its simplest level, this is a form of crude materialist determinism, implying that social institutions and values are derived from technology. It is probably more helpful to speak of technology as making a difference in people's lives or as contributing to change. For example, air conditioning and central heating certainly make it more pleasant to stay home, but it would be rather farfetched to argue that therefore people are brought into more intimate contact with one another in the home or even that families had fewer children in order to purchase fully equipped homes. To speak of a meaningful link between cultural forms and technology we must look for patterns and the conjunction of many technological elements.

We will return to the materialist position, which sees changes in technology as leading to, or making possible, changes in the mode of production, which in turn affects social institutions. An example of this is the breakdown of feudalism and the rise of capitalism in Europe during the sixteenth century. Under feudalism, agriculture was well developed, given the available technology. But feudalism, as Dobb (1946) stated, had a central contradiction: it was an inefficient system of production. "The amount that could be wrenched from the land and from the peasant reached its limits, and the ruling class had growing revenue needs. The needs strained the system beyond what it could stand. Some of the pressure was simply demographic" (McNall, 1981:8). The feudal population was growing, and so was warfare. There were new markets, and a cash economy was developing in the towns. In short, something had to give, and it did.

Agriculture was radically transformed as a system of production. For example, systematic crop rotation and fertilization were tried. People grew a surplus and sold it for cash. These changes contributed to the evolution of a new social order, in which a cash economy dominated and the people became wage laborers. The technology, and therefore the way in which people were organized to work, changed.

In the nineteenth century, the railroad was a technological complex that involved not just the steam engine and the tracks but also a system of marketing, the towns that sprang up along the lines, the immigrant towns that developed because immigrants were hired to lay the cross-country lines, the financial schemes needed to pay for it, and the political schemes devised to persuade Congress to drive the Native Americans from their homes and open the Western frontier.

Population

In the shift from feudalism to capitalism, the growth of the population also helped change the agricultural practices. The early evolutionary theorists saw the growing population as a factor in the move from simple to more complex societies— more people meant more potential interactions and thus a more complex division of labor.

The character of a population also can change and affect the social system. Sociologists often construct population pyramids that show the number of males and females in different age categories. In the early 1800s, for instance, there was a true pyramid: a few elderly people at the top, with more females than males, and a larger number of children on the bottom. But now our population is aging, and the pyramid is beginning to look like an hourglass, with fewer people in the middle and younger years and a growing number of older ones at the top. Advances in medical technology that allow people to live longer and that reduce infant mortality have contributed to this shift. Our aging population has made Congress aware of the elderly as a powerful political force. Medicare and Medicaid, social security, and other government programs have been created by the needs of the elderly, just as the baby boom of the 1950s contributed to the expansion of our educational system at all levels.

The Environment

One of the most famous statements about the relationship between land and values was made by the historian Frederick Jackson Turner (1920), who asserted that the American frontier was responsible for our democratic institutions: "The existence of an area of free land, its continuous recession, and the advance of American settlement westward, explain development" (Turner, 1920:1). As Americans moved westward, they left behind the outmoded cultural patterns of Europe: "Moving westward, the frontier became more and more American" (4). The frontier promoted democracy because it promoted individualism. To sum up Turner's position, "the frontier of settlement advanced and carried with it individualism, democracy, and nationalism, and powerfully affected the East and the Old World" (35).

Turner recognized that the frontier experience produced several economic changes that affected America's value complex. The frontier weakened America's dependence on Great Britain because British merchants could not supply the pioneers in the interior. American merchants themselves, therefore, opened inland trade routes and moved the supplies. Because the pioneers "needed the goods of the coast, the grand series of internal improvement and railroad legislation began, with potent nationalizing effects" (Turner, 1920:24).

The first frontier was the East Coast. Later frontiers were the Ohio River Valley, the Great Plains, and the Oregon Territory. But wherever the frontier was, it was a powerful force for change, and Turner saw its closing as the loss of an important sense of opportunity. President John F. Kennedy tried to capitalize on the American image of the "land of opportunity" by labeling his administration the "New Frontier" and suggesting that we could recapture a pioneering spirit by turning our energies and attention to solving problems of poverty and unemployment.

Alterations in the environment certainly affected the Great Plains people's behavior. Grasshopper plagues and the Dust Bowl storms of the 1930s drove people from the land. But it was the land itself—the unbroken miles of grass—that determined the kind of agriculture that was possible. The lack of rain in the western Great Plains initially meant that dry farming was the main form of agriculture. (The technology of deep-well irrigation has, to some extent, changed that.) The environment necessitated large farms, which in turn required farm machinery. Age-old patterns of farming behavior were drastically altered in response to the land.

Ideas

When the Populist orator Mary Lease insisted, "Kansans should raise less corn and more hell," she was speaking of the role that ideas could play in social change. The idea that the farmers could take action against the railroad trusts, the shippers, and those others who controlled their economic destiny was an important force. Likewise, the belief that slavery was an abomination and contradicted the ideals of a Christian or democratic nation helped move some to action. Roy Davis, whom we read about in Chapters 6 and 7, believed that World War II pitted the forces of enlightened democracy against the forces of ignorance and tyranny.

Ideas, though, do not exist in a vacuum but in a social context, and in turn, they influence, and are influenced by, that context. Many communities on the Great Plains were settled by members of particular ethnic or religious groups. The Mennonites, who migrated to the Great Plains from Russia, survived because their ideology helped them to be successful farmers.

Human Action

We have seen that individual action helps transform social structures. When Vi Mercer was asked why she stayed with farming when she was raising her two boys, she answered, "I didn't have a *choice.*" But she then went on to explain why she wanted to do what she did. We do not question the values that determine our choices; we sense them as part of our selves and not of our circumstances.

Claude Fisher (1977) and his associates wrestled with the relationship between the individual and the larger society. Like Stanley Milgram (1977), they saw people as "linked to their society primarily through relations with other individuals: with kin, friends, coworkers, fellow club members, and so on" (Fisher et al., 1977:vii). Each of us stands at the center of a complex web of interconnecting ties. We are friends with person X, who knows Y, who knows Z, who is related to M, who in turn knows us. These strands, connections, webs, and ties constitute our personal social networks. Through these networks, which ultimately form the social structure of our society, the larger society affects us, altering the choices we can make.

We can choose our friends, acquaintances, and spouses. But to take the example of marriage, our networks constrain our choices. We do not marry just anybody, but generally someone who is a member of the same social class. Social class is a structural variable that affects personal choices. According to Marx, "Men make history, but not in circumstances of their own choosing."

Social psychologist Stanley Milgram (1977:278) used a helpful term, *microdeed,* in seeking to explain how the individual is linked with the larger social order. To Milgram, the social world is composed of individual communications, or microdeeds, which are cumulative. Henry Martin, for instance, decided to move to Kansas. Once he made that decision, a number of others were set in progress: his marriage would be postponed while the farm was established, and he would return later for Lucy, his wife. Lucy's decision to marry meant leaving her parents for a life in an unknown wilderness. These decisions were made within a social structure that constrained their choices. Men were enterprising and could demonstrate this in a variety of ways, but women had to marry the men they had promised to marry.

The role of either individual human action or social structure in influencing social change must be examined in the context of a specific historical event. The families whose members suffered or died in World War I or II felt that they were being used by history. Yet this sense existed side by side with their belief in the justice of each of those wars and the value of human courage and endurance.

Thus we disagree with the authors of *Middletown Families* (a contemporary study of the town examined by Lynd and Lynd in *Middletown* and *Middletown in Transition*), who asserted: "Middletown does not make its own history but patiently suffers the history made outside....Change, for Middletown, is something flowing irresistibly from the outside world" (Caplow et al., 1982:5). They chose to focus on the lack of change in Middletown and neglected to explore the ways in which individuals in Middletown were linked to the larger social order, which they helped change or retain.

STABILITY

We stated earlier that stability was as important as change in analyzing societies and noted that social institutions are partly responsible for this stability.

The Family

The myth of the decline of the family began, in part, with the failure to understand the families of earlier periods. In Chapter 1, we explained that the size of the colonial family was much smaller than generally thought; that people did not live in large extended families, but in single-family households; and that the structure of the family has been stable for a long time. The authors of *Middletown Families* found that "the Middletown family is in exceptionally good condition...and Middletown families are reasonably similar to American families in general" (Caplow et al., 1982:323). Why has the family been stable?

Again, in the Middletown study, which helps us answer the above question, the authors explain that "the family, with its complex of attitudes and practices for regulating the relationships between the sexes and between the generations, is too massive and deep-rooted an institution to be rapidly transformed under any circumstances" (Caplow et al., 1982:19). Furthermore, the institution does not change because its structural features remain the same. People still get married at about the same age, have about the same number of children, and generally live in single-family housing. In addition, "changes in patterns of intimate human relationship are necessarily much slower than technological changes..." (Caplow et al., 1982:19).

Caplow and his colleagues recognized the family as a complex pattern of attitudes and practices, a view similar to the one we outlined in Chapter 3. As such, the complex as a whole can remain stable while its individual parts change. For instance, the family today is much more egalitarian than it was in the past, and sex-role behavior is changing. For example, husbands may spend more time with their wives and young children, and more women may work outside the home, but the family as a whole remains more or less the same. Even what seem to be new forms, such as the single-parent household, existed in the past.

The family is stable also because its structure has remained the same. This is true of other social institutions, as well. The economy today has not changed completely since the early 1900s. People still sell their labor power, workers disagree with employers, and unemployment and recessions come and go. The government now plays a much larger role in regulating the economy, but the average citizen's relationship to the economy is not much different.

The Community

Another popular myth is that the sense of community has disappeared. In his review of the literature on the community, Fisher (1977) separated fact from fancy and demonstrated that although the form of community has changed, it has by no means disappeared. In regard to just one element of the myth, he found that people today were less likely to be geographically mobile than at other moments in our country's history. We have only to recall the rush for land during the late 1800s, the movement of substantial numbers of people from established settlements to the Western frontier, and the influx of immigrants, in order to understand this. Of course, there have also been real changes "...in human communities with the advance of industrial organization. They have grown larger, more complicated, more interdependent. Yet none of these transformations guarantees a loss of solidarity. When we look at the smaller, simpler, more independent communities in which men used to live, we find them divided, stratified, oppressive—not always, by any means, but often enough to make us realize that the picture of the old rural community with which people commonly compare today's cities and suburbs is a myth" (Tilly, 1974:187).

The social institutions of today—the family, the community, the economy—are different from those that existed at earlier times. In describing continuity and change in the American national character, Inkeles (1979) found, for instance, that over a span of two hundred years, Americans have valued self-reliance, autonomy, and independence and have believed in the necessity for working together and helping one another, especially their neighbors. But they also have changed, according to Inkeles, for people's attitudes toward work are different from those of the Puritans, and people now are generally more tolerant of others' differences than they were previously.

Values

In an early work, Seymour Lipset (1961) took issue with David Riesman's thesis in *The Lonely Crowd* (1953). Riesman contended (see Chapter 9) that the capitalist economic order had spawned a new type of social being—an other-directed being who wanted chiefly to "get along" with others. Gone were the inner-directed persons, who were individualistic, self-reliant, and cared only for their own opinions of themselves, rather than those of others. One of Lipset's concerns was that Riesman used a materialist explanation of values and viewed them as the simple response to material changes such as urbanization and the rise of the white-collar class. Lipset carefully traced continuities in the American character, attempting to show that Americans have always been somewhat other-directed. Lipset's main point, though, is important:

> Basic alterations of social character or values are rarely produced by chance in population or in the means of production, distribution, and exchange *alone*. Rather, as a society becomes more complex, its institutional arrangements adjust to new conditions within the framework of a dominant value-system. In turn, the new institutional patterns may affect the continuity of the socialization process which, from infancy up, instill the fundamental traits of personality. Through such a process, value change develops slowly, or not at all. There are

constant efforts to fit the "new technological world into the social patterns of the old, familiar world." (1961:319, emphasis in original)

We have been careful to avoid talking about the general society's needs. We have not looked at the family or the community as fulfilling society's needs, although stable family systems and communities may in fact contribute to stable social orders. Many argue that the family is a microcosm of the larger capitalist social order: it reproduces the patriarchal relations of the work place, contributes to the sex-role division of labor and, in short, guarantees the survival of the larger system (Zaretsky, 1976:Chap. 2). Even so, we cannot maintain that capitalist society actually *needs* the prevailing type of family system. As Giddens (1981) insisted, "Not even the most deeply sedimented institutional features of societies come about, persist, or disappear because those societies need them to do so. They come about *historically*, as a result of concrete conditions that have in every case to be directly analysed; the same holds for their persistence or their dissolution" (18, emphasis in original).

To use our earlier terms, in order to understand the present, we need to understand how the separate and semiautonomous spheres have been related over time. Our political and economic institutions and our ideology are the result of countless concrete responses to every aspect of concrete historical conditions; nevertheless, we can find patterns in change and in stability.

From the Hawaiians, to Henry Martin, to Etta Sue Higbee, and to Vi Mercer, people have lived their lives in a historical setting that they have created and that constrains their actions. As we follow the routines of our everyday lives, we transform the very social institutions that provide us with our structure, whether the family or the larger political order. The small, apparently inconsequential events in which we all participate lead to major qualitative changes. Each of us is human history; each of us contributes to it.

*   *   *

Bibliography

BOOKS AND PERIODICALS

Althusser, Louis
1969 *For Marx.* Tr. Ben Brewster. New York: Pantheon.
1970 *Reading Capital.* London: New Left Books.
American Historical Society of Germans from Russia
1975 *Newsletter.* Volume 1, January. Topeka, Kansas: American Historical Society of Germans from Russia, Northeastern Kansas Chapter.
American Youth Commission
1942 *Youth and the Future.* Washington, D.C.: American Council on Education.
Aronowitz, Stanley
1973 *False Promises: The Shaping of American Working-Class Consciousness.* New York: McGraw-Hill.
Arp, Julius Bernhard
1919 *Rural Education and the Consolidated School.* New York: World Book.
Banton, Michael
1965 *Roles: An Introduction to the Study of Social Relations.* New York: Basic Books.
Barr, Elizabeth S.
1918 "The Populist uprising." Pp. 1113–1195 in William E. Connelley (ed.), *A Standard History of Kansas and Kansans.* Volume 2. Chicago: Lewis Publishing.
Bauman, Zygmunt
1973 *Culture as Praxis.* London: Routledge & Kegan Paul.
Beadle, John H.
1873 *The Undeveloped West: Or Five Years in the Territories.* Philadelphia: National Publishing.
Bell, Daniel
1976 *The Cultural Contradictions of Capitalism.* New York: Basic Books.
Bell, Howard M.
1938 *Youth Tell Their Story: A Study of the Conditions and Attitudes of Young People in Maryland Between the Ages of 16 and 24.* Washington, D.C.: American Council on Education.
Bender, Thomas
1978 *Community and Social Change in America.* New Brunswick, N.J.: Rutgers University Press.

Bennett, John W.
 1969   *Northern Plainsmen: Adaptive Strategy and Agrarian Life.*
        Chicago: Aldine.
Bernard, Jessie
 1966   *Marriage and Family Among Negroes.* Englewood Cliffs, N.J.:
        Prentice-Hall.
Billington, Ray Allen
 1949   *Westward Expansion: A History of the American Frontier.* New
        York: Macmillan.
Blau, Peter M., and Otis Dudley Duncan
 1967   *The American Occupational Structure.* New York: John Wiley.
Bonnifield, Paul
 1979   *The Dust Bowl: Men, Dirt, and Depression.* Albuquerque:
        University of New Mexico Press.
Braly, Colonel William C.
 1947   *The Hard Way Home.* Washington, D.C.: Infantry Journal Press.
Braverman, Harry
 1974   *Labor and Monopoly Capital: The Degradation of Work in the
        Twentieth Century.* New York: Monthly Review Press.
Brookings Centennial Commemorative Book Committee
 1979   *Brookings Centennial Commemorative Book, 1879–1979.*
        Brookings, South Dakota.
Brookings Daily Register
 1946–47
 1951–52
 1954–56
 1954   Diamond Jubilee Edition. August 15.
Brookings League of Women Voters
 1956   *This Is Your Town.* Brookings, South Dakota.
Brooks, Van Wyck
 [1915] *America's Coming of Age.* Garden City, N.Y.: Doubleday/
 1958   Anchor.
Broom, Leonard, and Philip Selznick
 1963   *Sociology.* 3rd ed. New York: Harper & Row.
Brown, Martey
 1973   "The use of oral and documentary sources in historical archeol-
        ogy: Ethnohistory at the Mott farm." *Ethnohistory* 20:347–
        360.
Buck, Ricker
 1979   "The new sweatshops: A penny for your collar." *New York
        Times Magazine* (January 29):6–8.
Calhoun, Craig
 1981   "The political economy of work." Pp. 272–299 in Scott G.
        McNall (ed.), *Political Economy: A Critique of American
        Society.* Glenview, Ill.: Scott, Foresman.
Caplow, Theodore, Howard M. Bahe, Bruce A. Chadwick, Reuben Hill, and
        Margaret Holmes Williamson
 1982   *Middletown Families: Fifty Years of Change and Continuity.*
        Minneapolis: University of Minnesota Press.
Carney, Mabel
 1912   *Country Life and the Rural School.* Chicago: Row, Peterson.

Childe, V. Gordon
    1942 *What Happened in History.* Baltimore: Penguin Books.
Chodorow, Nancy
    1978 *The Reproduction of Mothering: Psychoanalysis and the Sociology of Gender.* Berkeley and Los Angeles: University of California Press.
Clark, John G., David M. Katzman, Richard D. McKinzie, and Theodore A. Wilson
    1977 *Three Generations in Twentieth Century America: Family, Community, and Nation.* Homewood, Ill.: Dorsey Press.
Cochrane, Willard W.
    1979 *The Development of American Agriculture: A Historical Analysis.* Minneapolis: University of Minnesota Press.
Cohen, Sol
    1974 *Education in the United States: A Documentary History.* New York: Random House.
Coleman, James S., et al.
    1974 *Youth: Transition to Adulthood—Report on Youth of the President's Advisory Committee.* Chicago: University of Chicago Press.
Coleman, John S., Jr.
    1978 *Bataan and Beyond: Memories of an American P.O.W.* College Station: Texas A & M University Press.
Comte, Auguste
    1853 *The Positive Philosophy.* Tr. Harriet Martineau. 2 volumes. London: J. Chapman.
Cooley, Charles Horton
    1902 *Human Nature and the Social Order.* New York: Scribner's.
    [1907] *Social Organization.* New York: Scribner's.
    1937
Coon, Carleton S.
    1971 *The Hunting Peoples.* Boston: Little, Brown.
Creigh, Dorothy Weyer
    1977 *Nebraska: A Bicentennial History.* New York: Norton.
Cubberley, Ellwood P.
    1922 *Rural Life and Education: A Study of the Rural-School Problem as a Phase of the Rural-Life Problem.* New York: Houghton Mifflin.
    1934 *Public Education in the United States: A Study and Interpretation of American Educational History.* Boston: Houghton Mifflin.
Dalla Costa, Mariarosa
    1972 "Women and the subversion of the community." Pp. 15–29 in Mariarosa Dalla Costa and Selma James, *The Power of Women and the Subversion of the Community.* Bristol, England: Falling Wall Press.
Davis, Allison, Burleigh B. Gardner, and Mary R. Gardner
    1941 *Deep South: A Social Anthropological Study of Caste and Class.* Chicago: University of Chicago Press.
Davis, Kingsley
    1949 *Human Society.* New York: Macmillan.

Davis, Kingsley, and Wilbert E. Moore
    1945   "Some principles of stratification." *American Sociological Review* 10:242–249.
Davis, Maxine
    1936   *The Lost Generation.* New York: Macmillan.
De Crevecoeur, J. Hector St. John
    [1782]
    1925   *Letters from an American Farmer.* New York: Albert & Charles Boni.
Dick, Everett
    [1937]   *The Sod-House Frontier, 1854–1890: A Social History of the*
    1979   *Northern Plains from the Creation of Kansas and Nebraska to the Admission of the Dakotas.* Lincoln: University of Nebraska Press.
Dobb, Maurice
    1946   *Studies in the Development of Capitalism.* London: Routledge.
Dobriner, William D.
    1963   *Class in Suburbia.* Englewood Cliffs, N.J.: Prentice-Hall.
Doyle, Dan H.
    1978   *Social Order of a Frontier Community: Jacksonville, Illinois, 1825–1870.* Urbana: University of Illinois Press.
Drake, William E.
    1955   *The American School in Transition.* Englewood Cliffs, N.J.: Prentice-Hall.
Dreiling, Norbert R.
    1976   *Official Centennial History of the Volga-German Settlements in Ellis and Rush Counties in Kansas, 1876–1976.* Hays, Kansas: Volga German Centennial Association.
DuBois, Cora
    1955   "The dominant value profile of American culture." *American Anthropologist* 57:1232–1238.
Durkheim, Emile
    [1893]   *The Division of Labor in Society.* Tr. George Simpson. New
    1947   York: Free Press.
Dykstra, Robert R.
    1976   *The Cattle Towns.* New York: Atheneum.
Edwards, Newton, and Herman G. Richey
    1947   *The School in the American Social Order: The Dynamics of Education.* Boston: Houghton Mifflin.
Elkins, Stanley, and Eric McKitrick
    1954   "A meaning for Turner's frontier." *Political Science Quarterly* 69:321–353, 565–602.
Emigh, Tula R.
    n.d.   *The Story of Lincoln Park, Cawker City, Kansas and the Marvelous Chautauquas Held There at the Turn of the Century.* Cawker City, Kans.: Lithographed by the *Cawker City Ledger.*
Erikson, Kai T.
    1966   *Wayward Puritans: A Study in the Sociology of Deviance.* New York: John Wiley.
Esquire
    1970   "Nine Happy Places" (December):146–153.

Ewen, Stuart
1976 *Captains of Consciousness: Advertising and the Social Roots of the Consumer Culture.* New York: McGraw-Hill.
Faragher, John M.
1980 *Women and Men on the Overland Trail.* New Haven, Conn.: Yale University Press.
Fischer, Christiane, ed.
1977 *Let Them Speak for Themselves: Women in the American West, 1849–1900.* Hamden, Conn.: Shoe String Press.
Fisher, Claude S., Robert M. Jackson, C. Ann Steuve, Kathleen Gerson, Lynne McCallister Jones, with Mark Baldassare
1977 *Networks and Places: Social Relations in the Urban Setting.* New York: Free Press.
Fite, Gilbert C.
1966 *The Farmers' Frontier, 1865–1900.* New York: Holt, Rinehart & Winston.
Flint, Herbert
1916 "Journalism in territorial Kansas." Volumes 1 and 2. Master's thesis, University of Kansas.
Franklin, Benjamin
[1730] *The Autobiography of Benjamin Franklin.* New York: Modern
1944 Library.
Frieze, Irene H., Daniel Bar-Tal, and John S. Carroll, eds.
1978 *Women and Sex Roles: Social Psychological Perspective.* New York: Norton.
Gates, Paul W.
1936 "The Homestead Law in an incongruous land system." *American Historical Review* 41 (July):654–681.
1960 *The Farmer's Age: Agriculture, 1815–1860.* New York: Holt, Rinehart & Winston.
Giddens, Anthony
1981 *A Contemporary Critique of Historical Materialism.* Berkeley and Los Angeles: University of California Press.
Giles, Nell
1943 *Punch In, Susie! A Woman's War Factory Diary.* New York: Harper & Bros.
Gouldner, Alvin W.
1976 *The Dialectic of Ideology and Technology.* New York: Seabury Press.
Green, Hardy, and Elizabeth Weiner
1981 "Bringing it all back home." *In These Times* (March 11–17).
Guettel, Charnie
1974 *Marxism and Feminism.* Toronto: Women's Press.
Gusfield, Joseph R.
1955 "Social structure and moral reform: A study of the Women's Christian Temperance Movement." *American Journal of Sociology* 61:221–232.
1975 *Community: A Critical Response.* New York: Harper Colophon.
Gutman, Herbert G.
1976 *The Black Family in Slavery and Freedom: 1750–1925.* New York: Pantheon.

1978   "Persistent myths about the Afro-American family." Pp. 467–489 in Michael Gordon (ed.), *The American Family in Socio-Historical Perspective*. 2nd ed. New York: St. Martin's Press.

Hall, Calvin S., and Gardner Lindzey
1957   *Theories of Personality*. New York: John Wiley.

Harris, Marvin
1974   *Cows, Pigs, Wars, and Witches: The Riddles of Culture*. New York: Random House.

Harrison, Harry P.
1958   *Culture Under Canvas: The Story of the Tent Chautauqua*. New York: Hastings House.

Hart, Joseph K., ed.
1913   *Educational Resources of Village and Rural Communities*. New York: Macmillan.

Hartmann, Heidi I.
1981   "The family as the locus of gender, class, and political struggle: The example of housework." *Signs* 6:366–394.

Henry, Jules
1963   *Culture Against Man*. New York: Random House.

Hicks, John D., George E. Mowry, and Robert E. Burke
1965   *The American Nation*. 4th ed. Boston: Houghton Mifflin.

Hofstadter, Richard
1955   *Social Darwinism in American Thought*. Boston: Beacon Press.

Hollingshead, A. B.
1949   *Elmtown's Youth*. New York: John Wiley.

Hoopes, James
1979   *Oral History*. Chapel Hill: University of North Carolina Press.

Horner, Charles F.
1954   *Strike the Tents*. Philadelphia: Dorrance.

Householder, S. L.
1937   "A study of the educational and social backgrounds of the enrollees in the Civilian Conservation Camps in Kansas with the relationship of these backgrounds to leadership status." Master's thesis, University of Kansas.

Howe, Florence
1971   "Sexual stereotypes start early." *Saturday Review* 54 (October):76–77, 80–82, 92–94.

Inkeles, Alex
1979   "Continuity and change in the American national character." Pp. 390–453 in Seymour Martin Lipset (ed.), *The Third Century: America as a Post-Industrial Society*. Stanford, Calif.: Hoover Institution Press.

Jeffrey, Julie Roy
1979   *Frontier Women: The Trans-Mississippi West 1840–1880*. New York: Hill & Wang.

Jencks, Christopher, Marshall Smith, Henry Acland, Mary Jo Bane, David Cohen, Herbert Gintis, Barbara Heyns, and Stephan Michelson
1972   *Inequality: A Reassessment of the Effect of Family and Schooling in America*. New York: Basic Books.

Kansas Rural School Bulletin
1922   Topeka: State Department of Education.

Kansas State Department of Education
  1933   Topeka: *Handbook on Organization and Practices for the Secondary Schools of Kansas.* Kansas State Department of Education.
Kansas State Historical Society
  1954–56   *Annals of Kansas, Volume 1: 1886–1910.* Topeka: Kansas State Historical Society.
Kasarda, John, and Morris Janowitz
  1974   "Community sentiment in mass society." *American Sociological Review* 39:328–329.
Kelly, Maria Patricia Fernandez
  1981   "Development and the sexual division of labor: An introduction," *Signs* 7:268–278.
Koch, Fred C.
  1977   *The Volga Germans: In Russia and the Americas, 1763 to the Present.* University Park: Pennsylvania State University Press.
Koeppel, Barbara
  1978   "The new sweatshops." *The Progressive.*
Kohlberg, Lawrence
  1966   "A cognitive-developmental analysis of children's sex-role concepts and attitudes. Pp. 82–173 in Eleanor E. Maccoby (ed.), *The Development of Sex Differences.* Stanford, Calif.: Stanford University Press.
  1969   "Stage and sequence: The cognitive-development approach to socialization. Pp. 347–480 in David A. Goslin (ed.), *Handbook of Socialization Theory.* Chicago: Rand McNally.
Kramer, J. Howard
  1976   *South Dakota State University: A History, 1884–1975.* Brookings: South Dakota State University.
Lally, Francis J.
  1962   *The Catholic Church in a Changing America.* Boston: Little, Brown.
Lasch, Christopher
  1977   *Haven in a Heartless World: The Family Besieged.* New York: Basic Books.
  1979   *Culture of Narcissism.* New York: Norton.
Laski, Harold J.
  1948   *The American Democracy.* New York: Viking.
Leacock, Eleanor
  1978   "Women's status in egalitarian society: Implications for social evolution," *Current Anthropology* 19:247–275.
Lenski, Gerhard, and Jean Lenski
  1978   *Human Societies: An Introduction to Macrosociology.* 3rd ed. New York: McGraw-Hill.
Lerner, Max
  1957   *America as a Civilization.* New York: Simon & Schuster.
Life
  1941   "How to tell Japs from Chinese." 11 (December):81–82.
Lindley, Betty, and Ernest K. Lindley
  1938   *A New Deal for Youth: The Story of the National Youth Administration.* New York: Viking.

Lipset, Seymour Martin
　1961　"A changing American character?" Pp. 310–349 in Seymour
　　　　Martin Lipset and Leo Lowenthal (eds.), *Culture and Social
　　　　Character*. New York: Free Press.
Lynd, Robert S., and Helen Merrell Lynd
　1929　*Middletown*. New York: Harcourt, Brace & World.
　1937　*Middletown in Transition: A Study in Cultural Conflicts*. New
　　　　York: Harcourt, Brace.
McMurtry, John
　1978　*The Structure of Marx's World View*. Princeton, N.J.: Princeton
　　　　University Press.
McNall, Scott G.
　1974　*The Sociological Experience*. Boston: Little, Brown.
McNall, Scott G., ed.
　1981　*Political Economy: A Critique of American Society*. Glenview,
　　　　Ill.: Scott, Foresman.
McWilliams, Carey
　1942　*Ill Fares the Land: Migrants and Migratory Labor in the United
　　　　States*. Boston: Little, Brown.
Maier, Henry M.
　1965　*Three Theories of Child Development*. New York: Harper &
　　　　Row.
Martineau, Harriet
　1837　*Society in America*. Volumes 1 and 2. London: Saunders and
　　　　Otley.
Marx, Karl
　[1847]　*Poverty of Philosophy*. Ed. Friedrich Engels. Moscow: Progress
　1966　Publishers.
Marx, Karl, and Frederick Engels
　[1846]　*The German Ideology*. Moscow: Progress Publishers.
　1964
　[1848]　*The Communist Manifesto*. New York: International Pub-
　1948　lishers.
Mead, George Herbert
　1934　*Mind, Self and Society*. Chicago: University of Chicago Press.
Meyer, Adolph E.
　1965　*An Educational History of the Western World*. New York:
　　　　McGraw-Hill.
Milgram, Stanley
　1977　*The Individual in a Social World: Essays and Experiments*.
　　　　Reading, Mass.: Addison-Wesley.
Mills, C. Wright
　1951　*White Collar: The American Middle Classes*. New York:
　　　　Oxford University Press.
　1959　*The Power Elite*. New York: Oxford University Press.
Minehan, Thomas
　[1934]　*Boy and Girl Tramps of Ameria*. Seattle: University of
　1976　Washington Press.
Montgomery, David
　1972　"The shuttle and the cross: Weavers and artisans in the
　　　　Kensington riots of 1844." *Journal of Social History* 5:411–
　　　　446.

Morison, Samuel Eliot
　　1965　*The Oxford History of the American People.* New York: Oxford University Press.
Morison, Samuel Eliot, Henry Steele Commager, and William E. Leuchtenburg
　　1980　*The Growth of the American Republic.* Volume 2. New York: Oxford University Press.
Mould, David
　　1980　*The Kansas Immigrants.* Lawrence: University of Kansas Press.
Nebraska Legislative Council Committee on the Reorganization of School Districts
　　1954　Lincoln, Nebraska.
Nisbet, Robert
　　1966　*The Sociological Tradition.* New York: Basic Books.
Novack, George
　　1971　*An Introduction to the Logic of Marxism.* New York: Pathfinder Press.
Nugent, Walter T. K.
　　1963　*The Tolerant Populists: Kansas Populism and Nativism.* Chicago: University of Chicago Press.
Olmstead, Clifton E.
　　1960　*History of Religion in the United States.* Englewood Cliffs, N.J.: Prentice-Hall.
Olson, James C.
　　1955　*History of Nebraska.* Lincoln: University of Nebraska Press.
Parsons, Stanley B.
　　1973　*The Populist Context: Rural Versus Urban Power on a Great Plains Frontier.* Westport, Conn.: Greenwood Press.
Person, Ethel
　　1974　"Some new observations on the origins of femininity." Pp. 289–302 in Jean Strouse (ed.), *Women and Analysis.* New York: Grossman.
Peshkin, Alan
　　1978　*Growing Up American: Schooling and the Survival of Community.* Chicago: University of Chicago Press.
Piaget, Jean
　　[1932]　*The Moral Judgment of the Child.* New York: Free Press.
　　1948
　　1950　*The Construction of Reality in the Child.* London: Routledge & Kegan Paul.
Rader, Melvin
　　1979　*Marx's Interpretation of History.* New York: Oxford University Press.
Rainey, Homer P., Arthur L. Brandon, M. M. Chambers, D. L. Harley, Henry H. Moore, and Bruce L. Melvin
　　1937　*How Fare American Youth?* New York: Appleton-Century.
Redfield, Robert
　　1941　*The Folk Culture of Yucatan.* Chicago: University of Chicago Press.
　　1947　"The folk society." *American Journal of Sociology* 52:293–308.

Reissman, Leonard
   1959   *Class in American Society.* New York: Free Press.
Ridge, Martin, and Ray Allen Billington
   1969   *America's Frontier story: A Documentary History of Westward Expansion.* New York: Holt, Rinehart & Winston.
Riesman, David, Nathan Glazer, and Reuel Denney
   1953   *The Lonely Crowd: A Study of the Changing American Character.* Garden City, N.Y.: Doubleday/Anchor.
Robertson, James Oliver
   1980   *American Myth, American Reality.* New York: Hill & Wang.
Robertson, Ross M.
   1973   *History of the American Economy.* 3rd ed. New York: Harcourt Brace Jovanovich.
Rothman, Sheila M.
   1978   *Woman's Proper Place: A History of Changing Ideals and Practices, 1870 to the Present.* New York: Basic Books.
Russo, David J.
   1974   *Families and Communities: A New View of American History.* Nashville: Vanderbilt University Press.
Sahlins, Marshall D.
   1981   *Historical Metaphors and Mythical Realities: Structure in the Early History of the Sandwich Islands Kingdom.* Ann Arbor: University of Michigan Press.
Sanday, Peggy Reeves
   1981   *Female Power and Male Dominance: On the Origins of Sexual Inequality.* New York: Cambridge University Press.
Schafer, Roy
   1974   "Problems in Freud's psychology of women." *Journal of the American Psychoanalytic Association* 22:459–485.
Scheff, Thomas J.
   1968   "Negotiating reality: Notes on power in the assessment of responsibility." *Social Problems* 16:3–17.
Schell, Herbert S.
   1975   *History of South Dakota.* 3rd ed. Lincoln: University of Nebraska Press.
Schlebecker, John T.
   1975   *Whereby We Thrive: A History of American Farming, 1607–1972.* Ames: Iowa State University Press.
Schrag, Peter
   1970   "Is Main Street still there?" *Saturday Review* 53 (January 17):20–25.
Schur, Edwin M.
   1971   *Labeling Deviant Behavior: Its Sociological Implications.* New York: Harper & Row.
Sennett, Richard
   1981   *Authority.* New York: Random House.
Seward, Rudy Ray
   1978   *The American Family: A Demographic History.* Beverly Hills, Calif.: Sage Publications.
Sewrey, Charles
   1959   *A History of South Dakota State College, 1884–1959.* Brookings: South Dakota State University.

Shannon, Fred A.
  1945 *The Farmer's Last Frontier: Agriculture 1860–1897.* New
        York: Farrar and Rinehart.
Sheridan, Richard
  1956 *Economic Development in South Central Kansas: An Eco-
        nomic History, 1500–1900.* Lawrence: University of Kansas,
        School of Business.
Smith, Daniel Scott
  1974 "Family limitation, sexual control, and domestic feminism in
        Victorian America." Pp. 119–136 in Mary S. Hartman and Lois
        W. Banner (eds.), *Clio's Consciousness Raised: New Perspec-
        tives on the History of Women.* New York: Harper & Row.
Snyder, Ralph
  1953 *We Kansas Farmers: Development of Farm Organizations and
        Co-operative Associations in Kansas.* Topeka: F. M. Stevens
        and Sons.
Sorokin, Pitirim A.
  1947 *Society, Culture and Personality.* New York: Harper.
South Dakota State College and University
  1946 Announcements for 1946–1947 School of Agriculture. Vol-
        ume 39.
  1945 Annual Catalogue, 1945–1946. Volume 38.
  1953 Annual Catalogue, 1953–1954. Volume 46.
  1959 General Catalogue, 1959–1960. Volume 51.
  1959 *Agricultural Research in South Dakota.* 72nd Annual Station
        Report, July 1, 1958, to June 30, 1959. Agricultural Experi-
        mental Station, Brookings, South Dakota.
Spencer, Herbert
  1898 *The Principles of Sociology.* New York: D. Appleton.
Spengler, Oswald
  [1918] *The Decline of the West.* Tr. Charles Francis Atkinson. New
  1926 York: Knopf.
Steele, Ronald
  1980 *Walter Lippman and the American Century.* Boston: Little,
        Brown.
Stinchcombe, Arthur L.
  1978 *Theoretical Methods in Social History.* New York: Academic
        Press.
Stoller, Robert J.
  1968 *Sex and Gender.* New York: Jason Aronson.
Stratton, Joanna L.
  1981 *Pioneer Women: Voices from the Kansas Frontier.* New York:
        Simon & Schuster.
Tavris, Carol, and Carole Offir
  1977 *The Longest War: Sex Differences in Perspective.* New York:
        Harcourt Brace Jovanovich.
Taylor, Paul Schuster
  1941 "Goodbye to the homestead farm: The machines advance in the
        corn belt." *Harper's* 82:589–597.
Thayer, Vivian Trow
  1960 *The Role of the School in American Society.* New York: Dodd,
        Mead.

Thompson, Paul
1978 *The Voice of the Past: Oral History.* Oxford, England: Oxford University Press.
Thompson, Robert
1969 *The Golden Door.* London: Allman and Son.
Tilly, Charles, ed.
1974 *An Urban World.* Boston: Little, Brown.
Tilly, Charles
1981 *As Sociology Meets History.* New York: Academic Press.
Tonnies, Ferdinand
[1887] *Gemeinschaft and Gesellschaft.* Tr. Charles P. Loomis as
1940 *Fundamental Concepts of Sociology.* New York: American Book.
Toynbee, Arnold J.
1934–54 *A Study of History.* 10 volumes. New York: Oxford University Press.
Tumin, Melvin M.
1953 "Some principles of stratification: A critical analysis." *American Sociological Review* 18:387–393.
Turner, Frederick Jackson
1920 *The Frontier in American History.* New York: Henry Holt.
United States Bureau of the Census
1893 *Report on Population of the U.S. at the Eleventh Census: 1890.* Washington, D.C.: U.S. Government Printing Office.
1964 *Statistical Abstract of the United States, 1964.* Washington, D.C.: U.S. Government Printing Office.
1969 *Statistical Abstract of the United States, 1969.* Washington, D.C.: U.S. Government Printing Office.
1977 *Statistical Abstract of the United States, 1977.* Washington, D.C.: U.S. Government Printing Office.
1980 *Statistical Abstract of the United States, 1980.* Washington, D.C.: U.S. Government Printing Office.
United States Children's Bureau
[1929] *Infant Care.* Washington, D.C.: U.S. Government Printing
1945 Office.
United States Commissioner of Labor
1899 *Thirteenth Annual Report (1898): Hand and Machine Labor.* Washington, D.C.: U.S. Government Printing Office.
United States Committee on Education
1939 *Educational Activities of the Works Progress Administration.* Staff Study 14. Washington, D.C.: U.S. Government Printing Office.
United States Department of Agriculture
1901 *Miscellaneous Series, Bulletin No. 18.* Washington, D.C.: U.S. Government Printing Office.
United States Department of Commerce
1947 *County and City Data Book, 1947.* Washington, D.C.: U.S. Government Printing Office.
1949 *Historical Statistics of the United States, 1789–1945.* Washington, D.C.: U.S. Government Printing Office.
1952 *County and City Data Book, 1949.* Washington, D.C.: U.S. Government Printing Office.

1953 *County and City Data Book, 1952.* Washington, D.C.: U.S. Government Printing Office.

1960 *Historical Statistics of the United States, Colonial Times to 1957.* Washington, D.C.: U.S. Government Printing Office.

1962 *County and City Data Book, 1962.* Washington, D.C.: U.S. Government Printing Office.

1971 *Historical Statistics of the United States, 1790–1970.* Washington, D.C.: U.S. Government Printing Office.

United States Department of Commerce and Labor
1910 *Statistical Abstract of the United States, 1909.* Washington, D.C.: U.S. Government Printing Office.

United States Department of Labor
1979 *The Earnings Gap Between Men and Women.* Washington, D.C.: U.S. Government Printing Office.

Van Ravensway, Charles
1977 *The Arts and Architecture of German Settlements in Missouri: A Survey of a Vanishing Culture.* Columbia: University of Missouri Press.

Veblen, Thorstein
1912 *The Theory of the Leisure Class.* New York: Macmillan.

Vidich, Arthur J., and Joseph Bensman
1960 *Small Town in Mass Society: Class, Power and Religion in a Rural Community.* Garden City, N.Y.: Doubleday.

von Miklos, Josephine
1943 *I Took a War Job.* New York: Simon & Schuster.

Walker, Kathryn E., and Margaret E. Woods
1976 *Time Use: A Measure of Household Production of Family Goods and Services.* Washington, D.C.: American Home Economics Association.

Warner, Lloyd W., and Paul S. Lunt
1941 *The Social Life of a Modern Community.* New Haven, Conn.: Yale University Press.

Warner, Lloyd W., and Marcia Meeker and Kenneth Eells
1960 *Social Class in America.* New York: Harper & Row.

Webb, Walter Prescott
1931 *The Great Plains.* Boston: Ginn.

Weber, Max
[1904] *The Protestant Ethic and the Spirit of Capitalism.* Tr. Talcott
1958 Parsons. New York: Scribner's.

1946 *Max Weber: Essays in Sociology.* Tr. and ed. Hans H. Gerth and C. Wright Mills. New York: Oxford University Press.

1946 Max Weber: Essays in Sociology. Tr. Hans H. Gerth and C. Wright Mills. New York: Oxford University Press.

Whyte, William H., Jr.
1957 *The Organization Man.* New York: Simon & Schuster.

Wilder, Daniel Webster
1875 *Annals of Kansas.* Topeka: G. W. Martin.

Williams, Raymond
1973 *The Country and the City.* New York: Oxford University Press.

Williams, Robin M.
1961 *American Society: A Sociological Interpretation.* New York: Knopf.

Wilson, Sloan
1955   *The Man in the Gray Flannel Suit.* New York: Knopf.
Women on Words and Images
1972   *Dick and Jane as Victims: Sex Stereotyping in Children's Readers.* Princeton, N.J.: Women on Words and Images.
Worster, Donald
1979   *Dust Bowl: The Southern Plains in the 1930s.* New York: Oxford University Press.
Wright, Erik Olin
1978   *Class, Crisis and the State.* London: New Left Books.
Zaretsky, Eli
1976   *Capitalism, the Family, and Personal Life.* New York: Harper & Row.

COLLECTIONS

Elam Bartholomew, Diary, 1871–1907. Topeka: Kansas State Historical Society.

Anne E. Bingham, "Sixteen Years on a Kansas Farm, 1870–1886." Lawrence, Kansas: University of Kansas, Kansas Collection.

Clark Family Letters, 1873–1900. Lawrence, Kansas: University of Kansas, Kansas Collection.

Sarah G. Clark, Family Correspondence, 1859–1911. Lawrence, Kansas: University of Kansas, Kansas Collection.

Anna Cooley Collection, 1891–1950. Topeka: Kansas State Historical Society.

Engler Family, n.d. Privately printed and circulated. Topeka, Kansas. University of Kansas, Kansas Collection.

Clara Frost, Letters, 1840–1893. Lawrence, Kansas: University of Kansas, Kansas Collection.

Hansen-Bales Collection, 1860–1975. Lawrence, Kansas: University of Kansas, Kansas Collection.

William Cyrus Howard Collection, 1858–1966. Lawrence, Kansas: University of Kansas, Kansas Collection.

Samuel Emmons Hudson, Diaries, 1881, 1902–1904. Lawrence, Kansas: University of Kansas, Kansas Collection.

P. J. Jennings Collection, 1871–1894. Topeka: Kansas State Historical Society.

Kansas League of Women Voters, Papers, 1926–1978. Lawrence, Kansas: University of Kansas, Kansas Collection.

Harry E. Kelley, Letters, 1887–1905. Lawrence, Kansas: University of Kansas, Kansas Collection.

Minerva Club, Records, 1948–1956. Lawrence, Kansas. Privately held.

J. M. Clipping Newton, "Women and Maternity: From a Mother of Seven," 1869. Lawrence, Kansas: University of Kansas, Kansas Collection.

Pillsbury-Weston Papers, 1828–1896. Lawrence, Kansas: University of Kansas, Kansas Collection.

Stewart-Lockwood Collection, 1859–1950. Lawrence, Kansas: University of Kansas, Kansas Collection.

Vawter Collection, 1878–1913. Lawrence, Kansas: University of Kansas, Kansas Collection.

Warthen-Searcy Collection, 1884–1949. Lawrence, Kansas: University of
Kansas, Kansas Collection.
Dr. Lewis Watson, Diaries, 1871–1885. Topeka: Kansas State Historical
Society.
West Side Study Club, Papers, 1901–1978. Lawrence, Kansas: University
of Kansas, Kansas Collection.
Donald Worster, Thirteen cassette tapes: "Reminiscences of the dust bowl
in Haskell County, Kansas, and Cimarron City, Oklahoma." Law-
rence, Kansas: University of Kansas, Kansas Collection.

Index